S0-AVQ-206

The VNR Dictionary of Business and Finance

The VNR Dictionary of Business and Finance

David M. Brownstone
Irene M. Franck
Gorton Carruth

R
658003
B885

A HUDSON GROUP BOOK

VAN NOSTRAND REINHOLD COMPANY
NEW YORK   CINCINNATI   ATLANTA   DALLAS   SAN FRANCISCO
LONDON   TORONTO   MELBOURNE

COLLEGE OF THE SEQUOIAS

LIBRARY

Van Nostrand Reinhold Company Regional Offices:
New York   Cincinnati   Atlanta   Dallas   San Francisco

Van Nostrand Reinhold Company International Offices:
London   Toronto   Melbourne

Copyright © 1980 by Litton Educational Publishing, Inc.

Library of Congress Catalog Card Number: 79-25532
ISBN : 0-442-20949-5

All rights reserved. No part of this work covered by the copyright hereon may
be reproduced or used in any form or by any means—graphic, electronic, or
mechanical, including photocopying, recording, taping, or information storage
and retrieval systems—without permission of the publisher.

Manufactured in the United States of America

Published by Van Nostrand Reinhold Company
135 West 50th Street, New York, N.Y. 10020

Published simultaneously in Canada by Van Nostrand Reinhold Ltd.

15 14 13 12 11 10 9 8 7 6 5 4 3 2 1

Library of Congress Cataloging in Publication Data

Brownstone, David M
    The VNR dictionary of business and finance.

    1. Business—Dictionaries.   2. Finance—Dictionaries.
I. Franck, Irene M., joint author.   II. Carruth,
Gorton, joint author.   III. Van Nostrand Reinhold
Company.   IV. Title.
HF1001.B7   658'.003   79-25532
ISBN 0-442-20949-5

Preface

We have long believed that anyone associated in any way with business and finance needs a clear, concise, up-to-date dictionary containing all the key words and phrases encountered in the course of work and study—yet no such dictionary was in print.

The VNR Dictionary of Business and Finance is our attempt to fill that need. It contains all those key words and phrases, drawn from every major business, financial, and professional area. These areas include finance, management, computers, statistics, law, accounting, government, industrial relations, advertising, marketing, merchandising, research, quantitative management, operations, packaging, real estate, securities, insurance, general business, and the many interfaces between government, business, and the professions. Throughout the dictionary, we have included practical examples of current usage.

We have made every effort to be clear and concise. In selecting entries, we have, whenever appropriate, tried to consolidate several related words into one usable definition, rather than defining several forms of the same word. We have selected those words and phrases that are most often encountered in general business and financial practice rather than words that are of interest only to particular disciplines.

The VNR Dictionary of Business and Finance is designed to be the basic business and finance desk dictionary. Those practicing in special areas will benefit most from having both this general dictionary, covering the whole world of business and finance, and a specialized dictionary. For example, a computer specialist should have both a general business dictionary and a computer dictionary; a lawyer should have one or more law dictionaries along with a general dictionary of business and finance.

A clear and concise dictionary should have as few cross-references as possible. Thus, to minimize page-flipping by busy readers, we have most often briefly defined terms that might otherwise have been cross-referenced. Key words in the definitions will, however, lead interested readers to wider definitions, where appropriate. Where two or more terms are synonymous, in general the most commonly used term is defined, and the less commonly used terms are cross-referenced.

Many of the terms commonly encountered in business and finance have quite different meanings in different contexts. Sometimes these differ from each other as well as from general nonbusiness usages. For such terms, we have numbered the various meanings in their general order of importance, giving the most general meanings first, except where a very narrow meaning is that meaning most often encountered.

The alphabetizing style we have chosen is "letter by letter" rather than "word by word." This method should enable users to find desired words and phrases quickly and easily.

This dictionary is intended for use by people in both large and small businesses; people in all the professions associated with business and finance, including law, accounting, insurance, securities, banking, consulting, and advertising; people in government; students and teachers; librarians and those using libraries. In short, this dictionary is designed for people at all levels who need a concise dictionary of business and finance, written in precise, easy-to-understand, business English.

Any such dictionary is by its very nature selective, reflecting the authors' decisions regarding which terms will prove most useful to its users. While including as many new terms as possible, they must seek to select only those terms of lasting value and exclude the jargon of the moment. Nevertheless, should there be any significant omissions, we take full responsibility.

DAVID M. BROWNSTONE
IRENE M. FRANCK
GORTON CARRUTH

The VNR Dictionary of Business and Finance

A

ABA: See American Bankers Association.

abandonment: 1. The total, irrevocable and voluntary giving up of any property and of all possible rights to that property. Once abandoned, the property becomes the possession of the first to claim it. **2.** In marine insurance, the giving up of wrecked ships to the underwriters in return for the settlement of claims, a practice now specifically prohibited by many insurance policies.

abatement: 1. A decrease; for example, a reduction in taxes on real property due to special circumstances or on imported goods due to spoilage in transit; also a legally acceptable decrease in payments due or received for any reason. **2.** The total destruction of a plaintiff's cause of action at law, but leaving the plaintiff the ability to commence another cause of action based on the same set of facts.

abend: To *abnormally end,* specifically referring to a computer program that does not run properly, for whatever reason; also called abort.

ability to pay principle: The belief that taxes levied should depend on the relative abilities to pay of those taxed. The practical applications of this belief included both progressive income taxes and wealth taxes.

ab initio: Latin for from the beginning, describing the legal status of a condition or transaction, whether by its very nature or constructed from subsequent matters; for example, as applied to a contract that is void from the start, or to a legal entry later construed to have been a trespass from the start due to the subsequent actions of the trespasser.

abort: To terminate a program in the process of being executed, whether by machine or human intervention, when an irretrievable malfunction or error occurs.

above par: Above listed, or par, value. Any stock selling for more than its listed value is selling above par.

above the line: 1. Describing any normal, customary item on an accounting statement; unusual items are described as *below the line.* **2.** In marketing, describing costs for advertising, while other sales promotion costs are called below the line.

abrogation: The destruction or repeal of an existing law, whether by legislative, judicial, or executive act, or by practice.

abscissa: The horizontal distance from 0 on the base line of a graph, or the number of units a point is from the origin on the x-axis; one of the two coordinates necessary to describe a point on a rectangular or Cartesian graph, the other being the ordinate.

absentee: One who is not present when expected by others, especially for a scheduled work period.

absenteeism: The rate of absence from scheduled work by one or more workers. If ten workers are due to work a shift and three are absent, the absentee rate is 30%. Of if over a period of ten shifts, an average of four workers are absent per shift, or 40 out of 100, the rate of absenteeism is 40%. Permissible rates of worker absenteeism are

1

often negotiated and made part of modern collective bargaining contracts.

absentee ownership: The ownership of wealth-producing assets by those who neither work nor manage those assets, a common form of industrial ownership. Often used as term of opprobrium by local people who feel that absentee owners care little about local people and their interests but only about profits.

absolute coding: Computer coding in machine language usable by the central processing unit being coded, rather than in symbolic language.

absolute sale: A sale which is consummated in full at the moment of formal agreement, with no conditions of any kind accompanying the sale, as distinct from a "conditional" sale, which becomes fully consummated only upon the occurrence of specified later events.

absorbed cost: Any additional, determinable cost which might either be passed on whole to the buyer or paid by the seller, but which is paid by the seller, such as postage or handling charges.

absorbent packing: Packing material capable of absorbing liquids, used in packages containing liquids that might either leak or exude moisture during storage and shipment.

absorption: See freight absorption.

absorption costing: A method of allocating all or part of fixed and variable production costs to goods in production, goods sold, and inventory.

abstract: A written summary of the contents of a longer work, such as a brief digest of a legal decision or of any other document or set of documents.

abstract of title: A summary statement of all transactions affecting title to land, all interests held by anyone in that land, and all liens, charges, or other claims upon that land. It is a basic document needed by all purchasers of land.

accelerated depreciation: Any method of cal-

culating depreciation of land, buildings, or other fixed assets so that the stated value of the asset diminishes faster than if it lost its value in equal proportions, period after period, as is the case when *straight line* depreciation is used. It is used widely as a tax avoidance device, especially in real estate and generally throughout American industry.

acceleration clause: A clause in a debt instrument, such as a mortgage, which makes the entire amount of the debt due and payable on demand if the conditions stated in the clause are not met. For example, the entire amount of a mortgage may become immediately due if a single payment of interest or principal is missed.

acceleration principle: The theory that when demand for consumer goods rises, investment in capital equipment rises even faster; conversely, that when consumer demand drops, capital equipment investment drops faster.

acceptable quality level (AQL): That proportion of goods which must reach a pre-set standard. For example, an acceptable quality level of 96% means that a 40% rejection rate on inspection of a shipment received is acceptable to the buyer, while a 5% rejection rate may cause return of the entire shipment.

acceptance: Agreement to a transaction with intent to carry through that transaction. It is usually expressed and indicated by acts such as signing a contract, writing "accepted" on the face of a time draft or bill of exchange, receiving and holding delivered goods, or registering a deed. Acceptance may be implied, conditional, or partial, as when property is received and held, but the question of the receivers' intent to keep it can be disputed. Some common examples are banker's acceptances, bills of exchange, and trade acceptances.

acceptance bank: A banking firm that specializes in handling bills of exchange.

acceptance sampling: A method of partial inspection of goods in which those inspecting examine a relatively small part of a lot and statistically infer the condition of the entire lot. For example, 100 out of 1,000 pieces may be examined; if 3 of 100 are defective, a rate of 3%, or 30 in 1,000 for the entire lot is inferred.

accession rate: A figure derived by dividing the number of employees newly hired and rehired in a given period by the total number of those employed in that period. The Bureau of Labor Statistics computes the accession rate in United States manufacturing industries monthly.

access time: The time it takes for a computer to transfer information between its storage and processing units.

accident frequency rate: The number of disabling injuries per one million hours actually worked; a figure computed by the Bureau of Labor Statistics.

accident insurance: 1. Insurance against claims of others who allege the insured's involvement in claimant's accidents; a kind of liability insurance. **2.** Insurance covering an insured for damages to person or property stemming from an accident; for example, workmen's compensation.

accident prone: Describing those who tend to become involved in far more accidents, usually both at work and in their private lives, than their contemporaries under roughly similar conditions.

accommodation endorsement: See accommodation party.

accommodation paper: A debt instrument which is co-signed by one who does not receive the borrowings, but who is signing as guarantor that the borrower will repay or, if not, that the co-signer will repay the debt.

accommodation party: One who signs a debt instrument and undertakes co-liability for borrowings while not receiving any of the proceeds of those borrowings.

account: 1. A written record of transactions, kept in one or more ledgers and usually, though not always, expressed in money or money equivalents. **2.** A customer, one who has a bank or brokerage account, or one who regularly buys and is extended some kind of business credit.

accountability: Responsibility to others for properly accomplishing tasks, as of subordinate to superior in a corporation or any other human organization. The term is also used more generally, as in accountability of governments to those governed.

accountancy: Accounting theory and practice. In modern usage, it is synonymous with accounting.

accountant: One who practices accounting, such as a Certified Public Accountant or public accountant.

account balance: See balance.

account executive: An employee responsible for handling the relationship between a firm and one or more of its clients; widely used in advertising, but also in other service industries, such as consulting, securities, and insurance.

accounting: 1. Reporting, classifying, summarizing, and interpreting transactions, partly or wholly of a financial nature. **2.** Any formal report of an entity's transactions during a specific period, usually including a summary of the entity's current status as of the beginning of the period.

accounting period: Any period for which an accounting is prepared, usually monthly, quarterly, and yearly.

accounting practice: 1. The professional practice of a Certified Public Accountant or public accountant. **2.** The normal and generally accepted practices of accountants regarding commonly encountered professional matters.

accounts payable: Money a firm owes others for goods purchased and not yet paid for; does not include such obligations as notes, bonds, and other debts.

accounts receivable: Money owed a firm by its customers for goods purchased and not yet paid for; does not include income from such sources as investments and bank deposits.

accounts receivable financing: Use of money owed a firm in receivables to secure funds, either by the sale of those receivables to others, a process known as factoring, or by their use as loan collateral.

accretion: In general, any gradual increase in size; in business the meaning has expanded to mean any increase in value of any asset for any reason and at any rate of speed.

accrual: 1. The process of adding to and accumulating. Also refers to anything that is added to and accumulates. **2.** In accounting, continuous or periodic change in the amount of any account, including increases and decreases, income and expenses. Also refers to the specific account item that is changed by the process of accrual.

accrual basis: An accounting method which records income and expenses for accounting purposes when they are earned and incurred rather than on a cash basis, when they are actually received and spent. For example, on the accrual basis, goods bought are charged against the day they are actually bought rather than the day they are paid for, which may be considerably later; goods sold are recorded as income, minus any necessary reserves for uncollectibles, when sold rather than when the money due for them is collected.

accrue: 1. To increase, accumulate and accrete over some extended period of time. **2.** To reach the point where an increase is gained, as when pension rights accrue to their holders at the moment of vesting, or inheritance rights accrue to their holders on the death of the testator. **3.** In accounting, to record accruals in the appropriate accounts.

accrued: Describing any item which, for accounting purposes, has been earned or incurred but which has not yet been received or spent.

accrued dividend: Dividends thought to be due, undeclared, and unpaid. In fact, dividends are not due until declared by a firm's board of directors, so this phrase describes a situation that can exist only in certain private securities sales situations.

accrued expense: An expense incurred and recorded in one accounting period which is due and payable in a future accounting period, under an accrual basis accounting method.

accrued income: Income earned and recorded in one accounting period which is to be actually received in a future accounting period, under an accrual basis accounting method.

accrued interest: Interest earned that is not yet due and payable, as with fixed interest bonds earning interest every day which is payable quarterly or semi-annually.

accumulated dividend: See dividend in arrears.

accumulated income: Net and undistributed corporate income which is not offset by losses. How much corporate income can be held undistributed without being subject to tax is the focus of a considerable body of tax law.

accumulated profits: See accumulated income.

accumulated surplus: See accumulated income.

accumulation: The acquisition of marketable securities or goods over a period of time, in such fashion as to avoid public notice, which might drive up the market price of that which is being accumulated. For example, securities might be so acquired during a period of depressed prices; a kind of collectible might be accumulated before it becomes popular; or the shares of a company might be accumulated by a potential acquirer in anticipation of a takeover attempt.

ACH: See automated clearing house.

acid test: The ratio of liquid assets, including

cash, trade receivables, and marketable securities, to current liabilities. Used to assess the credit-worthiness and liquidity of a business, with a ratio of 1:1 generally thought acceptable. Also called quick ratio.

acquired surplus: Accumulated income of a company which is taken over when that company is acquired by another.

acquisition: 1. The process of gaining ownership of anything. Also that which is acquired. **2.** In business, the process of gaining full or partial but controlling ownership of a business entity. Also, the business entity which is acquired.

acquisition candidate: A company that others are seriously thinking of acquiring or trying to acquire, whether or not that company desires to be acquired.

acquittance: A document that completely discharges a financial debt or other performance obligation; usually issued upon settlement of a financial obligation.

acreage allotment: The amount of land that a farm may use for production of a specific crop; part of the national farm price support program, which seeks to limit supply in order to keep prices at minimum specified levels.

acronym: A word constructed from the first letters of a series of related words, as in NASA for National Aeronautic and Space Administration, or ALGOL for *Algo*rithmic *L*anguage.

across the board: Referring to a group of numbers that have all risen or fallen together; for example, the prices of securities listed on an exchange or uniform wage increases for all employees in a plant or industry.

action: The pursuit of a claimed legal right by any kind of legal process in a court of law. Also refers to the legal proceeding itself.

active account: An account that is used relatively often, with transactions occurring fairly regularly, such as a checking account or a stock brokerage account.

active market: Any market in which trading is heavy. Examples are, a day of large share turnover on the New York and other stock exchanges; a period of heavy trading on the commodities exchanges; or a week of active trading in currencies.

activity charge: A monthly bank service charge on a depositor's checking account, where the average monthly balance in the account is below the minimum which the bank sets to cover the costs of handling the depositor's checks. Special checking accounts have no minimum but charge a flat sum per check drawn.

act of God: An event beyond control or planning; usually a cataclysmic natural event such as earthquake, famine, flood, and pestilence, which precludes contracted performance without penalty or is a stated exception to insurance coverages.

actuary: An insurance mathematics and statistics expert, whose work includes the setting of insurance premiums through the calculation of all the kinds of risks involved.

additional capital: See paid in surplus.

add-on contract: A kind of installment buying contract, in which the purchaser can buy one item, start payments, then add other items, and have them consolidated with the earlier purchase into a single contract, often for a longer repayment period than that provided by the original installment buying contract.

address: In computer systems, the characters that specify the location or destination of any kind of data source.

address of record: An address stated for legal purposes, such as a legal residence statement for tax and voting purposes, or an address stated for purposes of legal notification under the terms of a contract.

ad hoc: On a one time basis. For example, an ad hoc committee is one formed for a single purpose, to be dissolved after that purpose has been achieved or abandoned; an ad hoc rule is one adopted for a single situation and is not intended to set any precedents.

adjudication: The judgment or decree of a court, usually after the completion of the legal process as to an action.

adjusted gross income: For income tax purposes, gross income minus all deductions from gross income provided by statute, such as business and some other expenses connected with property and wealth.

adjuster: One who examines, evaluates, and negotiates settlement of insurance claims. Adjusters are usually employed directly or indirectly by insurance companies to assess and settle claims on behalf of those insurers.

adjusting entry: A change in existing accounting records to correct entries or to modify them to reflect changing circumstances, such as reserves for bad debts and uncollectibles, accruals and writeoffs.

adjustment: 1. Any satisfaction of a claim, as in the granting of credit to a customer for unsatisfactory merchandise purchased, or the settlement of an insurance claim. **2.** Any necessary change, as an adjusting entry in accounting.

administered price: A price mainly controlled by one or more organizations rather than by marketplace supply and demand factors. While direct price-fixing collusion among companies is prohibited by law, groups of companies in substantial control of industries can and do informally set narrow price ranges for many of their products, amounting to effectively administered prices.

administration: 1. The management of matters, businesses, and other organizations. **2.** The organizational entity created to accomplish the work of managing matters, companies and other organizations. **3.** In law, the process of managing an estate.

administrative action: Action taken by administrators to further the day-to-day work

of management, relying generally upon organizational policies but not upon specific actions of policy-making bodies. For example, an administrator empowered to hire and fire within the bounds of company policies need not consult the board of directors on a hiring decision.

administrative agency: A governmental body set up to administer a specific law or laws. Examples are the Securities and Exchange Commission, charged with administration of federal securities laws and state motor vehicle bureaus which administer laws regulating motor vehicles.

administrative budget: Management's operating budget, controlling normal ongoing business operations, usually on a yearly basis.

administrative discretion: Power to act as one's own judgment indicates within the framework of legislative intention indicated by statute and supporting material. For example, the Public Health Service in its discretion may undertake emergency action to quarantine goods entering the country while investigations proceed as to the health hazards created by those goods.

administrative expenses: Expenses incurred to accomplish the management of matters and organizations. In business, the expenses of management as management, rather than by specific productive functions.

administrative law: The body of law created by the interplay between statutes, administrative agencies, and the courts, in areas of government regulation of the lives of its citizens and their organizations. Composed of statutes and their interpretation in contrast with common law, which is composed of cases and their development.

administrator: One who manages matters and organizations. In business, an executive in charge of some aspect of management. In law, one who manages an estate.

ADP: Automated data processing. See electronic data processing.

ADR: See American Depositary Receipt.

ad valorem tax: A tax computed on the basis of the value of the taxed item; usually expressed as a percentage of that value. Examples are many excise, most property, and all value-added taxes.

advance: 1. To move forward, as in a general rise of stock prices. **2.** A loan, as in payment to an employee to be repaid out of future earnings. **3.** A non-refundable prepayment, as in a royalty advance to an author and most types of commission prepayments to outside salespeople.

advance billing: Billing submitted for payment before services or goods billed have been performed. Rarely encountered in business unless requested for tax purposes, but practiced by some public and quasi-public organizations.

Advanced Linear Programming System (ALPS): A set of programs used to help solve operations research problems carrying many variables; used in a number of business applications.

advance order: Purchase of goods considerably earlier than needed, usually with shipment deferred until goods are required by the purchasers. Often used when goods desired are or may soon be in short supply or when the seller offers incentives for early ordering.

advance refunding: An offer by a bond issuer to bondholders to exchange new bonds for old bonds at favorable rates, to forestall early redemption of the old bonds. Treasury bondholders often take advantage of advance refunding offers.

adverse possession: Legally acceptable assertion of title to real property by one claiming title but without clear title; usually including some claim to title, and actual and exclusive physical occupancy for a minimum number of years as required by the applicable statute.

advertise: To announce something publicly, especially aiming to sell, purchase, or hire goods or services.

advertised bidding: A mode of obtaining bids to perform contracts, in which the purchaser publicly solicits bids for the work to be performed. Bidders for the contracts must respond with very specific and detailed proposals in competition with all others bidding. This mode of contracting is widely used by governmental bodies and is often required by law; it is seldom used by private industry.

advertising: 1. An attempt to sell anything through paid public distribution of selling material. **2.** Selling material publicly distributed through any channels of communication, such as newspapers, broadcasts, mail and films, and in a wide range of possible forms, such as print, radio, and television commercials, direct mail promotions and records.

advertising agency: A business that specializes in the creation, preparation, and placement of advertisements for its clients.

advertising allowance: An amount granted by a manufacturer to independent sellers to advertise the manufacturer's products. The amount is usually expressed as a percentage of the direct costs incurred by the seller in advertising the manufacturer's products, up to a fixed dollar limit.

advertising manager. The employee responsible for overseeing a company's advertising activities. Depending on the company, this manager may run the company's advertising department as if it were an in-house advertising agency, or may mainly work as liaison with outside advertising agencies.

advertising medium: Any channel of communication which is used for communicating the sales messages of advertisers, including all available print and broadcast vehicles.

advertising rates: Amounts charged by advertising media for carrying advertisements placed by advertisers and their agencies; rates vary widely, depending on the size and type of markets reached.

affidavit: A written statement as to facts,

sworn to or otherwise affirmed by its maker before someone legally authorized to administer and verify that oath or affirmation.

affiliate: A company that is closely associated with another company, through partial stock ownership, largely shared boards of directors, shared marketing facilities, or other such relationships, but that stops short of subsidiary status, which requires majority stock control.

affirmative action: Action undertaken, by employers, unions, and others concerned with employment and equal economic opportunity, to reduce discrimination against minority groups and women. The basic statute mandating such actions is the Equal Opportunity Act of 1972, since followed by other administrative and legal actions.

affluent society: John Kenneth Galbraith's ironic term for an American society rich in material goods but poor in social services and human values. Now often merely used as a synonym for wealthy society.

AFL-CIO: Abbreviation of American Federation of Labor-Congress of Industrial Organizations, the major labor federation in the United States, formed in 1955 by merger of the American Federation of Labor, composed mainly of craft unions, and the Congress of Industrial Organizations, composed mainly of industrial unions.

after date: Describing when a debt is due to be repaid, a specific time after it is incurred; for example, a note payable 90 days after the date on which it was executed and the money loaned is payable 90 days "after date."

after sight: Describing when a debt is due to be repaid, a specific time after legal presentation and acceptance of the debt instrument; for example, in "This note is payable 30 days after sight," the debt is due 30 days after acceptance of the note.

agency: 1. A relationship in which one party acts for or represents another, under authority granted by the other. The agency may be express or implied, exclusive or shared, general or limited. **2.** A business organization, mainly engaged in the representation of other organizations; for example, an insurance selling organization that represents and handles business for an insurance company.

agency agreement: A formal and written contract between principal and agent, setting forth all terms and conditions of the agency arrangement; for example, the agreement between an insurance company and one of its general agents.

agency contract: See agency agreement.

Agency for International Development (AID): A United States Government agency responsible for programs of aid to underdeveloped countries.

agency shop: A collective bargaining agreement that requires all employees in a bargaining unit to pay union dues or fees equal to dues to the bargaining agent, whether or not they choose to join the union.

agenda: A list of things to be done. In business, usually an organized and often roughly timed list of matters to be taken up at a meeting.

agent: 1. One who acts for or represents another, under authority granted by the other. Where the agency is a formal business relationship, it is usually governed in every major way by the provisions of an agency contract. **2.** One who sells goods and services for another, as do insurance, real estate, and other sales agents.

aggregate demand: The total demand for goods and services during a defined time period.

aging of receivables: A periodically issued statement of accounts payable, listing them in groups by the length of time the listed sums have been owed; part of a firm's financial control system.

agio: The premium paid for exchanging one nation's currency for another's or for handling a foreign bill of exchange.

agribusiness: Those industries, companies, and individuals engaged in agriculture and agriculture-related activities, as big business, including farming and other agricultural production, processing, distribution, equipment, and supporting financial and service functions; in contrast to small family farming.

agricultural carrier: A motor vehicle used in carrying farm products to market and exempted by law from Interstate Commerce Commission rate regulation.

agricultural cooperative: A producer's cooperative, in which farmers pool resources to buy supplies and equipment, harvest and process their crops, and then market those crops collectively.

agriculture: Farming to produce crops and animals. Until recently, it has always referred to working the land, but now also refers to working the sea, using such techniques as hydroponics.

AIB: See American Institute of Banking.

AID: See Agency for International Development.

air express: Shipment of goods by air, in which all aspects of shipment are left to the air shipping company, which picks up, ships, and delivers.

air freight: Shipment of goods by air, in which the originator of the shipments gets the goods to the airline, the airline functions solely as carrier of the goods shipped, and the receiver of the goods arranges pickup from the carrier.

airline: A company licensed by the Civil Aeronautics Board to transport people and goods by air.

air rights: Proprietary rights to air space above owned land. Often leased or sold to others for building purposes, as in the instance of apartment buildings over bridge approaches in some major cities.

ALGOL: An international procedural language used in computer programming systems, primarily for scientific data processing; an acronym for *Algo*rithmic *L*anguage.

algorithm: A set of well-defined steps for solving a mathematical or logical problem, as in the conversion of a Fahrenheit temperature to Celsius. Algorithms are basic to computer programming because they provide rules for solving problems without the use of judgment.

Alliance for Progress: A multi-national set of programs aimed at assisting the economic growth of Latin American Countries, in which the United States and most Latin American countries are members. Mainly financed through the United States Agency for International Development.

allied products: Products that are most often used jointly, as are corn flakes and milk or shaving cream and razor blades.

allocate: 1. To distribute according to a plan or set of rules, as in distribution of scarce commodities by government in time of emergency. 2. To distribute expenditures and revenues according to function among various accounts in an accounting system. For example, the direct costs attributable to order processing may be distributed among the various products for which orders were processed.

allocation: See allotment.

allocation of resources: See resource allocation.

all or any part: In underwriting new securities issues, a term indicating that a firm bidding for the issue will buy the entire issue or any available part of the issue, for resale to the public.

all or none: 1. A commitment by new securities issue underwriters to sell the entire issue within stated time limits or void the issue, then returning all funds received to the issue's buyers. 2. An instruction from principal to broker, that the entire purchase requested be consummated or no purchase be made, thus specifically prohibiting a partial purchase.

allotment: 1. Distribution according to a plan or set of rules. **2.** A portion of that which is distributed. Examples include a portion of scarce commodities distributed by government in time of emergency; or a portion of a new securities issue sold to a firm by an underwriting syndicate.

allowance: 1. A sum granted by an employer for reimbursable employee expenses, as in a daily fixed expense allowance for traveling salespeople. **2.** The amount of quality or quantity deviation that will be acceptable by a buyer without penalty to the seller. **3.** The amount taken off a debt to offset claims by the debtor for such matters as defects in delivery or goods delivered. **4.** Sums set aside as advance offsets for such matters as bad debts and uncollectibles.

all-risk insurance: See comprehensive insurance.

alongside: See FAS.

alpha error (α): See Type I error.

alphameric: See alphanumeric.

alphanumeric: Referring to a set of characters containing letters, numerals, and often other special characters; synonymous with alphameric.

ALPS: See Advanced Linear Programming System.

altered check: A check that has undergone unauthorized change after issuance, usually by addition or erasure, so that such matters as payees, amounts, and dates have been materially altered.

alternative cost: See opportunity cost.

alternative hypothesis: In research, the theory that the researcher sets out to prove, with the experiment designed so that if results are statistically significant, the null hypothesis— that results are due to chance alone— can be disproved, though subject to Type I and Type II error.

ALU: See arithmetic and logic unit.

AMA: See American Management Association.

amalgamation: See consolidation.

American Arbitration Association: A nonprofit private organization functioning as impartial arbitrator of disputes, especially in all areas of business and collective bargaining. Many commercial and labor contracts provide for arbitration by the American Arbitration Association, and such arbitration is often binding upon the parties.

American Bankers Association (ABA): The largest national organization of commercial banks, and one of the oldest trade associations in the United States. It is involved in legislative representation of the banking industry, professional development programs, development of industry standards, and publishing in banking areas.

American Depositary Receipt (ADR): Receipts issued by American banks in place of foreign stocks held in trust by those banks. Relatively few foreign stocks are directly traded in the United States, but instead become tradable through the device of the depositary receipt.

American Federation of Labor: See AFL-CIO.

American Institute of Banking (AIB): Professional development arm of the American Bankers Association; awards professional certificates and publishes texts and other materials.

American Management Association (AMA): The largest national non-profit organization of management professionals, with membership drawn from both business and academe; heavily involved in professional development, publishing, and research in all management areas.

American National Standards Institute (ANSI): A standard-setting organization for the computer industry, composed of industry people and computer users.

American Standard Code For Information Interchange (ASCII): A proposed set of standards for characters to be used in the transmission of data in computer code over telephone lines and in the transfer of such data between the equipment of different manufacturers.

American Stock Exchange (ASE): The second largest United States stock exchange. Formerly called the Curb Exchange, it originated as an outdoor securities market.

amicus curiae: Latin for "a friend of the court"; one who is not a party to a case before a court, but who volunteers discussion or argument of a matter before the court; usually an attorney on a matter of law.

amortization: 1. The reduction and ultimate wiping out of any amount over a specified period, as in retirement of a mortgage debt through installment repayments that include both interest and principal until the full debt is repaid. **2.** The process of writing off the premium on a bond bought above par. **3.** The reduction and ultimate wiping out of the stated value of a fixed asset over a specified period, including all forms of depreciation, write-offs, and depletion of assets of limited life; of special tax significance in the form of accelerated depreciation.

amortization schedule: 1. A table showing the mathematics of amortization, as the obligation or asset is gradually reduced and eliminated. **2.** A table showing the mathematics of amortization as the premium paid on a bond is gradually reduced.

amortized loan: A loan repaid in equal installments over the life of the loan, each payment containing both interest and principal repayment; interest is high and principal repayment low at the start of the period, with principal repayment high and interest low toward the end of the period. Home mortgage loans are usually made on this basis.

Amtorg: The foreign trading agency of the Soviet Union, with branches in many countries; an acronym for its Russian name.

analog computer: A type of computer that continously measures, unlike a digital computer that counts, solves problems by translating what is being measured into analogous quantities within the computer, and produces analogs as output; often used in simulation applications.

analysis of variance: A statistical test designed to measure the degree of similarity between one population and another; if the relationship is close enough, statistically, the assumption is that information about one population can be used to make predictions about another.

annual audit: Thorough examination of a firm's books and records for a year's activities, usually conducted by outside accountants.

annual closing: The closing of a firm's books for the fiscal year, including the posting of closing entries in those books.

annual improvement factor: A collective bargaining contract provision that attempts to tie wage increases to productivity increases; also called productivity clause.

annualize: 1. To derive an annual rate from partial figures. For example, under certain conditions costs incurred in one month can be multiplied by twelve to get a projected annual rate of expenditure. **2.** In taxation, to compute for tax purposes when operations are taxable for only part of a year, as in change from a fiscal to a calendar year on a one-time basis.

annual report: A formal report of a firm's operating results for the year and its year-end financial condition, containing a balance sheet, operating statement, auditor's report, and often other financial materials and management comments; submitted by the board of directors to the firm's stockholders and often to other interested parties.

annuitant: One who has the right to receive an annuity.

annuity: A sum paid periodically in equal installments to annuitants under terms of an insurance policy or bequest. It is usually a form of retirement insurance, in which the insured buys an insurance policy, making periodic premium payments, a single lump sum, or some combination of both: then on maturity of the policy the insured receives payments in one of several alternative payment modes. In the recently introduced variable annuity, insureds may receive payment in shares of an annuity fund that varies with the fortunes of the securities in which it is invested.

ANSI: See American National Standards Institute.

answering time: The elapsed time between receipt of and response to a signal.

antedate: To date a document earlier than the real date on which it is executed, as in dating a gift earlier than the actual date of its giving to qualify for favorable, and often illegal, tax treatment.

anticipation: 1. Any expectation of change; generally used to describe the impact of events and reactions to them on stock market fluctuations, consumer buying patterns, and other economic trends. **2.** In accounting, recording costs and revenues before they actually occur, as in recording all proceeds from a multi-year magazine subscription as if they had already been received, even though payment is yearly.

anticipation factor: The idea that the economic expectations of those in a marketplace to some extent influence marketplace activities, becoming self-fulfilling prophecies; for example, that widespread expectation of market decline on the part of investors can be and often is a substantial factor leading to market decline.

anticipatory breach: A breach of contract occurring before other parties have obligations to perform under the terms of that contract, such as a direct statement of intent not to perform, or bankruptcy clearly making it impossible to perform.

antidumping tariff: An import duty levied to prevent dumping, which is the sale of manufactured goods at export prices far lower than those charged in the country of manufacture; the duty, levied by importing countries, is the difference between the normal home market price and the export market price. Such tariffs are often the subject of considerable international dispute, with importing countries charging that exporters dump to create unfair competition with home-produced goods, while exporting countries charge importers have unfair and exclusionary protective tariffs.

antitrust statutes: Laws aimed at curbing and reversing the spread of monopolies, monopolistic practices, and all practices and actions that function as restraints to free trade and the development of free markets. The Federal Trade Commission is charged with enforcement of antitrust laws, the main ones being the Sherman Antitrust Act of 1890, the Clayton Antitrust Act of 1914, the Federal Trade Commission Act of 1914, the Robinson-Patman Act of 1936, and the Celler Act of 1950.

APL: A programming language primarily used for remote computer terminal applications; an abbreviation for *A Programming Language.*

appeal: An attempt to secure a hearing in a higher court, after adjudication by a lower court and exhaustion of all other relevant processes, asking overturn of the lower court's decision.

applications research: Research aimed at finding products that will have specific uses, such as a new drug, weapon, or industrial process.

apportionment: Any proportional division, as in the division of revenues and expenditures between principal and interest in estate administration; the charging of current costs over several periods in accounting, relating costs to benefits; the allotment of shares among buyers who have oversubscribed a new securities issue; or the division of a tax levied among those who must pay it, according to rules developed by the taxing authority.

appraisal: The development of a formal estimate of value of any real or personal property, usually by an appraiser and in writing; also refers to the document so produced.

appraiser: One who sets value on properties for a wide variety of legal, taxing and transacting purposes, who is generally recognized as an expert in the kinds of properties being appraised, and who often possesses such credentials as a course of study, professional certification, and professional society membership.

appreciation: 1. An increase in the value of any property. **2.** An increase in the value of a fixed asset over its book value. **3.** An increase in the market price of a security.

appreciation potential: The likelihood that an investment will increase in value, and the probable size of that increase; always an estimate.

apprentice: One who is in the process of learning a trade while employed in that trade, usually for a fixed period. Certification to practice that trade often depends on satisfactory completion of the apprenticeship period.

apprenticeship training: The training of relatively unskilled workers to become skilled tradespeople, in programs sponsored by government, labor, and industry, often as part of affirmative action programs developed in compliance with Federal and state antidiscrimination laws.

appropriation: 1. In government, an expenditure authorized by a legislature for the accomplishment of a public purpose. **2.** In the private sector, expenditures authorized by the policy-making body of an enterprise to accomplish a major purpose, such as plant expansion.

approval sale: See trial sale.

APT: One of several computer languages used in programming a wide variety of numerically controlled machine tools; an acronym for *A*utomatically *P*rogrammed *T*ools.

aptitude test: A test used in assessing a person's potential for learning and successfully developing skills, especially for a specific area of work.

AQL: See acceptable quality level.

arbitrage: The practice of buying something in one market and simultaneously selling it in another or the same market, with the aim of taking advantage of price differences existing at the moment of purchase and sale. The usual subjects of arbitrage are currencies, currency futures, securities, precious metals, and other such commodities. For example, the British pound may be selling in Paris at $1.80 and in Tokyo at $1.81. An arbitrageur who buys a large quantity of pounds in Paris at $1.80 and simultaneously sells a large number of pounds in Tokyo at $1.81 can make a substantial profit.

arbitrageur: See arbitrage.

arbitration: A dispute-settling process, in which the parties in dispute submit their cases to a third party, either a single arbitrator or a panel, for a settlement that will be binding upon all parties. Arbitration is usually voluntary and written into contracts, such as labor-management and commercial contracts, but sometimes it is compulsory, being imposed by government on the parties, as in some labor disputes occurring in times of national emergency. Although arbitration is a quasi-legal proceeding that is usually binding upon the parties, it can in some circumstances be appealed through the courts.

arbitrator: One who functions to settle disputes between parties and whose decision will be binding upon those parties.

area sampling: A geographic sampling technique used in statistics, as in collecting data on all residents of several selected communities to try to arrive at statistically sound information on an entire area.

arithmetic and logic unit: That part of the central processing unit of a computer in which arithmetic and logical operations, such as comparison, addition, or division take place.

arithmetic mean: See mean.

arithmetic overflow: In computer operations, the development of a number too large to fit in the location assigned to it; also refers to that part of a number that is excess, such as the two extra digits in a 10 digit number which overflows an 8 digit register.

arithmetic progression: A sequence of numbers in which the numbers increase by a uniform amount, as in 2, 4, 6, 8, 10, 12, where the increase is always 2; in contrast with a geometric progression, in which each number in the sequence is a fixed multiple of the previous number.

arm's-length: Describing a transaction engaged in by parties who are absolutely independent of each other as regards the transaction. For example, wholly unrelated buyers and sellers can deal with each other at arm's-length.

array: In statistics, the listing of all values being examined by size, as in a listing of all companies being analyzed for financial performance by some measure of size of company, such as assets or gross revenue.

arrears: Debts such as installment payments, rent, and bond interest, which are owing and past due but unpaid on their normal and acceptable payment dates. Occasionally used to describe debts which are due, but not yet overdue.

arrival draft: A bill for goods shipped. The shipment's originator sends the bill and shipping documents directly to a collecting bank, where they arrive before the shipment itself arrives. When the shipment arrives, the bill must be paid before the shipping document will be released by the collecting bank to the shipper, so that the delivery cannot be completed without the bill being paid.

articles of association: A document embody-ing an agreement between those forming a company under the common law, that company in legal effect being a partnership rather than a corporation.

articles of incorporation: A document embodying an agreement between those forming a private corporation under the general corporation law, a statute specifying the limited liability of corporate shareholders and otherwise defining the special nature of that form of doing business.

articles of partnership: A document agreed to and signed by parties forming and organizing a co-partnership.

ARU: Audio response unit. See voice answer back device.

ASCII: See American Standard Code For Information Interchange.

ASE: See American Stock Exchange.

Asian Development Bank: An international bank composed of many Asian and non-Asian nations, including the United States. Formed to spur economic development in the Far East, it provides loans and technical assistance to both governments and private companies.

as is: Describing a sale made without any express or implied warranty; usually describes merchandise for sale, and is not always a bar to recovery under United States consumer protection laws.

asking price: The price at which anything is offered for sale; usually used in real estate and other substantial transactions to mean that the price being asked is negotiable, rather than firm.

assemble: In computer processing, to translate a program from a low-level language, in which a programmer wrote the instructions, into machine language, which the machine uses; in contrast, high-level languages are translated by a compiler.

assembler language: A computer language used to translate a symbolically coded program, one written in a language such as

COBOL or FORTRAN, into machine language that can be used by a computer; consists mainly of brief instructions that correspond one-to-one with the computer's data and instruction formats.

assembler program: A computer program that uses assembler language to translate programs written in a symbolic language, such as COBOL or FORTRAN, directly into machine language.

assembly line: A system of manufacturing, in which a conveyor carries parts through a series of work stations. At each work station, a specific operation is done, with the entire process producing finished goods at the end of the line. Modern assembly lines are usually partly or wholly automated.

assessed value: The value placed on real and personal property by government for property tax purposes.

assessment: **1.** A tax on real property, whether a recurring tax or a special tax for a single property-related purpose, such as sewers or sidewalks. **2.** The process of determining the assessed valuation of property as a basis for a tax to be levied. **3.** An amount levied by such companies as banks, insurance companies, and stock companies on shareholders and other parties holding some form of ownership interest to compensate for such matters as unanticipated losses and impaired capital positions. **4.** The amount of damages set to be paid to the winner of a lawsuit. **5.** Any special and temporary charge levied by an organization on its members.

asset: 1. Any owned item that can be converted into cash. In the widest sense, anything of value. **2.** In accounting, any source of wealth that can produce future value for its owner, including both tangible and intangible items, such as real property and cash.

assigned risk: An insurance risk that is shared by two or more companies pooling a group of very poor risks to minimize the liability of a single company; often applied

when auto insurance is legally required for all motorists.

assignee: One to whom legal rights belonging to a contracting party have been transferred, as in the transfer of rights to collect a debt, receive purchased property, or publish a book.

assignment: The act of transferring legal rights belonging to a contracting party to some other party.

assignor: One who possesses legal rights arising from a contract and transfers those rights to some other party. The assignor may be a party to the original contract or a previous assignee who is transferring the rights once again.

association: 1. Any group of persons joining together for a common purpose. **2.** An unincorporated organization, functioning much like a corporation, but without a corporate charter or the protections and obligations afforded corporations under the general corporation law.

assumed liability: A liability taken over from another, as when a company takes over assets and liabilities of an acquiring company in a corporate merger.

assurance: Generally a synonym for insurance, especially in referring to some aspects of life and marine insurance.

at market: An instruction by a securities buyer or seller to a broker to buy or sell immediately at the best available price, rather than at a specific price.

at or better: An instruction by a securities buyer or seller to a broker to buy or sell at or higher than a specified price.

at sight: Describing a negotiable instrument, such as a bank draft, on which payment is due immediately on presentation.

attachment: A court order authorizing seizure by legal authorities of property belonging to the defendant in a legal action. The seized property may be physically seized and held safe, as with cash, paintings, and other small portable items; may be held in place with a lien against its sale, as with realty; or may be frozen, as with a bank account with the defendant unable to draw upon it. If the defendant loses the lawsuit, the attached property may then be used to satisfy damages and expenses.

attest: 1. To affirm, verbally or in writing, the truth of a statement or the existence of a fact. **2.** To witness, and to sign a statement that verifies the signing of a document by another. **3.** To certify that a document copy is genuine; usually done by a court officer licensed to fulfill this function. **4.** To offer a professional opinion supporting stated facts and opinions, as when an accountant verifies a financial statement.

attestation: The formal and written witnessing of a document's signing by another, at the request of the other.

at the close: An instruction by a securities buyer or seller to a broker to buy or sell at the best available price near the closing of the market for the day.

at the opening: An instruction by a securities buyer or seller to a broker to buy or sell at the best available price at the opening of the market for the day.

attorney in fact: A status conferred by the signing of a valid power of attorney, by which one empowers another to act as his or her attorney for purposes specified in the document.

attorney of record: That attorney on record, in the documents relating to a specific case, as representing a party in that case, and to whom service of process and other communications are to be directed.

auction: Any sale to two or more potential buyers in which those buyers bid against each other, with whatever is being sold going to the highest bidder.

auctioneer: One who conducts an auction, offering goods for sale, taking bids, and ultimately selling to the highest bidder.

audio response unit (ARU): See voice answer back device.

audit: To examine and substantiate the accuracy, completeness, and internal consistency of books of account and the transactions recorded in them by one professionally qualified to do so. Also refers to the examination and substantiation process.

auditor: See audit.

auditor's report: A report issued by auditors on completion of their audit of company financial statements; such reports are usually brief, standard, and in language generally acceptable to the accounting profession.

audit period: The period covered by an audit, usually a year.

audit standards: Those standards for conducting audits that are acceptable to the accounting profession, as set forth by its professional associations and, to an increasing extent, as interpreted by courts and regulatory bodies.

audit trail: In accounting records and computer systems, references from entries back to the source materials from which the entries were generated; used in a wide variety of applications, including tax examinations.

audit year: The kind of year being examined for auditing purposes—fiscal or calendar.

authorization card: A document signed by a worker in a workplace being organized by a union, authorizing a union to be his or her collective bargaining representative.

authorized capital stock: The amount of capital stock a corporation is authorized to issue, as specified in its articles of corporation. A corporation may issue less, but may not issue more, than its authorized amount of capital stock without amending its certificate of incorporation.

authorized dealer: A dealer authorized by a manufacturer to act as agent for a product or group of products made by that manufacturer, whether on an exclusive or non-exclusive basis.

authorized shares: See authorized capital stock.

author's alterations: Changes made by an author on a manuscript after type has been set, except for corrections of printer's errors.

autocode: To use computers themselves to develop programs in machine language from human-developed symbolically coded programs.

automated clearing house (ACH): An interbank facility, clearing bank transactions for member banks through a central automatic data processing system.

automated data processing (ADP): See electronic data processing.

automated tellers: Machines that take the place of human tellers, handling a wide variety of bank functions formerly performed by humans, such as cash receipts and disbursals.

Automatically Programmed Tools: See APT.

automatic premium loan: A straight life insurance policy feature under which the company will, by agreement with the insured, loan the insured money to pay premiums out of the cash surrender value in the insured's policy.

automatic stabilizers: Economic factors built into the economy that are thought to exert counter-pressures on both inflation and recession, therefore tending to smooth out the boom-and-bust features of the business cycle; examples include social security, unemployment insurance, and welfare payments.

automatic teller: See cash machine.

automatic wage adjustment: Any wage increase or decrease tied to changes in economic factors, such as cost-of-living increases, productivity increases, or profit increases.

automation: The development of machine controlled production processes throughout the world of business, usually replacing human labor; a worldwide trend throughout the twentieth century, and causing very substantial opportunity development and adjustment problems in all countries.

automobile insurance: Insurance that includes a considerable range of coverages and options, such as coverage for damages caused by an owned car to the persons and property of others, as well as to the person and property of the insured.

autonomous investment: In economics, an investment made for reasons stemming from the nature of the investment itself, rather than being in any way directly tied to current or near-term anticipated economic conditions.

auxiliary storage: In electronic data processing, data storage capability other than that of the main computer system, such as on magnetic tape; also called secondary storage or when the storage is outside the computer system itself, external storage.

available assets: Any unencumbered assets available for general business purposes.

available cash: Cash in hand and in the bank, minus outstanding checks, that can be used for general business purposes.

avails: See net proceeds.

average: 1. An arithmetic mean, found by adding two or more items and dividing their sum by the number of items. **2.** Any number expressing the center or typifying a set of numbers of which it is part, such as a median, weighted average, or moving average. **3.** In shipping, losses suffered by ships or cargo and related payments made by owners, insurers, and other interested parties. **4.** In the securities markets, an average of a series of stocks; several such averages are generally cited as barometers of securities market health, including the Dow-Jones Industrial, Standard and Poor's, New York Stock Exchange, and New York Times averages and indexes.

average balance: The amount of deposits maintained in a bank by one using bank-extended credit, with the deposits expressed as a percentage of credit in use. An average of $5,000 in outstanding loans coupled with an average of $1,000 in deposits for the same period would result in a 20% average balance.

average cost: An inventory valuation, the total cost of all salable or usable items in the group of items being measured divided by the number of such items.

average deviation: The average difference from the median or some other selected point in collected data, ignoring plus and minus signs. For example, if five items show deviations from median of $+3$, $+1$, 0, -1, -3, the deviations are added together as $3+1+1+3=8$; 8 is then divided by the number of items, which is 5, for an average deviation of $8/5 = 1.6$. In statistics, the standard deviation is a more important measure.

average income: See income averaging.

average life: The projected useful life of a group of depreciating assets, taken together and weighted for relative original costs.

averaging: An investment technique, consisting of buying the same securities at successively lower prices as a stock goes down or "averaging down," or of buying the same securities at successively higher prices as prices go up or "averaging up." By lessening the risks involved by spreading purchases over a range of prices, averaging is thought to be a mode of insurance against wide stock price fluctuations.

aviation insurance: See property insurance.

award: To make a judgment in favor of a party or parties; for example, a sum given to an injured employee by a board in a workmen's compensation case; damages given a plaintiff by judge or jury; an arbitrator's judgment in an industrial dispute, as between disputing contracting parties or between labor and management; or the giving of a job to the lowest of several bidders. Also the judgment, sum, or job so given.

B

baby bond: A bond originally valued at less than $1000, sometimes at as little as $10; calculated by issuers to appeal to very small investors. These bonds are not routinely accepted for sale or as collateral by banks and brokers, requiring specific agreement to handle.

back: To place oneself behind a plan or project, materially, as in financing a project; by word, as in speaking for a political candidate; or both.

backdating: To date a document earlier than its actual date of execution; for example, the dating of contributions as if they were given in December 31 of one year, rather than on January 2 of the next year, in an attempt to evade timely income tax payments on the money given.

backdoor financing: The means by which a Federal agency raises money for operations other than by direct appropriation, as in the issuance of bonds under general authority previously granted by the legislature or by direct borrowing from the treasury under previously granted authority.

backdoor selling: Attempts to sell directly to users rather than going through company-designated purchasing people; an increasingly rare selling technique, as both selling and buying companies tend to discourage the practice.

background processing: Computer processing turned on automatically when higher priority or foreground processing is not preempting the computer.

backhaul: To transport a shipment past or in any other fashion away from its destination and then back to that destination, as in shipping goods from New York to Altoona by way of express shipment to Pittsburgh and shipment back to Altoona.

backlog: All unfilled orders from customers. A distinction is often made between total backlog, which includes all unfilled orders, and active or current backlog, which includes only orders in process or for which material is on hand.

back order: An order accepted and held for future delivery, usually because the item ordered is out of stock.

back pay: 1. Money payable by an employer to an employee as a result of any award to that employee after successful prosecution of a grievance, court case, or any other action charging the employer with contract or law violations. **2.** Any wages owed an employee that have not been paid as of the date such wages were due and payable.

back spread: In arbitrage, a smaller than normal difference in price in two or more markets on the currencies, securities, or commodities being traded. For example, if the normal price difference between the New York and Tokyo prices of a given stock is $2, and the difference becomes $1, the back spread is $1; then an arbitrageur who buys and sells the stock at the same time in both markets, may make a profit on the transactions.

back taxes: Taxes previously due, and now overdue and unpaid; for example, property taxes due which may ultimately result in forced sale by government to satisfy those taxes.

back-to-work movement: An attempt, usually initiated by the employer, to break a strike by starting a movement to get striking workers to return to work without a collective bargaining settlement.

backup system: A system that is designed to operate a machine or process when normal operating systems fail; for example, emergency operating systems in commercial nuclear plants.

bad debt: An uncollectible debt. Businesses often hold reserves against such uncollectibles; commercial banks are required by law to hold minimum bad debt reserves against possible loan losses.

bad delivery: In stock sales, a physical transfer of the stock sold which does not conform to stock exchange rules; the defects in delivery must be corrected for the transfer to be completed.

bad faith: Intent to deceive or defraud, usually in relation to a contract; often applied to the state of mind of one committing a willful breach of contract, beyond honest mistake or simple negligence.

bad title: Title that is so defective or otherwise encumbered that it cannot be transferred.

bail: A bond given by one to guarantee the appearance of another in court, forfeitable if that appearance does not occur.

bailee: One who holds property for another, and returns that property after specified purposes are accomplished, as in the instances of a freight shipper, broker, or bank.

bailment: The delivery of property to be held in trust by one for another, and the creation of an express or implied contractual relationship between owner and bailee, in such areas as banking, transporting, warehousing, and rental-purchase agreements.

bailor: One who entrusts property to another

for the accomplishment of specific purposes, and to whom that property is to be returned after those purposes are accomplished.

bait and switch: An illegal and unethical selling technique, in which the seller advertises an item for sale at an unusually low price, as bait to draw prospective buyers into a store; then attempts to switch the prospect to a more expensive item once in the store, by telling the prospect that the advertised item has been sold out or that the shipment hasn't arrived, or by using some other pretext.

balance: 1. The plus or minus total in an account after all debits and credits have been added and subtracted within that account. **2.** The amount needed to equalize credits and debits in an account. **3.** To equalize credits and debits in an account.

balanced budget: A budget with equal income and expenditures for a given period; the stated but unmet goal of the United States government for most of this century.

balanced fund: A kind of mutual fund that invests in several kinds of securities, including both stocks and bonds, in contrast to some other kinds of mutual funds that focus on specific kinds of securities investments, such as growth stocks or municipal bonds.

balance due: That sum still due and unpaid on a debt obligation; usually an installment debt obligation or one on which a partial payment has been made, to be followed by full payment.

balance of indebtedness: The balance of all amounts owed between a country and the rest of the world in a period. If all amounts owed by a country and its citizens are smaller than the amounts owed to them by the rest of the world, the country is an international creditor; if the reverse, an international debtor.

balance of payments: The balance of all transactions between a country and the rest of the world in a period, including individual, business, institutional, and governmental transactions. It consists of the current account, which includes all exports and imports of goods and services; the capital account, which includes all exports and imports of investment capital; and the gold account, which includes all financial reserves of any kind exported or imported to bring total exports and imports into balance.

balance of trade: The balance of all merchandise transactions between a country and the rest of the world in a period; a major element in the balance of payments. More merchandise exports than imports give a country a favorable balance of trade; more imports than exports are an unfavorable balance of trade.

balance sheet: A financial statement, indicating the financial condition of a business or other organization as of a specific time, including all assets, liabilities and ownership equities. Balance sheets vary in size and the amount of detail included, from the closely detailed statements of some small businesses to the summary statements of major corporations.

balloon: In finance, a far overpriced item of value, such as a security, market, or company; usually so much overpriced in relation to its underlying values that some form of manipulation is suspected.

BAM: See basic access method.

bank: **1.** Any organization lending, handling, holding, investing, or otherwise servicing money and other instruments of and claims to value; includes commercial, savings, mortgage and investment banks, savings and loan associations, trust companies, credit unions, and government banks of several kinds. **2.** To place money or other instruments of value in the hands of a banking organization for saving or holding purposes.

bank account: Money deposited in a bank for saving or holding. In a checking account the money is payable on demand; in a savings account, payable on notice to the bank of intent to withdraw funds, a requirement that is generally waived by the bank; in a

time deposit, sometimes called a long-term savings account, payable at a stated time after deposit has been made.

bank charter: See articles of association.

bank check: A check by a bank drawn on itself; usually used by bank customers as a means of cashless payment or in transferring funds.

bank credit: **1.** Credit available from banks as bank loans and investments grow, as federally regulated by current monetary policies and reserve requirements. **2.** Credit to the bank account of a borrower, now available for the borrower's use.

bank discount: See discount.

bank draft: A check to a specific payee drawn by a bank on its own funds on deposit with another bank. For example, a bill rendered in Swiss francs to an American may be paid by a bank draft purchased in the United States by the American, sent to Switzerland and cashed there with a correspondent bank of the American bank that issued the bank draft.

banker's acceptance: A negotiable time draft or bill of exchange traded in money market. These instruments usually originate in international trade, resulting from export or import transactions in which a bank accepts an obligation to pay the seller if the buyer defaults; they also originate in domestic shipping transactions and in the storage of staples in the United States and abroad.

banker's bank: **1.** A large, centrally located bank having a large volume of transactions with smaller banks. **2.** A central bank, such as a Federal Reserve Bank or the Bank of England.

bank examination: **1.** A thorough and formal official inspection of a bank's financial condition and related affairs, as required by applicable banking laws. National banks are inspected at least twice yearly by Federal bank examiners; most states require twice yearly inspections of state banks by state bank examiners. Examinations may be conducted more than twice yearly as required by regulating authorities; may sift any aspect of bank activities; and may go beyond legal compliance questions into any aspect of bank management. **2.** Inspection of the bank's financial condition and related affairs by the bank's own internal auditing staff.

bank examiners: Those empowered to examine any and all aspects of banking activity within their jurisdiction pursuant to law.

bank failure: The temporary or permanent closing of a bank because it is unable to meet the withdrawal demands of its depositors; such failure may be "hidden," when the failing bank is taken over by another bank that is able to meet depositors' demands. After the widespread bank failures following the stock market crash of 1929, a combination of regulation and Federal deposit insurance has served to minimize depositor losses from bank failure.

Bank for International Settlements: A European international banking organization, in which many European central banks are stockholders; functions as agent and handles international transactions for several supranational European financial and administrative organizations, such as the European Payments Union and the International Monetary Fund.

bank holding company: Any company owning a controlling interest in one or more banks. Such companies are regulated by applicable Federal laws; they may and often do engage in non-banking activities under conditions specified by law and the regulating authorities.

bank holiday: Any day on which the banks are closed by law or official proclamation in a given jurisdiction.

banking law: The body of laws, regulations, administrative decisions, and court cases that form the legal framework within which the banking industry operates.

bank money: Money held in bank checking accounts as demand deposits; this is the most common form of money.

bank money order: A money order sold by banks, usually for a somewhat smaller fee than a postal money order. It is a kind of cashier's check, and a negotiable instrument that may be signed by many successive endorsers.

bank moratorium: See moratorium.

bank note: A form of currency, issued by a bank and backed by that bank's promise to pay the bearer of the note on demand. In the United States today, the only bank issuer of such currency is the Federal Reserve System, operating as a national bank.

bank of issue: Any bank that has the power to issue bank notes; such central banks as the Federal Reserve Banks, the Bank of Canada and the Bank of England are banks of issue.

bank reserve: The amount of money banks are required by law to hold as a reserve against possible depositor demands, composed of vault cash on hand and currency reserves on deposit with a Federal Reserve Bank. These legal reserves are expressed as a percentage of deposits. In banking practice, primary reserves are vault cash, Federal Reserve deposits, and demand deposits in correspondent banks; secondary reserves are highly marketable short-term securities supplementing the bank's more liquid assets.

bank run: Unusually heavy withdrawals by depositors, due to a loss of confidence in the bank's ability to satisfy those demands, often leading to a crisis of bank liquidity and bank failure.

bankrupt: Describing a corporation or individual who has been declared to be in a state of bankruptcy by court proceeding. Often used more loosely to describe a person or firm that is insolvent, whether or not so declared by the courts; used even more generally, describes something of no further value, such as a bankrupt policy.

bankruptcy: The condition of a debtor who

has been declared insolvent by court proceeding, and whose financial affairs are being administered by the court through a receiver or trustee. Bankruptcy may be voluntary, when applied for and granted to an insolvent debtor by the court, or may be involuntary, when petitioned for by creditors and granted by the court. Businesses and individuals going into voluntary bankruptcy often use the court as a shield against their creditors while they attempt to solve their financial difficulties.

Banks for Cooperatives: A Federal lending agency established by the Farm Credit Act of 1933, consisting of a central bank and twelve district banks that loan money to farm cooperatives.

bank statement: 1. The balance sheet of a bank, issued periodically, covering assets, liabilities, and net worth. **2.** A statement as to the condition of a depositor's account, usually sent to a depositor monthly.

bar: All those who are licensed to practice law; originally referring to that portion of the courtroom in which an action at law physically took place, which was literally separated by a bar from that portion occupied by the general public.

bar association: A membership organization limited to those who are licensed to practice law and are therefore members of the bar; membership in a bar association is not required for the practice of law.

bar chart: A graph that uses horizontal bars or vertical columns to compare several items in terms of one or two characteristics, or to show the differing proportion of components in several items; widely used in statistical reports for popular consumption and for financial summaries; also called a histogram.

bargain: 1. A contract or agreement, as in to strike a bargain. **2.** To negotiate a contract or agreement. **3.** Anything bought or sold at a price significantly below what it would normally get in its market.

bargain basement: That portion of a retail establishment devoted to the sale of reduced price items; often literally in the basement of the establishment.

bargain counter: A securities industry term for a market in which a wide range of securities are for sale at prices considerably below the underlying value of the securities themselves: often widely used in a period of stock market decline.

bargain hunter: 1. A securities industry term describing a buyer who looks and waits for bargain counter securities, then buys as low as thought possible; often widely encountered in a period of stock market decline. **2.** Anyone searching for a bargain in any market.

bargain hunting: See comparative shopping.

bargaining: See collective bargaining.

bargaining agent: The union certified by that government agency having jurisdiction as representing the majority of employees in a bargaining unit and having the exclusive power to negotiate with the employer as to wages, hours, and all other matters affecting employment. An employer may choose to bargain with a union that has not been officially certified as the bargaining agent, but will not be protected against the organizing efforts of other unions by doing so.

bargaining power: The relative strengths and weaknesses of parties in a bargaining situation, especially in collective bargaining situations.

bargaining rights: The legal right of a union to represent those in a bargaining unit in collective bargaining negotiations with their employer, as certified by the appropriate government agency.

bargaining unit: A group of employees represented by a union empowered by them to negotiate with their employers as to their wages, hours, and other matters affecting employment. A bargaining unit may be certified as such by an official agency or be recognized as such by the employer without certification.

are shown separately on accounting statements. Such items are described as "below the line," while customary items are "above the line." **2.** In marketing, sales promotion costs other than advertising are "below the line," while advertising is "above the line."

bench: The judiciary; originally that portion of the courtroom occupied by judges.

benchmark: A reference point, from which calculations and predictions stem; for example, a major court decision, providing a basis for evaluating probable future court decisions on closely equivalent matters.

benchmark problem: A problem used to evaluate computer hardware and software, by comparing its performance with either system specifications or comparable hardware and software.

bench warrant: A warrant issued by a court, rather than by a justice of the peace or other official empowered to issue warrants. Such a warrant "from the bench" is issued by the court to bring in a subpoenaed witness, who has not appeared, one who has been indicted, or one who has been judged in contempt of the court.

beneficial interest: The right to benefits flowing from an insurance policy, a will, or a contract.

beneficiary: One who is legally entitled to benefit from a will, trust, insurance policy, or contract. A beneficiary may benefit from property legally held by another, as in many trusts, or may hold ownership of the property, as in a lump sum payment of all proceeds of a life insurance policy to survivors.

benefit: 1. Something providing gain, service, or any form of advantage. **2.** An item of compensation, other than wages, received by employees, such as a vacation, a pension plan, or health insurance.

benefit society: A voluntary association formed to provide accident, health, death and associated benefits to its members and their families in time of need.

benefits-received theory: The idea that taxes should as much as possible be levied on the basis of the taxpayer's use of the facilities and services being paid for; for example, a bridge, tunnel, or highway toll.

Benelux: An acronym for Belgium, the Netherlands and Luxembourg, which have formed a partial economic union with the stated policy of moving into complete economic union.

benevolent association: See benefit society.

bequest: A gift of personal property conveyed by the terms of a will; in contrast a willed gift of real property is called a devise.

Bernoulli distribution: See binomial probability distribution.

best efforts: In the issue of new securities, a commitment by the investment banking organization or group handling the new issue to sell the securities as an agent of the issuing party, rather than as underwriter of the entire issue. While an underwriter buys the entire issue, pays the issuer a fixed price, and takes possession of the securities, a best efforts seller acts as agent, does not take possession, and returns unsold securities to their issuer. New securities issues sold "best efforts" will often provide that unless a specified minimum portion of the issue is sold, the new issue will be withdrawn and the investors' money will be refunded.

beta (β) error: See Type II error.

Better Business Bureau: A private organization sponsored by business owners to foster ethical business practices among its members and in the entire business community; in many communities, a major handler and source of adjustment of consumer complaints directed against local businesses.

betterment: In accounting, spending that increases the value of a fixed asset in terms of operating efficiencies and useful life, rather than spending that maintains a fixed asset at present levels. A repair of an existing part is simply maintenance; replacement of that part with one that causes the machine to use less power than the machine used with its original part even when new, is betterment.

bias: 1. A tendency to select and interpret data based on preconceived conclusions. **2.** Systematic error in a statistical test, usually resulting from invalid selection of test groups. **3.** A synonym for discrimination.

bid: 1. An offer to buy immediately at a specific price. **2.** In the securities markets, an offer to buy at a specific price, which, if accepted by a seller, becomes a firm transaction. **3.** A formal quotation of the price a seller will require to do a job for a potential purchaser.

bid and asked: The price quotation on a stock, "bid" being the price at which the stock is wanted and "asked" the price at which it is offered for sale.

Big Board: A popular term for the New York Stock Exchange.

big business: In popular usage, the largest privately held enterprises in the country, taken as a group.

Big Steel: In popular usage, the United States Steel Corporation.

big ticket: In selling, a colloquial description of a high priced item or a large sale.

bilateral trade: Trade proceeding between two nations functioning as major trading partners, and wholly or largely excluding other nations. In practice, such trade is usually a one-way arrangement, with a dominant nation free to trade with many other nations and a subservient nation forced to confine its trade to the dominant nation, to its great economic disadvantage; a standard colonial arrangement.

bill: 1. A written, formal statement of specifics. Some of the many kinds of bills important in commerce are the bill of exchange, bill of lading, and bill of sale. **2.** A list of charges, as in an invoice for goods and services. **3.** A piece of paper money, such as a dollar bill.

billboard: An advertising poster or structure,

usually placed outdoors and aimed at catching the attention of travelers.

billing: The act of submitting a bill for payment, and the bill submitted.

billing machine: A business machine used to prepare invoices and related documents and to handle customer records.

billings: 1. The dollar amount of advertising placed by an agency for its clients during a specified period. **2.** The gross business done by an organization.

bill-only trading: The policy of a government's central bank, such as the Federal Reserve System, in trading only the short-term securities of its own government; in the United States, part of Federal manipulation of money and credit, through partial control of commercial bank reserves available for lending.

bill of credit: A written request to extend credit, and a guarantee of the credit extended, usually directed to correspondent banks abroad on behalf of a traveler.

bill of exchange: A written, unconditional order from one party instructing a second party to pay a specific amount of money to a third party. The order may be to pay on demand or at a specified future time.

bill of lading: A receipt for goods received for shipment by a carrier, which also serves as a contract for the shipment of those goods. A "straight" bill of lading designates the specific receiver of the shipment, and is non-negotiable, while an "order" bill of lading consigns the shipment to any named person and is negotiable.

bill of sale: A document signed by a seller passing title to personal property sold; usually a receipt for money paid by the buyer.

bimodal: See mode.

binary coded decimal (BCD): The expression of decimals as binary numbers for use in computer systems; since binary numbers are expressed using only two digits, 0 and 1, the decimal number 2 is expressed in binary code as 10, the decimal 3 as binary 11, the decimal 4 as binary 100, and so on.

binary number system: A number system based on only two digits, 0 and 1, in contrast to the decimal system, which is based on ten digits, 0 through 9. The binary digits 0 and 1 can also correspond to "on" and "off," "yes" and "no." Digital computers convert all data into binary digits, called bits, for storage and processing.

binder: 1. An interim agreement given to one applying for insurance, subject to full acceptance by the insurance company on the terms indicated in that policy. **2.** A relatively small "good faith" payment by buyer to seller in a real estate or insurance transaction; usually returnable if the transaction is not consummated.

binomial distribution: See binomial probability distribution.

biodegradable: Materials that by their chemical nature ultimately resolve themselves into their component parts, such as detergents that, after use, decompose into harmless substances.

biometrics: The measurement and assessment of biological information, using the tools of statistical analysis.

binomial probability distribution: A frequency distribution showing the number of times an event will occur, when only two possibilities exist and the observations are random and independent. This theoretical estimate, based on a mathematical formula by Jacob Bernoulli, is used to help researchers identify when data varies significantly, beyond chance variation, from the theoretical distribution; if the statistical test has been properly designed, the assumption is that if a significant variation exists, it is because of the factor being studied.

bionics: That branch of engineering which attempts to relate biological principles to the development of electronic and computer systems.

bit: 1. A single segment of information to be stored, usually the smallest piece of data capable of being stored in an information system. **2.** An abbreviation for binary digit.

black box: A device or theoretical construct in which functions are known or specified, but the true nature and inner workings are unknown; most often applied in electronics.

blackleg: See scab.

blacklist: 1. A list of employees whom a group of employers overtly or covertly agree not to hire, usually for union activity, but sometimes for such reasons as unpopular political beliefs. **2.** A list of those whom any group agrees to discriminate against, such as the Arab blacklist of companies doing business with Israel.

black market: Any marketplace in which something is traded contrary to law; an illegal marketplace. Black markets exist throughout the world in many commercial and financial areas, ranging from the illegal sale of meat in countries where meat is rationed to illegal trading of currency in countries where such trading is restricted or prohibited.

black money: Money or other stores of value gained illegally, such as the proceeds of bribery, embezzlement, and drug dealing.

Black Thursday: October 24, 1929, the day of the stock market crash which preceded the Great Depression of the 1930's.

blank check: 1. A check signed by its maker but with key information, such as payee or amount, omitted. **2.** A colloquial expression of the delegation of virtually unlimited responsibility or agency to another, as in "He has a blank check" to do something.

blanket bond: See fidelity bond.

blanket insurance policy: An insurance policy covering a group of related items, rather than a single item. Buildings and their contents are often covered by blanket policies, as are such related items as a fleet of company cars.

blanket mortgage: A mortgage loan secured

by more than one property, and which encumbers all properties so mortgaged. The mortgagee must pay back the entire amount of the mortgage before any of the properties are mortgage-free.

blanket order: See standing order.

blanket rate: A shipping rate that is uniform for all shipments of the same kind within a geographical area, whatever the shipping and receiving points within that area.

blind entry: An entry into accounting records that simply states the amount of the entry, but that is unsupported by additional information, explanation, or documentation.

blind trust: A popular term for an arrangement whereby a person places some or all financial affairs in trust, beyond that person's personal control; often an attempt by a public official to avoid charges of a conflict of interest.

block: 1. In the securities markets, a large number of shares of a single security traded as a group, as in the purchase or sale of a thousand shares of the common stock of American Telephone and Telegraph by a single buyer or seller. **2.** In computer operations, a group of records stored together and transferred from one area to another as a unit, to save both storage space and processing time.

blockade: The physical blocking of one or more ports by the armed forces of a country or group of countries, usually in wartime.

block booking: In the movie industry, a form of "tie-in sale," in which exhibitors are required by distributors to rent many films for distribution in order to secure any films; a form of forced distribution of films less desired by distributors by tying them to highly desired films.

blockbusting: The creation of an atmosphere of fear and hysteria in a community by real estate speculators, aiming to force homeowners of a certain race or group to sell at low prices, followed by quick resale at inflated prices to homeowners of another race

or group; most commonly employed to dislodge white homeowners and victimize black homeowners.

block diagram: In electronic data processing, a diagram of a system, instrument, or computer showing the main parts and annotating them to describe them and their interrelationships.

blocked account: A bank account or a store of money or credit that has been restricted by the country in which it is located, so that it cannot be drawn upon for use in other countries. Such blocked bank accounts are often also "frozen," that is held where they are, with any kind of use prohibited.

blocked exchange: A government policy that allows only specified kinds of foreign exchange transactions. This kind of exchange restriction is usually part of attempts to control current or potential balance of payments and international currency valuations problems.

block trader: In the securities industry, a trader who specializes or is largely engaged in the purchase and sale of substantial blocks of securities, working as a direct broker with buyers and sellers, and bypassing the organized stock markets. Large institutional traders, such as banks and mutual funds, work directly with block traders.

blotter: A place of first entry in a record-keeping system; for example, a daily record of commercial transactions kept by a business or of police matters kept by a police organization.

blowoff: A period of extremely heavy securities buying at the top of a rising market; almost always followed by a sharp, though sometimes brief, price break.

blowup: A substantially enlarged copy of a photograph or any other form of ink on paper.

BLS: See Bureau of Labor Statistics.

blue chip: A common stock that is highly esteemed as an investment, for its relative safety, consistent earnings, consistent dividend payout, and strong future prospects; often applied to the thirty industrials used in the Dow Jones Industrials average, but can refer to many other stocks as well.

blue collar worker: A non-supervisory worker primarily engaged in the production of goods and services, rather than in handling and accounting for transactions involving those goods and services; for example, a factory production worker, truck driver, miner or construction worker.

Blue Cross, Blue Shield: A private hospital and surgical insurance plan subscribed to by millions of Americans. For many, the plan is wholly or partly paid for by an employer, either voluntarily or as part of a collective bargaining agreement; for others, the plan is directly subscribed to by an individual or family.

blue laws: Laws prohibiting some kinds of activities on Sundays, including restrictions on the kinds of businesses allowed to open, the hours of operation and the kinds of goods that can be sold.

blue sky: Statements unsupported by facts or contrary to facts, and made with intent to deceive or defraud; "That has a lot of blue sky in it," is a common reaction to what is perceived as an over-imaginative sales approach.

Blue Sky laws: State securities laws aimed at the regulation of many aspects of securities industries practice and procedure, from the issuance of new securities to day-to-day procedures in the industry, with particular attention to questions of fraud and deceptive practices.

board: 1. In popular usage, the board of directors of an organization. **2.** In the securities industry, the device by which securities prices are posted in a brokerage office; usually no longer a board but an electronic data processing display terminal.

board lot: The standard minimum lot traded on a stock exchange, usually set by the rules of that exchange. For example, the New York Stock Exchange sets 100 shares as the standard lot of common shares traded, with a relatively small number of specific exceptions. Lots of less than 100 shares are called "odd lots."

board of directors: A group elected by a corporation's stockholders as the chief policy-making body of the corporation. The board of directors is responsible to the stockholders for the overall direction and control of the corporation and usually selects all major corporate officers.

Board of Governors: See Federal Reserve System.

board of trade: 1. An organization composed of member businesses, usually in a geographical area, which promotes group business and community interests. **2.** A name adopted by some commodity exchanges, as in the Chicago Board of Trade.

board room: 1. A room set aside by companies for meetings of the Board of Directors. In general usage, the term has come to mean any room set aside for formal meetings, including management, staff, and training meetings of all kinds. **2.** In the securities industry, a room set aside by brokers for customers, in which the latest quotations are posted.

body shop: An employment agency, especially one specializing in executive openings.

bogey: An informal work standard set by a group of workers, usually working on an incentive basis, in which the workers agree not to exceed the standard set; a strategy aimed at preventing employer incentive pay cuts, especially in piece work situations.

bogus: Describing that which is counterfeit or otherwise false, such as counterfeit money and other financial instruments.

boiler plate: A popular term for all standard clauses in legal documents, such as contracts and wills; sometimes used more loosely to describe any conventional often-encountered body of language.

boiler room: In the securities industry, any firm that uses high pressure selling tactics to deceptively and often fraudulently sell securities. Sales are usually made by phone out of minimally equipped offices, using techniques that are specifically prohibited by the securities laws.

bona fide: 1. In good faith; applies to one who contracts, holds, buys, or sells, innocent of any knowledge or intent that could be construed as bad faith or fraudulent intent. **2.** A popular term for guarantees of good faith, as when one party to an agreement wants to see the other party's "bona fides" before proceeding to agreement.

bond: 1. An interest-bearing debt instrument issued by a goverment or a corporation, which promises to pay specific sums at named times, with interest paid in installments and principal paid in a lump sum. **2.** An instrument pledging one as surety for another, as when a bonding company issues a surety bond to cover work to be performed by a contractor, or a bail bondsman issues a bond pledging payment of bail set in a criminal proceeding. **3.** Any stipulated amount that must be paid by a specified date. **4.** Describing taxable goods held pending payment of taxes or duties; such goods are described as being held "in bond."

bond circular: An advertisement offering bonds for sale, which fully describes the nature of the bonds being offered and any conditions attached to the offer; usually placed by banks, bond brokers, and bond underwriting syndicates.

bond discount: The difference between the face amount of a bond, or kind of bond, and any lower price at which it is actually sold.

bond dividend: A dividend issued by a corporation to its stockholders in the form of corporate bonds.

bonded debt: the amount of debt being carried by an entity, as indicated by the total amount of bonds outstanding.

bonded warehouse: A government-licensed warehouse that holds taxable goods pending payment of customs duties and other taxes due.

bond fund: 1. A mutual fund specializing in bond trading. **2.** A special fund set up by government to handle the proceeds of a bond issue.

bondholder: The owner of a bond and therefore the one to whom payment is owed. Ownership is evidenced by either the simple holding of bearer bonds or being the named owner of registered bonds.

bond house: A securities firm engaged in buying, selling, and underwriting bonds, sometimes exclusively and sometimes in conjunction with other securities industry activities.

bonding company: A company in the business of providing surety bonds.

bond market: A general term for all markets in which bonds are traded, including both stock exchanges listing bonds traded on those exchanges and the major over-the-counter transactions occurring between institutions.

bond premium: The difference between the face amount of a bond, or kind of bond, and any higher price at which it is actually sold.

bond ratings: Evaluation systems established by private companies to assess the investment quality or relative risks of bonds offered for sale. Moody's and Standard and Poor's are the two main bond risk evaluators. The Moody's system rates on a scale from Aaa to C; the Standard and Poor's scale runs from AAA to D.

bonus: 1. Anything freely given over and above what is due under the terms of a contractual relationship, as in a Christmas bonus given to employees or stock given to officers of a corporation by its board of directors. **2.** In industrial relations, payments made pursuant to incentive plans; also generally applied to some "fringes," such as overtime and holiday pay. **3.** In commercial contracts, sometimes used to describe premium payments, the addition of a fixed sum to be paid by one party to another on top of normal contract terms. For example, a lender in a tight money market may add a "point" to a mortgage loan, forcing the borrower to pay one extra percent of the entire amount loaned, payable immediately upon execution of the loan agreement, out of the proceeds of the loan.

bonus stock: Common stock given as a bonus to buyers of bonds or preferred stock, often in company start-up situations as extra payments to promoters and other "insiders." This practice is either prohibited or severely restricted in most states.

book: 1. To enter a transaction into a book of account. **2.** In the securities industry, a trading specialist's order book. **3.** A shorthand term for book value. **4.** To make a reservation.

book inventory: See perpetual inventory.

bookkeeper: One who handles a business' books of account on a day-to-day basis, short of an accountant's broader responsibility, such as preparing summary statements.

bookkeeping: The handling of all or part of a business' books of account, but stopping short of such account responsibilities as preparing summary financial statements and designing accounting systems. In practice, many bookkeeping and accounting functions are often difficult to separate.

book of account: Any record that is part of an accounting system, including both transaction records in permanent form and supporting papers, such as memoranda and invoices.

book of original entry: Any journal or other record of the day-to-day transactions of a business, kept in permanent form and serving as a source of entries into an accounting system.

book value: 1. The net assets of a business, derived by subtracting all liabilities from all assets. The book value of a share of common stock consists of net assets minus the value of all preferred stock outstanding divided by the number of shares of common stock outstanding. **2.** The net value of an asset, or a kind of asset, as carried on the books of account of a business entity, such as the book value of a company car.

Boolean algebra: A kind of algebra that deals with situations having only two possible states or values; developed by English nineteenth-century mathematician George Boole. It is basic to modern computer systems because it allows logical operations, used in switching and decision-making, to be handled through mathematical procedures; the two possible states may be "yes" and "no" or the values may be 0 and 1, the two digits in the binary number system used in computers.

boom: A period of strong and sustained economic growth; usually applied to an entire economy, but sometimes used to describe a company or section of the economy.

boom and bust: Describing the unrestrained operation of the business cycle; for example, the boom of the 1920s, followed by the bust that was the Great Depression of the 1930s.

boondoggling: A derogatory expletive used to characterize the wasteful handling of money and materials by governments and other bureaucracies.

bootlegging: The manufacture or smuggling of goods without payment of taxes legally due; for example, the interstate shipment of cigarettes without payment of taxes due.

bootstrapping: The generation of activity and development of business with limited means, depending for growth upon resources generated by the business.

borrowing: The process of getting a loan from others with a promise to repay, usually within a certain period at a specified rate of interest.

BOS: See operating system.

bottleneck: Anything tending to restrain the

development of a process. Examples are a single machine breakdown that may cut down the production of an item even though all other productive factors are operating at full capacity, or a single key executive whose absence may halt the decision-making process.

bottleneck inflation: Price rises in all or part of an economy caused by substantial and usually unanticipated increases in demand or decreases in supply for one product or a small group of products.

bottom: 1. In the securities industry, that time during a substantial stock prices swing in which average stock prices are lowest. During the course of such a swing, many successive estimates are made as to when the market has "touched bottom"; when estimates must be revised to conform with current realities observers often say "the bottom has dropped out of the market." **2.** A ship.

bottom line: The net of profit or loss; use of the term has expanded to include any result thought to be final, or to refer generally to the financial result of any endeavor, whether or not it is subject to accounting procedures. It is sometimes used as synonymous with "ultimate result."

bottomry: A loan secured by a vessel and often by its cargo as well.

bottomry bond: A document in which a shipowner pledges a ship as security for a loan. Under some conditions, as when a ship needs major repairs far from home, the ship's master may execute such a bond.

Boulwareism: A collective bargaining technique developed by the General Electric Company and named after a company officer, Lemuel Boulware, in which the company places a "take it or leave it" offer before the union at the start of negotiations, puts the terms of that offer into effect for non-union employees and represents itself as willing to undergo a strike if the union rejects the offer.

bourgeoisie: 1. In French, middle class. **2.** In Marxist theory, a term for the ruling or capitalist class, as distinguished from the proletariat or working class.

bourse: 1. The French stock exchange. **2.** European stock exchanges generally, with the exception of those located in the English-speaking countries.

boutique: A small business or department of a business selling goods, mainly clothing, put forward as fashionable and chic.

boycott: A concerted effort to harm a business by refusal to patronize or in any way deal with it, and to convince others to do the same, sometimes accompanied by acts of intimidation; often associated with union activity but widely used by citizens groups as well. A primary boycott is one directed by a union, its members, and sympathizers against an employer for collective bargaining goals. A secondary boycott is one directed against those who deal with that employer. Secondary boycotts are prohibited by statute, but court interpretations of primary, secondary, and consumer boycotts are in flux.

brainstorming: A technique aimed at stimulating the generation of as many solutions to a problem as possible; consists of a meeting, usually lasting no more than an hour, chaired by a strong moderator, who stimulates idea quantity and encourages building upon and modification of ideas expressed. Properly used, brainstorming encourages expression of all ideas, no matter how seemingly off-beat, and completely bars criticism of any ideas expressed; but it is sometimes misused, as when the moderator is ineffectual, the technique is misunderstood, criticism is allowed to develop, or the meeting wanders away from the specific problem addressed. The technique has been very successfully used in such areas as advertising and product development.

branch bank: The local office of a bank headquartered elsewhere. Branches of banks range widely in size and the scope of the functions performed. A large commercial banking branch may cover the whole spectrum of commercial bank functions and handle as much banking business as the home office, while a very small branch of a commercial bank, savings bank, or savings and loan association may be little more than a single room with a drive-in window.

branch banking: A system of banking authorized by law, by which banks are enabled to have a home office and many branch offices. In the United States, banks have limited ability to branch, being confined to states, metropolitan areas, cities, and in some instances to single home office installations, with only foreign branch operations unrestricted. In many other countries, banks are national, can branch without restriction, and therefore in some instances have thousands of branches.

branching: 1. Selection from among alternate courses of operating action by a computer at a decision point during execution of a program; also called jumping or transferring control. **2.** A form of organization of material, allowing humans or machines to choose alternative courses of action resulting from previous choices made. Commonly used in programmed instruction and computer-assisted instruction to allow students to build a body of knowledge based upon choices, with positive reinforcement resulting from correct choices.

branch manager: One who holds the job of managing a branch of a retail organization; for example, the manager of a bank branch.

branch store: The local outlet of a retailing company. Usually, one store in a market area is designated the main store, while the others are designated branches; but where a company operates several large, multi-department stores in a single market area, the distinction between "main" and "branch" stores becomes meaningless.

brand: A specific or general name, often accompanied by a distinctive mark, that identifies a product, a group of products, or a company making those products. For example, the General Motors Company makes a group of cars called Cadillacs, one of which is the Eldorado model; all three names are brands. As brand names alone, they are not trademarks, which must be uniquely identifiable and registered by law, but they are protected by law, so that no other auto maker can use these brands.

brand consciousness: The extent to which consumers are influenced in their buying decisions by their regard for a particular brand or company.

brand image: The total product picture created for a brand, usually a compound of company intentions, product performance facts, and actual marketplace conditions. A product's ideal brand image, as hoped and worked for by a company and its marketing staff, must be distinguished from its actual brand image.

brand recognition: The extent to which consumers literally see a brand when displayed among other brands; usually a key to buying preference.

breach of contract: Failure by a contracting party to do or allow to be done something that is required by the terms of the contract; or clear renunciation of the contract before it goes into effect. Such failure or renunciation can lead to invalidation of the contract and to the assessment of damages.

breach of warranty: See warranty.

break: In the securities markets, a very sharp downturn in prices, often following a period of relatively narrow price movement.

break even: To conclude any commercial transaction with neither profit nor loss; often used narrowly, to describe only the money factors in the transaction, failing to take into account many very real costs, such as overhead.

break-even analysis: An analysis of expense and revenue factors, often expressed graphically, aimed at determining at what cost and price points a product, product line, or company break even. Because break-even charts indicate alternate break-even points as cost and price assumptions are changed, this kind of analysis is especially useful in profitability studies, new product proposal evaluation, pricing, and in a large number of corporate planning applications.

break-even chart: A chart used to represent graphically the results of break-even analyses.

break-even point: The intersection of costs and prices in a break-even analysis. In planning, break-even points change as assumptions change; in profitability studies the actual break-even point of a product, product line, or company is a crucial success indicator.

break points: The points at which discounts for higher quantities purchased apply; for example, when a discount moves from 5% to 10% for over 100 units purchased, the break point is at 100 units.

Bretton Woods Agreement: An agreement stemming from the 44-nation conference held in Bretton Woods, New Hampshire in July, 1944, under which the International Monetary Fund and the Bank for Reconstruction and Development were established.

brief: A written document submitted to a court on a pending matter and serving as a basis for argument to be presented to the court on that matter.

broad market: In the securities industry, a market in which trading is very active and many kinds of shares or commodities are traded; used to describe wide and heavy volume, without reference to upward or downward trends in market prices.

broadside: A piece of advertising matter, consisting of a single sheet of paper that contains the entire advertising message. The sheet of paper is often, but not always folded down to a smaller size for ease of distribution.

brochure: A booklet devoted to advertising matter, often illustrated, printed on expen-

sive paper, and using a good deal of display type. Brochures vary widely in size and style, ranging from a small, folded broadside to a substantial booklet virtually indistinguishable from a small book.

broken lot: A group of items for sale in a smaller than usual lot. For example, if a retailer may normally buy from a wholesaler by the dozen, any lot of less than a dozen offered by the wholesaler is a broken lot. In the securities industry, broken lots are called "odd lots."

broker: One engaged in the business of bringing buyers and sellers together for a fee, who acts as a limited agent for purposes of purchase or sale. A broker acts in another's name, as distinguished from commission merchants or factors, who act in their own names, buying and selling goods belonging to others. A broker is an agent, as distinguished from a middleman, who brings parties together, but not as agent for any of them. There are many kinds of specialist brokers, include stock, insurance, real estate, commodities, ship, money, and mortgage brokers.

brokerage: 1. Fees to brokers for transactions arranged between buyers and sellers; such fees may take many forms, including percentage commissions, fixed fees per transaction, and a wide variety of special arrangements in specific situations. **2.** A business run by a broker or brokers.

broker-dealer: See dealer.

broker's loan: A loan made by a bank to a securities broker or dealer to finance securities carried, underwritten, and purchased for customer margin accounts, the securities acting as collateral for the loan.

bubble: An investment that may or may not be intrinsically and dangerously speculative, but which becomes so as irrational buying pushes it higher and higher, far beyond the real value of its underlying assets. At some point in every bubble, speculative confidence weakens, actual or adverse facts begin to be asserted and panic selling begins as "the bubble bursts."

bucket shop: A fraudulent stock brokerage operation, which either takes customer orders and money, doesn't execute the orders, keeps the money, folds and disappears very quickly; or takes customer orders and money and doesn't execute the orders in a timely way to the detriment of the customer and the advantage of the bucket shop operators.

budget: 1. Any formal estimate of future income and costs. A budget is a primary financial planning tool for public and private purposes. The operating budget, usually prepared from year to year, functions as both a forecasting device and performance yardstick; the capital budget functions to forecast expenses and consequent capital needs. **2.** To estimate future income and to attempt to establish a spending plan that conforms with income estimates.

budgetary variance: The amount that actual income and expense differ from the estimates made for budget purposes.

budgeting: The formal process of developing a budget. In business organizations, budget development is often a process involving a series of formal estimates made by every responsible member of management, the working of those estimates into coherent company-wide forecasts, a series of refining and reworking steps, and ultimately the production of the budget as a primary working tool for all of management.

budget period: The time covered by a budget. Operating budgets are normally developed on an annual basis, with results stated monthly and the budget reviewed quarterly, annually, or at any time variances from forecasts cause management to undertake a special review. The period of a capital budget varies with the projects budgeted.

buffer: In electronic data processing, a device that temporarily stores information being passed from one section of a computer system to another; often used when one part of a system processes information too fast for another part to handle.

buffer device: In computer technology, a temporary information storage vehicle, in which information is allowed to accumulate until it is of sufficient volume to permit efficient computer processing.

buffer stock: 1. Any materials held in inventory to meet unusual demand. **2.** Surpluses held by producing nations for sale in years of poor production, under some international commodity agreements, thus controlling supply and fixing prices.

bug: 1. A covert listening device; often used by criminals, law enforcement officials and others seeking access to otherwise private information. **2.** An error or defect in any system, program, machine or process.

bugging: The process of installing and operating a covert listening device.

building and loan association: An early form of the name for what has become the savings and loan association. As early "building associations" began to focus more and more on the savings function, the general name for this kind of banking organization changed as well.

building code: A set of local laws and regulations controlling all substantial construction activities within each jurisdiction. Building codes cover most kinds of new construction and associated activities, such as service roads and water supply. They also cover modifications of existing construction, often requiring the filing of specifications and the granting of official approval for relatively small modifications.

building permit: An authorization granted by local authorities to a builder to pursue construction activities.

built-in stabilizer: Any integral portion of an economic structure that tends to smooth out the "boom-and-bust" tendencies of the business cycle, including such features as unemployment compensation, social security and private pension payments, welfare payments, price supports, and tuition assistance plans. Built-in stabilizers are to be distinguished from such potential stabilizers as money supply control, which depends on conscious acts of manipulation.

bulge: In the securities markets, any relatively small, unanticipated, and short-lived increase in the general level of securities prices.

bulk cargo: A substantial amount of goods, unpackaged and usually measured, bought, and sold only by the vehicle in which it is shipped, such as a freight carload of goods, or part or all of a ship's hold.

bulk freight: See bulk cargo.

bulk sale: 1. The sale of any large, unpackaged quantity of goods. **2.** The sale of most or all of the assets or stock of a business, to avoid creditors or as part of a bankruptcy proceeding. Such sales to avoid creditors are prohibited by law.

Bulk Sales Act: A kind of statute aimed at the prohibition of secret bulk sales of assets or stock by businesses to avoid the claims of creditors.

bull: One who feels that an entire market, or one or more securities or commodities traded in that market, will rise, and acts accordingly; the opposite of bear. Bulls often buy when they think the market is rising or about to rise, and optimistically hold on when the market is falling.

bullion: Gold and silver in any form other than coins, and available for coinage. Bullion may be in bars, ingots, lumps, or nuggets; may be of ore or refined; and may be refined and put to other non-coinage uses, such as dishes or jewelry. In international markets, gold and silver are usually encountered in standard bars of minimum specified fineness or quality.

bullion dealer: A private person or organization buying and selling gold or silver bullion.

bullion value: The value of a coin as measured by the market value of its gold or silver content at current market prices, treating the coin as if it were a commodity.

bull market: A market in which prices rise over a long enough period of time to indicate an upward trend; normally used to describe trends measured in months or years, rather than short-term swings, no matter how sharp the move upward or how heavy the volume traded.

bumping. The pushing of one worker out of a job by another worker with great seniority, who is able to do the job. The seniority involved may be voluntarily recognized by management or provided by a union contract, and may be plant-wide or department-wide.

bureau: 1. Any organization, as in Better Business Bureau; usually a branch of a large organization. **2.** An administrative division or subdivision of government, as in the Bureau of Printing and Engraving.

Bureau of Customs: See Customs Service.

Bureau of Employee's Compensation: A bureau of the Department of Labor, responsible for administering Federal workmen's compensation laws and also generating a variety of industrial safety programs.

Bureau of International Commerce: A Federal agency responsible for assisting the American business community in a wide variety of international matters, including exporting and licensing, and for representing the United States government in dealing with international trading authorities.

Bureau of International Labor Affairs: A Bureau of the Department of Labor, responsible for policy advice and analysis of international labor developments affecting the United States and for officially representing the United States on international labor bodies.

Bureau of Labor Statistics (BLS): A bureau of the Department of Labor, responsible for research and publication in the field of labor statistics, and a major publisher of a wide variety of important publications in the field, including the Consumer Price Index, the Monthly Labor Review, the Occupational Outlook Handbook, and the Handbook of Labor Statistics.

Bureau of Printing and Engraving: A bureau of the Treasury Department, responsible for the total production of all currency and other financial printing, and a wide variety of other items for the United States government.

Bureau of Standards: A bureau of the Department of Commerce, responsible for the development of a wide variety of industrial standards.

buried offer: A solicitation to buy placed rather obscurely in the body of an advertisement, rather than being clearly stated; usually intended to make an attempt to sell seem an offer to send something free.

business: **1.** Any gainful activity. The gain sought is generally commercial or financial, but the term is so broad that it includes activities engaged in for personal development and emotional gain. **2.** An organization engaged in any form of commerce. **3.** An amount of trade engaged in, as in "Total business for the day was $1,000."

business activity: The general level of business transactions within an economy, taking into account such indicators as the number of transactions, their total value, employment and loans.

business advisor: See consultant.

business agent: A full-time union official who handles the affairs of one or more local unions, including major grievances, financial and insurance matters, some aspects of negotiations, and most other day-to-day administrative affairs.

business barometer: See indicators.

business combination: Any fusing of two or more businesses into one, however achieved. Such combinations may take the form of acquisitions by one of others; of consolida-tions forming new businesses; of purchases; or of mergers of interest.

business cycle: A widely observed general tendency of the United States and other similar economies to alternate periods of economic prosperity and depression, boom and bust. In recent decades the intensity of cyclical swings has generally been thought to have diminished; causes of cycles and variations in their intensity are the subject of considerable theoretical speculation.

business environment: A complex of social, political and economic factors surrounding a business, and impinging on its ability to operate. Such factors as government regulations, taxes, local zoning restrictions, consumerism, and local union activity are elements that combine to create a business environment.

business ethics: An attempt to apply the highest ethical standards of the larger community to the business community; business ethics are in no way different from any other ethical conception, and constructs in this area vary as widely as they do in the larger community.

business failure: A firm that ceases doing business primarily because of inability to meet its obligations. Failure may be involuntary, as in bankruptcies, foreclosures, assignments, and attachments; or it may be voluntary, as in cessation of business leaving unpaid debts or making an agreement to pay part of creditors' claims.

business firm: An organization doing business for profit and organized as a corporation, partnership or individual proprietorship.

business forecasting: Attempting to predict future business trends and events through the use of a considerable variety of analytical approaches and tools. Forecasting usually involves the use of statistical techniques, often featuring mathematical modes and computerized analyses. Business forecasting is far from precise, and invariably includes political and social analyses and a good deal of speculation.

business game: A decision-making exercise, usually encountered in business courses and other training situations, in which the players enter a business case simulation, receive data, make decisions, and then evaluate success in terms of the rules of the exercise. Some of the more complex business games use computer programs as game-playing and evaluative tools.

business indicator: See indicator.

business insurance: Any kind of insurance taken by a business for business purposes, including such insurance on property and the conduct of business as fire, casualty, theft, credit, and business interruption; and such business-related insurance as life, health, and accident.

business interruption insurance: Insurance covering an insured against losses caused by cessation of business, usually in addition to coverage for direct damage to property; for example, a sum paid to the owners of a restaurant for a proportion of profits lost by inability to do business caused by a fire, between the time the fire occurred and the time the restaurant reopened after repairs.

business law: See commercial law.

business panics: See panics.

business paper: Notes or trade acceptances used as payment for merchandise, instead of cash or checks; synonymous with "trade paper."

business risk: For credit and investment purposes, an estimate of the skills and performance of management, of such marketplace factors as relative prices and the strength of competition, and of the over-all conduct of and prospects for the business.

business situs: A legal determination as to where a business is located for tax purposes, more popularly referred to as "doing business at."

business trust: See Massachusetts Trust.

business unionism: A philosophy of unionism stressing economic, rather than social and political objectives as primary goals. It is the dominant trend in the American trade union movement, in contrast to the primarily political and social goals of most of the world's other trade union movements.

bust: A deep, major, protracted downward swing in the business cycle; an economic depression. There have been several substantial downward swings in the business cycle since 1945, but the last generally recognized "bust" was the Great Depression of the 1930s.

buy American: 1. A protectionist slogan, aimed at fostering the purchases of American-made goods and services by Americans. **2.** A series of laws and regulations designed to mandate purchase of American-made goods and services by the American government, except in instances of very large price differentials between American-made and foreign goods and services.

buyer: A purchasing executive for a large retail store or group of stores, mainly purchasing finished goods for resale to the public, rather than materials and services to be used in the creation of goods, which is the normal function of a purchasing agent.

buyer's market: Any market in which supply exceeds demand, giving buyers leverage over sellers in such areas as prices, quality guarantees, and delivery timing.

buying: See purchasing.

buying in: A bidding technique in which the bidder makes a lower-than-cost bid to get a job, hoping to secure through that job other, more profitable jobs or to develop billings in excess of estimates during the course of the job.

buying office: A purchasing office for a large retail store or group of stores. While the buying office of a large retail chain will buy exclusively for that chain, an independent buying office may represent many smaller stores which are pooling their buying efforts.

buying on margin: See margin.

buyout: 1. A purchase of controlling owner-ship in a business organization. **2.** A pur-chase of any entire stock of goods for sale.

buzz words: Fashionable jargon; those words and phrases currently in vogue in any trade or area. Such words are used widely for a rel-atively short time, and then, with few excep-tions, quickly pass out of active use.

by-laws: 1. The rules of a corporation, gov-erning the conduct of its own internal affairs and supplementing the articles of incorpora-tion. **2.** Generally, any set of rules adopted by an organization to govern the conduct of its own internal affairs.

by-product: Any additional product stem-ming from activity primarily aimed at pro-ducing something else. For example, coke ovens work primarily to turn coal into coke for use in the steelmaking process; however, the gases released from the burning coal are captured and refined into a series of highly profitable by-products.

byte: In computer languages, the shortest se-quence of binary digits which the computer will recognize and work with, such as the eight-digit, or 8-bit, sequence used to repre-sent a character in the IBM 360 system; the basic unit of the Extended Binary Coded Decimal Interchange Code.

C

©: The symbol for copyright.

CAB: See Civil Aeronautics Board.

cable transfer: A means of sending money abroad quickly by cable or other electronic means, through a bank or other transmitting agency.

cable rate: The rate charged by a bank for sending money abroad via cable or other electronic means. The purchaser of the bank draft being transmitted pays the cost of the cable plus a somewhat higher rate than would be charged for a check, reflecting cable handling costs plus the issuing bank's loss of interest on the funds so quickly transmitted, which if transmitted by check, would take as long as several weeks to clear.

c.a.f.: See cost and freight.

CAI (computer-assisted instruction): See programmed instruction.

calculator: A machine that does arithmetic and in some instances solves other mathematical problems. The term is generic, including all such machines, from the simplest adding machine to the most complex computer.

calendar variation: See seasonal variation.

call: 1. An option to buy a specific amount of stock at a fixed price and within a specified time. The option buyer is speculating—buying an option for a set amount now and hoping that the stock will rise more than the amount paid within the period covered by the option. If the stock does rise the option buyer may profit greatly by exercising the option, buying the stock, and then immediately reselling it. But if the stock goes down, the option buyer will lose some or all of the money spent for the option. The opposite of a "call" is a "put." **2.** A demand for payment of the balance due on a purchase of capital stock. **3.** A repurchase of outstanding preferred stocks or bonds by a corporation, if authorized by the terms of the issue. **4.** In computer systems, to transfer control to a named sub-routine.

callable bond: A bond that may be redeemed by its issuer at any time before maturity, usually with a premium payment to the bondholder at the time of redemption. The "callable" feature of the bond is specified by the terms of the issue, often on the face of the bond itself.

callback: A selling call on a prospect who has been previously called on, in an attempt to sell goods or services presented earlier.

callback pay: Pay for work performed after an employee has finished a regular workday and has been called to return to work, usually because of unforeseen circumstances or emergency. Such pay is usually at premium rates and is often a guaranteed minimum sum for the callback.

call-in pay: A minimum amount of pay guaranteed to workers who report for work as scheduled, but are then sent home early because of insufficient work. Usually, call-in pay is provided under a union contract; occasionally it is provided voluntarily by an employer.

call loan: A demand loan, which either

lender or borrower may terminate at will and without notice. In the securities industry, it is a standard form of loan from bank to stockbroker, amounting to a special line of credit on which interest is computed daily at that day's rate.

call money: Money lent by banks on which repayment may be demanded at any time and without notice.

call pay: See call-in pay.

call premium: The amount of the premium payment due a bondholder when a callable bond is redeemed before maturity by its issuer, as specified by the terms of the bond issue. That amount may vary with redemption date, the premium diminishing as the bond matures.

call report: 1. A written report made by outside salespeople to management, specifying and usually describing selling and service calls they have made on prospects and customers. **2.** Formal statements of condition made by banks to regulatory authorities, usually at times and in forms specified by law. A bank's call report is often termed its "legal" statement.

cancellation: 1. The legal termination of an instrument or agreement on maturity or completion, such as termination of an insurance policy pursuant to the terms of the contract, whether before or at end of the term covered by the contract, or the retirement of a debt instrument upon payment in full. **2.** The termination of an order for goods or services, often prior to fulfillment of that order.

cancellation clause: A contract provision allowing termination of the contract by a party, usually under specified circumstances.

cancelled check: A check which has been drawn against a bank account, paid by the bank holding that account; marked, perforated or otherwise voided; and returned to its maker. Cancelled checks serve as evidence that banks have cashed them and that bills have been paid; they also provide hard evidence for use in tax and accounting audits.

canned presentation: A fully prepared sales presentation, presented exactly as written, either by a seller who has memorized it or by use of a recording device.

canvassing: 1. Making a count, as in the conduct of a poll. **2.** Searching for sales prospects by means of personal calls on those who might be prospects; sometimes used as a synonym for selling.

capacity: 1. The ability of a business to produce goods and services with its present physical equipment. Usually stated as full theoretical capacity, it differs from practical full capacity, which takes into account unavoidable production losses caused by such factors as machine breakdowns and worker absences. **2.** In extractive industries, the amount of material that can be extracted in a given period by present equipment, such as the amount of coal a mine or oil a well can produce in twenty-four hours. **3.** The amount of freight a carrier can carry, as the weight of freight a truck can bear or the volume of goods a boxcar can take. **4.** A synonym for "business risk."

capacity ratio: The relationship between theoretical and practical full capacity, expressed as a ratio.

capacity utilization rate: See operating rate.

capital: 1. Any kind of tangible wealth that is or can be used to produce more wealth. In this sense, money invested to start a business is capital. Intangibles, such as a good reputation of one starting a business, are often loosely called capital, but the term is then stretched so far as to make it lose its useful meaning. **2.** The net worth of a business. **3.** Amounts invested by shareholders in a business, called "paid-in" capital.

capital account: 1. An account or group of accounts indicating ownership equities. They are designated proprietorship, partnership, or capital stock accounts, depending on the business' form of organization. **2.** Any fixed asset account.

capital appropriation: A sum authorized for capital expenditure by the policy-making group of a business organization, usually the board of directors.

capital asset: Any asset held and used for the production of goods and services, including fixed assets, such as land, plant, raw materials sources, and reserves; investments in owned and afiliated companies; and some long-term intangibles, such as patents.

capital budget: A budget or part of a budget which handles the acquiring and financing of capital assets. Capital budgets may be developed by private organizations or governments; may be short-term or long-term; and may be financed out of current revenues or debt instruments or both.

capital coefficient: The amount of new capital investment needed to produce one new unit of output capacity. The figure can be derived for a whole economy or any portion of an economy, and it varies widely from enterprise to enterprise and industry to industry. For example, the capital coefficient, or the amount of new investment, needed in the oil refining industry, which requires heavy plant expenditure to increase capacity and employs relatively few people, is much larger than the capital coefficient of the garment industry, which requires relatively small plant expenditure to increase capacity and employs a great many people.

capital costs: An estimate of what the money tied up in inventories might earn if applied to other investments. For example, if $1,000 tied up in inventory might earn $80 per year, the capital cost of carrying that much inventory for one year would be $80.

capital expenditure: 1. An expenditure to acquire capital assets. **2.** In accounting, an expenditure which wholly or mainly benefits future accounting periods rather than the current period.

capital flight: See flight of capital.

capital flow: The movement of funds in and out of an enterprise, as recorded in a cash flow statement.

capital formation: In an economy, the total net private investment in capital assets, derived by totalling gross capital assets investments and subtracting depreciation and other relevant deductions. The rate of capital formation is an important long-range indicator of the future health of any economy.

capital gains: The profits realized from a sale or exchange of capital assets, usually securities or realty. Long-term capital gains are given preferred treatment for tax purposes, since they are taxed at substantially lower rates than short-term gains, which are treated as ordinary income for income tax purposes.

capital goods: Capital in the form of fixed assets used to produce goods, such as plant, equipment and rolling stock. The term is used to describe the assets themselves, rather than the amount or kinds of funds used to acquire them.

capital-intensive: Any kind of business or economic unit requiring large amounts of capital investment relative to the number of people employed in it. For example, the nuclear industry requires far more investment per employee than the garment industry. The nuclear industry is then described as capital-intensive, while the garment industry is described as the opposite—labor-intensive.

capital investment: See capital expenditure.

capitalism: An economic system characterized by private ownership of capital and investment of that capital in the means of production and other wealth-producing ways. Private ownership and the pursuit of profit are essential features of capitalism. In many countries, economies mix public and private ownership, but where a major private sector controls substantial industries, capitalism can be said to exist.

capital issues: The stocks and bonds issued by corporations and governments to finance the purchase of capital assets or to permanently increase the pool of working capital funds. In modern corporate practice, some long-term notes and lines of credit also function as part of the long-term fund pool, though they are treated differently than stocks and bonds for accounting purposes.

capitalization: The total value of a corporation's stocks, bonds and surpluses. The term includes stocks, normally carried at par rather than market values, and bonds and debentures carried at their face values, but does not include other debts, such as bank loans.

capitalize: To carry forward capital expenditures for accounting purposes. Investments in the acquisition of capital assets then appear as expenditures in future profit and loss statements, and are associated then with any benefits derived from those assets.

capitalized value: The current value of assets that will yield future earnings, derived by projecting both anticipated earnings and interest on the money invested as if it had been borrowed forward over the life of the asset.

capitalized expense: An expense charged to a capital asset account which would normally be charged to a current account and would appear on the current profit and loss statement; for example, tax and interest payments on a plant being built but not yet in operation.

capital market: The long-term debt obligations market, dealing in long-term loans and bonds, with the proceeds of the obligations normally used to finance the purchase of capital assets. The distinction between long- and short-term loan markets tends to blur in modern practice, as most major lending institutions engage in both long- and short-term financing, with financing "packages" often including loans in several forms and of varying durations.

capital movements: The movement of capital, both government and private, between countries, including long- and short-term loans, credits, deposits, and any other form in which capital can move. The total of all such capital movements forms the capital account portion of a country's balance of payments.

capital-output ratio: See capital coefficient.

capital restructuring: See recapitalization.

capital spending: See capital expenditure.

capital stock: The ownership stock in a business, representing the equity held by its owners. Not all of the capital stock need be distributed; some may be held in the business. Sometimes stock issued and outstanding is bought back, wholly or in part, by a business.

capital sum: The principal of an investment plus any sums that have been added to that principal but not yet accounted for as income.

capital surplus: See paid-in surplus.

capital turnover: The speed with which the net worth of a business turns over relative to that business' sales in a given period; usually a period generally accepted and used as a basis of comparison by those in that industry. For example, a business with net worth of $2,000,000 and sales of $4,000,000 in a year experiences capital turnover of 2:1 in that year. Each industry has its own optimum and average turnover rates, and those considering the extension of credit to a business take capital turnover into account in assessing the health of a business, with relatively slow turnover an indication of possible problems.

captive audience: An audience that cannot, practically, escape from a message being broadcast or otherwise communicated to them; for example, those employed in a workplace, or those travelling in an airplane.

captive company: A company entirely owned by another company, and organized for the purpose of providing a particular kind of service or performing a certain kind of function for the owning company; for example, the Western Electric Company, which provides telephone equipment for American Telephone and Telegraph, or a real estate company that functions solely to hold and manage parent company installations.

captive item: An item that is both produced and used by a single firm. For example, telephone equipment is both manufactured and used by American Telephone and Telegraph through its Western Electric Company subsidiary.

captive market: A market that has little real choice as to which seller to buy from; for example, the market for electric power, which is substantially dominated by one supplier in each area.

captive shop: See captive company.

card: In electronic data processing, a machine-processable piece of paper or cardboard, holding information which the computer will accept and hold.

cardinal number: A number that indicates amount or quantity, such as 1, 2, 3, 100, 200, or 300, in contrast to an ordinal number, which indicates a specific position in a series of numbers, such as first, second, or third.

card punch: See keypunch.

card reader: A computer input device that reads information from punched cards, and translates that information into machine language for computer use.

card reader-punch device: A computer card reader that also punches the data read into additional sets of computer-readable cards.

card-to-magnetic tape converter: A machine that reads punched cards directly onto magnetic tape, which may then be used in a computer system, rather than reading the cards directly into the computer.

card verifier: A machine that allows an operator to manually verify the accuracy of card punching for computer input purposes.

career ladder: A series of generally related jobs in which each job attained provides the qualifications for getting the next higher position. The term is often used to mean any set of upwardly mobile career moves.

cargo: Materials of any kind being shipped by sea or air, but normally applied to international shipments.

carloadings: The number of freight cars loaded by American railroads every week. Carloadings are a major indicator of business activity, though not as important now as before alternate means of transportation cut the relative amount of freight carried by the railroads.

carrier: A transportation company, such as a railroad, airline, shipping company, trucking company, taxi company or bus line.

carrot and stick approach: A negotiating and managing theory that posits the value of alternating and sometimes simultaneously presenting both "soft" and "hard" positions; a variation on Theodore Roosevelt's "speak softly and carry a big stick."

carry: To extend credit to a customer beyond normal practice. For example, a supplier, who normally requires payment within sixty days after delivery of goods and will cut off credit arrangements if a payment is not made, may decide to extend credit and deliver more goods to help a customer through a cash flow problem; a bank may carry a borrower by extending a loan for the same reason.

carrybacks: For business income tax purposes, those current operating losses that can be used to offset profits from preceding years, thereby diminishing taxes for those years.

carryforwards: For business income tax purposes, those current operating losses that cannot be absorbed as carrybacks to diminish taxes on income of previous years, but can be used as deductions carrying over and thrown forward into succeeding years.

carrying charge: Any normal and repeated charge stemming from asset ownership, such as interest charged by brokers on margin accounts and charges for warehousing goods.

carrying cost: The cost of holding an asset, such as inventory or equipment, for a given period, including both actual costs, such as maintenance and warehousing, and opportunity costs, such as the interest that might have been earned at current rates on money tied up in inventory and spent in warehousing.

carrying value: See book value.

carryovers: See carrybacks and carry forwards.

cartel: 1. A group of business entities functioning as a monopoly. **2.** A group of companies or countries functioning together to control a world market. A recent example is the Organization of Petroleum Exporting Countries.

cartridge: A container holding materials or information, inserted as a unit into a device for use or display of that material or information; for example, fountain pen ink holders, television program cassettes, and containers holding computer tape.

cartwheel: A colloquial name for the silver dollar.

case law: The body of law formed by preceding cases and therefore possessing value as precedents for use in deciding current cases, as distinguished from the body of law formed by laws, regulations, and other sources. In practice, cases, statutes, regulations, and other sources form an intertwined body of law.

case method: A mode of teaching that stresses a case-by-case problem-solving approach rather than an exposition of general principles. Long practiced in law schools, the illustrative use of cases has also become widely adopted in business schools.

cash: 1. Money in any form that can be directly and immediately used as legal tender, including paper money and coins. **2.** For accounting purposes, anything immediately usable or almost immediately convertible into legal tender, including paper money, coins, checks, net bank balances, and some other negotiable instruments. **3.** To turn a negotiable instrument of any kind into cash, as in cashing a bond.

cash and carry: A way of doing business that requires the buyer to pay cash immediately for goods and to carry away the goods bought. Cash and carry is often used in private sales, auctions, and cut price sales conducted by businesses.

cash assets: Assets that are either in ready cash form, such as currency and coins on hand, or that can be easily turned into cash while continuing business as usual, such as bank deposits and trade acceptances.

cash basis: An accounting method that records and keeps books on the basis of when cash is received and spent, rather than accruing income and expenditures. While most individuals operate on a cash basis, most businesses are on an accrual basis.

cashbook: A book in which cash transactions are recorded.

cash budget: An income and expenditure estimate based solely upon cash receipts and cash spent for a certain period. In a cash budget, nothing is accrued or in any way deferred.

cash customer: One who pays for purchases in cash. "Cash" in this sense is used broadly, and includes currency, coins, checks, negotiable money orders, and other readily negotiable instruments.

cash discount: A price reduction for early payment of a bill for goods or services. For example, an industrial company may offer its customers a 2% discount if goods are paid for within ten days after delivery, rather than within the thirty days usually allowed for payment. Or a retailer may offer a discount for an immediate cash payment rather than a payment made by a credit card or charge account.

cash dividend: A dividend paid in cash. Most

dividends are paid in cash, although some are paid in stocks, bonds, or other forms.

cash equivalent: What something would be worth if immediately converted into cash. The term is normally encountered in a sale or exchange in which items that are paid for in ways other than money are valued by the transacting parties at agreed-upon levels.

cash flow: The movement of cash into, through, and out of an entity. Cash flow may be traced for an individual or a major corporation; for a single product or a line of products or services.

cash flow statement: A statement accounting for the movement of cash through an entity during a specific period.

cashier: 1. One who directly handles and records receipts and expenditures for a business. 2. In banking, an officer in charge of the bank's funds, who is directly responsible for all disbursements and must personally authorize them.

cashier's check: A bank's check, signed by a cashier of the bank, and functioning as a direct obligation of the bank. Cashier's checks are issued for many purposes, including deposit transfers, bill payments, and loans.

cash in transit: Cash in motion to or from an entity which, at a given moment, has not yet been received or expended and which therefore does not appear on the entity's books as a receipt or expenditure.

cash machine: A machine for dispensing cash, used by banks as a mechanical means of handling depositor transactions, often in hours when banks are closed.

cash market: A market in which commodities are sold for immediate delivery in return for a cash payment.

cash on delivery (COD): The payment terms of a purchase in which buyer and seller agree that payment will be made in cash immediately upon delivery and acceptance of the goods, with completion of delivery contingent upon cash payment.

cash price: The price of goods or services when payment is made either on delivery or within a specified period thereafter. Normally, cash prices assume payment within 30 days of delivery.

cash rich: Describing a company holding a relatively large amount of cash or easily convertible-to-cash assets for a company of its size and kind of business.

cash sale: 1. A sale paid for immediately in cash, either at the point of sale or on delivery, as in most non-credit retail stores. 2. A sale paid for soon after delivery, often within a specified 30-day period, as in many industrial sales.

cash statement: A periodic statement of cash flow for specific, usually short periods, such as days or weeks. The statement shows cash balances on hand at the beginning of the period, cash in and out during the period, and the balance on hand at the close of the period.

cash surrender value: The amount an insurance policy holder or other contracting party can recover upon cancellation of a contract. The term is most often applied to "whole" or "straight-line" life insurance policies, which incorporate both death insurance and savings features, and is the net of previously paid premiums plus interest minus sums actually paid for the insurance portion of the policy and certain other deductions.

casual labor: Work that is irregular, often temporary, and usually requires little or no skill. Such work is often seasonal and performed in several successive locations, as is much farm labor. The term is also used to refer to those who do that kind of work.

casual laborer: See casual labor.

casualty insurance: A now somewhat outdated term, generally describing all the kinds of insurance other than life, fire and marine insurance; now covered by multiple line companies, writing all property insurance, including fire and casualty.

casual worker: See casual labor.

cathode ray tube (CRT): A vacuum tube, such as a television picture tube or a computer system display device, used to show images of data or designs; especially useful in settings where information often needs to be modified or rearranged.

cats and dogs: In the securities industry, a colloquial term for highly speculative and thoroughly unpromising securities; securities that may have seemed promising once, but are now seen to be very nearly worthless.

cause of action: Any set of circumstances recognized by a judicial body as valid for purposes of bringing an action against another at law or equity, whether or not that action w.". ultimately be successful.

caveat emptor: Latin for "let the buyer beware," an underlying theme in commercial transactions of all kinds. This maxim places the burden of prudence on the buyer, except for specific warranties or misrepresentations made by the seller. To some extent, consumer-oriented statutes and court decisions have redistributed burdens in this area, resulting in the creation of a large number of implied warranties binding on sellers, so that "caveat emptor" now has rather limited significance.

caveat venditor: Latin for "let the seller beware," placing the burden of truthful representation on the seller. Short of specific and willful misrepresentation, "caveat emptor" has been the far stronger maxim in the marketplace; but recent legislative and judicial trends have created a large number of implied warranties binding upon sellers, which to some extent have changed the balance between "caveat venditor" and "caveat emptor."

CBOE: See Chicago Board Options Exchange.

CC: See communications controls.

CD: See certificate of deposit.

cease and desist order: An order issued by an administrative body with quasi-legal powers, such as the Federal Trade Commission or the National Labor Relation Board, demanding that a particular activity, such as an allegedly unfair trade or labor practice, be stopped.

ceiling price: The maximum price that may legally be charged on an item covered by government-imposed price controls.

census: A collection of quantitative data for a given area of inquiry, such as a government count of population and its characteristics or of types of businesses and their characteristics within an industry, a local area, or the entire country. The Bureau of the Census conducts massive and continuing censuses, touching on every aspect of business activity.

center spread: In a publication, two facing pages at or near the center of the publication. A center spread is sometimes a preferred position for advertising.

central bank: A bank funded by and representing a national government, responsible for the development and execution of national money and credit policies and for the health of the nation's banking system. In the United States, the Federal Reserve System functions as a central bank through twelve regional banks and its Board of Governors; in most other industrial countries the central bank is a single bank, such as the Bank of England and the Bank of Canada.

centralized network functions: Those functions in a computer or communications system that are performed in a single central location, such as allocation of resources or assignment of jobs.

centralized planning: In fully planned economies, government control through an agency of the state, of all major economic functions. In mixed economies, a tendency toward central planning of some major economic functions.

central limit theorem: See normal distribution.

central processing unit (CPU): The arithmetic or logic unit of a computer, which includes those circuits responsible for interpreting and executing of instructions. A synonym for "main frame."

central tendency: See normal distribution.

cents-off-marketing: A pricing technique that sets prices at a few cents less than a whole dollar amount so that prospective buyers will be induced to buy more readily than if the whole dollar price were quoted. For example, prices may be quoted at $2.98 rather than $3.00, or $49.95 rather than $50.00.

certificate: A document stating that something has been done or complied with. The document is usually issued by an established public or private institution, such as a government agency or a college, though in the widest sense a "certificate" may be issued by any person or organization for any purpose not specifically covered by existing law.

certificate of beneficial interest: An ownership share in a Massachusetts, or business, trust.

certificate of deposit (CD): A receipt for a bank deposit, in certificate rather than passbook form. Time certificates of deposit are payable either on a specific date or after passage of a specific amount of time, can bear interest, and are therefore widely used by companies and institutions as short-term investment vehicles. They are also negotiable and widely traded as short-term paper in the money markets. However, demand certificates of deposit are payable at any time on endorsement and therefore are not available as money market instruments.

certificate of incorporation: A document forming a private corporation signed by the parties so incorporating and filed in the public office of appropriate jurisdiction.

certificate of indebtedness: The short-term promissory note of a corporation or institution, unsecured by specific property but generally interpreted as carrying the same obligation as a bond. There is some question about whether it operates as a lien prior to the liens of general creditors or whether it is merely an unsecured promissory note that is no more than equal to the claims of other general creditors.

certificate of occupancy: An official document certifying that a building is in compliance with applicable ordinances and regulations and may therefore be occupied and otherwise used.

certificate of origin: A statement by an importer specifying the country of origin of imported goods. All United States importers must make this statement about all goods imported, and in most instances attach this information to the goods themselves.

certificate of public convenience and necessity: A license or permit issued by the government, authorizing the business operations of utilities, communications companies, transportation companies, and other regulated businesses serving the public.

certification: **1.** In labor relations, the formal recognition by government of a union's status as the recognized collective bargaining agent. **2.** The licensing of any activity by governments or by institutions recognized by government as having licensing authority.

certified check: A check drawn on a depositor's account which a bank endorses and accepts, usually on the face of the check, after first setting aside enough of the depositor's funds to cover the check. The check then becomes a bank obligation, backed by the full resources of the bank, and short of bank failure will be paid if properly endorsed on presentation. Certified checks are widely used as payment in transactions requiring sure immediate payment of large amounts of money and immediate passage of title, as in many securities and real estate transactions.

certified copy: A copy of a document such as a deed or birth certificate, held by a public official, signed and certified as a copy by that official.

certified public accountant (CPA): An accountant holding a state license to practice public accountancy, granted after passing a written examination and other examining procedures. This license is not necessary for the practice of accountancy, but no uncertified person may use the title "certified public accountant" in those states issuing this license.

certiorari: A writ issued by an appellate court, calling for review of the action of a lower court or other lower judicial body, bringing all records of the lower court action into the appellate court; used by an appellate court to force review of a lower court action in place of adjudication of an appeal, when the appellate court is not satisfied that appropriate appeal has been made and wants to fully review a case.

cestui que trust: One who holds a beneficial interest in a trust, but not legal title to that trust, as a beneficiary who gets money distributed by a trustee.

CETA: See Comprehensive Employment and Training Act.

CFTC: See Commodity Futures Trading Commission.

chain banking: The ownership of three or more banks by one person or a group acting as one in terms of mutual interests and joint policies.

chain discount: A series of discounts offered on merchandise, each successive discount being a percentage of the previously discounted price. For example, three successive 10% discounts on a $100 list price would mean a first discount of $10, or 10% of $100, leaving a discounted price of $90; a second discount of $9, or 10% of $90, leaving a discounted price of $81.; a third discount of $8.10, or 10% of $81, leaving a discounted price of $72.90. Total discounts come to $27.10 or 27.1% of the $100 list price.

chain of command: A set of reporting relationships within an organization, defining the unbroken line of superior-subordinate relationships starting with the top person in an organization, who reports to no one in an operating sense, and ending with those, usually in relatively unskilled jobs, to whom no one reports. In management, individuals within an unbroken chain of command are often described as "line" people; those in advisory and service capacities are described as "staff" people.

chain store: A retail store that is part of a group of commonly owned, centrally managed stores, usually having quite a similar look. Some examples of chains are the Woolworth, J. C. Penney, Grand Union, A & P, and Safeway stores.

chairman of the board: The head of the corporation's policy-making body, the board of directors. The chairman of the board can be the most powerful person in the corporation, but such factors as ownership equities and the realities of operating control must be taken into account.

chamber of commerce: An organization formed for the stated purpose of promoting the interests of the business community it represents. Chambers of commerce operate in cities, and in regional, state and national groupings.

change of venue: A change of the location at which a pending legal case is to be tried; for example, a move of a scheduled trial from one federal district court to another, or from a state court to a federal court.

character: In computer usage, a basic element within a piece of information. In human-readable form, characters are expressed as letters, decimal digits, and other symbols; in machine-readable form, they are expressed by bits, or binary digits, arranged in groups, which are often called bytes.

charge account: A buy-on-credit arrangement a seller offers to its retail customers. Charge account credit arrangements vary, including open or regular accounts, which usually specify payment in thirty days and are similar to normal industrial sales arrangements; extended payment plans, usually for large purchases and often as options offered in conjunction with regular charge accounts; and revolving charge accounts, usually with specified, fairly limited credit limits, much like national Mastercharge and Visa credit card arrangements. Interest is normally charged on all but open accounts.

charge-off: See write-off.

charges forward: See free-on-board.

charter: A document issued by government defining and granting the basic legal rights and obligations of corporations and other private and public organizations. A charter, which is a grant of government, should not be confused with articles of incorporation or association, which are private documents.

charter rate: The cost of leasing a ship or a substantial part of the cargo space of a ship.

chartist: In the securities industry, one who wholly or in large part believes that current and future market fluctuations can largely be predicted on the basis of previous fluctuations, as graphically represented in charts. Many securities analysts, traders, and investment advisory services subscribe to this view.

chart of accounts: In accounting, a list, classification, and systematized organization of a company's account, including names, numbers, and other identifying information.

chattel: Any personal property, except for freehold title to real estate, including both movable and fixed items of property. For example, clothing, dogs, automobiles, and real estate leases are chattels, while wholly owned real estate is not.

chattel mortgage: A mortgage loan using chattels, such as vehicles and paintings, as security for the loan. If there is default on repayment of the loan, the chattels become the property of the lender. Chattel mortgages are substantially similar to real estate mortgages.

cheap money: See easy money.

check: **1.** A draft or order drawn on funds belonging to the drawer and on deposit with a banking organization. Checks are payable on demand. **2.** An examination of a process or of materials to see if they are functioning properly or are as previously specified; for example, a sampling of a grain shipment to see if it is up to standard specifications, or one of a series of tests built into a computer to see if results meet prescribed conditions.

check digit: One or more digits generated and held in a computer system and used to check processing accuracy within that system.

checking account: A bank account holding credit balances against which a depositor may draw checks. Although there have traditionally been sharp differences between checking and savings accounts, those differences have in recent years tended to diminish. For example, checks may now be drawn against balances in savings accounts, in some states, and checking accounts sometimes pay interest on deposit balances.

checking copy: A copy of a publication containing advertising sent to advertisers or their representatives for review of accuracy, placement, and such matters as quality of reproduction of photos.

checkoff: The deduction of union dues from employee's paychecks and direct payment of those dues by the employer to the union. Even when checkoffs are authorized by union contracts, under federal law employees must consent in writing to them, renewing that consent yearly. Several state laws similarly limit the use of checkoffs.

checkpoint: A point at which a procedure or process is formally examined for conformance to specifications and standards.

Chicago Board of Trade: A major commodities trading exchange handling large quantities of both current cash and futures trades in corn, wheat, soybeans, oats, and associated materials. An affiliated organization is the Chicago Board Options Exchange (CBOE), which handles a very large volume of options trades.

COLLEGE OF THE SEQUOIAS

LIBRARY

Chicago Board Options Exchange (CBOE): See Chicago Board of Trade.

Chicago Mercantile Exchange: A major commodities trading exchange, handling large quantities of both current cash and futures trades in many dairy, meat, and natural resources items.

child labor: The illegal employment of children who are under legal age. The legal age at which children may be employed is set by the states, and is usually in the 14–18-year-old range. Exceptions are often specified, especially in agriculture and in family businesses. The employment of under-legal-age children of migrant agricultural workers, in disregard of laws requiring that they not be employed during school hours, is widespread.

Chi square (χ^2) test: A statistical test used to help determine the probability that a given sample was drawn from a particular population; if that probability is high enough, statistically, researchers can make predictions about that population based on experimentally derived information about the sample.

Christmas club: A special-purpose savings account, stressing the regular deposit of specified sums, usually each week for fifty weeks a year, to be withdrawn at the end of the year and used for Christmas expenses.

chronic unemployment: Long-term unemployment related to economic factors, such as protracted recession or technological unemployment, and affecting those willing and able to work but unable to find jobs.

churning: In the securities industry, the unethical and sometimes illegal practice of turning over customer accounts faster than necessary for the customer's investment purposes, in order to create brokerage commissions.

c.i.f.: See cost, insurance, and freight.

CIO: Abbreviation for the Congress of Industrial Organizations, formed in the 1930's to organize industrial workers by enterprise rather than by craft, as was the practice of the then competing American Federation of Labor; for example, steelworkers as a whole rather than pipefitters and all the other crafts found in a steel plant. The CIO is now part of the AFL-CIO.

circulating capital: That portion of a business' capital that is invested in current and continuously working assets, such as materials and labor.

circulation: The number of copies of an issue of a periodical that are in any way distributed. Circulation is often composed of paid copies and complimentary, or free, copies. The average number of copies distributed in a given period is a publication's "average circulation."

circulation guarantee: The number of copies of a periodical publication its publisher states as the current average circulation figure; often verified by an independent auditing organization. The publisher's circulation guarantee plays a major part in developing their advertising rates.

circumstantial evidence: Indirectly derived evidence, constructed from a consideration of the facts surrounding a case, rather than from direct testimony.

civil action: An action at law involving private rights and wrongs rather than criminal questions. In the widest sense, any action at law that is not a criminal action.

Civil Aeronautics Board (CAB): A Federal agency charged with responsibility for regulating the United States air transport industry, both within the United States and worldwide.

claim: Any demand for payment for any stated legal reason, but most often a demand for payment made by an insured of an insurer under the terms of an insurance policy.

class action: An action at law brought by one or more on behalf of a larger number, all alleged by those bringing the class action as being commonly interested and commonly damaged. The class action has been a widely used form of complaint in suits brought against businesses and institutions by such groups as consumers and stockholders.

classification of risks: In the insurance industry, the setting of premium rates for various kinds of things insured, as in the setting of a range of accident insurance rates for occupations based on the differing degrees of risk involved in each.

classified advertising: Brief advertisements, usually carried as a group within newspapers and other periodicals, usually describing job openings or selling goods or services.

class interval: In frequency distributions, the size of the groups in a series. If the class interval is six, for example, the series may run in such groups as 201–206, 207–212, 213–218.

class one carriers: Under Interstate Commerce Commission rules, the largest overland transportation firms, together handling the overwhelming bulk of goods transported. Class two and class three are the smaller carriers, handling the balance of goods carried.

class price: A selling price that is set for one kind of buyer or group of potential buyers that is different from the prices charged others. When class prices are judged in restraint of trade, they are violations of antitrust law.

class rate: A price set by a seller which applies to particular kinds of goods or services sold. For example, freight carriers set class rates for kinds of goods carried, such as eggs, milk and automobiles, while communications media charge class rates for advertising placements.

class three carriers: See class one carriers.

class two carriers: See class one carriers.

Clayton Act: A basic Federal anti-monopoly statute, passed in 1914, which places legal sanctions on tie-in and competition-restricting sales arrangements; price discrimination; interlocking directorates; and other practices tending to operate in restraint of trade and to foster the growth of monopolies and monopolistic practices.

clean bill of exchange: An undocumented bill of exchange; that is, one unaccompanied by such documents as bills of lading.

clean bill of lading: One which in no way restricts the transporter's responsibilities and liabilities by words qualifying the language of the bill of lading itself. Literally, it is a bill of lading with no additional qualifying language written on it.

clean credit: A letter of credit without significant qualifications placed on the issuing bank's commitment to pay when presented with an undocumented bill drawn on that letter of credit.

clean hands: In law, the equity-derived concept that a party seeking redress of relief come into court untainted by fraud, dishonesty, or other attitudes or actions that discredit motives as to the matter at issue.

clear: 1. In law, entirely free of any kind of ambiguity, limitation, or encumbrance, as in ownership of a property "free and clear." **2.** To leave a port with all legal necessities completed and in receipt of all appropriate permissions and papers. **3.** To complete a financial transaction, most often as in the collection of a check that has been passed through a bank clearing house.

clearance: 1. Any permission to proceed with a course of action. **2.** Official permission for a vessel to proceed on its journey, having satisfied all legal port requirements and received evidence of such permission. **3.** Settlement of financial transactions.

clearance sale: A sale of retail goods to make way for new stock; in practice, a term used by retailers for many kinds of sales.

clearing house: A voluntary association of banks or brokers, acting to settle transactions between its members on a daily basis.

close: 1. The end of the trading day in a securities or commodities market. Many commodities trades are executed and securities price quoted "at the close." **2.** In accounting, the process of closing the books of a business at the end of a given accounting period.

close corporation: See closely held corporation.

closed circuit: A television system in which transmitter and reception are directly linked, as by cable, without the broadcast of a television signal.

closed-end investment company: An investment company owned by a limited number of stockholders and with an initially fixed amount of capital, which invests in other companies for the benefit of its stockholders. Investment company shares may not be redeemed by their holders as can mutual funds shares by their stockholders, but they are often traded on stock exchanges.

closed-end mortgage: A mortgage specifying that no further money can be borrowed on the property being mortgaged. Some bonds carry the same limitation.

closed out: 1. Lines of goods, accounts, and businesses that have been ended. **2.** Merchandise that is being discontinued, and is therefore on sale. **3.** A margin account sold out by a broker when a customer has failed to raise necessary additional margin.

closed shop: An employer that hires only members of a specified union or unions, and in which union membership is a condition of continuing employment. Although closed shops are illegal under federal and many state laws, they continue to remain substantially in effect in some industries.

closed stock: Goods sold in sets, such as silverware, which may not be in any way replaceable if part of a set is damaged, in contrast with open stock, which is interchangeable and replaceable.

closed union: A union which is substantially closed to membership for all but current

members and sometimes a favored few applicants sponsored by current members.

closely held corporation: A company that is owned by a small number of people, all or most of whom are directly involved in the conduct of the business, with little or none of its stock in the hands of outsiders.

closeout: See closed out.

closing: 1. The consummation of a real estate transaction, in which buyer and seller exchange purchase price and deed and title passes. **2.** In accounting, the process of closing the books at the end of an accounting period.

closing costs: The costs attendant to the closing of a real estate transaction, such as title insurance, lawyer's fees, and recording fees.

closing date: In accounting, the date the books of account are closed for accounting purposes, and the date of preparation of all financial statements derived from the books of account.

closing entries: In accounting, a series of entries closing the books as of the end of an accounting period, which serve to balance the books and prepare them to be the basis for preparation of the financial statements.

closing price: The price of a security listed on an exchange as of the end of the trading day on that exchange.

cloud on title: A potential threat to a clear title. Such claims as tax liens, mortgages, and prior judgments may cloud title and must be settled before the title can be conveyed unencumbered.

COD: See cash on delivery.

codetermination: In labor relations, the representation of labor on the policy-making boards of enterprises. Though codetermination has been adopted by some European companies, it is rare in the United States.

codicil: An addition to a will, in some way modifying or explaining that will. A codicil may be drawn at any time and must be executed as formally as the will itself.

codification: The compilation of a body of statutes into a system covering a body of law, called a code.

coding: Developing a sequenced set of computer instructions used to accomplish a desired result within a computer system.

coding check: A manual check on the accuracy of a set of coding instructions for a computer program.

coin: 1. A piece of metal stamped by government and used as a form of money. In very few United States coins now in use is the underlying value of the metal in the coin worth more than a small fraction of the stated value of the coin. **2.** To process metal into coins.

coinage: The physical production of coins by government at a government mint.

coincident indicator: An economic indicator that moves at about the same time as the economy moves, in contrast to leading or lagging indicators that move earlier or later; examples are current retail sales, personal income, and industrial production.

coinsurance clause: A provision in most property insurance policies dividing the risk between insurer and insured, usually at an 80-20 ratio. The provision comes into play in the event of a partial loss, as when there is a $40,000 loss on a property really worth $50,000, but which has been insured for only $40,000. In that event, the insurance will pay 80% of the $40,000, or $32,000, rather than the $40,000 of actual loss. If the property had been insured for its real value of $50,000, then 80% would have been $40,000, the amount of the loss.

COLA: See cost of living adjustment clause.

cold call: A sales call made without an appointment, and usually without any prior notice to the prospect, who is often a stranger.

collateral: Security for a loan, in the form of real or personal property belonging to the borrower which is formally pledged to the lender, and which can become the property of the lender upon default on the loan. Collateral is property of determinable value that can be fairly readily sold and converted into cash, such as securities, real estate, saving account passbooks, and commodities.

collateralize: To provide collateral as security for a loan. A loan is described as "collateralized" when it has been so secured.

collateral loan: A loan secured by collateral, usually applied to a short-term loan in which the collateral security is physically held by the creditor.

collateral trust bonds: Bonds secured by other bonds and sometimes stocks of the issuing company. The securing bonds and stocks are placed in trust as collateral for the bonds being issued.

collateral value: The value of assets pledged as collateral for a loan. In setting collateral value lenders will consider such factors as the collateral's current market value, its stability, and its convertibility into cash.

collating: The process of merging separate groups of sequenced documents, such as the pages of a report or groups of computer records.

collectible: 1. A balance due, which a creditor is legally justified in collecting from a debtor. **2.** An item, whatever its age, that is acquired, held, and traded, and for which a market of any kind, formal or informal, has developed. In the widest sense, the term embraces antiques and works of art, as well as such well-defined collecting areas as stamps, comic books, and many kinds of glass.

collection: The process of securing payment for outstanding debts. Collection may range from a simple billing and payment to a long series of efforts, including letters, telephone calls, and legal action.

collection agency: A firm that is engaged in the business of collecting overdue accounts for others.

collection letter: See dunning letter.

collection period: A measure of how long it takes to collect outstanding receivables, derived by comparing the average annual receivables generated by company credit sales with the average dollar value of outstanding receivables for the period being measured. For example, if receivables for a year are $365,000, an average of $1,000 per day, and average daily receivables for a 30-day month are $30,000, then the average collection period is 30 days.

collective bargaining: The process of negotiation between employers and organized employees acting through their designated representatives, resulting in a labor-management agreement covering any or all aspects of work and work-related matters, including wages, hours, working conditions, and pensions.

collect on delivery: See cash on delivery.

college recruiting: Employment interviewing and selection directed at college students by companies and institutions, featuring campus visits, interviews, subsequent checking, and re-interviewing.

collision insurance: A kind of motor vehicle insurance coverage, which insures the owner of a vehicle against property losses resulting from collision damage to the owner's vehicle.

collusion: A secret agreement by two or more parties to commit fraud or other illegal actions against others.

collusive bidding: Seemingly competitive bidding carried on by two or more bidders which is actually pursuant to a secret agreement between them to commit fraud by attempting to control bidding to their advantage.

column: A vertically arranged body of figures or digits.

COM: See computer output microfilm.

co-maker: One who signs a debt instrument with others and is therefore responsible for repayment, often without being in any way a recipient of the money borrowed.

combination: Any formal or informal joining of individuals for common purposes. In business, any joining of business organizations, including such formal joinings as mergers and consolidation and such informal joinings as pools, syndicates, and interlocking directorates.

combination in restraint of trade: Any business combination prohibited by law. The phrase is the language of the basic United States anti-trust statute, the Sherman Act of 1890, and refers to such combinations as trusts, pools, cartels, discriminatory freight rate arrangements and interlocking directorates.

combination rate: Any rate joining two or more individual rates together, usually at a discount when compared to the individual rates themselves. For example, a combination rate is often quoted for transporting goods by two or more different kinds of carriers.

COMECON: See Council For Mutual Economic Assistance.

commerce: Any and all trade and commercial intercourse between individuals, organizations, peoples, and governments. The term is so wide as to be used synonymously with "business" and "trade."

Commerce Department: See Department of Commerce.

commercial bank: A bank primarily in the business of holding demand deposits and making business loans. Commercial banks have many other functions, however, including a wide variety of consumer loans, trust functions, finance and securities industry service and selling functions, and a large number of services usually described as "full service banking." Commercial banking is the major form of banking in the United States.

Commercial Code: See Uniform Commercial Code.

commercial credit: Credit customarily extended by lenders to businesses, to satisfy fluctuating and seasonal cash needs, finance inventories, and satisfy other short-term cash needs.

commercial credit company: A company in the business of lending money to other companies using the borrowers' accounts receivable as collateral, or of buying those accounts receivable at a discount and collecting them.

commercial law: A very wide and imprecise term generally used to describe all matters in the law relating to commerce, trade, and the people and organizations engaged in commercial practices.

commercial paper: 1. All short-term, negotiable debt instruments issued by businesses, including all bills, notes, and acceptances arising from the normal conduct of business. **2.** Short-term notes issued by large, well-established and well-regarded businesses, usually in the $100,000 to $1,000,000 range. Such notes are traded in the money markets, rated by private rating organizations as to their degree of investment safety, and often provide short-term, relatively low-cost financing to their issuers.

commercial property: Property classified as usable for commercial purposes, and so zoned by local zoning authorities; such property may be used for residential purposes as well.

commingling: Mixing funds, as when the administrator of several estates mixes funds owned by those estates with his or her own private funds; often accompanied by illegal misuse of the funds held in trust.

commission: A sum paid by a principal to one acting in some sort of representative capacity. Commissions are usually figured as a percentage of the transaction consummated. Both independent representatives, such as real estate brokers, and employees, such as salespeople, are often compensated on a commission basis.

commission agent: An independent businessperson or company, selling goods for another on a commission basis.

commission plan: A sales compensation plan, in which salespeople are wholly or in major part compensated on the basis of a percentage of sales made. Such plans are often tied to other aspects of compensation, such as non-refundable advances against future commissions and base salaries.

commodity: Any item which may be traded, broadly including every item of value. In a somewhat narrower sense, any one of a considerable group of materials and products traded on commodities exchanges.

commodity agreement: An international arrangement between producers to control production and prices of a commodity.

Commodity Credit Corporation: The bureau of the United States Department of Agriculture responsible for a wide range of farm-support aids, including cash payments, crop purchases, loans to farmers, the management of farm surpluses, and the encouragement of domestic consumption and foreign trade in agricultural commodities.

commodity exchange: A market for the sale and exchange of commodity futures contracts and current or spot cash commodities contracts. United States commodity exchanges trade a wide range of agricultural, agriculture-related, and natural resource contracts, such as pork bellies, cotton, wool, soybeans, corn, wheat, gold, silver, lumber, coffee and rubber.

commodity futures: Contracts between buyers and sellers specifying the prices, terms, and delivery locations of commodities that are to be delivered at some stated future time. These contracts are instruments of value that are traded on "futures" markets.

Commodity Futures Trading Commission (CFTC): A Federal agency responsible for the regulation of United States trading in commodity futures, including the setting up of the machinery of regulation.

commodity paper: Negotiable bills of exchange payable on sight or demand, and backed by the value of staple commodities, properly stored and insured, as evidenced by appropriate shipping or storage documents, such as bills of lading.

commodity price index: Any price index that measures the average price of a group of commodities, including both current or spot prices and futures prices. Both the United States government and private sources, as well as including commodities in wider price indexes, publish such current and future indexes.

commodity rate: A very widely used railroad freight rate applying to specific kinds of commodities and products, such as cotton, coal, and grain. Rates apply for shipments of these commodities between specified points, and sometimes also apply to any shipments of the commodities within a given area.

common area: In computer systems, a temporary data storage area that can be used by and for more than one program or module at once.

common carrier: A carrier accepting any and all goods or persons within stated classes and fixed areas for transportation at fixed rates. Common carriers are usually licensed and regulated by the government.

common field: In a computer program, a field capable of being accessed by more than one routine.

common language: A computer language capable of being used by several related kinds of computers and compatible peripheral equipment as well.

common law: That body of law developed in England and other English-speaking countries, which has been built case by case and precedent by precedent, rather than depending upon statutory bases. Much of our civil law, adjusting the private relations between private parties, is based upon the common law. Much of the relationship between pri-

vate parties and governments is based upon statues, and upon regulations and cases interpreting those statutes.

common-law trust: See Massachusetts Trust.

Common Market: The European Economic Community, a partial economic union of most of the nations of western Europe, organized to stimulate trade and production and to help provide the economic basis for a wider European political and economic union.

common software: Programs that can be used compatibly in many computer systems, and often among several kinds of computers.

common stock: An ownership share in a corporation, in the form of capital stock which is neither preferred nor in any way limited, and therefore fully shares the risks and opportunities created by corporate operations. It is the standard form of stock ownership in American corporations.

common trust fund: A fund administered by a bank or other trust investment organization which pools the funds of two or more individual trusts and manages the pooled funds as one. The aim is to gain the flexibility and leverage offered by the larger pool of funds, while cutting administrative costs.

common user network: A multi-user data communications network, connecting many computers with large data bases.

communications controls (CC): In data communications systems, devices providing for direct linkages between remote computer memories.

Communications Satellite Corporation (COMSAT): A privately owned United States communications company, owning and carrying responsibility for operation of all United States commercial communications satellite operations.

communications system: Any network of communicating devices providing the ability to communicate between several remote locations, such as a telephone system; also a computerized data transmission system providing direct computer-to-computer transmission.

communism: 1. A theory positing total common ownership of all resources and means of production, total planning of all economic aspects of life, and distribution of all goods and services according to need. **2.** That system of government based on the theories and practices of Marx, Engels, Lenin, as well as of Stalin, Mao, and other leaders, which now rules in the Soviet Union, China, and many other countries in which the Communist Party is the dominant force.

community property: Property owned jointly by wife and husband, which in some states includes all property acquired during marriage but not including property owned before marriage or some kinds of property acquired during marriage but specifically exempted from community property provisions of the law, such as property acquired as a bequest.

compaction: In computer systems, the condensation of data to achieve economies of transmission and storage.

company: 1. A very broad term, meaning any business entity, including corporations, partnerships, and sole proprietorships. **2.** A group joining together to pursue common interests for profit.

company store: A retail store, owned and operated by a company and selling only to its own employees. Company stores were once widespread in the United States, and were used as major instruments of employee control by some companies. Today, company stores exist mainly in remote locations, such as exploration and drilling sites, except in agriculture, where they are still widely used to keep some farm laborers in virtual peonage, by selling food and other goods at high prices and on credit, building up sums owed to the company by the workers, and thus guaranteeing that those workers will never catch up on their debts.

company town: 1. A community literally owned and organized by a company, in which its workers live, pay rent on company-owned houses, and buy from company-licensed or operated stores. Once widespread in the United States, the company town in this sense is a fast disappearing phenomenon. **2.** A community dominated by one or more large employers in which all significant governmental functions are controlled by those directly or indirectly working for those employers.

company union: 1. A union or association of employees that is controlled by company management; often a union that has been organized by management and recognized by management as a bargaining agent, and one that bargains collusively with management. **2.** A union nominally independent of management, but which in fact bargains collusively with management to the detriment of the interests of its members.

comparative advantage: The ability of a country or of any other economic unit to produce an item at less cost than another country or economic unit. For example, if the Japanese television industry can produce television sets of comparable quality cheaper than American industry can, the Japanese industry has the comparative advantage.

comparison: In computer operations, to check the equality or inequality of two items of data; with the result often used as the basis for a branching decision by a computer, and also used to check the accuracy of the machine's processing.

comparison shopping: The practice of shopping more than one retailer to compare the prices and quality of goods for sale. Professional comparative shoppers are employed by consumer and government organizations and by some large retailers to assess the goods of their competitors. Comparison shopping is also a standard practice of many individual consumers.

compensable injury: A work-related injury which qualifies for compensation to be paid to the injured under the workmen's compensation law.

compensating balance: An amount kept on deposit by a borrower, in a non-interest-bearing regular account in a bank holding active loans of that borrower. Many commercial banks informally but very firmly require that borrowers keep deposits of approximately 20% of the amounts currently borrowed on deposit. As the deposits do not bear interest, the loans in fact cost considerably more than they seem. For example, $100 borrowed at a simple interest of 6% costs $6 in interest. But if $20 must be kept on deposit, $6 in interest is being paid on 80 usable dollars, a real interest rate of 7.5% or 20% more than it seems.

compensation: **1.** Any payment made to satisfy the just claim of another. **2.** A popular abbreviation for Workmen's Compensation.

compensation award: A money settlement made to the victim of an industrial accident or illness pursuant to workmen's compensation laws.

compensation specialist: One who is professionally engaged in the development and administration of compensation plans; usually either part of personnel or labor relations functions within an organization or an outside consultant.

compensatory tariff: A tariff levied on imported goods to equal taxes levied within a country on the same kinds of goods manufactured domestically, or to compensate for taxes levied on imports used to make domestic goods.

competition: In any marketplace, rivalry between sellers to persuade customers to buy their goods or services. Competition may be between sellers of essentially identical goods, such as competing aspirin manufacturers; may be between sellers of somewhat different kinds of goods satisfying similar needs, such as different lines of clothing or household goods; or may be between sellers of vastly different kinds of goods, as in the contest between sports car and boat manufacturers to capture the discretionary income of potential customers.

competitive price: A price quoted by a seller which realistically reflects the facts of marketplace competition, comparing favorably with, or at least equal to, prices quoted by other sellers for similar goods or services.

compile: **1.** To gather and organize any body of information. **2.** In computer programming, to prepare a machine-language program from a program written in higher level computer language, one that is in symbolic form which is easier for humans to read.

compiler: In computer processing, a program that will convert a program written in symbolic language into machine language, which the computer can use.

compiler language: A computer language that translates from higher level computer languages, such as FORTRAN or COBOL, into machine languages.

complaint: The first pleading of a plaintiff in a civil action, setting forth the facts alleged to constitute a cause of action against the defendant.

compliance: Action by private parties to comply with government-set rules, regulations, and procedures, usually referring to actions by business to comply with government regulation; for example, to adhere to government-set pollution control, health, and safety regulations.

complementary products: Products generated from the same raw material or industrial process, as when coal used to produce blast furnace coke in steel mills also generates many chemical by-products, which are sold separately.

composite demand: The total demand from all sources for a product or service. For example, the composite demand for legal services includes many kinds of public and private demands, only part of which are met by lawyers in private practice.

composition: 1. An arrangement between a debtor and all creditors to satisfy the entire body of debt outstanding for less than the totals due and on a pro rata basis. For example, a debtor owing a total of $10,000 to five creditors, composed of four $1,000 debts and one $6,000 debt might reach agreement to repay on a 50% basis, and then repay each of the $1,000 debts at $500 and the $6,000 debt at $3,000. Composition is a common-law arrangement between debtor and creditors, arrived at voluntarily and not as part of a bankruptcy settlement. **2.** A synonym for typesetting.

composition in bankruptcy: Substantially the same arrangement as composition (above), but arrived at by operation of law in pursuit of a settlement of outstanding debts during bankruptcy.

compound entry: In accounting, a single entry that combines three or more elements; often used to record a series of related transactions, clarifying the nature of those related transactions as a single complex transaction.

compound interest: A system of computing and paying interest that takes the original sum on which interest is to be computed, adds simple interest, and then uses the resulting amount as the basis for the next computation of interest. For example, payment of compound interest on $100 for two years at 5% per year would result in a first year interest payment of $5. With the $5 added to the original $100, second year interest would be 5% of $105, or $5.25.

compound tariff: A customs duty that combines both an ad valorem tax, in which a percentage is added to the value of the imported item, and a specific tax, such as $10 per set for imported television sets.

Comprehensive Employment and Training Act (CETA): A Federal statute providing and funding programs to provide jobs and job training for the unemployed and disadvantaged.

comprehensive insurance: Property insurance covering all risks related to the property insured, except for stated exceptions, such as war and certain natural disasters.

comptroller: See controller.

compulsory arbitration: See arbitration.

computer: A device that processes data at high speeds following logical and mathematical procedures; usually not just a single device, but a system of several electronic components, including a central processing unit and input/output devices. The two main computer types are digital and analog.

computer-assisted instruction (CAI): See programmed instruction.

computer console: See console.

computer crime: A crime committed by entry into an illegal use of a computer system; for example, the use of a bank's computer system to cause issuance of checks when no balances exist validating those checks.

computer-dependent program: A program written solely for a particular kind of computer.

computer hardware: See hardware.

computer language: A set of characters and symbols that are put together according to well-defined rules and are used to code instructions in a computer program. Computer languages exist on several levels, from symbolic languages readily understandable by humans to machine code in which the computer actually operates.

computer letter: A letter that is mass produced but is personalized by individual details inserted by a specially programmed computer; most often used for sales solicitation or fund raising.

computer network: A chain of interconnected computer components, including various processing units and input and output devices, often some distance apart.

computer operator: The person who handles

the main manual control functions of a computer system from its console.

computer processing: See electronic data processing.

computer program: A series of instructions, written in an appropriate computer language, that defines how the computer system should process given data.

computer output microfilm (COM): Microfilm that is printed directly from computer output, in contrast to computer output resulting in line printout or magnetic tape generation.

computer software: Written or printed materials, and related facilities and services, used in carrying out computer functions; as opposed to the hardware, which are the machines themselves.

computer system: In general, a central processing unit, input and output devices, and any other related components that work together to process data; often simply called a computer.

computer terminal: See terminal.

COMSAT: See Communications Satellite Corporation.

concentration ratio: The extent to which business in a single industry is concentrated among the leading firms in that industry, in terms of either the amount of business done or the size of the firms involved, as a proportion of the whole industry.

concession: 1. Any reduction in price, usually offered by a seller as an incentive to buy. A concession may be a simple price reduction on goods for sale; it may be an incentive offered by government to business in the form of a tax holiday, cut rate, or rebate in return for moving into an area; or it may be a selective tariff cut or any other move resulting in lower price. **2.** A permission, usually in the form of a lease granted by government or a private owner, granting the right to conduct a given kind of business in a specific area. For example, a stadium management may sell a business the right to sell food at events conducted in the stadium.

conciliation: The process of attempting to assist in the settlement of a dispute between two or more parties by means of third party intervention aimed at keeping negotiations going, opening up and developing areas of agreement between the parties, and moving toward settlement of outstanding differences. It is most often used in collective bargaining, with government often acting as conciliator. A synonym for mediation.

condemnation: The taking of private property by government for public use. Condemnation is a legal process by which government conducts a forced sale to itself of private property. For example, condemnation may be used to clear a highway right-of-way.

conditional branch: A computer instruction that is executed only under certain circumstances specified in the applicable computer program.

conditional sale: A sale in which the buyer takes possession of goods at the time of sale, but must meet certain conditions before actually receiving title to the goods. A typical form of conditional sale is the credit purchase, in which the buyer takes possession of goods on sale and agrees to pay for them over a period of time, usually in fixed installments. The seller retains title, which passes only if the buyer completes payment. If the buyer defaults on payment according to the terms of the sales contract, the seller may reclaim possession of the goods.

conditional value: In statistics, an event or events influenced by related events; for example, a consumer's buying decision may be influenced by a rise in prices.

condominium: A housing unit, usually an apartment in a multiple occupancy building, which is separately owned, just as if it were a single family house standing alone. It may be purchased, sold, mortgaged; and in all other ways handled as any other wholly-owned building. Condominium owners also own a share of communally used elements, such as land or land lease, lobbies, basements, stairs, roof, heating, and cooling systems.

conference call: A telephone call linking three or more parties at different locations in a simultaneous discussion.

confidence interval: See level of confidence.

confidence level: See level of confidence.

configuration: A group of machines operating together as a single computer system.

confirmation: A document expressly validating a previously made oral or in some other way voidable purchase, agreement, or contract. For example, a telephoned order for goods must often be followed by a written confirmation, signed by the ordering party.

confirmed credit: Credit that cannot be withdrawn or altered in any way, usually in the form of a letter of credit.

confiscation: The taking of property without compensation by government. A government may confiscate the property of its own citizens or may confiscate property in its control belonging to the citizens of other countries or to other governments.

conflicting evidence: Elements of evidence that seem to point to differing conclusions. The term is somewhat amorphous, as much evidence seemingly conflicts before conclusions can be drawn.

conflict of interest: Any contradiction existing between the responsibilities created by a position of trust and the other interests of the holder of that position. For example, a government official awarding public contracts who has a substantial stock interest in a company bidding for those contracts has a clear conflict of interest.

conflict of laws: Differences in the legal treatment of persons and situations stemming from differences in the laws of various governments and jurisdictions; also, the body of legal theory and practice addressed to these kinds of differences.

conglomerate: A large, diversified organization, doing business in a number of more or less unrelated areas. A conglomerate usually acquires many of the unrelated portions of its operations, instead of developing them from the kinds of business it originally conducted. An example is the International Telephone and Telegraph Corporation, which does business in dozens of areas unrelated to its communications activities.

Congress of Industrial Organizations: See CIO.

consent decree: An agreement between parties to an action at law, entered by the court in the form of a legally binding decision. A consent decree is normally an agreement by the defendant to meet certain demands of the plaintiff.

consent election: A collective bargaining representation election jointly agreed to by labor and management, in which all interested parties waive National Labor Relations Board hearings and agree to immediate elections to determine what union, if any, the workers in a bargaining unit choose to represent them.

consent order: See consent decree.

consequential losses: Indirect losses, such as the damage caused by the water used to put out a fire, which are recoverable from insurances.

conservation: A term used to describe a wide variety of theories and practices aimed at preserving or restoring the physical environment and at saving depletable natural resources, including such energy sources as oil and coal and such other natural resources as water, air, timber, and metal ores.

conservatism: A term connoting a stance resistant to change rather than defining a coherent social and political philosophy. In politics and economics, the term "conservative," like the term "liberal," implies a value judgment: it is used approvingly of a person or policy by those who share resistance to change; disapprovingly by those who disagree.

conservator: One appointed by a court to guard and protect the property of another who is found by the court to be incompetent to manage his or her own interests. The conservator acts toward an incompetent as a guardian acts toward a ward.

consideration: In the law of contracts, an inducement sufficient in the eyes of the law to cause a party to make a contract. The inducement must have enough value to be deemed a sufficient inducement and must be thought by a contracting party to confer a perceptible benefit.

consignment: 1. A general term for a shipment of goods or for the goods themselves. **2.** A method of selling, in which an agent sells goods owned by another, receiving payment for the sale either as a percentage of sale or a flat fee per sale or some combination of both.

consistency: In accounting, adherence to the same accounting methods over a period of time, so that statements of operating results and financial position will not be distorted by material changes in accounting methods within a period or from one period to another. Consistency demands that when a substantial change is introduced, its nature and impact must be fully disclosed and explained in the financial statements.

console: That portion of a computer system which may be operated by a human, containing controls such as start and stop keys for both computers and peripheral equipment, as well as monitoring devices.

consolidated balance sheet: A balance sheet covering a parent company and all its subsidiary companies as a single business organization.

consolidation: The joining of two or more business organizations into a single succeeding organization, with the previous organizations ceasing to exist.

consortium: A group of large companies participating in a joint venture; most often applied to international ventures involving the development and exploitation of the resources of less developed nations.

conspicuous consumption: The acquisition and use of material things for the purpose of enhancing status rather than satisfying needs. Originally posited by Thorstein Veblen as part of his theory of leisure class behavior, the term has come to describe any ostentatious and wasteful display and use of goods and services.

constant: An element that does not change, in contrast to other elements that may be variables; for example, an unchanging element in an equation or body of data being processed by a computer system.

constant cost: See fixed cost.

constant-dollar value: The value of an item as if the dollar had constant value, neither inflating or deflating. This is done by adopting a given year as a base year and figuring the values of items as if the dollars used to buy them purchased as much as they did in the base year. For example, a car purchased this year for $8,000 may be worth $4,000 in "1970 dollars," if the dollar's purchasing power is now 50% of what it was in 1970.

construction contract awards: An economic indicator used to assess future investment in construction and therefore the impact of that investment on the economy. Since construction contracts indicate the money appropriated or otherwise set aside for payments of awarded contracts, this is a relatively hardy indicator of future economic prospects.

constructive contract: A contract which a court will literally construct out of the relations between the parties before it, when no written contract actually exists; for example, under some circumstances, a binding agreement springing from oral agreements and subsequent actions stemming from those agreements, without a written contract.

consular invoice: An invoice for imported

goods, issued in the country of origin by the consular office of the country receiving the goods. The invoice repeats and certifies the information contained in the seller's invoice and is sent to the customs offices of the receiving country, where it is held and then compared with the seller's invoices accompanying the actual goods. The goods cannot clear customs without the consular invoice.

consultant: A very broad term, designating individuals and organizations that hold themselves out as qualified to counsel others in the conduct of their businesses and personal activities, in such areas as the consultants claim professional skills and competence.

consumer: One who purchases goods and services for personal rather than business use.

consumer cooperative: A firm owned by its customers, who buy goods and services through the firm in order to gain price and sometimes quality advantages through bulk purchases, quantity discounts, and professional buying. Consumer cooperatives are often managed by their own members; often sell to nonmembers as well as members, with the members sharing any resulting profits; and sometimes operate as wholesalers serving businesses as well as consumer members.

consumer credit: Any credit used by consumers for purchases, including such short-term sources of credit as installment purchases; credit cards; bank loans for consumer purchases such as automobile and general-purpose personal loans; finance company loans; and revolving credit or overdraft loans. While the normal repayment period distinguishing consumer credit from longer term loans was until recently stated as six months to three years, the development of a wide range of revolving credit and longer fixed term repayment plans has blurred the distinction between intermediate and long-term credit. Consumer credit is now best described as credit granted for the purchase of consumer goods.

consumer debt: See consumer credit.

consumer expenditures: See personal consumption expenditures.

consumer finance company: See finance company.

consumer goods: Goods used directly by consumers, as distinct from goods used by businesses to produce other goods for business or personal use. Only end products consumed by individuals are consumer goods.

consumerism: A very general term describing the growth of group consciousness among consumers and the development of organizations advocating consumer-oriented positions on public issues, as well as the formulation and passage of legislation protecting consumers; for example the proposal and passage of truth-in-lending laws.

Consumer Price Index (CPI): A national monthly index generated by the United States Bureau of Labor Statistics, which compares a weighted average of prices with the same weighted average for a previous year selected as a base year. It is a basic measure of increases in the cost of living, and was formerly called the "cost of living index."

consumer protection laws: A general term for a substantial number of United States statutes protecting consumers in the marketplace, extending as far back as the Pure Food and Drug Act of 1906, and including such major statutes as the Food, Drug and Cosmetic Act of 1938; the Hazardous Substances Labeling Act of 1960; and the Truth in Lending Act of 1969. Consumer protection laws are administered by several major agencies, including the Federal Trade Commission and the Food and Drug Administration.

consumer research: Research aimed at determining consumer preferences, focusing on such matters as product and brand choices and identifications, the development of effective promotional approaches, and the kinds of consumer responses elicited by new products and approaches.

consumption: The use of goods and services by consumers and producers to the extent that they are, at least in part, worn out or used up. For example, food eaten is consumed; a car driven is partially consumed even though it will be used again and again and even though as scrap it will be used again and again.

consumption tax: A tax levied on that which is consumed, usually as a percentage of the value of the original purchase and usually as a sales tax; for example, a sales tax on meals consumed in restaurants.

containerization: The packing and shipping of goods in large, standard containers, which are easily handled, stacked, and stored by loading and unloading equipment, considerably cutting labor and other costs throughout the transportation industry.

contingency model: A management theory, developed by Fred Fiedler, that a group's success depends on the style of the leader and on the amount of control the leader has over the group, the task, and the outcome. Application of the theory involves matching a leader's style with an appropriate situation, which is called the leader match approach.

contingency reserve: In accounting, a reserve kept to meet possible and unspecified liabilities. It is composed of funds in no way encumbered by any other claims or allocations.

contingent liability: A liability which does not now exist, but will come into being if some now-perceived event occurs; contingent liabilities are potential, not probable. When considered probable, they become contingent but real, and are treated as real in accounting statements.

contingent profit: Possible but not certain profit, which may be realized if a perceived event occurs.

continued bonds: Bonds that are not re-

deemed when mature, but instead are carried on as interest-bearing obligations, though not necessarily at the same rate of interest.

continuous audit: In accounting, an audit that is carried on, at least in part, throughout the period being audited rather than entirely during a relatively short time at the end of the audited period.

continuous inventory: A partial physical inventory that continues during the period between complete physical inventories. It consists of the constant checking of physical stock against perpetual inventory records to find and correct discrepancies between them. Physical inventories are actual counts of materials, contrasting with perpetual inventories, which are records of material movement in and out of inventory.

continuous process: An industrial process that continuously receives raw materials and processes them through to completed products, as in the 7-days-a-week, 24-hours-a-day coke oven process.

contra account: In accounting, an offsetting account; that is, an account such as a depreciation account, that is wholly or partially subtracted from the balance in one or more other accounts.

contraband: Goods prohibited by a country into which they are being taken. Any goods imported contrary to a country's laws are contraband, but the term is usually applied to goods imported with intent to break those laws.

contract: 1. A legal agreement in which two or more parties, for adequate consideration, make and accept promises to do or not to do specified things. Also the written record of that agreement, agreed to and signed by the parties. **2.** To make a legal agreement with one or more parties, for adequate consideration, to do or not to do certain things.

contract carrier: A transporter making a contract to carry specific people or goods, in contrast to a common carrier, which agrees to transport classes of people and goods.

contraction: An imprecise euphemism for a recession or depression as in a "contraction of economic activity."

contract of sale: A formal agreement between buyer and seller, in which the seller agrees to supply specified goods and services and the buyer agrees to pay for those goods and services at agreed-upon prices.

contractor: One who contracts to do a job for another, operating independently although often under very specific terms of agreement covering such matters as materials to be used, quality of work to be performed, schedules, and deadlines. A contractor may contract an entire job as "prime" contractor or may contract with a prime contractor to do part of a job as subcontractor.

contrapuntal reverberation: In macroeconomics, a major contradiction between leading and lagging indicators, pointing toward temporary economic stasis.

contributed capital: The money invested in a firm by its owners, including both money invested in capital stock and money they later put into the firm for operating purposes.

contribution: 1. A share payment made to accomplish a purpose, as in a contribution to capital or to payment of any joint obligation. **2.** For tax purposes, any gift which is defined by law and regulations as tax-free.

contributory negligence: Negligence by a party claiming damages at law or in the course of pursuing an insurance claim, which contributed to the situation causing the damages and sometimes to the severity of those damages; a finding of contributory negligence therefore can partially or wholly invalidate the claim of the claimant.

contributory pension plan: A pension plan which is jointly financed by contributions from employees and employer, in contrast to a non-contributory plan, which is financed wholly by the employer.

control: 1. The provision of adequate checks and safeguards within a system designed to accomplish an organization's goal. **2.** To be able to direct organizations and individuals toward the accomplishment of one's own goals or the goals of one's own group. Also, the ability to so direct, as in "to have control of." **3.** That portion of a computer system that ensures the execution of instructions in sequence according to the programs being run.

control account: In accounting, an account containing summarized transactions, with the details of those transactions appearing in subsidiary documents.

control card: In a computer system, a punched card that specifies initial information or modifies a program for particular applications.

control chart: A diagram used in statistical quality control to distinguish between random and nonrandom variations of products and processes, so that sources of nonrandom variation can be identified and controlled.

control function: In a computer system, a function or action that affects the operation of the system as a whole, such as stopping or starting.

control group: In an experimental situation, the group that does not receive the special treatment under examination; results of the control group and the experimental group, which did receive the treatment, are compared to see if any differences between them are statistically significant, and therefore are presumably due to that special treatment.

controllable cost: 1. A cost that can literally be controlled by management, usually within limits set by production and distribution requirements. **2.** A synonym for *variable cost*.

controlled account: In the securities industry, a trading account that is controlled by someone other than the owner of that account.

controlled circulation: A periodical which

distributes all or most of its copies free to selected subscribers, usually either because it is primarily an advertising medium or because it is circulated mainly to the members of an organization.

controlled company: A company that is under the control of another company, such as a subsidiary.

controlled price: See ceiling price.

controlled substance: A drug that may not be distributed without a doctor's prescription.

controller: The chief accounting officer of an organization. A variant spelling is "comptroller." The controller is normally that internal officer responsible for the development and supervision of such functions as tax management, budgeting, internal control systems, and all direct money handling functions.

controlling interest: That percentage of ownership of the common stock of a company which enables one or more stockholders to secure effective control over the operations of the company. The percentage necessary for control varies from 51% of some closely held companies to less than 20% of some very large and widely held companies.

control program: In a computer system, a previously prepared special-purpose program that can be attached to many other programs, eliminating the need for rewriting them each time; for example, a general-use program concerning the handling of errors occurring within a specific kind of computer system.

convenience foods: Foods that can be consumed with very little preparation, including a wide and growing range of prepared ready-to-eat, often partially or wholly precooked foods, such as TV dinners.

convenience goods: Goods that are usually bought at the first or handiest encounter with little regard for minor differences in price and quality, such as toothpaste, chewing gum, magazines, and cigarettes.

conversational language: A computer language such as BASIC that stresses the use of letters and words, so that computers and computer users may most easily communicate; a higher level, symbolic language, in contrast to lower level languages that are closer to machine language and are hard for humans to read and understand.

conversational mode: A terminal-computer communications style in which operator and computer respond to each other on a one-to-one basis.

conversion: **1.** The unauthorized taking of another's property, whether by direct physical taking or by an action which in law can be construed as unauthorized taking. **2.** The act of exchanging one instrument of value for another, as in conversion from paper money to the precious metal, usually gold, backing that money and as in conversion from bond or preferred stock to common stock by the terms of a stock issue. **3.** The act of processing raw materials into more finished materials; for example, coal into coke. **4.** The act of changing from one system or process to another; for example, from a computer system to a more advanced computer system.

conversion cost: **1.** The cost of processing materials into more finished materials and finished products, including all direct and associated indirect costs. **2.** The cost of moving from one kind of equipment or production to another, as when introducing new machinery or moving from wartime to peacetime production.

conversion price: The specific price at which a security, usually a preferred stock or bond, can be converted to the common stock of the issuer.

convertible: A bond or stock that may be exchanged for a specified number of shares of the common stock of the same corporation at a specified price, as defined by the corporation on issue of that instrument; the convertible shareholder may or may not choose to exercise that conversion privilege. Both bonds and preferred stocks may be issued carrying such conversion privileges attached.

conveyance: The transfer of legal title to land and the document transferring that title. The term has developed a much wider meaning as well, and is now used to describe any transfer of title to real or personal property.

cooling-off period: Any period prescribed by state or federal law, requiring the parties to an industrial dispute to stay a strike or lock-out action for a specified period of time so that mediation and further collective bargaining can be undertaken by both government and the parties to the dispute.

cooperative: A form of business in which a group of individuals or firms jointly organize some aspects of production or consumption. Producers may jointly buy equipment and supplies, as in a farm cooperative, or may sell their products together, as in a milk producers' cooperative. Consumers may buy food together and sometimes resell it at a profit to cooperative members, as in a food cooperative.

cooperative advertising: Advertising paid for by both the originator of the product or service being advertised and its distributors; for example, the cost of a book advertisement may be shared in a specified proportion between publisher and retailer.

cooperative apartment: A form of conditional apartment ownership, in which a tenant in a multiple occupancy building owns a share in the building, holds an open-end lease on the apartment occupied, and shares on a pro rata basis with other tenants the total cost of running the building. The tenants are stockholders in the building, in contrast to condominium owners, who own their portions of their dwellings.

coordinates: The two points necessary to specify the location of a point on a rectangular or Cartesian graph, with the abscissa identifying the horizontal location and the ordinate identifying the vertical distance from 0; often called Cartesian coordinates,

after René Descartes who developed the system.

coordination of benefits: A provision of many insurance plans, especially group health insurance plans, providing for payment of benefits only up to the amount of the claim, and attempting to avoid duplicate payments for the same claim from more than one insurer.

copy: 1. In the communication industries, the text, or words-on-paper portion, of the written communication, as distinct from any visual material used. The text of a news story or advertisement is its copy; any accompanying photographs or graphics are visual materials, although the captions explaining those visual materials are part of the copy. **2.** An exact duplicate, as in a photograph, or photocopy; and the process of making such a duplicate. **3.** A duplicate, put forward as an original, and the process of making such a duplicate.

copy editor: In publishing, one who is employed to work over copy already written and prepare it for publication, both by improving the clarity of exposition and by specifying spacing and layout of the copy to the compositor.

copywriter: In advertising, one who is employed to write advertisements. Many copywriters do considerably more than writing copy, working with every aspect of the advertisement, including its conception and a visual workup.

copyright (©): The right of ownership in literary and artistic property, under laws vesting the right in the creator of that property for specified times, and extending it by international agreement to much of the world. The owner of a copyright often sells or leases rights in that property to another for publication or other broadcast communication.

core: See magnetic core.

core memory: See core storage.

core storage: The storage of information by

a computer in its main memory, literally in magnetic cores, allowing high-speed, direct access to that body of information by the computer.

corner: In the securities and commodities markets, to obtain enough control of the available stores of a commodity or outstanding shares of a stock to be able to control price and supply. Although cornering was a commonly employed competitive technique in the last century, it is seldom encountered now because federal and state laws and regulations substantially preclude its use.

corporate bond: See bond.

corporate income tax: A tax levied by government on corporate profits. Profits are normally stated by corporations as pre-tax, or net-before-taxes. Corporate income taxes are graduated according to taxable income, as are personal income taxes.

corporation: A business entity created under law, which functions in all ways as an individual under law and is regarded as an individual in the eyes of the law. Corporations may be formed by a single individual or by an unlimited number of individuals joining together as stockholders. In the main, the liability of stockholders for the actions of the corporation is limited to the resources of the corporation, so that in the event of bankruptcy stockholders may lose only the value of their ownership interests; in contrast the individual proprietor and partners' liability is personal and unlimited.

corpus: A physical body; a body of value, as in the corpus or body of an estate. The corpus of an estate can earn money or can be used for other purposes; but the body of value itself remains as a physical perceivable entity.

correlation coefficient: A statistical measure of the closeness of the relationship between two variables, such as age and reaction time, as shown on a scattergram; a 0 correlation coefficient indicates no relationship, while a $+1$ indicates a positive linear relationship and a -1, a negative linear relationship.

correspondent bank: A bank maintaining a direct relationship with another, holding deposits and performing services for the other. In United States banking, the use of correspondent banks is widespread, with large banks in major cities, and especially those in New York City, performing a wide variety of services for less centrally located banks and holding substantial deposits from those banks.

co-signer: See co-maker.

cost: **1.** The price to be paid for anything, whatever medium of exchange used for payment. **2.** In economics, the amounts committed to pay for the factors of production, including all expenses necessary for production. **3.** To determine what something will cost, applying all necessary expense factors, as in "to cost out" an item.

cost absorption: The payment of some costs, usually not directly associated with production, by the seller, rather than the passing on of those costs to the buyer. For example, mailing costs may be passed on by seller to buyer, or may be paid by the seller, who is then absorbing this extra cost.

cost accountant: An accountant who is employed in cost accounting and who normally claims special competence in that area of accounting practice.

cost accounting: A branch of accounting devoted to the gathering, analysis, control, and reporting of costs and to the development of methods and systems aimed at accomplishing these functions.

cost and freight (c.a.f.): A price quoted, usually in international transactions, which includes both the cost of the merchandise offered for sale and the freight charges for shipment of the goods to the buyer.

cost basis: In accounting, the valuation of assets based upon their original cost minus any depreciation and without allowance for the addition of intangible factors, such as goodwill or developing antique value.

cost-benefit analysis: In planning, the weighing of projected costs and possible benefits by incurring those costs against alternative costs and benefits. The process may be informal, as it often is in very small companies, or formal and involved, depending on the resources and skills available for planning purposes. In some very large companies, cost-benefit analysis is a highly complex, computer-oriented process.

cost center: Any portion of an organization for which direct costs are separately figured and allocated, and for which someone has formal responsibility. There are often cost centers within cost centers, as a major department may be a cost center and every machine and activity within that department may also be a cost center.

cost consciousness: Awareness on the part of those working in a business of the importance of controlling and minimizing costs, usually accompanied by a specific program to accomplish these goals.

cost control: A general term embracing all those management techniques aimed at keeping costs to a minimum while still maintaining current quality and quantity standards.

cost curve: A graph representing the cost of producing a product at various levels of output. It is widely used in production planning to help identify the relationships between fixed and variable costs.

cost depletion: See depletion allowance.

cost effectiveness: An evaluation of whether or not to do something based on the cost-benefit relationship resulting from the move.

cost escalation: See escalation.

cost flow: In accounting, the tracking of costs through every step of the process of producing goods and services, from raw materials to sales, including all overhead functions.

costing: See cost.

cost, insurance and freight (c.i.f.): A price quoted that includes the cost of the merchandise offered for sale and the freight and insurance charges for shipment of the goods to the buyer.

cost of goods purchased: The total cost incurred for goods purchased, including prices paid, transportation charges, receiving costs, storage, and all associated overhead and in-plant costs.

cost of living: The level of expenditure necessary to maintain a current standard of living for families and individuals, as measured against previously necessary levels of expenditure. The Consumer Price Index, formerly called the Cost of Living Index, is a major United States cost of living indicator.

cost of living adjustment: Wage changes tied to increases or decreases in indexes that measure change in the cost of living, such as the Consumer Price Index.

cost of living adjustment clause (COLA): A collective bargaining provision mandating pay raises tied to the cost of living index; usually determined several times during the life of a collective bargaining contract.

cost of living allowance: Periodic wage increases incorporated into a pay plan to provide for anticipated increases in the cost of living, but not tied to actual increases in a cost of living index. The increases go into effect at stated intervals, usually during the life of a multi-year collective bargaining contract.

cost of living index: See Consumer Price Index.

cost of possession: See carrying cost.

cost of production: All costs associated with producing goods, including overhead, labor and materials. In manufacturing, the analysis and proper allocation of production costs is central to the pricing process.

cost of reproduction: An estimate of the cost of replacing present assets, usually buildings, and equipment, at current cost levels, and as they were when completed.

cost of sales: The total costs associated with

goods sold, as measured in accounting periods. In manufacturing, it is synonymous with the cost of production.

cost or market: Sometimes expressed "cost or market, whichever is lower," this is a method of inventory valuation that takes into account any decreases in the market value of inventory items. For example, pocket calculators in inventory during the 1970's often were marked down in evaluating inventory, as newer, more effective and much less expensive calculators reached the market.

cost out: See cost.

cost-plus contract: A contract in which the parties agree that the contractor will submit bills for payment based on costs actually incurred plus either a fixed fee or a percentage of those costs.

cost-plus pricing: The pricing of goods or services on the basis of costs plus an estimated necessary profit margin. This pricing technique is usually a budgeting planning device, rather than a means of reaching final marketplace prices, which must reflect the realities of competition and other market factors, including government regulation and public attitudes.

cost-price squeeze: A situation in which sellers are trapped between rising costs of production and sales on the one hand and marketplace resistance to price increases on the other, resulting in an erosion of their profits.

cost-push inflation: A type of inflation, caused largely by a wage-price spiral, that consists of upward pressure on the cost of production caused by wage increases, followed by price increases, then further wage increases and so on.

cost records: In accounting, the set of documents showing costs, including both ledgers and all supporting evidence, such as invoices, vouchers, and internal control materials.

cost savings: An unusual reduction in cost caused by a new procedure, such as a differ-

ent method of manufacturing or a change of suppliers. The cost reduction may be either a one time or a long-term saving.

cost standard: An estimate of what costs should be, to be compared with actual costs; usually part of a cost control system.

cottage industry: A system in which many small suppliers, working in their homes, supply goods to business as part of a production process. No longer widespread in manufacturing, it has taken on new meaning with the spread of part-time and home-work in the United States, with workers at home supplying a wide variety of services to business, such as typing and transcription services, preparation of visual materials and free-lance editorial services.

Council For Mutual Economic Assistance (COMECON): An Eastern European economic equivalent of the European Common Market.

counter check: A blank check available at a bank for the convenience of depositors who do not have their own checks with them. They must be cashed in person at the bank in which they are issued.

counterfeit: False, simulated, or imitating the genuine. The term often refers to bills and coins issued illegally by forgers, but is also used to refer to many other imitation articles of value.

counteroffer: An offer made in response to another's offer, usually as part of the process of negotiation.

country bank: A bank located in an "undesignated"city under Federal Reserve Board rules, which therefore can carry somewhat smaller legal reserves than banks located in designated Federal Reserve cities.

coupon bonds: Negotiable bonds payable to their bearer, carrying interest certificates or coupons which are clipped when mature and presented to the issuer of the bonds for payment. Coupon bonds need not be endorsed, either at passage of title in them or at the presentation of clipped coupons for payment.

convenant: A contract or part of a contract. In modern usage, the term describes a provision in a contract, usually one of the several kinds of real estate contracts.

cover: 1. In insurance, for an insurer to assume certain kinds of risks and potential liabilities when issuing an insurance policy, such as specified medical and surgical costs in a health insurance policy. **2.** In the securities markets, for a short seller to complete or cover short sales by buying stock.

coverage: See cover.

CPA: See certified public accountant.

CPI: See Consumer Price Index.

CPM: Critical Path Method. See Program Evaluation and Review Technique.

CPU: See central processing unit.

craft: A special skill, usually a skill used to make a living.

craft guild: An association of independent practitioners of a craft, organized for the pursuit of mutual interests and benefits. A major purpose of guilds is often the setting of craft standards and the limitation of memberships to restrict competition within the crafts.

craft union: A union of workers on the basis of shared crafts rather than on the basis of a shared workplace. The American Federation of Labor was in the main composed of craft unions; the Congress of Industrial Organization in the main organized workplace or industrial unions. The distinction between craft and industrial unions still exists though it has become somewhat blurred in practice.

Crash: The 1929 United States stock market collapse, which triggered the Great Depression of the 1930's.

credit: 1. The ability to secure goods and services now with a promise to pay later. Credit comes in many forms and from many sources, including both moneylenders and producers. It may be granted on the basis of a simple promise to pay, as in most routine commercial transactions between buyers and sellers, or may be granted only if completely covered by collateral, as with most home mortgages. **2.** In accounting, an entry on the right side of an account recording the reduction or elimination of an asset or expense, or the addition to or creation of a liability, net worth, or revenue item. In double-entry bookkeeping, each credit is accompanied by a debit entry to a balancing account, so that the books always reflect the current relationship between assets and liabilities.

credit account: See charge account.

credit approval: The granting of credit to a purchaser or borrower by a seller or lender; for example, approval of credit for an appliance purchase by a retail store manager or approval of an individual line of credit by a bank branch manager.

credit balance: In general, the excess of credits over debits in any account, as in banking, where the excess of credits over debits in a depositor's account indicates that the depositor has funds currently on deposit. When an account shows a debit balance, the depositor either has an overdraft in the account or is using an overdraft privilege or line of credit.

credit bureau: A private organization that maintains files containing credit information and often a good deal of personal data on those who have previously used or sought credit, for the use of commercial customers seeking to determine the creditworthiness of customers asking for credit; those listed in the files of credit bureaus are by law granted the right to examine their own files.

credit card: A document, usually in the form of a card, given as evidence that the issuing organization is extending credit to its holder. If the card is given for use only on the premises of the issuing organization, as in the case of a department store or gasoline credit card, it will be honored only on those premises. If the card is issued by a major national credit card company, it will be honored up to a certain limit, in thousands of establishments. Credit cards often carry with them a revolving credit arrangement in the form of an overdraft privilege in a participating bank.

credit control: Controls over national money and credit policies, credit and money supplies, and interest rates, vested in the Federal Reserve System and its Board of Governors, which affects the quantity and cost of credit available to private borrowers throughout the country, and can strongly influence the direction of the national economy.

credit instrument: A document evidencing debt, including all paper instruments other than paper money and coins. In a certain sense, even paper money and coins issued by a government solely on the basis of its full faith and credit, as in the United States, are credit instruments. The most widely used of all credit instruments is the check, accounting for well over 90% of all commercial transactions in the United States.

credit insurance: Insurance against uncollectibles, in which the insurer shares the risks developed by the extension of credit to customers.

credit investigation: Any investigation of the potential creditworthiness of one seeking credit entered into by a lender, seller, or one acting for a lender or seller, including the use of credit bureaus and direct checking of such matters as bank references supplied by the potential creditor.

credit investigator: One who is employed by a lender to gather information about the creditworthiness of a potential borrower. Credit investigators may be employees of a lending institution or of a private organization serving lending institutions.

credit line: An overdraft privilege granted by a lending institution, allowing a customer to borrow sums within a stated range without treating each loan as a new loan, requiring separate approvals and documents from the lender. Credit lines are often stated in fixed sums, such as a $50,000 credit line at the bank, but are in fact somewhat variable, depending on the borrower's bank balances, business and personal status, interest rates, and general economic conditions.

credit memorandum: A memorandum from creditor to debtor, decreasing the amount owed or creating a credit balance in favor of the debtor; due for example to a refund due to the purchaser of an item that has been returned for credit.

credit money: In economics, the concept that lending institutions create money when they grant credit to borrowers because money loaned does not really exist until the credit granted is used.

creditor: One to whom money is due. In the widest sense, one who has the right to collect anything of value from anyone for any reason, including the right to collect from another as a result of a legal proceeding.

creditor nation: A nation whose people and institutions have larger total investments outside their country than the total of all foreign investment inside their country.

credit rating: An assessment of the creditworthiness of a business or individual made by private organizations, such as Dun and Bradstreet, specializing in the gathering and evaluation of credit information. A credit rating may be expressed on a scale, such as A to D, or may be expressed in evaluative comments.

credit report: A report made by a credit investigator or bureau on the creditworthiness of one seeking credit.

credit risk: The degree of exposure to risk faced by a lender with respect to a specific customer, as in an evaluation of a not-very-credit-worthy firm as a "high" credit risk.

credit sale: A sale in which the seller passes title to the buyer and makes delivery, while the buyer pays over a period of time. The term is broadly used to include both credit sales in which title passes and conditional sales in which title is retained by the seller until payment is completed.

credit standing: See credit rating.

credit terms: The specific arrangements for repayment defined in a credit sales contract, including such matters as the length of time allowed for payment, the rate of interest, penalties for slow payment and actions in the case of nonpayment.

credit union: A cooperative that lends its members money out of funds deposited by its membership, usually at somewhat lower interest rates than those available from commercial lenders. Widespread in the United States, credit unions are often formed by such organizations as fraternal societies and trade unions.

creditworthiness: An estimate made by a lender as to how likely a potential borrower will be to pay back a requested loan. Lenders will base estimates on such factors as available collateral, the character of the credit applicant, the capital available to that applicant, presumed capacity to repay based upon such factors as current income and future prospects, and general economic conditions as of the time of application for credit.

creeping inflation: A slow inflation rate, about 2-3% per year. Creeping inflation is thought to be stoppable or reversible by some economists and government officials. The average rate of inflation has been far higher than 2-3% since World War II, however, so the term has lost most of its precise original meaning.

Critical Path Method (CPM): See Program Evaluation and Review Technique.

crop-lien system: See sharecropping.

crop insurance: Insurance for farmers against crop losses due to such unavoidable causes as weather, insects, and disease, under coverage provided by the Federal Crop Insurance Corporation, an agency of the Department of Agriculture.

crop production adjustments: A set of limita-

tions on farm production programs of the Agricultural Stabilization and Conservation Service. These programs limit the amount of acreage used to produce some crops, take some acreage out of production for certain periods, and limit the amount of some crops that can be sent to market.

crosschecking: Adding figures both horizontally and vertically, to check their totals. In accounting, the process is sometimes called crossfooting.

crossfooting: See crosschecking.

cross-validation: The application of predictions, based on earlier experiments, to new groups, to check the validity of those predictions.

CRT: See cathode ray tube.

cryogenics: The study of low temperature phenomena. In industry, cryogenics research is being increasingly applied to the storage and transportation of energy and to the development of alternatives to conventional sources of energy.

cum dividend: A stock which is transferred with a dividend declared, but not yet paid, which is payable to its new owner. Stock sold "ex dividend" is sold without the right to collect such a dividend.

cum rights: A stock which is transferred with rights to buy newly issued stock at prices somewhat lower than subscription prices attached, which may be exercised by its new owner.

cumulative distribution: In statistics, a form of frequency distribution in which each interval includes all the items from previous intervals, so that the final interval is 100% of the total group of items being considered; useful in assessing the number of items above or below certain break points.

cumulative dividends: Dividends due but unpaid on cumulative preferred stock that is entitled to fixed dividends and is in arrears. Cumulative dividends are paid out of corporate earnings before dividends are issued to common stock holders.

cumulative preferred stock: Preferred stock that is entitled to receive fixed dividends for a specified period if justified by corporate earnings, and that accumulates dividends if they are not paid or "passed." These accumulated dividends must be paid before common stock holders receive dividends on their stock.

cumulative voting: In elections to the boards of directors of corporations, the ability of a holder of a single share of stock to cast one vote for each director to be elected or to cast as many votes as there are elected directors for as few as one director. For example, a holder of ten voting shares of common stock in a situation in which ten directors are to be elected might cast ten votes for each of ten directors, 100 votes in all for the ten shares. Or the stockholder might choose to cast all 100 votes for one director, or to vote any variation between the two extremes, thus maximizing the possibility of minority representation on the board of directors.

curator: See conservator.

curb exchange: Any market in which trading takes place outdoors, as trading on the sidewalk or curb. The American Stock Exchange originated as one of many such curb exchanges, and was formally named the Curb Exchange for many years.

currency: All paper money and coins acceptable as legal tender, but not including negotiable paper, such as checks, even if it is freely transferrable from bearer to bearer. Currency is often used synonymously with paper money, but the term does include coins.

currency swap: A currency exchange between two countries at an agreed-upon rate of exchange, usually to help stabilize international currency values.

current account: An open account between buyer and seller, through which normal transactions flow, with payments due in the normal course of business and without any special billing or settlement terms specified between the parties.

current assets: Those assets that are held in cash or are relatively easy to convert into cash, including such items as collectibles, short-term investments, and inventory. They are normally convertible into cash within one year, but for accounting purposes some assets that take longer than a year to convert may still be classified as current.

current expense: A normal operating expense chargeable to an accounting period, as contrasted to extraordinary and nonrecurring expenses.

current income: Income attributable to an accounting period, normally as distinguished from cash receipts, which sometimes may not be treated as income in the accounting period in which they are received.

current liability: Any debt which is due and payable within a specified short period, usually one year, including both short-term debts and longer term debts maturing and payable within the period.

current ratio: The ratio of current assets to current liabilities. It is a key indicator of the current health of any business, and is carefully noted by investment analysts and potential lenders. A current ratio of $2 in current assets to $1 in current liabilities is minimally acceptable for credit-securing purposes in almost all businesses, with somewhat lower ratios acceptable in some instances.

current return: See current yield.

current yield: The relationship between the dividends paid in a year on a stock and its current market price. For example, a stock which paid $1 in dividends last year and is now selling at $10 has a current yield of 10:1, with a selling price 10 times the dividends paid.

customer service: That part of a business organization involved with the handling of business matters after sale, including billing, collections, complaint handling, and the day-to-day administrative functions involved in customer relations.

customer's man: In the securities industry, a woman or man who represents a securities firm in handling customers' buy and sell orders. This somewhat out-of-date term, has now been largely replaced by the synonymous "registered representative," or "account executive."

customs broker: One who is in the business of expediting the import and export of goods through the preparation of the papers and other aspects of legal compliance.

customs duties: Taxes levied by a country on imports and, in the United States, collected by the Customs Service.

customs house: A district office of the United States Bureau of Customs, which is charged with a wide range of responsibilities regarding tax assessment and collection, regulation, inspection, and control of transportation. There is a customs house in every major port of entry in the United States.

customs ports: Those ports at which ships carrying imports enter the United States and pay customs duties.

Customs Service: The Bureau of Customs of the United States Treasury Department, charged with a wide range of responsibilities regarding import duty collections, regulation, inspection and law enforcement.

customs union: A trading union between two or more countries, which establishes common levies on imports from all other countries and eliminates all or most taxes on imports and exports passing between the countries in the union. The European Common Market is such a customs union.

cutback: A drop in the amount of work available, causing a business to cut its work force. The term has come to be widely used to describe any cut in work force, whether or not necessitated by business conditions.

cutoff date: Any date at which something is stopped, as in a cutoff date for extension of credit or a cutoff date for accounting purposes, which sets the end of an accounting period.

cutthroat competition: Ruthless competition between businesses, using a substantial number of unfair and often illegal competitive practices, and especially the device of temporary price-cutting to drive competitors out of business; sometimes practiced by large, better capitalized companies to drive out weaker, marginal companies, and by new competitors in a field to establish a sales position.

cybernetics: The broad field of systems control and communications involving the development of self-regulating logical systems through the use of feedback, patterned after analysis of human information-handling processes. One very simple cybernetic system is the heater-thermostat which controls heat production according to changes in temperature. Developed and named by Norbert Weiner in the late 1940's, cybernetics is basic to the development of modern computer theory and has wide applications in areas such as engineering technology, forecasting, policy analysis, and systems modeling.

cycle: Any repeated sequence of events. A cycle can be measured by the passage of time, as in the twenty-four hours of a day; by the passage of events, as in the events comprising the "business cycle"; or by both time and events, as in the start-to-finish time of a closely timed, sequenced production cycle.

cyclical industry: An industry that is particularly sensitive to economic upswings and downturns caused by the operation of the business cycle. For example, the travel industry, because it depends to a significant degree on the spending of discretionary income, which tends to dry up in periods of economic downturn, is more cyclical than the grain industry.

cyclical unemployment: Unemployment

D

damages: Compensation due for loss or injury, gained by legal process.

data: 1. Generally, a synonym for information. In electronic data processing, information that is ready or easily made ready for input into a computer system. **2.** In research of any kind, the raw material of the study.

data bank: In electronic data processing, a large single or substantial group of data bases, all capable of being reached, or "accessed," as one.

data base: 1. Any body of information that can be used as raw material for studies, products or specific information. **2.** In electronic data processing, a body of information in a computer memory that can be reached into by computer, or "accessed," for information.

data base management: The handling of a computerized data base by its human managers to most effectively collect, store and use that data.

data communications: The transmission of data in the form of computer code to remote locations through communications systems, such as telephone lines.

data processing: A general term for the processing of information in a systematic way. The major way of processing data in modern business is electronically, through computers, the descriptive terms being "electronic data processing" and "computer processing."

data processing system: See computer system.

data reduction: The transformation of raw data into usable form.

data retrieval: See information retrieval.

data transmission: The movement of information between two or more geographically separate points, as in the transmission of documents over telephone lines with input of the printed document at the sending point and printout of the document at the receiving point, or as in transmissions between computers in a network.

dated billing: A postdated billing, resulting in a credit extension beyond the normal terms offered; for example, an order sold in May for immediate delivery on net 30 day terms would normally become payable some time in June, but if billed in July would become payable in August, an effective two month credit extension.

date of issue: The date on which an instrument of obligation, such as an insurance policy, or bond or other debt instrument, becomes operative. The instrument bears that date rather than the date on which the instrument is executed or any other date.

daybook: A journal of original entry for business transactions, in which a chronological record of transactions is maintained for later entry into an accounting system. Once widely used, the daybook has in the main been replaced by the journal. It survives, however, in the records kept by people conducting business away from their offices, such as outside sellers.

day loans: Unsecured loans to stockbrokers made by lending institutions at the start of the business day, and for that day only, as a means of supplying working cash for that day. The loan is in the form of a line of credit for the day, to be used by the borrower as transactions necessitate, and is secured by the collateral resulting from the securities transactions themselves as they occur.

day order: In the securities markets, a customer buy or sell order that must be consummated on the day it is placed. If not so consummated, it is automatically nullified at the end of that business day.

days of grace: See grace period.

day worker: One who is employed on a day-to-day basis, rather than for any longer period or as a regular employee, usually for temporary or difficult-to-schedule work.

deadheading: In the transportation industry, the carrying of people or freight free; also the movement of empty carriers, as in returning home empty after a delivery of freight or in traveling empty for part of the journey between distant points.

deadline: A time set for delivery of anything, such as copy for a newspaper article, advertising matter, or performance under the terms of a contract.

dead stock: Stock on hand that for any reason either sells so slowly as to be uneconomic to continue to hold and sell, or that cannot be sold at all.

dead time: See down time.

dead weight: The weight of any vehicle empty. The term is usually used to describe vehicles used in transporting people and freight.

deal: In general, an agreement. Deals range from contracts with full legal force to verbal agreements with little or no legal force, intended to lead to contracts. Deals may lead to development of a single contract or of a number of legal instruments which together embody the agreements reached.

dealer: Any person or organization buying or selling goods and services who takes title to whatever is bought and passes title on whatever is sold, as distinct from brokers and agents, who represent and deal with buyers and sellers but do not take or pass title. Dealers are sometimes also brokers or agents, as in the securities industry, where many securities dealers buy and sell for themselves through their own accounts while, acting as brokers, they also transact business for their customers.

dealer service representative: A person who sells and services goods sold to dealers, and is therefore usually employed by a manufacturer or wholesaler.

death tax: Any tax levied on the property of the dead, whether directly or indirectly, whether estate or inheritance taxes.

debasement: In business or finance, a reduction in the value of metal used in coins, especially as regards the value as metal of the precious metals used in coinage. The term has also come to be used loosely as describing erosion in the value of currencies caused by inflationary processes.

debenture: Any long-term debt instrument issued by a company or institution, secured only by the general assets of the issuer. Debentures are usually issued as bonds, primarily by corporations and governments. They are therefore only as good as their issuer's ability to meet the debt obligations they create.

debenture bonds: Unsecured debt obligations issued by governments and corporations backed only by their promise to pay, and only as good as the repayment ability of their issuers.

debit: In accounting, an entry on the left side of an account, recording addition or creation of an asset or expense, or the subtraction or elimination of a liability, net worth or revenue item.

debit balance: A debit amount left in any account, as in a credit account showing an amount still owed by buyer to seller or a bank account with a minus balance, showing money owed to the bank by the customer.

debit memorandum: A memorandum reducing the amount owed, as in the reduction of a debit balance by a lender or other creditor due to correction of an arithmetic error in favor of the creditor.

debt: A fixed sum owed by one to another, payable now, and collectible at law by the creditor. In a somewhat wider sense, all debts owed by one to all others, as in a "national debt." The term is also loosely used to describe any obligation, however unenforceable, as in the "moral debt," or "debt to society."

debt ceiling: See debt limit.

debt limit: The maximum lawful debt which may be incurred by any government. Debt limits are set by law, and for sovereign states may be revised by law, as in the instance of the United States, which has often raised its own debt limit. Most states need state constitutional amendments to raise their own debt limits, but in fact are at least as much influenced by bond market considerations as by statutory constraints. Most municipalities need state approval for debt limit changes.

debt monetization: The issuance of new debt obligations by government to pay existing debts, and therefore the expansion of money supply; for example, the issuance of new short-term United States Government securities, providing a larger money supply and consequent expansion of credit available in the economy; a primary cause of inflation.

debtor: One who is legally responsible for the payment of debt, however that debt was incurred. One liable for payment of a judgment is just as much a debtor as one responsible for repayment of a loan.

debtor nation: A nation whose people and institutions have smaller total investments outside their country than the total of all foreign investment inside their country.

debt service: The amounts a debtor must pay a creditor to keep a debt currently paid up, including due and payable interest payments and principal repayments. Debt service often also refers to the total of all such payments due on all debts by a single debtor in a specified period.

debugging: 1. The process of finding and removing the flaws and errors in any process, product or program, as in the final checking, adjustment and correction processes involved in a new automobile model, computer program, or customer relations handling process. **2.** The finding and neutralization of wiretaps and other covert listening devices, such as those used in international and industrial espionage.

deceased account: A bank account held in the name of someone who is deceased. A bank must freeze such an account on notification of the death of the accountholder, pending legal process leading to the close of the account and payment of the sums in it as directed by a court after probate.

decedent: A dead person.

decentralize: 1: To remove decision-making power and operating authority from a single entity and vest it in several entities. For example, a company with a single operating head and no divisions may be split into several operating divisions, each with its own operating head and responsible only to an executive committee. This kind of decentralization is often accompanied by, but need not involve, physical moves. **2.** To separate elements of an entity and disperse them into various locations. For example, some nations have dispersed or decentralized their vital industries during wartime.

decertification: Removal of National Labor Relations Board certification of a union as bargaining agent for a group of employees in a bargaining unit, after those employees have voted to remove the union and replace it with another union or no union at all.

decile: See percentile.

decimal coinage: The organization of a nation's coinage system on a decimal basis, with a base of 10. The United States has a decimal coinage system.

decision-making process: The process of identifying, illuminating, and analyzing alternative courses of action, and of making informed decisions based upon that process. Considerable attention is paid to the development of sound decision-making processes, because they are so important to management skill and success.

decision rule: A rule prescribing fixed patterns of response in similar situations, usually relatively complex mathematical and statistical situations, especially in computer applications.

decision tree: A graphic treatment of the decision-making process, identifying and following key probabilities and their effect on further probabilities.

declaration: 1. A listing of items to be imported or exported, and their values. **2.** A listing of insurable items, attached to an insurance policy.

declaratory judgment: A judgment declaring the rights of the parties before the court, rather than requiring execution of the court's judgment.

declining balance method of depreciation: A method of figuring depreciation by applying a fixed percentage to each year's balance, which remains after the previous year's depreciation.

deck: A set of punched cards, organized and prepared for use in a computer system.

decree: The judgment of a court of equity, ordering execution of the provisions of that judgment.

dedicated: Any equipment set aside for stated purposes. The term is most often encountered in electronic data processing, referring to computers, data transmission equipment and related hardware and software devoted to the accomplishment of specified purposes, such as a computer employed solely to handle a specific kind of customer service function.

dedicated computer: See dedicated.

deductible: 1. In the insurance industry, the amount of the insured's loss which will be borne by the insured before the insurance company's risk starts. For example, a "$200 deductible" provision in an automobile collision insurance policy means that the first $200 of damage to the insured's automobile will be borne by the insured, with insurance company liability starting after that $200 deductible. **2.** In taxation, any expense item which serves as a subtraction from taxable income.

deduction: See deductible.

deed: A document legally conveying current title in real property from one to another. The document must be signed, sealed, witnessed, delivered, and conveyable. There need be no consideration for conveyance of a deed, as it may be a gift.

deed in trust: A form of mortgage, conveying property to a trustee as real property security for a loan.

de facto: Literally, "in fact." Often used to describe the realities of a situation, as distinct from its appearance or legalities. For example, a "de facto" government may be in actual possession of state power, but may not have been accorded legal or "de jure" status.

defalcation: The misappropriation or other illegal use of funds by one in a position of fiduciary trust. The term is normally used in relation to corporate or government officials who have so abused their trust.

defamation: A legally actionable attack on an individual that tends to injure that person's reputation, through personal and slanderous or libelous utterances.

default: 1. Failure to do a legally required act, and subsequent liability for the resulting consequences. For example, failure to make payment on a loan may make a debtor liable for immediate payment of the entire loan amount, or a corporate bond default may force a corporation into bankruptcy. Failure to defend an action at law may result in a judgment by default, in favor of the plaintiff. **2.** In computer operations, the alternative selected by the system at a choice point, when the user has not specified the alternative to be chosen.

default judgment: See default.

defendant: One named by a plaintiff as the object of a lawsuit.

defensive investment: An investment aimed primarily at the conservation of capital, rather than at its aggressive growth. For example, an investor during a prolonged downward turn in common stock prices may sharply limit common stock investments and turn to less volatile and probably considerably safer investments, giving up the possibilities of aggressive capital growth inherent in common stocks for slower-growing, capital-conserving defensive investments.

deferral: Any item of expense or revenue that should be carried forward for accounting purposes so that it is attributed to the period in which the benefits stemming from the expense are received or the revenue is earned.

deferred annuity: An annuity that starts payments only after a certain period or after reaching a specified attained age; for example, a pension plan that vests, or guarantees later payments after 10 or 20 years of employment, but will start payments only at retirement age.

deferred charge: A charge that by its nature should be spread, all or in part, over future accounting periods rather than be treated as a current operating expense. For example, research and development costs are often properly spread over future years, with little or no charges expensed into the current period.

deferred credit: See deferred revenue.

deferred delivery contract: A contract to purchase goods in which one party pays consideration due and the other takes delivery at some future date. While under many circumstances, this is a normal commercial arrangement, the device has been widely used to defraud the unwary, in such areas as precious metal sales to small investors.

deferred dividend: A dividend that has been announced but on which payment has been postponed, either until a specific future date or until the occurrence of a specifically stated event.

deferred income: See deferred revenue.

deferred revenue: Advance payment received but not actually yet earned, and therefore for accounting purposes held for attribution to the period in which it is earned.

deferred tax: A tax that will result from current income and transactions at some later date beyond the current taxing period; for example, money earned in a current year and accrued in a profit-sharing plan, which will be taxable only when the money in that plan is paid out.

deficiency: 1. An amount claimed by a taxing authority over what a taxpayer has actually paid. **2.** In accounting, the amount by which liabilities exceed assets, which normally must be balanced by capital contributions to avoid insolvency.

deficiency letter: A formal notice from a taxing authority, notifying a taxpayer of alleged taxes due, usually in addition to taxes already paid.

deficit: The amount of deficiency, or excess of liabilities over assets, at a specified time, as at the end of an accounting period. In a much wider sense, the term is used as a synonym for "loss," and is often used to describe a process rather than a fixed sum at a specific time, as in "We are running at a deficit."

deficit financing: Government spending in excess of income, year after year on a long-term basis, with a corresponding very large and continuous increase in the national debt. It is most often used as a term of opprobrium by critics charging excessive government spending.

deflation: A sustained drop in the general price level of goods and services: the opposite of inflation. The last substantial deflation in the United States was the Great Depression following the stock market crash of 1929.

deflationary gap: A theory that deflation is wholly or largely caused by a relatively large proportion of saving in an economy, resulting in too little investment spending to fuel economic growth and substantially full employment.

degradation: A condition in which a computer system is being operated at less than normal levels of efficiency, usually due to equipment problems.

de jure: That which is legal and right according to law. For example, a government that is recognized as legitimate according to the past laws of a country, as interpreted by its legal institutions is "de jure," as distinct from a government that simply has power and exercises it, which is "de facto." In the modern world, the distinction between "de facto" and "de jure" as to questions of state power is somewhat blurred.

delegate: 1. To pass responsibility to another for performance of one or more tasks, while keeping full responsibility for the proper performance of those tasks. The delegator is not absolved of responsibility for the delegated tasks, but rather has the new tasks of checking and guaranteeing that the delegated tasks are properly performed. **2.** A representative, such as a union representative elected by other workers to represent them in grievance procedures under a collective bargaining contract.

delegation: 1. The process of delegating. **2.** A group of representatives.

delinquent tax: A tax that is overdue, unpaid, and usually accompanied by penalties for late payment.

delisting: The dropping of a stock from the list of those traded by a stock exchange. To be listed, and thus traded, stocks must meet a number of rules set up by a stock exchange, usually including minimum earnings, company size, and numbers of stockholders and shares of stock held by the public. When a stock ceases to meet these minimum qualifications for listing, a stock exchange may delist it.

delivered price: A price quoted by a seller that includes the cost of shipping the goods sold to the buyer. The price quoted may include the addition of the freight costs associated with a single sale, but more often will be a fixed price for delivery within an area or sometimes for delivery anywhere in the country.

delivery: 1. The legal transfer of possession of real or personal property. The transfer of possession may be by means of physical delivery or by means of an instrument of control, such as a bill of sale or deed; it may be absolute or conditional, actual or constructive. **2.** In commercial transactions, the actual physical delivery of purchased goods to their buyer, as specified by contract or common practice.

Delphi forecast: See jury of executive opinion forecast.

demand: 1. In law, the claiming of a specific right, asserted to be an absolute right under law, as in the demand for withdrawal of a demand deposit. **2.** In economics, the total of wants for a product, service, or body of products and services.

demand curve: A graph showing the varying relationship between demand and price, often used in pricing new products, to determine optimum price levels.

demand deposit: A bank deposit that may be claimed by the depositor without notice, either in the form of checks drawn upon it or by outright withdrawal of the deposited amounts. Legally, many such deposits may be held for up to 30 days, but practically they are almost always recoverable on demand, except in some instances of bank failure.

demand loan: A loan that has no fixed date of termination, but may be terminated at any time by either lender or borrower.

demand pull inflation: An inflationary spiral, with strong demand for goods and services, resulting in increased business and credit expansion, increased money supply, and still higher prices.

demography: The study of human population, focusing on such factors as population densities, growth rates, occupational trends, income levels of various strata, birth and death rates, and consumer behavior.

demonetization: Discontinuance of the use of a substance as legal tender, such as the dropping of gold and silver as legal tender.

demurrage: Charges levied by a carrier for longer than normal loading and unloading time, as when a freight car is held empty on a siding because the shipper is not ready to load it on time.

denationalization: The turning or returning of publicly owned businesses to private ownership.

denomination: The face value of ownership, debt, and currency certificates. While debt instruments and currency are issued in face value certificates, stocks are normally issued in multiple share certificates, such as a certificate for 100 shares; the denomination of a $10 bill being $10.00, and of each share whatever the par value of the single share.

department: A functional unit within any organization, described in any of several ways as a department, unit, group, cost center, division, office, plant or shop.

Department of Agriculture: A Federal department responsible for all executive branch matters dealing with agriculture, including a wide range of regulatory, enforcement, administrative, and educational functions.

Department of Commerce: A Federal depart-

ment responsible for all executive branch matters dealing with business and commerce, including a wide range of regulatory, enforcement, administrative, and educational functions.

Department of Energy: A Federal department responsible for a wide range of executive branch activities dealing with energy, energy conservation, and energy resource development.

Department of Health, Education and Welfare (HEW): A Federal department responsible for the nation's massive social security and welfare systems, and for related activities; this department handles a very wide range of regulatory, enforcement, administrative, and educational functions.

Department of Housing and Urban Development (HUD): A Federal department responsible for the development and administration of programs aimed at improving the quality and quantity of the nation's housing, with special attention to the needs of the poor and disadvantaged.

Department of Justice (DOJ): A Federal department functioning as the nation's chief executive branch legal arm, carrying substantial prosecuting and regulatory responsibilities.

Department of Labor: A Federal department functioning in those areas affecting labor and labor-management matters, and handling substantial regulatory, mediating, enforcement, administrative, and educational functions.

Department of Transportation (DOT): A Federal agency responsible for policy development and regulation in matters affecting national land transportation.

department store: A substantial retailer, carrying a considerable quantity of goods and organized into several subsidiary cost centers, accounted for separately and often separately staffed and managed.

dependent: One who may be claimed by another as a dependent for an income tax deduction. The amounts deductible and the circumstances under which dependency may be claimed change as the tax statutes are amended, and vary to some degree from state to state. A dependent need not be a relative and, under some circumstances, it is possible to claim someone as a dependent while that person also claims a personal exemption.

dependent variable: An unknown factor in an experimental situation; one of the objects of the experiment is to determine the value of the dependent variables involved.

depletable: Capable of being used up, usually referring to natural resources, such as coal, oil, metal ores and standing timber.

depleted cost: For accounting purposes, the cost that is left after accrued depletion has been subtracted.

depletion: The concept that natural resources can be and are used up over a period of time, and that tax policy and accounting practice must take into account that exhaustion of resources. Also refers to the amount of resources so used up.

depletion allowance: 1. In taxation, the amounts of the deductions from taxes allowed their owners for the using up of natural resources, such as oil, coal, metals and timber. Depletion allowances, when occurring, are set by law. **2.** In accounting, the value reductions set for depletion of specified natural resources.

deposit insurance: Insurance of bank deposits up to certain limits set by law. See also: Federal Deposit Insurance Corporation; Federal Savings and Loan Insurance Corporation.

deposition: Testimony, given pursuant to a pending legal action by order of the court or by applicable law, that is taken out of court, written down, and attested, for use as evidence by the parties during that court action.

depository: 1. A person, institution or place to store anything of value. Also spelled de-

positary, when referring to a person or institution entrusted. **2.** A bank authorized to receive and hold government, trust or other bank funds.

deposits: Amounts placed into bank accounts, which are then drawn upon for business or personal use or held for the accretion of interest, and which provide a base for the bank's ability to create credit and make loans.

deposit slip: A record of deposit filled out by a depositor and stamped by a bank which functions both as an entry document for the bank and as a legal and vitally necessary evidence of deposit for the depositor.

depreciable cost: The basis upon which an asset's depreciation will be taken, often the money cost of the asset to its current owner.

depreciation: The lessening in value of an asset due to age and use. Depreciation is an accounting estimate, essential both for avoiding overstatement of an asset's value and for tax accounting purposes. Although its tax significance is similar to that of depletion, it results from use rather than using up. A machine may be fully depreciated for tax and accounting purposes and still be whole and entirely useable, while a stand of timber may shrink year by year as it is used up or depleted.

depreciation reserve: Those valuation amounts set aside for accounting purposes to reflect the depreciation that has accumulated on an asset. Depreciation reserves are accounting estimates, rather than actual reserves.

depression: A long, deep economic crisis, with widespread unemployment and the collapse or near-collapse of major economic institutions. The last depression was the Great Depression of the 1930's. Depressions and recessions are distinguished by the length and depth of the business cycle downturn, with recessions much less severe than depressions.

depth interview: An interview attempting to

probe as widely and as exhaustively as possible into the interviewee's views and attitudes on the subject matter of the interview; both fixed and open-ended questions may be asked, in proportions depending on the design of the specific interview; also called a qualitative interview.

deregulation: The ending of government regulation of private activities, usually business activities; for example, the ending of government-imposed price controls on a product, such as gasoline.

derived demand: Demands for some products and services that are created by demands for other products and services. For example, demands for automobiles create a very large number of other demands for metals, fuel, accessories and services. In a highly integrated economy, the concept becomes somewhat blurred as an analytical tool.

devaluation: Redefinition downward of the precious metal content of a country's currency by that country, or of a country's currency in relation to other national currencies. Under conditions of international currency price-fixing, devaluation can be precise; when currencies float freely against each other, backed in a practical sense only by the full faith and credit of the issuing governments, devaluation is a matter of national policy and central bank control operating within a fluid international currency situation.

developing nation: A wide and imprecise term generally describing any nation that is not highly industrialized, often referring to those relatively unindustralized nations of Asia, Africa and South America thought to be aligned with neither the United States nor the Soviet Union in international power bloc matters. Although often used synonymously with the term "Third World," some highly industrialized unaligned nations, such as Brazil, cannot be properly described as "developing."

development expense: 1. An expense incurred in new product introduction. **2.** Any expense related to advertising and promotion. **3.** A cost directly or indirectly related to the exploration and exploitation of natural resources.

devise: A gift of real property by the terms of a will, consisting of land or any other kind of realty.

diagnostic routine: A computer program developed to find errors in existing programs and hardware.

dictum: A judge's comments, of some interest and possible future significance, but having no direct bearing on the disposition of a case currently before that judge.

differential costs: Those costs which can be associated with doing or not doing, adding or subtracting from something in being or planned. For example, the cost to make a milkshake without an egg may be 20 cents; with an egg 25 cents. The differential cost of the egg in the milkshake is 5 cents.

digital computer: A computer that continually counts, applying arithmetic and logic functions to ingested data.

dilution: As applied to securities, the lessening of an ownership share's earnings and assets equity, caused by the issuance of more ownership shares without corresponding increases in earnings and assets. Stock dilution can occur in several ways, including new common stock issues and the exercise of stock options and warrants.

diminishing balance method: See declining balance method.

diminishing marginal utility: See marginal utility.

diminishing returns: See law of diminishing returns.

direct access: See random access.

direct advertising: See direct marketing.

direct cost: A cost that can be specifically related to a product, such as labor and materials used in manufacture. The proper identification of direct costs and their control is a major management goal, and the number of unattributable and therefore "indirect" costs is constantly diminishing.

direct costing: In accounting, the continual identification and proper recording of direct costs as they are incurred.

direct investment: The purchase of active ownership interests, whether controlling or substantial minority interests, in other companies, in contrast to the purchase of shares in those companies for non-active investment purposes.

direct labor: Labor that can be directly attributed to a product, comprising a set of direct costs.

direct mail: See direct marketing.

direct mail advertising: See direct marketing.

direct marketing: The selling of goods and services directly to consumers without intermediary selling organizations and retail establishments. Most direct marketing is done by mail, to prepared lists of prospective customers, and the process was for many years called "direct mail" or "direct mail advertising." Direct marketing attempts to make a sale or start the process of directly making a sale immediately; in contrast, advertising is primarily aimed at moving the potential buyer toward the start of the direct sales process without actually starting that process.

direct material: All material which is part of a finished product, such as the steel used in a typewriter, and its cost for accounting purposes.

director: A member of the highest policy-making body of an organization, the Board of Directors.

directory advertising: Advertising placed in such printed materials as trade association and telephone directories.

direct overhead: Those overhead costs that can be directly attributed to goods and services produced, and can therefore be ac-

counted for as direct costs, in contrast to those unattributable costs which must be accounted for as indirect costs.

direct placement: The sale of securities directly to a limited number of purchasers, rather than to the general public; for example, the sale of a corporate bond issue to a single bank or a group of banks and other institutions, without resale by them to the public.

direct tax: A tax specifically directed to a taxpayer and paid by that taxpayer, such as an income tax, in contrast to a tax on goods or services, which can be passed along to the ultimate consumer of those goods, such as a sales tax.

dirty float: A currency float, or exchange rate, that does not float free as against other currencies, with relative currency prices determined by marketplace conditions, but rather is manipulated by government in pursuit of national policy; normally a pejorative term applied to what other governments do, but a most usual practice indulged in directly or indirectly by most governments under most conditions.

disability insurance: Insurance against working time lost due to total or partial inability to work. Disability insurance coverage is supplied both through the Social Security program and by disability insurance policies sold by private insurers. Private disability insurance plans are often sold on an individual basis and are sometimes available to employees as part of a company insurance program.

disbursement: The immediate actual payment of money, by check or cash. Disbursements are cash out, rather than expenditures, and affect cash flow, not profit and loss.

discharge: The firing of an employee by an employer, for whatever cause, but usually for allegedly good cause, and often for stated cause as provided for in a collective bargaining agreement.

disciplinary action: Any punitive action undertaken by an employer against an employee other than outright discharge, including such measures as loss of pay, suspension from employment and downgrading of employment status.

disclaimer: 1. A denial of responsibility, made in advance of any possible claim of responsibility or culpability, as in an accountant's disclaimer of responsibility for the figures underlying an unaudited annual report, or a seller's attempted disclaimer of responsibility for the quality of goods sold "as is." **2.** In law, rejection of a proffered right, property or previously asserted claim.

disclosure: Generally, the revealing of previously hidden or private facts about a person or situation. In modern business, the term has also come to mean the legally required process of revealing facts about people and organizations, as in the disclosure requirements surrounding a public stock issue or a corporate political contribution.

discount: 1. Generally, any specific subtraction from a sum due prior to payment. **2.** To make a specific subtraction from a sum before payment. In a wider sense, to evaluate skeptically assertions made by others. **3.** A reduction in price paid, usually but not always in advance of payment, as in a 2% reduction in stated price for payment received within 30 days of billing, or for quantity purchased. **4.** A reduction in the net proceeds of monies loaned, almost always in advance of payment of loan proceeds by lenders to borrowers, as in the subtraction of stated interest of 8% from the proceeds of a $100 loan. The amount of the loan is $100, the proceeds to the borrower are $92, and the borrower pays back $100. **5.** The amount by which a security is selling below its face value, as in a $1,000 bond being sold for $950, with a resulting discount of 5%. **6.** To make advance allowance for anticipated trends and events, as in discounting the impact of projected political events. In this sense, the term is often used in describing securities price fluctuations as stemming from anticipated financial events.

discounted cash flow: The evaluation of cash spent now on capital expenditures in terms of both the cash spent now and an assumed compound interest rate on that cash over the anticipated life of the asset acquired.

discount house: See discount store.

discount market: The market for bank and commercial paper of all kinds, composed of all those who buy and sell these kinds of money market instruments.

discount rate: 1. The rate of interest charged by a bank when discounting bank and commercial paper. Discount rates depend on a number of variables, including the kind of instrument being discounted and the market's assessment of the quality of the issue and issuer. **2.** The rate of interest set by Reserve banks on loans to member banks. This rate varies with both economic conditions and government money policy. Raising this discount rate makes money more expensive to borrow, and is thought to be deflationary; lowering it makes money less expensive to borrow and is thought to be inflationary.

discount store: A store which attempts to sell at lower-than-normal prices and thus achieve high volume at acceptable profit ratios. Such stores routinely sell below manufacturers' suggested prices. The term has sometimes been misused to describe all high volume operations, whether or not they were truly low price operations.

discovery: A legal procedure aimed at finding evidence in the possession of another party to an action, who is by law obliged to disclose all relevant facts and documents to other parties seeking such facts and documents.

discretionary account: A securities account in which a customer grants a broker partial or complete authority to buy and sell securities on behalf of the customer, with the broker controlling such matters as which securities to buy or sell or when, where and at what prices to buy and sell.

discretionary income: Income that need not

be committed to mandated expenditures, and that can be used as desired, for spending, saving and investing. The term is usually applied to individual income, with such items as rent, food and debt repayment seen as mandatory and such items as boats, savings accounts and stock purchases seen as discretionary.

discretionary order: See discretionary account.

discretionary spending: Money spent by consumers on goods and services that are not basic necessities, such as money spent on travel and entertainment; but in some areas, as with money spent on home improvements, the line between discretion and necessity can blur.

discrimination: Actions favoring one group over another, often prohibited by law and public policy, as in the many kinds of racial, sexual, religious, political, ethnic, trade, and other economic and social discrimination.

diseconomy of scale: A theory describing the tendency of costs to rise under certain conditions with increases in the size of enterprises; for example, cost increases caused by the development of bureaucratic overstaffing in some highly centralized private and public enterprises.

dishonor: To refuse to pay the amount due on an instrument presented for payment, as in a bank's refusal to pay a check that has been stopped by its issuer or the nonpayment of any money market instrument by its issuer when due.

disincentives: Incentives aimed at reducing private activity, usually supplied by government; for example, the supplying of government subsidies to agricultural producers for limiting crop production.

disinflation: The arresting of inflation without forcing recession, attempted through a series of governmental economic manipulations.

disintermediation: The flow of money to those savings vehicles yielding the highest interest, as in the flow of personal savings from savings accounts to government obligations when interest rates are higher on government obligations.

disk operating system (DOS): See operating system.

disk storage: The storage of computerized information on devices, each much like a pile of phonograph records, which can quickly be accessed when put into the computer system.

dismissal pay: See severance pay.

dispersion: See normal distribution.

dispersion of industry: See decentralize.

display: 1. To exhibit goods or information in such a way as to get attention, as in an attractive arrangement of goods in a store window. **2.** A visual presentation of information, usually on a cathode ray tube (CRT) at a computer terminal or in a stockbroker's office; often provided where formerly the information was presented in paper form in a computer printout or a ticker tape.

display advertising: Advertising in print media, such as newspapers, periodicals, billboards, and point of purchase materials, that uses prepared graphics to develop visual impact.

disposable income: That personal income available for consumer spending, savings and investment, consisting of all income minus taxes and other payments to governments.

disposal sale: A sale of goods and sometimes other assets at considerably lower than normal prices, or at less than claimed value, often made in the process of closing down all or part of a business. Commonly used as a synonym for clearance sale, or distress sale.

dispossession: A removal from real estate by means of legal action. The most usual dispossession proceeding is that of landlord against tenant, as for nonpayment of rent.

dissolve: To terminate or cancel. Business organizations of all kinds can be dissolved by legislative, judicial or voluntary action, although some matters may remain open in proprietorships and partnerships. Contracts can be dissolved as can legal proceedings and restrictions.

distraint: The seizure of property to satisfy a claim, as in the instance of seizure of taxpayer's property to satisfy a tax lien.

distress goods: Goods sold through the process of a distress sale.

distress sale: Sale of goods or other assets at lower than normal prices by a seller who needs to sell and is willing to forego profit or take loss in order to speed the sale. The term is often used synonymously with clearance sale or disposal sale.

distributed data processing system: A computer-based electronic data processing system linking information sources, computers and communications channels into one cooperative system, controlled by a central computer, often called the host computer.

distribution: 1. The process of moving goods and services from manufacturer to consumer, including all physical and marketing steps. Although marketing is sometimes used as a synonym, it is only part of the distribution process. **2.** Payments, including dividends, by business organizations to their owners, other than salaries and salary-related sums. **3.** In accounting, a synonym for allocation, the assignment of income and expenditures to accounts. **4.** In statistics, the mode of spreading related information over a given area. **5.** The allocation of the remainder of an estate after all legal costs.

distribution expense: A selling expense that is attached to the distribution of goods and services.

distribution of risk: The spreading of investments among several kinds of investments to provide some protection should one or more investments turn out badly, as in developing an investment portfolio that includes savings, insurance, bonds and common stocks, rather than common stocks alone. Similarly, the spread of a single large loan among several large lenders; and the spread of a large insurance risk among several insurers.

distributor: A business entity that buys from manufacturer or other distributor and sells to another distributor or retailer, or directly to consumers.

distributor discount: The discount allowed by manufacturer to distributor; synonymous with trade discount.

diversification: The development by a company of more than one line of products or businesses; for example, an office machine company's development of a line of related office products, or a company's acquisition of related and unrelated businesses.

diversion: 1. The privilege of changing or more precisely specifying the routing of goods in transit, by prior agreement between shipper and transporter. Diversion is common railroad practice, as when shippers send farm products east and, while the products are in transit, specify the final routes or destinations, depending on market conditions. **2.** The unauthorized rerouting of a watercourse to the detriment of someone further downstream.

divestiture: Disposal of a subsidiary, division or any other substantial portion of a company; normally accomplished by some kind of sale or liquidation, as in the sale of a subsidiary pursuant to pre-trial agreement or court order in an anti-trust prosecution by the federal government.

dividend: A payment of a portion of profits to owners of corporations and other business organizations. Payment is proportional to the amount of equity owned, with the owner of 200 shares getting the same amount of dividends per share as the owner of 100 shares, and therefore twice as much in payments. Payments may be regularly scheduled or exceptional, but each decision to pay dividends is a separate decision made by the organization's governing body.

division: In organizations, a substantial body of operating functions and responsibilities. The term is used to describe a wide variety of groupings, including a whole group of major companies comprising part of a large corporation as well as a single substantial function within an organization, such as a marketing division or a manufacturing division, where it is essentially synonymous with "group" or "department."

division of labor: The separation of work into component functions, as in the separation of the process of assembling an automobile into many functions and organizing it as an assembly line. In theory, and usually but not always in practice, such division of a job results in improved efficiency.

docking: Penalizing an employee by an employer by deducting amounts from pay for such matters as lateness for work, absenteeism, damage to materials, and infractions of work safety rules. The practice is subject to a number of legal and collective bargaining contract restrictions.

dock receipt: A receipt for goods delivered to a carrier by a shipper, acknowledging that the goods have passed into the hands of the carrier. This document is subsequently replaced by a bill of lading, which functions as the main shipping document.

document: 1. Any material carrying inscribed material which can be used in evidence, including such materials as paper, prints, canvas, stones, wood and leather; and such inscriptions as letters, numbers, drawings and photographs. **2.** To substantiate through the use of relevant documents.

documentation: In computer systems, a complete record of programs, routines and processes, so that software can be reproduced by others than those who initiated that software.

doing business: Act of conducting business within the geographical bounds of a regulating authority, and therefore becoming subject to the regulatory powers of that authority. The term is used to define several situations, but is most often encountered in taxation, as when a business is adjudged to be doing business for tax purposes in a jurisdiction, and may therefore be taxable within that jurisdiction.

DOJ: See Department of Justice.

dole: An imprecise but widely used term describing all government payments to those defined by government as being in need of public assistance, including welfare, child assistance and medical aid.

dollar: A currency unit, used in decimal coinage. The United States is one of many countries using dollar coinage units. Dollars used in the several national coinage systems differ in value, and those differences vary with fluctuations in the relative values of national currencies.

dollar bond: A bond wholly denominated in United States dollars, in which interest and principal are paid in those dollars. Any bond may be so denominated.

dollar cost averaging: The practice of periodically buying securities with fixed amounts of dollars, as in a monthly investment plan in which an investor buys $200 per month of the same common stock, over a long period, and without regard to whether the stock goes up or down in the short term. The theory behind the practice is that the long-term tendency of the stock market is up, and that by purchasing sound stocks steadily, a steady investment profit can be made. As a practical matter, both theory and practice suffer greatly in periods of long-term market decline, especially when accompanied by a pronounced inflationary trend and its negative impact on the value of the dollar.

dollar exchange: Bills of exchange and banker's acceptances payable in dollars, although drawn or payable outside the United States.

dollar gap: International currency situation in which dollars outside the United States are in short supply, tending to push the value of the dollar up in relation to the values of other currencies.

dollar glut: International currency situation in which dollars outside the United States are in oversupply, tending to push the value of the dollar down in relation to the value of other currencies.

dollar shortage: See dollar gap.

domain: The ownership of land and absolute right to dispose of that land, subject only to the overriding right of the state to ownership of that land, expressed as the right of eminent domain.

domestic: 1. Of a home or domicile. In business, the term usually refers to the original and legal domicile of transactions and legal entities. **2.** A worker employed in the home of another and doing work related to the place of work as a home. For example, someone employed by a family to clean their home is a domestic worker, while someone doing clerical work for a self-employed person working at home is not.

domestic corporation: A corporation chartered in a state and therefore described as domestic to that state.

domestic product: A product produced in a particular place, such as a state or nation, and therefore described as domestic to that place.

domicile: That place which in law is regarded as the main place of residence of an individual or business entity. Corporations are domiciled where chartered, but for some regulatory and other legal purposes may be considered domiciled in other locations.

donated stock: Capital stock given back to a corporation by its stockholders, without consideration. It is often stock originally issued to early shareholders in payment for start-up services rendered, now returned to the corporation for new financing purposes.

donated surplus: Surplus resulting from contributions of property to a corporation by its stockholders, including both real and personal property, cash and stock, usually as a means of supplying needed additional capital to the corporation.

door-to-door selling: The marketing of consumer goods directly to prospective purchases by salespeople going from door to door. Goods sold in this way include encyclopedias, minor household items such as brushes and notions, cosmetics, and vacuum cleaners.

dormant account: A financial account, usually a bank account, that has little or no activity for a protracted period, and usually very small balances on deposit.

DOS: See operating system.

DOT: See Department of Transportation.

double digit inflation: A rate of inflation of 10% or more per year.

double entry: A bookkeeping system in which every transaction results in corresponding debit and credit entries into the system. All credits equal all debits at all times and the net balance of credits and debits is always zero; the standard bookkeeping system used throughout the business world.

double indemnity: In life insurance contracts, a clause providing for double death insurance payments if death occurs under certain circumstances, usually through accident.

double option: See straddle.

double taxation: A term widely used to describe alleged double taxation of corporate earnings, once through corporate income tax and again through taxation of corporate dividends paid out of after-tax earnings to stockholders.

Dow Jones averages: Three United States stock price averages—industrial, transportation and utilities—which are widely quoted as indicating the general rise or fall of stock market prices. The best known of the three averages, and the one most often cited, is the Dow Jones industrial average, composed of thirty well known and highly regarded common stocks. Although other averages are also quoted, such as Standard and Poor's Composite Index and the New York Stock Exchange Common Stock Index, the Dow Jones averages continue to command the widest popular and securities trade attention.

down payment: A first payment made by a buyer to a seller when making a purchase. The seller may pass title and possession to the buyer on receipt of that first payment, taking deferred payment of the balance of the purchase price, or the seller may pass only possession, holding title until payment has been completed. Sometimes, the first payment is called a down payment, but is merely a returnable indication of the buyer's earnest intent to buy, as in a binder placed on a house, returnable for several possible reasons if the purchase is not consummated.

down time: Production time lost for any reason. The term is usually applied to machine breakdown or maintenance time and to any other unplanned production stoppages for reasons other than industrial disputes.

Dow theory: A popular stock market price forecasting theory based on the movement of the Dow Jones industrial and transportation averages. This theory attempts to predict general stock market price movements by interpreting parallel upward and downward movements of these two averages past stated price support points.

draft: A bill of exchange, called a draft in domestic commercial and securities transactions, in which a buyer pays a seller for goods received with a call upon the buyer's bank for the agreed-upon sum. The buyer, or drawer, makes a draft, instructing the bank, or drawee, to pay the sum to the seller, or payee.

drawee: The person or company upon which demand for payment of a draft is made, usually a bank responding to the draft of one of its clients.

drawer: A person or company making a draft, usually upon its bank, for payment of a sum to anyone.

drawing account: In some sales compensation plans, in which salespeople are paid wholly or largely on a commission basis, a continuing account the salesperson holds with the company, from which periodic salary advances are subtracted and into which commissions are paid, with periodic payment of commissions earned above salary advances, usually with a reserve held against future salary advances. Most such arrangements do not require repayment by salespeople of salary advances larger than total commissions earned on termination of employment.

drive-in: A business serving customers who generally do not leave their cars while business is being transacted. Examples are found in some fast food operations, movies, and banks.

drop shipment: A shipment from manufacturer directly to customer, eliminating the need to ship to a middleman who then reships to the customer, even if the middleman has made the sale.

drummer: A now obsolete popular synonym for traveling salesman.

drum storage: The storage of computerized information on the magnetic surface of cylinders, which provides random access to the information by the computer system.

dry goods: Clothing and other textiles and textile-related products. The term mainly described goods sold by the yard until the advent of factory-made clothing and other textiles, and has now expanded to include them.

dry hole: A well drilled in pursuit of oil or natural gas that produces neither.

dual pricing: That form of price discrimination that sets different prices for substantially the same goods and services to different customers; an illegal practice, but one that is widespread.

due bill: See IOU.

due date: The date on which any debt becomes payable, as in the maturity date of a bond or note.

due process of law: The right to enjoy equal protection and equal responsibility with all others under the law, including the right to be heard, to defend oneself, and to have one's day in court; and the right to be governed by laws and heard by courts that are not arbitrary, capricious, or discriminatory.

dummy: In business, one who substitutes for another in a business situation, such as a dummy stockholder, who holds a stock actually belonging to another, to shield the identity of the real owner; or a dummy corporation, holding property really belonging to another.

dump: To copy information stored in a computer system onto an external storage device, such as punched cards or tapes, to allow checking and to provide backup storage should any loss occur from the main memory.

dumping: **1.** The sale of large quantities of goods in foreign markets at prices lower than those being charged in the producing country's home markets, usually in an attempt to undersell similar goods produced in those foreign markets. **2.** The sale of large quantities of securities in the securities markets at whatever prices can be secured, with little or no regard for the adverse effects of the sale on the prices of the securities being sold.

dunning letter: A popular synonym for collection letter, which attempts to collect overdue debts.

durable goods: Goods purchased for personal consumption that normally last some years, such as major household appliances and automobiles.

dutiable goods: Goods on which import or export duties should by law be imposed.

duty: See tariff.

duty free: Imports that are by law free of customs duty payment obligations.

E

early retirement: Retirement from a company before the normal retirement date, but with eligibility to receive retirement benefits from company benefits plans wholly or in part, either on retirement or when they would have been received if normal retirement had been taken.

earmarking: The segregation and use of specific funds for specific purposes, as in the use of specific federal, state, and local tax proceeds for purposes specified by law, or the planned but non-binding setting up of specific funds for stated corporate purposes.

earned income: Income stemming directly from work performed, rather than from any other source.

earnest money: A partial payment given as evidence of good faith. The term as popularly used can apply to money paid as a returnable or non-returnable binder on a purchase, to a down payment, or to any partial payment in connection with a contract.

earning power: The amount of earnings a person or asset will return as a result of work or earning functions performed. A worker's reasonable pay expectation at a particular level of skills and experience is often described as earning power.

earnings: **1.** The profits of a business enterprise. **2.** The pay of a working person.

earnings per share: The net earnings of each share of outstanding common stock of a company, arrived at by subtracting taxes and preferred stock dividends from earnings, and then dividing the resulting net earnings by the number of outstanding shares of common stock of the company. For example, if earnings are $100, and taxes are $40, net after-tax earnings are $60. If preferred stock dividends are $10, net earnings for figuring earnings per share become $50. If there are 50 shares, earnings per share are $1.

earnings statement: See income statement.

easement: A right which one has in relation to land owned by another. The most common form of easement is right-of-way, as when a driveway is built on land belonging to only one person, but a neighbor has the right to use a common driveway.

easy money: An economic condition in which a nation's money supply is expanding, and credit is easy to obtain. In the United States, a period of easy money results in large part from federal manipulation of the amount and cost of money available for commercial bank reserves and, therefore, for bank credit available to potential borrowers. In addition to federal credit control, other factors, such as condition of the international money market, also affect available money supplies.

EBCDIC: See extended binary coded decimal interchange code.

ECOA: See Equal Credit Opportunity Act.

econometrics: A branch of economic theory and practice that uses mathematics, and especially statistical analysis, as its main means of measuring, analyzing, and forecasting economic matters. As an aid to decision making, econometrics relies heavily on modern computer capabilities to set up and follow alternate mathematical models to possible future conclusions.

economic: **1.** Relating in any way to the economy. **2.** Relating in any way to the study of economics. **3.** The most efficient and least costly way of handling an economic matter.

economic activity: All activity that is primarily concerned with the generation and distribution of goods and services.

Economic and Social Council (ECOSOC): A United Nations agency that develops and implements policies and activities in economic and related social welfare areas.

economic determinism: The theory that all human affairs occur as the result of economic events and have nothing to do with ideas and emotions. The term is popularly used to describe a wide variety of economic and historical theories, including Marxism.

economic forecast: A description of anticipated economic trends for any future period, usually focussing on such matters as expected growth in national product, employment, business investment levels, retail sales, prices, wages, profits, and other key indicators of the future health of the economy.

economic growth: The growth and maturation of an economy, usually measured by growth in average productivity per worker, the development of increasingly complex and sophisticated means of production and supporting structures, and Gross National Product.

economic indicators: A series of economic factors which, taken together, are used in attempts to measure the economy's tendency to cyclical movement. Major indicators, such as wages, prices, profits, and investments, and scores of less important indicators, are tracked, weighted, placed in composite indexes, and used as much of the raw material of economic forecasting.

economic life: See service life.

economic man: The concept that people behave in direct response to their perceptions of their own economic needs, based on the theory of economic determinism as applied directly to human behavior. Under this theory, such basic motives as love, hate, and sex are discounted as directly affecting human actions.

economic model: See model.

economic order quantity (EOQ): The most efficient quantity of goods or materials to be purchased or made for any stated economic purpose. The factors to be taken into consideration in developing optimum quantities include cost of materials, anticipated rate of use, cost of storage including capital tied up in the materials being stored, pricing, and overhead costs.

economic planning: The organization of production and distribution by government. Often referring to totally planned economies, in which all major industry is controlled by the state, the term is widely used in describing mixed economies, in which some major economic functions and sometimes industries are controlled by the state. In the United States and other major industrial countries, money supply control and manipulation is an example of economic planning, as is the use of taxing policy.

economics: That branch of the social sciences that deals with the organization and operation of the economic system and with the entire economic side of life, with primary emphasis on the production, distribution, and consumption of goods and services.

economic sanctions: Punitive economic actions taken by one government against another in pursuit of political goals, as in the refusal of one government to export strategic goods to another while a dispute over human rights is in progress between the two governments.

economic strike: A strike putting economic

demands, such as wages or working conditions, to management, as contrasted with the political strike, which raises questions that can only be solved by government. In the United States, the overwhelming majority of strikes have been and continue to be economic, rather than political.

economic unit: A single entity operating for common economic purposes. Working individuals, families, wholly or in part, that pool their income and expenditures, and organized businesses, ranging from the sole proprietorship to the conglomerate, are all considered economic units.

economy: **1.** The economic life and structure of a specified geographical area; usually applied to a city, county, region, state or nation. **2.** The prudent and efficient use of resources and material.

economy of scale: The theory that unit costs tend to decline as the size of the producing unit and the amount of production grow. In modern American practice, economies of scale have often seemed to be overbalanced by major efficiency and operating problems, resulting in attempts to limit the size of producing organizations and facilities through decentralization.

ECOSOC: See Economic and Social Council.

ECSC: See European Coal and Steel Community.

edifice complex: A term of derogation applied to those who cause large physical structures, such as office buildings, highways and malls, to be built with private or public funds under their control, when those structures are largely unnecessary and often both economically wasteful and destructive to the organizations and individuals building them; for example, the construction of a very large headquarters building by a corporation in deep financial difficulty, which shortly afterward goes bankrupt, in part due to the financial drain caused by that office building.

EDP: See electronic data processing.

EEC: European Economic Community. See Common Market.

EEOC: See Equal Employment Opportunity Commission.

effective date: The date on which an agreement goes into effect, as specified by contract, purchase order, insurance policy, or other specifying document.

effective rate: **1.** The real as distinct from the quoted rates of interest paid on borrowings, as in a bank's quoted 8% interest rate that is a real 12% rate on a personal loan. **2.** The real as distinct from the quoted yield on investments, figuring the yield as a percentage of market value, rather than as a percentage of face value.

efficiency: A measure of how inexpensively stated goals can be reached. Usually, those goals involve producing and distributing goods and services to acceptable quality standards at the least possible cost.

EFTA: See European Free Trade Association.

EFTS: See Electronic Funds Transfer System.

elasticity of demand: Changes in the demand for a product or service, as a result of price changes relative to other products or services. Such changes occur mainly in areas of buying discretion, rather than in areas of necessity. However, demand for seeming necessities can sharply diminish, as in the instances of gasoline and coffee.

elasticity of supply: Changes in the supply of a product or service, as a result of price changes relative to other prices or services. Under some conditions, producers will supply more products and services to take advantage of higher prices.

electronic calculator: Any modern calculating machine that has little or no memory; the line between calculator and computer has virtually disappeared with the advent of small personal computers and minicomputers of all kinds.

electronic data processing (EDP): The recording and processing of data by electronic means, using computers and computer-related machines, materials, and techniques. EDP is by far the widest use to which computers are put.

Electronic Funds Transfer System (EFTS): A centralized system for handling financial arrangements for transactions in decentralized locations, such as for sales made at local branch stores around the country.

eleemosynary: Connected in some way with charity and charitable organizations.

eleemosynary corporation: A not-for-profit corporation organized for charitable purposes.

eligible investment: See legal investment list.

eligible paper: Commercial paper, consisting of notes, bills of exchange, and acceptances that will be rediscounted by Federal Reserve banks on submission by member banks, and subject to Federal Reserve requirements as to form, maturity, kinds of transactions generating the paper, and total amount relative to current bank capital.

embargo: Any formal ban imposed on trade, including action by government and by private organizations. Most often, it is a ban on international trade imposed for national policy reasons by one government on the products or carriers of another government, with the scope of the ban ranging from a single product to a total ban on all products and carriers.

embezzlement: The fraudulent taking of valuables by one acting in a fiduciary capacity for their owner. The valuables taken may be in any form, including cash and all other kinds of property; the embezzler may be in any position of fiduciary trust, including employees such as bank tellers and company treasurers, public officials, agents, and representatives.

eminent domain: The right of government to take property from private holders at any time, with or without payment, temporarily or permanently, for public purposes. The right is absolute; the question of payment depends on factors that must often be adjudicated. In times of peace, such taking mainly arises around such public projects as roads and dams and almost always involves payment to the private holders; in times of war and other national crises, such taking may be uncompensated.

emoluments: See wages.

empathy: The ability to understand how another feels; the ability to empathize with a prospective purchaser is essential to sellers, as it is to all who negotiate and otherwise interact with others.

empire building: In organizations, the tendency of people to try to expand their own areas of responsibility and authority, usually through building larger areas of supervision, and often by the acquisition of more people to supervise, even when more people are not needed to get the job done.

employable: Anyone physically and mentally able to do any kind of compensable work and within the ages defined by law and practice as normal for the performance of that kind of work. The term is very widely defined in practice, and covers almost everyone who might be available for any kind of work, except for those relatively few who are clearly, by virtue of severe mental or physical impairment, unable to do any kind of work.

employed: Those working at any occupation that normally pays compensation, including both those working for others and those who are self-employed, whether they are working full-time or part-time. Those who are temporarily not working but planning to return to existing work, such as people who are ill, on vacation or on strike, are also considered to be employed.

employee: One who works for wages or salary for someone else.

employee association: An organization of the employees of a single employer, joining together for the pursuit of common interests regarding their employment. Civil Service workers have traditionally organized such associations. In industry, such associations have often attempted to substitute for unions, sometimes as company-initiated efforts to keep out unions, sometimes as voluntary attempts by employees to stop short of unions, and sometimes as pre-union organizations developed by those who want to organize unions.

Employee Retirement Security Act (ERISA): A Federal law that attempts to protect employee retirement benefit rights under existing and future private benefit plans, providing safeguards regarding adequate plan funding, administration, and structure, as well as dealing with certain Federal tax aspects of such benefit plans. It also provides the legal basis for the development of Individual Retirement Accounts.

employer: A person or organization employing others and paying them any kind of compensation for work performed under the supervision and control of that employer or its agents.

employer association: Two or more employers organized to pursue common interests on matters relating to employment, especially collective bargaining. Such organization may be involved in a wide range of economic and political matters, and may be limited to a single locality or national in scope.

employment: See employed.

employment agency: An organization that helps people looking for jobs to find them, and helps employers to find people to fill empty jobs. Private agencies charge placement fees to employers, employees, or both. The states and other publicly funded organizations run public employment services, usually at little or no charge to employers and employees.

employment discrimination: See discrimination.

employment history: The record of an employee's work history on a job, including such matters as hiring date, pay rates, promotions, and any other data thought relevant by those compiling the record.

employment security: See job security.

Employment Service: See United States Employment Service.

employment tax: See payroll tax.

EMS: See European Monetary System.

encounter group: A group seeking to accomplish greater understanding of themselves and sometimes of group dynamics as well, through development of any of a wide range of shared sensory experiences, including discussion.

encumbrance: A lien, right, claim, burden, charge, or liability on property, which does not necessarily serve to block passage of title to that property, but which usually lessens the value that property would have if unencumbered. The term is usually used in relation to real property, but is sometimes used in relation to personal property as well.

endogenous variable: A variable within a system that moves in relation to the other elements of the system, as do both demand and supply with a national economy; in contrast to an exogenous variable outside the system

endorse: 1. To sign a document, such as a check, bill of exchange, or other negotiable instrument, and thereby make passage of title possible. 2. To publicly approve of someone or something, as in recommendation of a product.

endorsee: One to whom an endorsement and delivery are made.

endorsement: The actual signature of the owner of a document, making that document negotiable and passage of title possible. That signature must be on the document or otherwise attached to the document. Where the endorsement is to a specific entity, both signature and the delivery of the signed instrument to the one specified is required for the transaction to be completed; where the endorsement is in blank, as on a bearer bond, only delivery is needed.

endorser: See endorse.

endow: To provide for another by giving valuables or the income from valuables.

endowment: Valuables or income from valuables given to provide for another. An endowment implies permanence, though the giving may be temporary, as in some short-term trusts. The term is most often used in institutional funding, as in the giving of funds by alumni to their schools for specific or general purposes.

endowment fund: A fund set up out of the proceeds of an endowment, from which payments are made, as in a gift of money from an alumnus to set up and continuously fund a chair in physics, or a sum of money donated by several givers and continuously refreshed by additional gifts, which may be used for various purposes.

endowment policy: A kind of life insurance policy which can become fully paid and payable to its purchaser, the insured, during the life of the insured. Or, if the insured dies before the premiums are fully paid up, the face amount becomes payable to the beneficiary of the policy.

energy: The power released by a change in physical state, as in the change from water to steam. The power so released can be unusable by humans, as in a thunderstorm, or usable, as in a power plant that generates the energy to heat a city by burning fossil fuels.

energy conservation: The saving of increasingly scarce and costly energy by application of a wide number of techniques aimed at reducing energy losses, switching to more available and sometimes less expensive sources of energy, and developing new energy sources; for example, the use of insulation to cut fuel waste and the development of solar energy to replace fossil fuels.

energy level: The characteristic vitality and amount of activity engaged in by individuals. A person who is active, who thinks and moves swiftly over a sustained period of time, is usually described as having a high energy level; one who tires easily and moves slowly is said to have a low energy level.

energy policy: The policies, plans, and actions of government regarding the use, conservation, pricing, finding, and developing of energy for public and private purposes.

Energy Research and Development Administration (ERDA): A Federal agency responsible for research and development activities in energy and energy-related matters, such as energy conservation and the development of alternative sources of energy.

energy source: Anything that can be used to produce energy; in practice usually referring to those sources that can now be used to produce energy for human purposes. Thunderstorms, therefore, are sometimes described as potential energy sources, but hardly ever as energy sources.

entail: Any restriction imposed by prior testators upon the free disposition of that estate by subsequent owners; quite commonly encountered in families seeking to provide an unbroken line of family inheritance, particularly as family-owned real property is passed by will for several generations.

enterprise: A business of any size, usually of some complexity. The term is sometimes used more widely, to describe any organzied form of endeavor.

entity: Any person or organization which is, in itself, a discrete unit.

entrepreneur: One who undertakes the conception and development of a new business enterprise, doing whatever is necessary to make the enterprise go, and taking ultimate responsibility for every aspect of development, from financing to distribution; and who takes major risks and can reasonably expect a major share of any profits.

Environmental Protection Agency (EPA): An

agency of the United States government, charged with monitoring, protection and standard-setting functions in such areas as air and water pollution and the regulation of harmful industrial wastes.

EOQ: See economic order quantity.

EPA: See Environmental Protection Agency.

Equal Credit Opportunity Act (ECOA): A Federal statute forbidding discrimination against borrowers by lenders.

Equal Employment Opportunity Commission (EEOC): A Federal agency responsible for enforcing that considerable body of Federal statutes and regulations dealing with prohibition of discrimination in employment and related matters, and with the fostering of affirmative action programs aimed at remedial action made necessary by past discrimination.

equal pay for equal work: A national policy stemming from the employment of women in war industries during World War II, and embodied in the Equal Pay Act of 1963, prohibiting pay discrimination because of sex, race or for any other reason, and stating that pay must be figured equally for all on the basis of the job performed.

equilibrium: That theoretical point at which a firm is most profitable.

equipment: Tools and materials that are used in production, such as machines and vehicles, and are fixed assets other than land and buildings. The term is also generally used to describe all tools used in an enterprise. Sometimes, as in new car advertising, products themselves are described as equipment, suggesting utility beyond their real uses as consumer goods.

equipment trust bonds: Certificates issued by companies buying heavy equipment, such as railroad cars, that in essence are mortgages on the equipment which are then sold to lenders. The lender owns the equipment and can foreclose the mortgage for nonpayment; the company has the equipment with very little capital investment.

equipment trust certificate: See equipment trust bonds.

equities: A popular synonym for securities.

equity: 1. The money value of that which is owned, arrived at by subtracting all that is owed from the value of the ownership to arrive at a net ownership value figure. Some examples are: the value of real property minus all mortgages and other borrowings; the market value of stocks in a margin account minus the borrowings in the account; and the value of all outstanding common and preferred stock in a corporation. In some instances, as in determining the value of stock in a margin account, the ownership value can be easily determined at any time, as both market value and borrowings are firm figures. But often, as in attempting to determine a homeowner's equity in a mortgaged home, equity is only an estimate because the market value of the home is only an estimate until the home is sold. **2.** The concept of fairness and justice applied to that portion of the English common law relating to the rights and duties of individuals. Once administered through a separate system of courts, called chancery courts, cases involving matters of equity are now handled within the regular court system.

equity financing: A stock issue, in which a corporation sells a piece of its ownership to others to raise money, as distinct from raising money by borrowing.

ERDA: See Energy Research and Development Administration.

ergonomics: A body of theory and practice aimed at increasing employee efficiency and designing efficient production techniques; closely allied to the aims and techniques of time and motion study, and the subject of considerable labor-management friction and negotiation.

ERISA: See Employee Retirement Security Act.

escalation: A contractual provision allowing or mandating cost increases on items covered by the contract, on the occurrence of stated events. For example, some labor contracts provide for automatic wage increases tied to specified rises in the cost of living index; many commercial leases provide for rent increases in the event of increased taxes or labor costs; and many government and private construction contracts provide for additional payments to contractors in the event of increased costs.

escalator clause: The specific clause in a contract allowing or mandating escalation under certain circumstances.

escape clause: A contractual provision allowing one or both parties to avoid contractual obligations under prescribed circumstances, as for non-performance of contractually defined duties by another party.

escheat: The taking of property by the national government when there is no other legal inheritor, on the theory that the state is the residual owner of all property within its boundaries.

escrow: The holding by a third party of something of value which is the subject of a contract or proceeding between two other parties, until that contract or proceeding has been consummated. A deed evidencing ownership of real property being sold is often so held by a bank until the entire transaction has been cleared and recorded, as is a payment on a contract pending completion.

establishment: 1. Any place of business. **2.** A popular term referring to any social, political or economic structure carrying some aspect of authority; also any authority-carrying group within such a structure.

estate: 1. Any and all individual ownership or interest and the total of all ownerships and interests in real or personal property, including absolute, conditional, and contingent interests. In economic and legal senses, the term describes anything owned on which a monetary value can ultimately be placed. **2.** The sum of all such individual ownerships and interests remaining after death.

estate accounting: Accounting practice and procedures dealing with matters connected with the administration of estates, as specified by law and administered by the courts.

estate income: Income derived from property held by estates.

estate tax: An excise tax upon the entire estate of the deceased.

estoppel: In law, actions or assertions that are barred because of previous actions or assertions, such as the commission of a previous fraud or illegal act; for example, a criminal may not sue for damages to his or her person caused by an arresting officer.

Euratom: See European Atomic Energy Community.

Eurocurrency: Strong currencies held on deposit in banks in other countries and used as sources of financing by a wide variety of borrowers throughout the world. As long as American dollars, backed by American gold, were regarded as key reserves throughout the world, they were the prime source of such financing; in recent years, other currencies have increasingly been used as well, and the financing mode in this portion of the money market has become international.

Eurodollars: American dollars held on deposit in banks abroad, serving as a basis for financing throughout the world; a form which has been replaced by the Eurocurrency market, which includes American dollars and several other harder currencies.

European Atomic Energy Community (Euratom): An international agency formed by the same nations that formed the Common Market, which sponsors joint programs aimed at the development of peaceful uses of atomic energy.

European Coal and Steel Community (ECSC): A predecessor to, and now effectively an agency of, the Common Market; it develops joint international policies in the area of coal and steel, and finances its activities through international taxes on coal and steel production in the member countries.

European Commission: The main administrative organization of the Common Market, developing budgets and proposals for legislative action and holding substantial regulatory power in several economic areas affecting commerce in and between the member states of the Common Market.

European Court of Justice: An international court operating within Common Market and responsible for interpreting and enforcing the policies and regulations of the Common Market. By international agreement, it has supranational powers in some economic areas, as defined by the 1957 Treaty of Rome.

European Economic Community (EEC): See Common Market.

European Free Trade Association (EFTA): A group of European countries outside the European Common Market, and including Austria, Finland, Iceland, Norway, Portugal, Sweden, and Switzerland, organized as a free trade area, and having special trading arrangements with the European Common Market.

European Investment Bank: An international bank and agency of the Common Market, charged with the development of financing policies and plans, including both grants and loans, which will benefit the members of the Common Market, especially the less developed member nations.

European Monetary System (EMS): The monetary control system of the European Common Market, which ties together the currencies of most national governments in the Common Market as against all other world currencies, functioning so as to adjust Common Market currencies to each other within a relatively narrow range, with the whole currency group therefore moving together in world currency markets.

European Parliament: An institution of the Common Market, consisting of a consultative assembly with representation from all the member countries of the Common Market.

even lot: See round lot.

event: **1.** In statistics, that which is being measured for frequency of occurrence. **2.** In the nuclear energy industry, a nuclear accident, however severe.

ever-normal granary: One of the basic concepts upon which the agricultural aid programs of the United States government are based. In years of good harvests, surpluses are stored and farmers get government loans, essentially using the stored farm products as collateral; in poor years, the stored products are sold.

eviction: The legal removal of a tenant from occupied realty. That removal is usually accomplished by a legal proceeding and judgment, although in some circumstances it is accomplished by the landlord's re-entry, if legal; but mere dispossession of a tenant by a landlord is not in itself a legal eviction.

evidence of insurability: Proof that one seeking insurance is free of conditions unacceptable to an insurer; for example, the results of a medical examination showing an insurance applicant to be free of physical problems that would cause an insurer to decline to issue the life insurance policy sought.

exception rate: A railroad freight rate that is lower than normal rates, and is set to enable the railroad to compete effectively with other lower-cost carriers.

excess loans: The amount of those loans made to one customer above the loan limits specified by law. Where such loans have been made, bank directors may be personally liable for resulting bank losses.

excess profits tax: A special tax set on corporate profits, beyond normal corporate tax rates, in circumstances in which those profits are exceptionally high due to national circumstances, especially war.

excess reserves: The amount of reserve funds held by a bank above legal requirements. Bank reserves are a percentage of deposits, and a bank may lend only those funds beyond its legal reserve. But it may hold excess reserves, above the legal limit, for a wide variety of reasons, including current economic conditions and specific bank policies.

exchange: 1. A specific marketplace, in which instruments of ownership, such as stocks and bonds are bought, sold, and traded. **2.** A marketplace transaction, in which valuables are bought, sold, and traded, as in the sale of a single orange or ten thousand shares of a common stock.

exchange controls: Wide-ranging governmental restrictions on the free international exchange of foreign currencies within its own borders, aimed at stabilizing the international price of its own currency.

exchange depreciation: A fall in the value of a currency as measured against other currencies, whether by market action, governmental manipulation, or both.

exchange rate: The rate at which one currency can be exchanged for another at any given time, as in a dollar being exchangeable for half a British pound or two Japanese yen at a given moment of a given day, with the pound and yen directly exchangeable with each other as well. Exchange rates, regulated by international agreement for many years following World War II, became unregulated in the late 1970's, with currencies floating freely and continuously seeking new values in relation to each other after that.

Exchequer: 1. The British treasury, a central account into which all national income is paid and from which all national expenditures are drawn. **2.** The British government's treasury department, generally performing the same kinds of financial administrative, taxing, and handling functions as the United States Treasury Department.

excise tax: A tax on two quite different kinds of activities: sales of goods and intangible privileges. It is usually described as a single kind of tax on the privilege of selling those goods and exercising those privileges.

Excise taxes are levied, either as a percentage of the selling price or a fixed amount per item sold, on a wide variety of goods, including such necessities as gasoline and such luxuries as handbags. They are also levied on a wide variety of privileges, such as franchises and licenses.

exclusion: Anything specifically excluded from a set of contractual obligations or insurance policy coverages.

exclusive agent: One who is the only agent representing another on a specific matter or kind of matter. Examples include the only agent authorized to sell a firm's products in a state or group of states, or the real estate broker who is the only agent authorized to represent the seller on sale of a house.

exclusive bargaining agent: A union that is recognized as the sole bargaining agent for all employees in a collective bargaining unit, including members of that union, members of other unions and associations, and non-union employees; until and if such recognition is upset by a new collective bargaining agent election among the employees in the bargaining unit.

exclusive contract: A contract specifying that the parties will deal only with each other on specified matters; usually a contract between buyers of goods and services and suppliers, as in an agreement between a restaurant and a supplier for supply of a kind of food at favorable price or credit terms in return for which the restaurant grants the supplier sole supplier rights for a specified period.

exclusive representation: Under the National Labor Relations Act, the application of a union contract to non-union as well as union members in the area covered by the contrct.

exdividend: Describing stock on which a dividend has been declared but not yet paid and which is then sold, with the declared dividend going to the seller rather than to the buyer, reflected in a somewhat lower selling price. Stock exchange rules normally define the length of the period after dividend declaration and before delivery of stock sold exdividend during which the stock will be so treated, and also provide for sales on a cash basis, with the dividend going to the purchaser.

execute: To do a piece of work, usually in accordance with a plan, as in planning and carrying through a plant expansion or performing an assembly line function; in computer operations, for the machine to carry out instructions according to the program being run.

executive: 1. One who is responsible for carrying out administrative decisions; a manager. **2.** The administrative branch of any organization.

executive branch: In the United States government, the administrative organizations of government, headed by the President, as distinguished from the legislative and judicial branches.

executive committee: A committee responsible for continuous functioning of an organization. It is often composed of members of the Board of Directors, the chief policy making body of an organization, and is responsible both for implementing overall policies and for developing and implementing interim policies.

executive routine: A controlling program, handling actual computer processing and the execution of other computer programs and routines; also called supervisory routine.

executive sales: The selling of goods and services to management personnel and moneyed individuals; usually outside selling.

executive trainee: One who is in the process of being formally trained for management pursuant to a policy and program developed by a business organization; often also applied to newly hired management personnel occupying entry level management positions but not really part of such a planned program.

executor: One who is appointed by the maker of a will to carry out the provisions of that will as nearly as possible consonant with the wishes of the maker, and who undertakes to do so after the decease of the maker.

executrix: A woman executor. The term is rapidly becoming obsolete, as both women and men performing the functions are now more commonly called executors.

exemplary damages: Damages awarded to a plaintiff beyond those directly provable as having been caused by the actions of the defendant; usually awarded for such matters as defamation and other damages to character and reputation, sometimes as specified by statute.

exempt employees: Those employees who are classified as salaried, rather than being employed at hourly or other rates measured by relatively brief periods of time, and who therefore are not covered by Federal and state wage and hour laws; for example, a member of management, who receives a fixed yearly salary, no matter how many hours are worked or where those hours are worked, is classified as an exempt employee.

exemption: An income tax deduction used in United States federal, state and local income tax systems, consisting of fixed sums for taxpayers and their dependents that are subtracted from gross income and are therefore non-taxable.

exhibit: 1. A document or any other tangible item produced and made part of the body of evidence developed during the course of a legal proceeding. **2.** A document or section of a document presented as part of the supporting or illustrative data in a book or report. The distinctions between exhibits, footnotes, notes, and other supporting material are imprecise. **3.** A display at a meeting, fair, or convention, often of goods for sale.

Eximbank: See Export-Import Bank of the United States.

exit interview: A meeting between a representative of management and a departing employee, in which management attempts to derive whatever information may be useful to it from the departing employee.

exogenous variable: A variable outside a system which has impact on the system, but which does not move primarily due to the internal motion of that system; for example, supply factors from outside a national economy are exogenous variables in their interaction with the total demand-supply picture within that economy, while internal supply factors would be endogenous variables.

expanding economy: An economic system experiencing a period of growth, usually but not always accompanied by prosperity for most of those living in that economy, and in constrast to contraction, which is relative decline of an economy.

expediter: One who moves orders through the production process, scheduling and seeing those orders through to fulfillment, and handling the factors of the production process so that production moves with maximum speed and efficiency.

expenditure: The act of spending to acquire an asset or to pay a debt; also the amount so spent.

expense: 1. A cost incurred in the course of doing business and attributable to the business done. **2.** A present operating cost. **3.** Outlays attributed to accounting periods, as determined by accounting systems and conventions used and by company objectives and financial management techniques.

experience rating: The setting of insurance premium rates to reflect past experience of losses and consequent payments due to claims originating in the individuals or groups so rated.

experimental group: In an experimental situation, the group that receives the special treatment under examination; results of the experimental group and the control group, which did not receive the treatment, are compared to see if any differences between them are statistically significant, and therefore are presumably due to that special treatment.

expiration: The ending of a term specified by contract, such as the end of a periodical subscription term or an insurance coverage period.

export(s): 1. Goods made in one country, sold, and shipped abroad for use in other countries. **2.** To send those goods abroad. **3.** Popularly, all goods and services originating in one geographic unit and sold for use in another. States are described as exporting goods abroad and to one another. Consulting services are sometimes described as being exported abroad.

Export-Import Bank (Eximbank): A United States bank functioning to stimulate United States international trade by a wide-ranging program of loans, guarantees, and insurance to domestic and foreign exporters and importers, as a major supplement to private financing available for these purposes.

export license: A document issued by government, authorizing an exporter to export otherwise controlled goods to a specific place at a specific time and in specific quantity.

export quota: A limitation placed by government on the kind and quantities of goods that may be shipped by its exporters. Such quotas normally serve either home industry protective purposes or more directly political national purposes, as in restrictions of the export of strategic materials.

ex post facto law: A law retroactively providing penalties for actions previously legal, or which changes the nature of the penalties assessed for previously illegal actions; an unconstitutional practice.

exposure: 1. The amount that is at risk by an insurer, on an insurance policy, usually measured by the maximum amount of insurance that may have to be paid in claims on that policy under conditions of maximum possible liability. **2.** A very general measure of the kind and quality of public notoriety or popularity achieved through advertising and publicity efforts. **3.** A very general measure of the risks involved in taking any course of action, and in business with special emphasis on money risks.

express warranty: A warranty specifically stated by a seller to a buyer, in writing or orally, and binding upon the seller if provable by the buyer.

expropriation: The taking of private property by government, usually under a government's power of eminent domain, with or without compensation, as in the governmental takeover and subsequent nationalization of the property of a foreign or domestic company operating within its borders.

exrights: A stock on which rights have been declared but not yet issued, and which is then sold without those rights attached.

Extended Binary Coded Decimal Interchange Code (EBCDIC): A standard computer code in which characters are represented by bytes, each of which consist of eight bits, or binary digits.

extended bonds: Bonds that come to maturity and on which the face value is not paid but held by the issuer, with interest payments instead continued and the original backing of the bonds unchanged. Issuers desiring to extend their bonds must offer to do so and have that offer accepted by their bondholders.

extended coverage: Property insurance coverage which is expanded beyond normal bounds to include risks beyond basic property coverage, as in the extension of basic coverage beyond fire and theft to include floods and earthquakes.

extended payment plan: See charge account.

extended term coverage: An option provided by some life insurance policies carrying cash surrender values, allowing the insured to use cash savings built up in the policy to pay current premiums and so keep the policy in force.

extensive cultivation: The farming of large tracts of land with relatively small amounts of labor and machinery, and often with little regard for the continuing health of the land in singleminded pursuit of the highest possible short-term cash yield; increasingly an outmoded way of using the land, as world population grows and land costs rise.

external audit: An independent audit conducted by auditors not directly employed by the organization being audited; an outside audit.

external debt: The total of all public and private debts owed by a country and its citizens to all other countries and their citizens.

external storage: In electronic data processing, information held in computer-usable form in facilities outside the computer system itself; for example, information stored on magnetic tape outside the system.

extractive industry: An industry that takes its materials from nature, as in the mining of coal, iron, and gold, and the drilling and taking of oil and natural gas.

extra dividend: A dividend that is declared by a corporation to be higher than the normal dividend paid, and that may not be repeated, as distinct from a corporate decision to move to a higher normal dividend rate.

extraordinary depreciation: Depreciation far beyond that ordinarily to be expected, caused by such unusual matters as protracted cold or precipitation, extraordinary use factors, and unanticipated obsolescence, but not including such property loss matters as fire, flood, and theft.

extraordinary expense: A very unusual and often entirely unanticipated expense, which must be taken into account separately for financial statement purposes, rather than being placed in with and to some extent therefore distorting normal expenses.

F

FAA: See Federal Aviation Administration.

face value: The amount stamped, printed, or otherwise affixed on an instrument of value, indicating its stated value when issued or at maturity. Coins, currency, notes, bonds, stocks, insurance policies, and other such instruments have such face values, with bonds and insurance policies carrying stated values as of their maturity dates, and stocks carrying par values that often have no real relation to their market values.

facilities management: The professional management of physical plants, and of the people, materials, and processes operating within those plants; for example, the management of a hospital or prison.

fact-finding board: A group appointed, usually by government, to find and state facts which may be relevant in securing the settlement of an industrial dispute; such a board is often part of formal mediation or arbitration efforts.

factor: 1. One who buys accounts receivable from a manufacturer, pays the manufacturer at a discounted rate for them and then assumes all risks and makes and keeps all collections of those accounts receivable. In many instances factors have also become lenders and suppliers of working capital in ways that go beyond their original factoring roles. **2.** A consignment agent, possessing control over the goods being sold, collecting commissions on sales, and remitting sales revenue minus those commissions to the goods' owners.

factors of production: The main elements involved in production, in orthodox economics normally described as land, labor, capital, and entrepreneurial contribution, though theorists disagree as to the inclusion of entrepreneurial contribution as a main element of production.

factory: Any building or portion of a building used for the production of goods.

factory costs: See manufacturing costs.

factory expense: Any manufacturing cost beyond raw materials and labor applied to production, therefore including all indirect manufacturing and overhead costs.

factory seconds: Factory-produced goods that have been rejected by the factory's own inspection processes and have been put on sale at reduced prices, although claimed to possess only minor defects and to be entirely suitable for most purposes.

factory system: production system in which most production is accomplished in factories by employees; it is the major production system in use in all industrialized countries.

fad: Something fashionable for a limited time, such as hula hoops, pet rocks, or some kinds of management jargon.

failsafe: A safeguard or body of safeguards designed to prevent the failure of a system or machine; for example, those safeguards surrounding the operation of a nuclear reactor are intended to be failsafes.

failures: 1. Those businesses that do not survive, going out of business voluntarily or involuntarily, solvent or in bankruptcy. **2.** Inability to achieve or to continue normal performance, as in the instance of a machine that breaks down or a human who makes an unusual error. The term is also sometimes used as a synonym for breakdown.

fair: A special market open daily from time to time, such as a county or trade fair, at which goods are bought, sold, swapped, shown, and usually awarded prizes. Some continuing markets are called fairs, but are more accurately described as markets.

fair credit and information reporting practices: A body of practices developed under the statutory authority provided by the Fair Credit Reporting Act and the Freedom of Information Act, providing those listed in public and private dossiers the ability to examine those parts of their files that have no effect on national security matters, and to dispute any portion of those dossiers they consider untrue, unfair, or legally actionable.

Fair Credit Reporting Act: A Federal statute that defines fair credit checking and reporting practices and provides a basis for regulating those practices, as well as providing recourse for aggrieved consumers.

fair day's pay for a fair day's work: A slogan adopted by both management and labor, each for its own purposes. It is almost always part of a negotiating and exhortative stance on the part of management and labor groups, as they attempt to define what is paid or sought as "fair."

fair debt collection practices: A body of practices described and prohibited under Federal law, aimed at preventing a substantial number of especially distasteful collection practices indulged in by some debt collection organizations, including harassment, abuse, and outright threats to the jobs, reputations, and even the persons of debtors.

fair employment practices: A body of practices, defined by a substantial number of federal, state, and local laws and regulations, aimed at prohibiting discrimination in employment on the basis of race, color, religion, political belief, age, sex, national origin, or any other basis defined in law.

Fair Labor Standards Act (FLSA): A Federal statute which defines and provides the basis for regulation of such wage and working conditions matters as minimum wages and child labor, and which also defines those workers who are protected by its provisions.

fair list: A list of employers regarded as fair to labor, compiled by labor organizations; by implication, employers not listed may be regarded as unfair, though that is not stated.

fair market value: The trading price of anything, at which a willing and informed seller and buyer will or would trade, and without either party possessing extraordinary trading leverage. The term is used widely in setting values for tax assessment and judicial purposes.

fair return: A theory and series of formulas developed by regulatory bodies and the courts to determine what rates of profit should be allowed to companies in highly regulated industries such as telephone, power supplying utilities, and railroads.

fair trade: A concept that producers, distributors, and retailers should be allowed to set minimum prices on their goods. Formerly supported by a series of statutes in many states, setting minimum prices on a wide range of goods, it is now mainly prohibited since repeal of federal laws that had barred application of the anti-trust statutes to this form of collusive price fixing.

family business: A business controlled by the members of a single family; examples range from a "Mom and Pop" corner grocery store to a corporation in which a controlling interest, though not necessarily a majority shareholding, is owned by a family.

Fannie Mae: See Federal National Mortgage Association.

FAO: See Food and Agriculture Organization.

farm: 1. To work the land or work on the land to produce crops and animals, for sale or personal consumption. **2.** A business producing crops and animals from the land for sale and exchange, with business size ranging from the very small farm operation, farmed part-time, in which some family members work at other occupations to massive farm enterprises known as agri-businesses.

Farm cooperative: See cooperative.

Farm Credit Administration (FCA): A Federal agency charged with the responsibility for administering a wide range of credit alternatives for American farmers, organized into a cooperative farm credit system that includes Federal land banks, Federal land bank associations, intermediate credit banks, production credit associations, and banks for cooperatives.

Farmers Home Administration: An agency of the Department of Agriculture, which loans money on favorable terms to farmers who might otherwise find affordable credit difficult or impossible to secure. Loans are available for a wide variety of purposes, including home and land ownership, operating expenses, and special projects.

farm out: To get a job done wholly or partially by other businesses located elsewhere, as when textile manufacturers subcontract work to a series of small shops and home enterprises.

farm surplus: Farm production which is unsalable at current market prices to available markets, and which is held or destroyed, often pursuant to government policy and accompanied by government support payments to farmers.

f.a.s.: A price quote, meaning Free Alongside Ship. The f.a.s. price is an export price, which includes all costs up to the point at which the goods sold are directly available for loading on the ship.

fascism: A theory and political organization aiming at total dictatorship over the state and all its inhabitants. In power, fascists have committed themselves to the destruction of civil liberties, to the elimination and sometimes mass murder of all opponents, including their fellow citizens, and to genocide.

favorable balance of trade: See balance of trade.

FCA: See Farm Credit Administration.

FCC: See Federal Communications Commission.

FCIC: See Federal Crop Insurance Corporation.

FDA: See Food and Drug Administration.

FDIC: See Federal Deposit Insurance Corporation.

FEA: See Federal Energy Administration.

feasibility study: A formal investigation of all relevant aspects of a proposed project, including such matters as costs and the possibilities of practical accomplishment.

featherbedding: Management's term for union insistence on the employment of union members in unnecessary jobs, usually expressed as demands to retain jobs that have become obsolete due to technological changes. Work efficiency and job retention are major subjects of negotiation between labor and management, and cross-complaints of featherbedding and speed-up are part of the normal course of such negotiations.

Fed: A popular term for Federal Reserve Board. See: Federal Reserve System.

Federal Advisory Council: A purely advisory organization attached to the Federal Reserve System, consisting of one member, often a banker, selected by each of the twelve Federal Bank boards of directors.

Federal Aviation Administration (FAA): A Federal agency, part of the Department of Transportation, charged with responsibility for national air safety and traffic controls, as well as with a wide variety of other registration, regulatory and information functions regarding aircraft, airports, and the aircraft industry.

Federal budget: The fiscal year budget of the United States, running from July 1 to June 30, and detailing all anticipated income and expenditures.

Federal Communications Commission (FCC): An independent Federal agency, responsible for watching and regulating all matters relating to national and international communication, and for interpreting national communications policy. The FCC holds licensing and construction permit powers and handles television and radio broadcasting and all other forms of communication.

Federal Crop Insurance Corporation (FCIC): A Federal agency, part of the Department of Agriculture, responsible for a national system of federally funded insurance against crop losses due to natural and unavoidable causes, such as weather and insects, rather than such avoidable causes as market conditions and uncompetitive work practices.

Federal debt: See national debt.

Federal Deposit Insurance Corporation (FDIC): An independent Federal agency that insures individual deposits up to certain limits in all national banks and in all state banks that are part of the Federal Reserve System, as well as in those other banks which apply for such insurance. The FDIC has substantial regulatory and supervisory powers as well.

Federal Energy Administration (FEA): An independent Federal agency, responsible for developing a coherent policy regarding United States energy resources and conservation, encouraging development of existing and new energy resources and conservation techniques. The FEA also functions as an information resource for energy users and developers.

Federal funds: Funds held by Federal Reserve member banks in excess of funds needed to comply with legal reserve require-

ments. These funds are traded among member banks on a short-term basis, allowing those banks with more-than-necessary reserve funds to loan them on a day-to-day basis to banks with less-than-required reserve funds. The sum of those trades comprise the "Federal funds market." Although banks with reserve fund needs may also borrow from the Federal Reserve, funds may be available in the Federal funds market at less than the Fed's discount rate, and banks that have borrowed up to their legal limit from the Fed find that market a useful source of short-term funds.

federal funds rates: The rates of interest paid on Federal debt obligations, and especially the various rates of interest paid on United States Treasury bills.

Federal Highway Administration: A Federal agency, part of the Department of Transportation, responsible for a wide variety of functions relating to administration, funding, safety and regulation of the Federal highway system.

Federal Home Loan Bank System: A federally organized and administered banking system, consisting of twelve regional Federal Home Loan Banks that supply credit reserves to all savings and loan associations, which must by law be members of the system, and to other lending institutions, including savings banks and insurance companies, engaged in home mortgage lending.

Federal Housing Administration (FHA): A Federal agency, part of the Department of Housing and Urban Development, responsible for a wide variety of mortgage and loan insurance functions covering all the forms of residential housing.

Federal intermediate credit banks: Part of the farm credit system administered by the Farm Credit Administration, consisting of twelve banks engaged in providing reserves for and lending to those institutions and organizations that lend directly to farmers.

Federal land banks: Part of the farm credit system administered by the Farm Credit

Administration, consisting of twelve Federal land banks, that make long-term mortgage loans at favorable rates and for a wide variety of purposes to the members of some hundreds of land bank associations throughout the country.

Federal Maritime Commission: An independent Federal agency, responsible for regulation and compliance matters regarding the shipping industry.

Federal Mediation and Conciliation Service (FMCS): An independent Federal agency, responsible for efforts in the mediation of labor-management disputes. It may offer its services to the disputants or those services may be requested.

Federal mortgage insurance: See mortgage insurance.

Federal National Mortgage Association (Fannie Mae): A federally sponsored private corporation which buys, sells, and otherwise deals in government insured or guaranteed mortgages to help provide liquidity in the secondary market for home mortgages and therefore a greater availability of mortgage money for borrowers.

Federal Power Commission (FPC): A Federal agency responsible for regulating the natural gas and electric power industries, the FPC exercises a wide range of powers in such areas as rate-setting, licensing, construction, and pollution.

Federal Reserve Bank: One of the twelve central Federal banks, each operating in one of the twelve Federal Reserve Districts in the United States.

Federal Reserve Board of Governors: The chief policy making body of the Federal Reserve System, composed of seven Presidentially-appointed, Senate-approved members, each serving seven years, and with terms expiring at different times to assure continuity within the Board. It is an independent body, with major power to influence the direction of the United States through its control of money and credit policies, tools which it openly and consciously uses to influence national and international economic trends.

Federal Reserve credit: The total of all Federal Reserve Bank credit outstanding, including government securities, loans to commercial banks, and checks outstanding; the base of the credit system of the United States, and a key government instrument of money and credit manipulation in pursuit of national purposes. As that credit outstanding increases, so does commercial bank lending power, at a multiple of that increase, fueling both economic activity and the tendency toward inflation; as it decreases, lending ability decreases and economic activity tends to diminish.

Federal Reserve System (Fed): The United States Federal banking system, operating as a central money and credit control organization and as a system of twelve regional banks implementing the policies of the central Board of Governors. One of the world's major banking systems, it has substantial impact on national and international economic events and trends.

Federal savings and loan association: A savings and loan association whose main business is home mortgage lending, and which is chartered and regulated by the Federal Home Loan Bank Board.

Federal Savings and Loan Insurance Corporation (FSLIC): A Federal agency, responsible for providing insurance on deposits in savings and loan associations. All Federal savings and loan association deposits are by law insured to certain limits; state savings and loan associations may apply for such insurance coverage.

Federal Trade Commission (FTC): An independent Federal agency, responsible for enforcing and interpreting anti-trust laws and a wide range of other laws relating to unfair competition, consumer protection, deceptive practices, and other matters affecting free and fair competition. The FTC is the main Federal trade regulatory body and has an extremely wide mandate.

Feds: A popular term for Federal officers,

applied loosely to all Federal law enforcement officers.

fee: A charge for a service. Usually applied to charges for professional services, such as those of doctors and lawyers. The term sometimes also used to describe legally fixed charges for services, such as those of government officers and notary publics, and more widely to describe charge for any service.

feedback: 1. Information sent back to its originator about any matter, whether in progress or recently completed; often used by the originator to modify and build currently developing processes and to evaluate developing and completed processes. **2.** In computer systems, the transfer of energy back to input from output.

feeder: A transportation line that is connected with one or more larger lines, giving the area it services access to main lines into much larger areas. The term is usually used to describe overland rather than ocean shipping lines.

fee simple: An absolute, unconditional ownership of land or other estate, which belongs to its holder during his or her lifetime and then passes to its inheritors.

felony: A serious, usually major crime, such as murder, arson, rape, and robbery involving substantial sums; but except where defined by statute, no longer definitively separated from the term misdemeanor.

FHA: See Federal Housing Administration.

flat money: Money that is backed by the faith and credit of its issuing government, rather than by any store of value, such as gold and silver. All United States paper currency and all currently issued coins are flat money.

FICA taxes: Payroll taxes levied under authority of the Federal Insurance Contribution Act, as part of the Social Security System.

fidelity bond: A policy insuring employers against losses caused by employee dishonesty, actionable negligence, and non-performance of obligations.

fiduciary: One who has a relationship of trust, including one holding specific and legal status as a trustee of any kind. A fiduciary may be an executor or administrator of an estate, as well as anyone holding any position of trust, as does a banker, lawyer, or company treasurer.

fiduciary accounting: A body of accounting practice relating to property being held by legally recognized fiduciaries, such as executors, administrators, and trustees.

fiduciary capacity: A relationship in which trust of an agent acting in money and property matters is central to the relationship between the parties. The fiduciary has a position of trust, either defined as such by the very nature of that position, as with trustees and executors, or capable of being so construed by law, as with lawyers, bankers, and corporate financial officers.

fiduciary money: See flat money.

field: In computer processing, an area that is assigned to hold similar information in each of a set of records.

field auditor: An employee travelling from location to location to do internal auditing of his or her own company.

field warehousing loan: See warehouse receipt loan.

fifo: See first in, first out.

file: A group of related records, whether held as information on paper in a file cabinet or in computer storage.

file maintenance: The continuous updating of materials in a file.

finance: 1. To raise and supply money for any purpose, as in securing of funds needed by an enterprise by borrowing, by selling shares, or from personal resources. **2.** The entire field of money, credit, and capital, including theories, practices, and institutions.

finance bill: A bankers' bill of exchange,

drawn on a bank in one country by a bank in another country, usually unsecured by anything other than the full faith and credit of the bank drawing the bill, and functioning as an advance of funds by one bank to another.

finance company: A company mainly in the business of making loans to individuals, businesses, or both, such as personal finance companies, specializing in loans to individuals; and sales finance companies, specializing in the buying and collecting of business accounts receivable.

financial accounting: A body of accounting practice concerned with matters relating to the financial side of a business, including income, expenditures, assets, and liabilities.

financial expense: A business expense directly attributable to financing, as are mortgage and bond interest payments.

financial position: The financial situation of a company or individual, as evidenced by current financial statements.

financial statement: Any formal statement that indicates the current financial position of a company or individual, such as a balance sheet, profit and loss statement, flow of funds statement, or any other summary document helping to illuminate that financial position, and including any supporting material.

financier: One who finances a business operated by others; usually one whose main business is the use of substantial sums of money to finance large businesses run by others, whether those sums are loaned or are venture capital.

finder: One who brings the parties to a financial transaction together, whose role in so doing is recognized by those parties, and who is in some way compensated by them for that role.

finder's fee: A fee paid to a finder by one or more of the parties to a financial transaction. Such fees are usually highly negotiable as between parties and finders and are often paid as a matter of practice rather than of contract.

fineness: The proportion of pure metal in a coin or ingot, usually referring to precious metals. For example, the degree of fineness of "silver" coin may be 40%, with the coin composed 40% of silver and 60% of other metals; or a gold bar may be 100% fine, consisting of pure gold.

finished goods: Goods that have been through the manufacturing process, are complete, and are now being held in inventory.

fink: A professional strikebreaker. The term's use has broadened to include anyone working while others are on strike.

fire: To discharge an employee for any reason, and most widely used to describe abrupt, unanticipated discharge.

fire insurance: A form of property insurance, providing protection against losses resulting from fires, often including extended coverage against other hazards such as smoke or windstorm.

fire sale: A sale of goods that have been damaged during a fire, either by the fire itself, by smoke, or by those agents used to extinguish the fire; often expanded to include the sale of any relatively large quantity of goods sold in damaged condition.

firm: 1. Any business organization, including corporations, partnerships and sole proprietorships. **2.** Non-negotiable, as applied to any aspect of a contemplated transaction by one of the parties involved. The term is most often encountered in price matters, where a potential seller quotes a fixed and non-negotiable price.

firm order: An order that has taken on the nature of an enforceable contract, either by a writing between purchaser and seller, or by generally accepted industry practice, such as a telephone order for which adequate evidence of placement exists.

firm price: A price that is non-negotiable or

minimally negotiable; normally found in a seller's market, in which demand is considerably in excess of supply.

firmware: Computer software that is part of a computer system, rather than being separate from and plugged into the system, regardless of whatever other software is plugged in.

first generation computer: An early computer, using vacuum tubes as major components, and requiring programming in machine language.

first in, first out (fifo): 1. An inventory evaluation method, which assumes that material being currently used is always the earliest purchased such material currently in inventory. Materials used in manufacture are generally costed at less than current replacement costs when this method is used, so profits and therefore taxes paid tend to be higher than when different inventory evaluation conventions such as last in, first out, are adopted. **2.** A queueing model in which each is served in order of arrival, as in those banks where all customers wait in order for the first available teller, rather than having to choose a line which may be delayed by a single lengthy transaction.

first-line supervisor: A supervisor whose primary responsibility is to supervise those who themselves have no supervisory powers, rather than other supervisors. For example, most foremen in manufacturing operations, office managers, and restaurant managers are first-line supervisors, but general foremen who supervise other foremen, administrative vice presidents, and restaurant owners are not.

first mortgage: A mortgage senior to all other mortgages, in that it is the first loan to be secured by the property mortgaged, and therefore is the first to be paid in the event of sale of property.

first mortgage bond: A bond secured by a first mortgage on part or all of the property of its issuer, as well as by the issuer's promise to pay.

first preferred stock: See preferred stock.

fiscal: That which refers to or describes financial matters; for example, a fiscal year, which is any 12-month period designated consistently for financialy reporting purposes.

fiscal agent: One who is empowered to handle financial matters for another, as with a financial institution that handles some kinds of receipts and expenditures for a corporate client.

fiscal policy: The over-all direction of a national government's spending and taxing policies aimed at accomplishing the current economic, social, and political goals of that government, and significantly affecting such matters as inflation, recession, expansion, and the taking and holding of national power.

fiscal year: 1. For tax purposes, a 12-month period ending with the last day of any month other than December, in contrast to a calendar year, which ends only on the last day of December. **2.** For accounting purposes, any year-long period, including any 12-month, 52-week, or other set of accounting periods running consecutively and adding up to a year.

fishybacking: A mode of transporting freight by truck, transferring the fully loaded trucks to water carriers such as barges, and then putting the trucks back on the road to continue on. It is a form of "piggybacking," like transferring railroad cars from tracks to road and back to tracks.

Five-Year Plan: A national economic plan that literally plans a major part of a nation's economic activity for a five-year period. First used by the Soviet Union in the late 1920's, five-year and other economic plans of varying durations continue to be used there as well as in a substantial number of other planned economies.

fixed assets: Assets that are part of the operating capital of a business, such as land, buildings, machinery and associated tangible production-related items.

fixed charges: Periodic and continuing financial overhead charges that must be paid, and that have no direct relationship to the level of activity of a business, including such charges as rent, interest, and depreciation.

fixed costs: Periodic and continuing operating overhead costs which are not directly and immediately affected by the level of operations, though they may be in the long term. Fixed costs include general administration and indirect labor and materials costs.

fixed income: Income that is set at specified dollar levels, such as the income from social security and from such investments as most bonds and annuities. In periods of inflation, the value of fixed incomes declines, often sharply, as the number of income dollars remains constant and the value of those dollars diminishes. In periods of deflation, however, fixed incomes appreciate in value.

fixed investment trust: An investment company that sells shares to investors and that may invest its assets only in a specified list of securities, usually in predetermined proportions.

fixed liabilities: See long-term liabilities.

fixed overhead: See fixed costs.

fixed price contract: A contract stating a firm price, in contrast to a contract stating a conditional price. For example, a contract to buy a house states a fixed price and is consummated at that price, while a government contract or any construction contract may have a number of possible price-increasing conditions built into its terms, such as materials costs and labor rate increases.

fixture: Something that has been attached to land or a building and has therefore, in law, become part of that to which it is attached, such as a fence, sink, or built-in cabinet.

flag of convenience: A national flag flown by a ship registered in other than the country of its origin for purposes of regulatory and cost advantage; for example, to avoid higher taxes, union contracts, high pay scales, and government safety standards.

flat: Describing the sale of a bond in which the purchaser receives all interest accrued on that bond since the last interest payment date. Most often, bonds are sold "full" and the seller receives that interest.

flat rate: A specific price for a task to be performed or for materials or services to be supplied. For example, a carpenter may charge a set price for a job to be done, including labor, materials, and possible profits, rather than charging separately and on a cost-plus basis.

flash report: A report on current conditions, based on as much information as is available at the time the report is generated, and to be superseded later by more complete reports based on fuller data. Such reports are often interim operating reports for intracompany use, to be replaced by formal and complete reports at the ends of accounting periods.

fleet policy: An insurance policy covering a group of company-owned vehicles, such as a fleet of company owned and operated trucks, buses, or taxis.

flexible budget: A budget carrying different expenditure levels for different levels of activity, with those alternatives spelled out in the budget from the start of the budgeted period.

flexible schedule: 1. A work schedule that varies to meet company needs, usually around a basic guarantee of minimum hours and pay. **2.** A work schedule that varies from the standard five-day week, eight-hour day arrangement, as in adoption of a four-day week, ten-hour day.

flexible tariff: A tariff that can be adjusted at the discretion of its administrators, usually within bounds specified by those legislating the tariff, and sometimes only on occurrence of specific events, such as specified unfavorable trade balances.

flight of capital: The movement of capital, including both long- and short-term investment money, from its home country to other countries offering more favorable conditions, such as higher interest rates, lower taxes and greater safety.

float: 1. In finance, the total value of checks outstanding and uncollected. **2.** To raise money, whether through a securities offering or a loan.

floater: A form of property insurance covering transportable property, including both personal and business property, and moving with the property insured. Floaters usually cover specific items at their appraised values, and are widely used to cover such valuables as jewels, art objects, money instruments, and equipment, often for all or almost all risks and sometimes worldwide.

floating capital: Capital that is currently circulating and being used for working purposes rather than being fixed and held for longer term purposes.

floating debt: The total of all current short-term debts, expressed in accounting as the current liabilities of a government of business.

floating exchange rate: The variable rate at which currencies can be exchanged with each other, which is the price of each currency as against all other currencies in the absence of governmental intervention into the world currency markets.

floating interest rate: An interest rate that is not fixed, but moves with other money market factors, especially with changes in the prime rate. As a practical matter, most businesses with bank lines of credit have de facto floating interest rates; in recent years, the concept has been formally extended to include such instruments as home mortgages, that previously had only fixed rates.

floating supply: The total amount of a common stock or bond issue that is actually available for purchase and sale at a given time, as distinguished from the amount outstanding, much of which is held for long-term investment purposes and therefore is not really available for trading.

flood insurance: Insurance coverage for flood damage; usually written by private insurers, but subsidized by the Federal government.

floor partner: A securities firm partner who handles transactions for his or her firm on the floor of a securities exchange.

floor trader: A trading exchange member who trades on the floor of the exchange for his or her own account or one in which he or she holds an interest.

flower bonds: Low denomination United States government bonds formerly widely purchased because of their preferential tax treatment in decedent's estates; hence their popular name; such special tax treatment has now been largely terminated.

flow of control: Within a computer system, the timely execution of instructions following the transfer of control at branching points in the computer program.

flow of funds analysis: A statement of the flow of money through any economic entity, following funds from entry to departure. In business accounting, this analysis results in a cash flow or funds flow statement; in national accounting, the result is a periodic national flow of funds analysis.

fluctuation: The movement of prices in securities and commodities markets, stated in such gradations as points, fractions of points, cents, and dollars.

FMCS: See Federal Mediation and Conciliation Services.

f.o.b.: Abbreviation for free on board, an agreement between buyer and seller that seller will be responsible for all risks and transportation costs connected with goods being sold until those goods are delivered to a specified point. Buyer takes over cost and risks at that point and after legal delivery.

For example, goods originating in New York sold f.o.b. Kansas City must be transported and insured as far as a Kansas City freight destination by the seller, and those charges are covered by the purchase price. On delivery, the buyer takes over costs and risks.

FOIA: See Freedom of Information Act.

Food and Agriculture Organization (FAO): A United Nations agency that is charged with developing programs in such areas as food production, distribution and nutrition, especially for developing nations, and that provides many services toward those ends.

Food and Drug Administration (FDA): A Federal agency charged with administering laws relating to the purity and safety of foods, drugs, cosmetics, and related materials, processes, and services. The FDA sets standards, exercising licensing powers, and does a great deal of product testing in all areas of its jurisdiction.

food cooperative: See cooperative.

food stamps: Coupons issued by the Federal government through the Food Stamp Program of the Department of Agriculture, enabling low income people to buy food at discount prices.

footnotes: In financial statements, comments keyed to financial items, to explain those items more fully to those reading the statements.

forced loan: A loan which is made by the lender due to the pressure of circumstances, rather than by choice, as in the payment of a customer's overdraft or the extension of an unpaid loan when due.

forced sale: A sale that is made by the seller due to the pressure of circumstances, rather than by choice, as in the involuntary sale of foreclosed property by law or the voluntary sale of goods at a loss to raise cash to save a business.

forecast: An estimate of future trends, events and results, such as an estimate of future stock market price trends made by a stock advisory service, or an estimate of its own future sales, costs, and earnings made by a business as part of a report to stockholders.

forecasting: Predicting future business trends and events through the use of various analytical tools, especially mathematical models using computer technology. In a wider sense, any systematic attempt to predict the future, as in weather or crop forecasting.

foreclosure: A legal proceeding, in which the mortgage holder takes possession of property on which mortgage payments are in default. The foreclosed property is normally sold at public auction, with proceeds used to pay the balance due on the mortgage and anything over that paid to the former owner of the property.

foreground processing: High-priority computer processing that is done in preference to lower priority, or background processing.

foreign aid: A national policy of supplying financial and technical aid to other countries, as in United States supply of outright grants and credits to war-damaged countries after both of this century's world wars.

foreign bill of exchange: A bill of exchange that is drawn on a drawee in another country and is payable in another country, including a wide variety of financial instruments.

foreign corporation: A corporation whose main domicile is in a jurisdiction other than the one in which a question is being considered. For example, a corporation domiciled in Delaware is a foreign corporation to a court in any other state; a corporation domiciled in Germany is foreign to any United States court.

foreign exchange: The means by which international financial transactions are handled, through the transfer of financial instruments, denominated in several currencies, between buyers and sellers, and the financial instruments themselves.

foreign exchange market: A worldwide market in the currencies of all countries, used for settling international financial obligations, trading in world currencies, and speculating in world currency futures, with participants located in financial institutions of all kinds throughout the world, rather than in a single central location.

foreign exchange rates: The prices of the world's currencies in relation to each other; the rate at which a unit of one currency will be exchanged for units of other currencies. For example, the number of American dollars it takes to buy one British pound expresses the exchange rate between the two currencies.

foreign exchange reserves: The amount of foreign currency and other financial instruments held by a government as reserve against foreign debts.

foreign trade: Trade between public and private parties in two or more countries.

foreign trade zone: See free trade zone.

foreman: A female or male supervisor, usually functioning as a first-line factory supervisor, but sometimes responsible for other foremen as well.

forfeiture: The loss of money or a right because of failure to fulfill obligations or the performance of illegal acts, as in forfeiture of a bond for nonperformance of a contract.

forgery: A false writing, made with intent to defraud. Also the written instrument so falsified.

formula investment plans: Investment plans that provide for specific moves on the part of investors in response to specific securities market behavior, with particular reference to the proportions of common stocks and bonds to be held in investment portfolios.

FORTRAN: An acronym for *For*mula *Tran*slator, a major computer language widely used in scientific programming, with many business applications as well.

forward buying: In commodity trading, buying at current prices for future delivery, in

anticipation of future advantageous price moves; for example, the purchase of contracts now calling for the future delivery of wheat.

forward exchange: Foreign exchange bought or sold at current prices for future delivery, in anticipation of future advantageous price moves.

forwarding agent: See freight forwarder.

forward movement: Any upward trend in the market prices of securities or commodities, and used to characterize price trends of as little as a few hours and as much as several years.

forward selling: In commodity trading, selling at current prices for future delivery, in anticipation of future advantageous price moves; for example, the sale of contracts now calling for the future delivery of wheat.

foundation: A tax-free, non-profit private organization that receives and distributes funds for charitable and other benevolent purposes, such as health research and support for the arts.

founders' shares: Capital stock carrying special privileges issued to founding members of a company in return for their role in the initiation and early promotion of that company.

FPC: See Federal Power Commission.

fractional currency: Any currency denominated in fractions of the main currency unit, as are pence to pounds and cents to dollars. All coins less than $1 in value are fractional currency in the United States.

fractional reserve banking: That system of banking, now in use in the United States and in all other industrial nations, in which banks carry only a relatively small liquid reserve against all deposits, on the theory that all deposits will never be withdrawn at once from all banks in the system.

fractional share: Any portion of stock less than a single share, as occurs in some stock dividend and dividend reinvestment situations.

frame: 1. In sampling, the total source group from which samples will be drawn; for example, the telephone books containing the numbers of all consumers from which a sample group will be drawn. **2.** In programmed instruction, a discrete segment of material, including application and feedback.

franchise: 1. An agreement between a business organization—the franchisor—and a retailing organization—the franchisee—providing the franchisee the right to deal in the franchisor's goods and services. Usually the franchiser provides such supporting mechanisms as financing, marketing, materials procurement, and management help in return for a share of the franchisee's revenues or profits. **2.** The right to perform stated functions, granted by government to a private organization or individual, in such areas of quasi-public and essentially monopolistic operation as power supply, lighting, telephone service, and public transportation.

franchised dealer: A dealer holding a franchise agreement with a producer, usually for a specific length of time and subject to certain terms and conditions involving minimum acceptable volumes of business done by the franchisee and acceptable modes of business behavior.

franchisee: See franchise.

franchise tax: A tax on a corporation's right to do business within a taxing jurisdiction.

franchisor: See franchise.

fraud: The intentional misstatement, distortion, and suppression of truth, actually or constructively leading to the damage or loss of legal rights of others. Under the English Statute of Frauds, enacted into law in almost all United States jurisdictions, some kinds of contracts, including real estate contracts, must be in writing before fraud can be alleged.

fraudulent conversion: The possession and illegal appropriation of money or property belonging to another for purposes of personal gain.

fraudulent conveyance: The illegal transfer of property owned by one to another, to avoid a legally due payment or performance of an obligation; for example, the transfer of corporate property to a family member to avoid payment to the corporation's creditors in the face of impending bankruptcy.

free alongside ship: See f.a.s.

free and clear ownership: See clear.

freedom of entry: The ease or difficulty for a newcomer to go into a kind of business and successfully compete with those already established in that business, taking into account such factors as the amount of money necessary to develop competitive manufacturing and marketing operations. Entry into the restaurant business is relatively easy and thousands of entrepreneurs open restaurants every year, providing powerful and continuing new competition for those in the field. In contrast, entrance into steel or gasoline production is expensive and difficult, with a consequent lessening of competition in those fields.

Freedom of Information Act (FOIA): A Federal statute establishing the right of the public to have access to public information, including access to legislative materials, personal dossiers, and investigative records, with some exceptions, such as information affecting national security matters.

free enterprise: A theoretical construct, positing the existence of perfectly free competition in all aspects of economic life, with a free marketplace regulating all economic developments. Given the present massive, interconnected, highly regulated, and heavily manipulated world economic system, free enterprise is far more a political slogan than an economic fact.

freehold: An estate in real property or that which is affixed to real property in perpetuity, such as the free and clear title to a piece of land.

freelance: Describing one who sells services as an independent contractor; usually applied to skilled creative people, such as writers, graphic artists, and some consultants, although many consultants function as full-scale business organizations rather than as small individual operators.

free list: A list of imports which may be brought into a country free of import duties.

free market: A market which is in no way controlled or manipulated, but which functions purely in response to supply and demand factors, as in the instance of some securities markets and the markets for some foodstuffs.

free on board: See f.o.b.

free port: A port operating as a free trade zone, where no duties are levied on either imports or exports.

free supply: Describing the physical amount of a commondity available for trading at any given time, arrived at by totalling the world stock and subtracting that which is held by governments; often a considerably misleading figure, as governments do release commodity stocks from time to time, in some cases suddenly adding to the free supply and tending just as suddenly to drive commodity prices and futures down. An example is United States sales of substantial gold stocks in the early 1970s.

free trade: A theoretical construct, proposing a system of international trade entirely without government-imposed barriers of any kind, such as tariffs, currency restrictions, and political restraints. Like free enterprise, free trade is more a political slogan than a current reality.

free trade area: A group of two or more countries that have agreed to free trade between themselves, eliminating all tariff and other trade barriers between them, while maintaining the ability to set individual trade barriers against other countries.

free trade zone: A duty-free area, often but not always in or near a port city, where no

import or export duties are placed on goods bought, sold, or processed.

freight: 1. Any goods transported by land, sea, or air. 2. Any charges for transporting such goods.

freight absorption: The payment of freight charges by the seller of goods, rather than charging those costs to the buyer.

freighter: A ship carrying primarily freight, and few if any passengers.

freight forwarder: A freighting firm that takes small shipments from many shippers, consolidates them, and then ships them, handling the necessary papers and securing any price advantage for larger shipments. Freight forwarders are heavily used in exporting.

freight line: A transportation company carrying primarily freight, and few if any passengers.

frequency distribution: In statistics, a representation of data to show frequency of occurrence within specified ranges, or class intervals, often shown graphically; an example would be a chart showing the number of people in each of several salary classifications within a company.

frictional unemployment: Unemployment caused by temporary labor market conditions, such as plant relocations, unemployment between jobs due to personal factors, lack of mobility, and similar miscellaneous factors.

friend of the court: See amicus curiae.

fringe benefits: Compensation beyond wages and salaries paid by employers to employees, including such items as pensions, sick leave, vacations, tuition assistance, insurance and profit-sharing.

front-end analysis: In training, the analysis of a situation to see what, if any, training materials need to be developed; the aim is to avoid producing materials when lack of training is not the problem or when the cost of the training would not justify the minimal gain.

front-end load: Sales and other administrative costs charged against some kinds of investment contracts at the start of a contract period. For example, an investor in a mutual fund may buy a five-year plan, want to sell it out after one year, and find that half the payments made during that year have gone to pay front-end costs and cannot be retrieved.

front-end processor: In computer systems, that device or group of devices controlling the interface between auxiliary devices and the central processing unit, especially between remote terminals and the computer in a data communications system.

front-line supervisor: See first-line supervisor.

front-load commissions: See front-end load.

frozen account: A bank account on which all transactions have been suspended, usually either by court order to avoid the account holder fleeing with the funds or by administrative order in pursuit of national policy, as in the freezing of the accounts of enemy nationals in time of war.

frozen asset: An asset that has been set aside and held by a legal body, and will not be returned to its owner until that legal body relinquishes it; for example, property held by a court pending the resolution of legal action or the property of aliens that is held by a government during and after a war.

FSLIC: See Federal Savings and Loan Insurance Corporation.

FTC: See Federal Trade Commission.

full: Describing the sale of a bond in which the seller receives all interest accrued since the last interest payment date, as opposed to a "flat" sale where the buyer receives that interest.

full coverage: Insurance coverage that pays the full amount of any loss incurred on that which is insured, in contrast to deductible coverage, which pays only losses over a specified amount.

full crew rule: A collective bargaining contract provision specifying the number of workers to be employed on a specific job. The full crew rule is the subject of a great deal of contention as technology changes and employers press to cut crews while unions resist such cuts.

full disclosure: See disclosure.

full employment: A labor market condition in which all who want to and are able to work are employed, other than an irreducible minimum who are literally between jobs. Full employment is more a goal than an actuality in the United States.

full faith and credit: Describing a promise to pay a contracted debt. If unsupported by collateral, the promise describes a general debt, supported only by the worth of the organization or individual making it.

full service: A company that provides a wide range of services to its customers, including all those main services supplied by any such company in its industry. For instance, a full-service department store provides many services a discount department store does not; a full-service bank provides a wide range of services to business and individual depositors.

full-service banking: See commercial bank.

full vesting: See vesting.

fundamentalist: One who believes that such basic economic facts as deep economic trends, specific company managements, and the condition of the money market are primary predictive factors in forecasting securities price fluctuations.

fundamentals: See fundamentalist.

funded debt: The total long-term debts of a business or government, in the form of such long-term debt instruments as bonds and long-term notes.

funding: 1. In the widest sense, the securing

of money for any purpose, as in the funding of college study through a combination of grants and loans. **2.** The creation of a pool of reserve funds to pay for future obligations, as in the development of pension funds to pay for future pensions. **3.** The conversion of short-term debts into funded debts, by the creation of long-term debt instruments.

funds flow statement: See flow of funds analysis.

fungibles: Goods of common quality, recognized in practice and in law as exchangeable for each other in satisfaction of contractual obligations, as in the instances of peas, eggs, or other agricultural products stored together in warehouses and supplied by grade rather than by specific lot.

furlough: A leave of absence, with or without pay, but normally without forfeit of seniority or fringe benefit eligibility and continuity.

futures: Contracts for commodities and other tangibles and intangibles, specifying future delivery or receipt of stated amounts at specific future times, specifying identical quality, quantity, and terms as all other such contracts, and traded on commodities and other futures exchanges according to the rules of those exchanges.

futures contract: See futures.

futures exchange: An organized exchange, on which futures are traded.

futures market: A group of commodity markets in which futures contracts are traded, organized into several commodities exchanges, such as the Chicago Board of Trade. Futures markets also exist in foreign exchange and in some government obligations.

G

gain: The net of any income over costs; in accounting, summed up by the entry "gain or loss." In the widest sense, any advance or profit.

gain sharing: A form of profit sharing, in which workers share in any profits attributable to increased production.

galloping inflation: A popular term for a relatively very high and seemingly almost impossible to control rate of inflation.

gambling: Risk taking with small factual bases, as in the instance of the entrepreneur who moves into a new business on the basis of predicting a new consumer buying pattern, or the investor who speculates on the basis of a "hunch."

games theory: A body of mathematical theory which handles a number of variables, some known and some unknown, develops a series of alternative models, and attempts to develop the best possible courses of action; widely used in conjunction with computer-generated simulations in business problem-solving exercises.

Gantt chart: A bar chart comparing scheduled with actual performance, named after its developer, H. L. Gantt, widely used in production control and computer scheduling operations.

GAO: See General Accounting Office.

garnishee: One who has by legal process been warned not to part with property or wages belonging to another who is defending a lawsuit, so that the court may direct payment to the plaintiff in that lawsuit if

warranted; for example, an employer directed by court order to withhold a portion of an employee's wages for possible satisfaction of judgment.

GATT: See General Agreement on Tariffs and Trade.

Gaussian distribution: See normal distribution.

GAW: See guaranteed annual wage.

General Accounting Office (GAO): A Federal agency responsible for checking, auditing, and reviewing all Federal expenditures, and reporting any irregularities found to Congress.

General Agreement on Tariffs and Trade (GATT): An international agreement and administrative organization participated in by most countries, outside the Soviet and Chinese areas of influence, dedicated to the removal of tariff barriers to trade throughout the world.

general fund: A fund that can be used for any normal organizational purposes, rather than being earmarked for use to accomplish specific tasks.

general ledger: The main accounting ledger of a business, containing either detailed or summary information on every aspect of business activities.

general mortgage bonds: Bonds backed by a general mortgage on all company property already subject wholly or partially to existing first mortgages.

general partner: One who shares in all profits and has unlimited liability, in contrast to a limited partner, who has sharply defined shares of profits and limited liability.

general purpose computer: A computer that can be programmed to solve many kinds of problems with relatively equal facility.

General Services Administration (GSA): A United States Government agency, responsible for miscellaneous management, construction, distribution, and purchasing functions on behalf of the Federal Government.

general store: A retail store carrying many lines of merchandise, and attempting to serve most or all of the retail needs of its customers. It is a fast disappearing kind of retailer, now found mainly in lightly populated areas.

general strike: A strike by workers in many industries simultaneously, for mainly political rather than economic ends. It is often confined to a single locality and lasts for a limited time, often being as much a demonstration as a strike. Such strikes have occurred rarely in the United States, but are more frequent in other parts of the world.

gentlemen's agreement: An agreement in which the parties sign no document and produce no other evidence of the agreement they have reached. Such agreements are often tacit, very often extra-legal; they have no legal force, and rely only on custom and the verbal assurances of the parties involved.

geographical differential: The difference between wages paid for substantially similar work in different locations, sometimes as a matter of common practice and sometimes as a matter of labor-management agreement.

geometric mean: A type of mean that is calculated from the logarithms of the values being averaged; used in complex statistical analyses such as calculations of indexes.

geometric progression: A sequence of numbers in which each succeeding term is a constant multiple of the last; for example, in the series: 1, 3, 9, 27, each term results from

the previous term being multiplied by the constant 3.

gift certificate: A certificate sold by a retailer for cash, enabling its holder to purchase goods up to the amount stated on the certificate from that retailer, and used by its purchaser as a gift to another party.

gift taxes: Federal and state taxes on the value of property given to others, the gifts being taxable to the recipient and graduated according to the value of the property given.

gigo: An acronym for "garbage in, garbage out," in computer industry slang, meaning that the computer can only process information in programmed ways, and that badly prepared and useless information fed into a computer system results only in output of the same quality.

gilt-edged: High grade and relatively safe securities, usually bonds; a popular term some generations ago, but now rarely used in the United States. In the United Kingdom "gilts" is a popular term for bonds.

Ginnie Mae: See Government National Mortgage Association.

glamour stock: A stock which is very popular with investors in any given period, far beyond its intrinsic value or current prospects, due to widespread expectation that the specific stock or the group of stocks of which it is part will rise in value far more quickly than most other stocks; for example, gambling stocks for a time in the late 1970s, or electronic stocks in the early 1960s.

glut: A market condition in which supply far exceeds demand at current consumption and price levels. Glut is traditionally encountered in agricultural commodity areas, given the wide variance in crop yields from year to year due to factors beyond farmers' control.

GNP: See gross national product.

goal setting: The fixing of organizational, group, or personal achievement levels; an indispensable part of the planning process.

go-go fund: Popular description of a kind of mutual fund, oriented toward investment in rather speculative common stocks, with the hope of very rapid appreciation.

going concern: A business that is in operation and is expected to continue operation, in contrast to a business that either has not yet started operations or is not expected to continue doing business.

going public: The sale of shares to the general public by a corporation that has been closely held, usually through the issuance of common stock.

going rate: Popular term for the customary rate for services or price for goods; generally refers to an approximation or acceptable range of rates, rather than to a fixed sum.

goldbricking: Covert failure to do a job, usually accompanied by an attempt to seem to be doing that job.

gold certificate: United States paper currency fully convertible into gold. Gold certificates are no longer legal tender and were withdrawn after the United States went off the gold standard in 1933.

gold reserve: The amount of gold physically held by a government. Although gold no longer directly backs the world's major currencies, gold reserves are still major elements indirectly supporting national currencies.

gold shares: The stocks of companies primarily engaged in gold mining, in many cases the stocks of South African companies.

gold standard: A monetary system in which gold provides a basic value for a national currency, stated as a unit of currency being worth a specified quantity of gold. Gold standards throughout the world began to be modified and then abandoned during the Great Depression of the 1930s.

good delivery: Delivery of securities, in ready-to-transfer condition to be sold or held by a bank or broker.

good faith bargaining: A legal obligation set by Federal and state labor laws on labor and management to pursue collective bargaining as an honest attempt to settle industrial disputes short of industrial action.

good faith payment: See earnest money.

goods: Anything bought or sold in the process of doing business, including materials and processed or manufactured items.

goods in process: Materials and products at any stage of the production process after entry into a system of production and before completion.

good-till-cancelled order. An order to buy or sell securities placed with a broker on an "open" basis, to be fulfilled at any time by the broker unless specifically cancelled by the customer who placed the order.

goodwill: The value of a business beyond the total of its tangible assets; normally determinable only in purchase or sale of the business and defined by the price that is paid for the business. It is sometimes, but relatively rarely, treated as an intangible asset and taken into books of account on that basis.

goon: One who is hired to use tactics of terror and intimidation on behalf of another. Management in many companies routinely hired goons to intimidate strikers and break strikes in the early days of union organization; some labor unions hired goons to intimidate non-strikers and union dissidents. Though greatly diminished, the practice continues to be used by some managements and some unions.

go public: To sell shares in a privately owned company to the public through a public securities offering.

gouging: The taking of unfair and unjust advantage of buyers by sellers in a sellers market, with resulting unusually high profits for those sellers; for example, the selling of milk at very high prices by retailers during a milk strike.

government accounting: That body of accounting practice and procedure that has developed to deal with the accounting requirements of Federal, state and local governments, including those requirements imposed by law.

government bill: A general term for any short-term government debt obligation, such as a 90-day Treasury note.

government bond: A bond issued by a government or an agency of government. In the United States, the term is reserved to describe United States Federal government debt obligations in the form of bonds.

Government National Mortgage Association (Ginnie Mae): A federally owned and financed corporation administered by the Department of Housing and Urban Development, which finances several kinds of mortgages pursuant to national policy, in relatively high risk areas that might otherwise have difficulty in securing financing; for example, inner city public housing and commercial development projects.

government ownership: See public ownership.

government sector: See public sector.

government spending: See public spending.

grace period: A period beyond the due date of a debt obligation, in which the creditor allows payment of the debt without penalty to the debtor.

grade labeling: The labeling of consumer packaged goods by quality, as in the stamping of Grades A, B, C and similar indicators on the labels of canned goods, meat and eggs.

grading: The classification and identification of commodities by grade, applying a set of specified quality standards.

graduated tax: A tax that increases in relative rate as the value of that which is taxed increases. For example, the tax rate on taxable income between $20,001 and $24,000 may be 30%, and then rise to 34% on taxable income between $24,001 and $28,000.

grandfather clause: A legal or contractual provision effectively precluding some people from existing activity, or exempting some people from new requirements, by providing that those who have been previously engaged in these activities are the only ones who can continue in them on current contractual or legal bases. Examples include a now illegal voting law providing that only those whose grandfathers previously voted can now vote, for some time an effective means of denying southern Blacks the right to vote; or a new zoning ordinance that exempts those now in place who would be violators of that ordinance if they had built after rather than before the ordinance was enacted.

grant: An outright gift of money to further the accomplishment of specified goals, usually from government or from a private institution such as a foundation or corporation. Grants are usually made in response to requests accompanied by detailed statements of purposes and methods.

grant-in-aid: An outright gift of money from government to government or by government to a sub-governmental unit, as from the federal government to state and local governments. Grants-in-aid are sometimes dependent on the supply of some matching funds by the recipient.

grapevine: An informal set of information channels in an organization; no organization is without one.

graveyard shift: The late night shift, worked from late at night to early the next morning, often from 11 P.M. to 7 A.M. or midnight to 8 A.M.

gray knight: In corporate takeover situations, a company that follows an antagonistic bid by a first company attempting takeover with a somewhat higher bid of its own; such a company usually holds out a more amicable takeover situation to the management and stockholders of the takeover candidate.

gray market: A market in which exorbitant

prices are charged for goods and services, usually those in short supply for some reason. Where those goods and services are being supplied legally, a gray market exists; where illegally, a black market exists.

Great Depression: The worldwide economic depression that began with the United States stock market crash in 1929 and continued in many countries until the beginning of World War II. In the United States, it was deepest between 1929 and 1933, with significant aspects remaining until 1941.

Great Society: President Lyndon B. Johnson's slogan, characterizing a wide range of Federal social programs developed during his administration.

greenback: United States paper currency. A popular term now passing out of the language, it was derived from the color of United States Treasury debt obligations issued by the United States government during the Civil War, which later became recognized as part of the national currency.

green hands: Those employees who are inexperienced in the performance of their jobs.

Green Revolution: Replacement of some crops with improved strains of those and other crops in large areas of the Third World, including much of East Asia, Sub-Sahara Africa, and Central and South America. Starting in the late 1950's these new crop strains have resulted in far higher and more nutritious crop yields in many impoverished, densely populated areas, though positive effects have often been vitiated by maldistribution and the susceptibility of some new crop strains to disease.

Gresham's Law: The observation that "bad money drives out good," attributed to Sir Thomas Gresham, Queen Elizabeth I's Master of the Mint, meaning that when two kinds of money, one of greater intrinsic value than the other, are circulated simultaneously at the same face values, the less valuable money will be used, and the more valuable money will go out of circulation due to hoarding, sale at greater than face values,

and such illegal devices as melting down the more valuable money for its metal content.

grievance: In labor relations, any complaint against each other by employees or unions on the one hand and employers on the other. The complaints may be formal or informal, may or may not result from collective bargaining agreement disputes, and may be subject to arbitration or only to collective bargaining.

grievance machinery: The procedures by which grievances are handled within the framework of an applicable collective bargaining agreement, as interpreted by law and government labor relations agencies.

gross: Total before any applicable deductions of any kind, but after any necessary corrections.

gross income: Total income from all sources, before subtracting any applicable deductions or other necessary subtractions, but after any necessary corrections.

gross margin: The remainder, after subtracting direct costs from sales revenue, but before making any other subtractions.

gross negligence: Failure to exercise the slightest bit of care, in clear disregard of consequences to others, and raising a presumption of willful carelessness, but falling short of intentional wrongdoing.

gross national product (GNP): The total market value of all goods and services produced by a nation within a period, usually a year, before any subtractions for depreciation and capital goods consumption.

gross profit: The remainder, after subtracting costs of goods sold, including factory overhead from net sales.

gross sales: The remainder, after deducting direct sales and excise taxes, cash discounts, and corrections from total sales, but before subtracting returns and allowances.

gross weight: The entire weight of anything, including all packaging and contents, and under some circumstances the weight of the carrier as well, such as in measuring the weight of a motor carrier at a highway weighing station.

ground rent: Rent paid under the terms of a lease of land; often a long-term net lease of land without usable structures.

group banking: The control of a group of banks by a single holding company, which may hold both the banks and other non-bank companies. The holding company has its own structure and personnel, as do each of the banks held.

group bonus: A bonus paid to employees for their performance as a group rather than as individuals, which is then divided among the members of the group, sometimes equally and sometimes in proportion to their other earnings.

group buying: The pooling of purchases by a group of buyers to gain such advantages as quantity discounts, delivery time leverage, and professional buying. For example, many medium-sized clothing retailers in smaller cities may pool their buying efforts by opening an office staffed by professional buyers in New York City.

group discount: A price reduction offered to a buying group, such as a group of travelers or health insurance purchasers.

group dynamics: The way people move, interact, and develop patterns of relationship within and as a group; of particular significance to those leading and seeking to participate successfully in business organizations, which by their nature move as groups rather than collections of individuals.

group insurance: Insurance which covers the members of a group at uniform amounts of coverage at uniform rates for all group members, usually offering more cost-effective and wider coverages than those available to individuals. Most group insurance plans, such as life, health, and accident coverages, are fringe benefits, in which employers pay all or part of the premiums for the insurance.

group rate: A special rate, usually discounted, offered to those purchasing as a group, rather than as individuals or individual businesses; for example, a discounted rate offered to a group of shippers by a carrier, a discounted rate offered by an insurer to those buying health insurance as a group, or a special rate offered by an agency or carrier to those travelling as a group.

growth company: See growth stock.

growth fund: A mutual fund oriented primarily to the purchase of the common stocks of companies thought to be growing fast, with stocks therefore thought to be excellent prospects for rapid appreciation.

growth portfolio: A portfolio of securities carried by an investor or investing organization, oriented primarily toward holding the stocks of companies thought to be growing fast, with stocks therefore thought to be excellent prospects for rapid appreciation.

growth recession: A recession in which economic growth continues, although at a considerably slower rate than that experienced during periods of prosperity.

growth stock: A popular term describing a common stock which is appreciating in value quickly, and which is thought to reflect the excellent future prospects of its issuing company.

GSA: See General Services Administration.

guarantee: 1. A legally binding assurance by one of the obligation of another to a third party, as in the assurance of payment of a loan to another. **2.** A legally binding assurance of product quality, issued in writing to the purchaser of that product; in this era of consumer protection, a guarantee can be implied as well as expressed.

guaranteed annual wage (GAW): 1. An arrangement between employer and employee, sometimes as part of a collective bargaining agreement, in which the employer pledges to provide a minimum yearly salary to the employee, whether or not there is work all year.

2. A government-funded minimum yearly income plan.

guaranteed bond: A bond issued by one business, which is guaranteed wholly or in part by another, as in the instance of a subsidiary, controlled, or affiliated company bond guaranteed by a parent company.

guarantor: One who makes a legally binding commitment to guarantee payment or performance due from another.

guidelines 1. General directions supplied by those leading a group or organization, within which all personnel in those groups or organizations are asked to function; for example, a general instruction to all sales personnel on the general limits within which refunds on merchandise previously sold will be granted. **2.** General requests by government to private parties, asking for voluntary compliance; for example, requests that price and wage increases be generally kept within certain bounds.

guild: An association of small business proprietors or independent craftspeople, who are themselves often small proprietors, to pursue mutual interests arising from their businesses or crafts.

gypsy: 1. An independent vehicle operator-owner, who hires out to do transportation jobs. **2.** An independent and unlicensed vehicle operator-owner, such as a taxi driver without a license to operate a taxi. **3.** One who moves from job to job, roughly at the same level, such as "gypsy scholars" who move from college to college on one- or two-year contracts, never receiving promotion or tenure.

H

habeas corpus: An action at law, started by a writ of habeas corpus served upon a law officer, aimed at bringing that officer into court to answer the charge that a prisoner is being unlawfully held.

hand-to-mouth: 1. Any business that is operating on a very thin financial basis, as expressed in such matters as lean buying, and difficulty in meeting financial obligations. **2.** In purchasing practice, the policy of holding purchases and therefore inventory to little more than enough to meet current output commitments, for any of several reasons, such as financial problems or anticipated new sources of supply at lower prices or better quality.

hard copy: Copy that is printed, as by a writer on paper or a computer on paper out of a line printer.

hard-core unemployed: Those who are unemployed for long periods of time, in relatively good times as well as clearly bad times. For example, a 60-year-old printing press operator, terminated because new developments in printing technology have made his job obsolete, might be unemployable for a very long period of time.

hardhat: One who works in basic industry, particularly in the construction industry; sometimes used as a synonym for blue-collar worker.

hard loan: An international loan that must be repaid in a currency which is not subject to rapid losses in value, such as those occasioned by inflation in the borrowing country; therefore, usually a loan that must be repaid in the currency of the lending country.

hard money: 1. Coins, rather than paper money, **2.** Cash or assets that can be quickly converted into cash.

hard sell: A popular description of very persistent, aggressive attempts by a seller to close a sale, usually over the resistance of an unconvinced and therefore highly resistant potential purchaser.

hardware: 1. Any machinery or other physical tools for doing a job. **2.** In computer technology, the machinery, consisting of the computers themselves and other associated physical devices, in contrast to software, or programming components.

harmonic mean: A type of mean that is calculated from the reciprocals of the values being averaged; used in complex statistical analyses.

Hatch Act: The basic Federal statute regulating corrupt political practices by office holders and by those who would seek to illegally influence their actions.

hazard: The dangers specified in a property insurance policy, against which something insured is covered. For example, a policy covering a retail store and specifying the hazard of fire will cover the store for fire. The same policy, not mentioning or specifically excluding flood as a hazard, will not cover the store for flood.

head hunter: A popular description of an executive recruiter who will use a wide variety of means, often unethical, to get the desired person to fill a job. the term has widened to include all executive recruiters and recruitment firms, no matter how ethical.

health insurance: Insurance covering illness and illness-related expenses, including all or part of hospital, surgical, dental, drug, disability, or related expenses.

heavy industry: The basic industries, such as metal production, machine tools, mining, and other extractive industries.

heavy market: A securities or commodities market in which prices are falling.

hedge fund: A speculative mutual fund, aiming to make quick profits with a combination of borrowed money and highly leveraged transactions, requiring relatively small cash and carrying relatively high risks.

hedging: An attempt to reduce the risks inherent in a situation or transaction by developing alternate courses of action that minimize the risks, as in the instance of a gambler who places two almost contradictory bets simultaneously, hoping to alter the overall odds in his or her favor. In the securities or commodities markets, hedging is the simultaneous execution of present and future transactions in the hope of minimizing risks.

heuristic: Learning through independent investigation leading to the step-by-step solution of problems with little or no attention paid to preconceived solutions; in general, it is a pragmatic approach to problem solving.

HEW: See Department of Health, Education and Welfare.

hexadecimal: A number system based on 16 digits, the usual decimal digits, 0–9, and the first six letters of the alphabet, A–F; used in computer systems that operate on the extended binary coded decimal interchange code (EBCDIC).

hidden agenda: A plan of action covertly held by an individual group, or organization, in contrast to announced objectives and plans.

hidden assets: Assets that are not in an accounting sense assets at all, but rather are company advantages to be considered by potential investors and acquirers; for example, a very favorable market position, or a new and very promising product or process.

hidden inflation: A reduction in the real value of goods sold, by changing the quantity and quality of the goods supplied and without or with small dollar price increases. Examples are machines that are less well made, reflecting far poorer material and less labor than the same goods in prior years; and packaged foods that come in smaller quantities but larger packages and are adulterated with less expensive and usually far less nutritious ingredients. These very real price increases do not show up in the Cost of Living Index, yet are quite normal features of the American economic landscape.

hidden liabilities: Liabilities that are not in an accounting sense liabilities at all, but rather are company disadvantages to be considered by potential investors and acquirers; for example, an increasingly unfavorable market position, or a product made obsolescent by new developments in its field.

hidden reserves: Assets that are substantially understated in company financial statements, causing company net worth to be understated, as in the instance of regulated utilities which may understate assets in an attempt to hide growth in net worth as part of a strategy aimed at securing rate increases.

hidden tax: A tax on goods that is not separately stated to the buyer at point of purchase; often encountered in the sale and purchase of imported goods at retail, as with the price of an imported television set which includes, but does not separately state, the import duties that have been paid on it.

hierarchy: A group of people organized by rank and authority, such as the pyramidal organization of the modern American company.

hierarchy of needs: A list of basic human needs ranked in order of necessity, postulated by the psychologist Abraham Maslow, which provides a substantial portion of the theoretical underpinning of modern American personnel practices and procedures, with their stress on effectively manipulative human relations as a prime means of developing industrial efficiency and productivity.

high energy level: See energy level.

high finance: A popular way of describing financing functions, implying complex, speculative, and somewhat dishonest financial practices on the part of people and organizations involved in financing activities.

high flyer: A stock that is appreciating in value very quickly, when compared to other stocks in the markets in which it is traded; often but not always a speculative stock, subject to wide price variations both up and down.

high grade securities: Securities carrying little risk of loss, such as United States government debt obligations; some state, local, and corporate debt obligations; and the common and preferred stocks of some well-established and carefully managed corporations.

high-level language: In computer programming, a symbolic language, such as FORTRAN, COBOL or BASIC, which is relatively easy for humans to write in, but which must be translated by a compiler into machine language, before it can be used by the computer; in contrast, low-level languages require a simpler translation process.

high technology company: A company significantly involved in producing goods or providing services resulting from the use of complex modern technologies; such as companies in the aerospace, computer, and nuclear energy industries.

highway trust fund: A Federal fund dedicated to the development and preservation of the national highway system.

hiring hall: An employment organization, operated by a union, that sends union members to available jobs in shops with which the union has collective bargaining agreements; usually found in industries in which closed shops were the rule before they were outlawed by the Taft-Hartley Act. The present law requires that union-run hiring halls also send non-union members out on jobs, if they are registered with the hiring hall, but as a practical matter that is rare.

hiring rate: See accession rate.

histogram: See bar chart.

hoarding: Storing anything that is in short supply, whether for personal use, business use, or resale at anticipated higher scarcity prices. Examples are the storage of gasoline for personal use during a fuel shortage and the storage of metal money during a period of ruinous inflation.

holder: One who by delivery or endorsement, lawfully possesses the right to be paid the value of a money instrument.

holder in due course: One who legally holds a money instrument which has been received for value in good faith and timely, and without knowledge of any defect in the lawful right to be paid.

hold harmless clause: A contract provision absolving a contracting party from all liability arising from stated circumstances and placing that liability with another of the contracting parties. An example is a clause in a contract between author and publisher, in which the author takes all responsibility for defending libel suits and consequent damages from the contracted book. Courts may hold such clauses invalid as regards suits brought against both author and publisher.

holding company: A company that is primarily in the business of controlling other companies, fully or in part, usually directly owned subsidiaries.

holding the line: Resisting increases in prices and wages in an attempt to moderate or stop the pace of inflation; usually part of national economic policy.

holdover tenant: A tenant who has occupied property under the terms of a lease, and then continues to occupy after the lease term has ended; usually then going to a month-to-month tenancy with the consent of the landlord.

holiday pay: Pay for unworked holidays and extra pay for holidays worked; for example, double time on top of regular pay for a holiday worked, as provided in many collective bargaining agreements.

Hollerith code: A punched card information-representation system, coding alphabetical, numerical, and special information; named after its inventor, Herman Hollerith.

home computer: See microcomputer.

homeowner's insurance: Property insurance covering a wide range of hazards intrinsic to home ownership, such as fire, weather, theft, and some kinds of personal liabilities.

home relief. See relief.

homework: Work performed at home rather than at an employer's place of business. Quite common in the 18th, 19th, and early 20th centuries, homework had diminished considerably later in the 20th century. However, the recent widespread move toward flexible hours and part-time work has revived the practice, with free-lance and homeworking employees now commonly found in many industries.

home-work industry: See cottage industry.

honor: In finance, to pay or fulfill. For example, a bank honors a check by paying its lawful holder its face amount when it is presented for payment; a contracting party honors a contract by fulfilling it.

Hooper rating: The audience share achieved by radio programs, as measured by surveys conducted by the Hooper organization.

horizontal acquisition: The acquisition by one company of other companies doing essentially the same kinds of business as the acquiring company. Such combinations among companies that are significant factors in their industries are often considered by federal regulatory authorities to be combinations tending to diminish competition, in violation of antitrust laws.

horizontal transfer: A change of job within a company, resulting in different functions performed, but no real advance in either pay or responsibility.

hospital and surgical insurance: Insurance covering hospital, surgical, and related charges, such as anesthesia, nursing, medicines while in hospital, and intensive care; widely provided by Blue Cross, Blue Shield, and other private insurers.

hospitalization insurance: A group of insurances covering hospitalization and sometimes related expenses; a mixed set of arrangements, including individual, private, group, state and Federal insurance.

host computer: The controlling central processing unit in a computer-based distributed data processing system.

hot cargo: Goods made or distributed by a non-union or struck company, and handled under protest or not at all by unionized workers.

hot goods: Goods illegally acquired, such as the proceeds of a robbery.

hot issue: A stock in great demand; usually just after original issue, and therefore experiencing a considerable runup in market price.

hot money: 1. Investment capital that is repeatedly moved from one investment vehicle to another, and usually also internationally, seeking the highest possible short-term returns. **2.** Currency illegally acquired, such as the proceeds of a bank robbery or drug smuggling.

house brand: A brand name placed on a

product by a distributor or retailer, rather than a manufacturer. For example, air conditioners sold by several major retailers under their own brand names may be basically the same air conditioner, sometimes identical and sometimes with very small cosmetic differences between them, all manufactured by a single company.

housecleaning: The firing of a substantial number of employees all at once or within a short time span, usually during the course of a reorganization.

household: Any habitation occupied by a group of people living together or by one person living alone.

house item: See captive item.

housekeeping: In computer systems, programs and routines that are directly related to successful execution of programs, but not to the solution of specific problems.

house organ: A continuing publication created by a company or other organization for its own people, focusing on intra-organization matters; sometimes also distributed to outsiders, such as customers and distributors.

house-to-house selling: Outside selling directly to consumers, in which salespeople make direct calls on potential customers at home, with or without appointments. Examples are brush, vacuum cleaner, and encyclopedia salespeople. This kind of selling has become somewhat restricted due to Federal Trade Commission regulations on selling practices, but is still widespread in the United States.

HUD: See Department of Housing and Urban Development.

human engineering: An attempt to develop and apply production techniques that maximize efficiency and best use employee capabilities; quite closely related to the aims and techniques of time and motion study, and equally a matter of considerable labor-management friction and negotiation.

human relations: In business, the study of the interactive processes between people in work situations, and a body of personnel and management development theory and practice aimed at achieving corporate goals through humane management of those processes.

human resources administrator: A specialist in personnel development, charged with responsibility for human resources planning and administration.

human resources planning: Organizational planning aimed at maximizing job satisfactions, securing maximum efficiency of output, and the training, retraining, and general development of those employed. Although historically part of the overall charge of those handling personnel, many larger organizations have in recent years set up separate administrative groups to maximize employee development and avoid confusion of this function with industrial relations functions and negotiations.

hush money: Blackmail or bribes paid to try to cover up illegal activities or legal activities the payer does not want known: for example, blackmail paid to cover up embezzlement or to cover up a public official's drinking problem.

hybrid computer: A computer that shares some of the qualities of both digital and analog computers.

hydroponics: The raising of plants in water rather than in soil; it is the object of considerable research and development attention by government and industry, aimed at helping solve world food shortages.

hype: Exaggeration aimed at securing a sale or promoting a person or activity; short for hyperbole.

hyperinflation: See runaway inflation.

hypothecated stock: Stock that has been used as loan collateral, and that is therefore so encumbered as to be incapable of being traded, as clear title cannot be passed.

hypothecation: The use of pledged collateral to secure a loan. In law, possession of the pledged collateral stays with the owner of the collateral, though the lender has the right to force sale of the collateral to cover default of the loan. In practice, collateral which cannot be delivered, such as a ship, stays with the borrower; collateral which can be delivered, such as securities and warehouse receipts, usually are physically moved to the lender.

hypothesis: See alternative hypothesis.

I

ICC: See Interstate Commerce Commission.

ICFTU: See International Confederation of Free Trade Unions.

iconic model: A research model, constructed to simulate as closely as possible real products and situations, as in replication of a moon rocket launch under controlled laboratory conditions.

IDA: See International Development Association.

IDB: See Inter-American Development Bank.

idle capacity: Unused ability to produce on the part of a production facility, measuring the time allocated to production against the time that would be allocated to production if the facility were in full normal use. For example, a steel plant that normally operates seven days a week and 24 hours a day is operating at only two-thirds of capacity if it is working seven days a week and 16 hours a day; but an electronic assembly plant normally operating five days a week and 16 hours a day may, for accounting and reporting purposes, be operating at full capacity.

idle time: Unused production time within a period of otherwise normal use, due to any of the supply, machine, people, or business breakdowns that can impede the orderly flow of production.

IDP: See integrated data processing.

IFC: See International Finance Corporation.

illegal strike: A strike in violation of law, contract, or prohibiting injunction; for example, a strike by public employees in the face of a law or injunction prohibiting that strike, or a wildcat strike while a collective bargaining contract is in force.

illiquid: Describing a company or individual not in possession of sufficient cash to meet its cash needs and facing difficulty in raising that cash.

ILO: See International Labor Organization.

image: The public impression of an individual or organization. The object of a great deal of advertising and public relations attention, and an increasingly important part of a personal or business reputation, favorable public image is much sought after by politicians, some celebrities, and many business organizations.

IMF: See International Monetary Fund.

immunity: A legal status exempting one from the performance of normal citizens' obligations; for example, an exemption from jury duty because of one's occupation.

immunity from prosecution: A very special status granted by special circumstances, such as the granting of that immunity by a grand jury in return for testimony.

imperfect competition: A construct in economics that posits a marketplace in which some sellers can influence such market factors as prices and supplies, in contrast to a marketplace that is in theory entirely free, with supply and demand the sole factors influencing prices.

implied: In the law, an intent which is inferred from the circumstances surrounding a situation or transaction, and which becomes the legal equivalent of an expressed intent, as with implied contracts or implied trusts, which under some circumstances become equivalent in the law to written contracts and trusts.

implied contract: See contract.

implied trust: See trust.

implied warranty: See warranty.

import: 1. Goods made in other countries, purchased abroad, and shipped into the buying country. 2. To procure those goods abroad and bring them into a country. 3. Popularly, all goods and services originating in one geographic unit and brought into another. States are described as importing goods from other states. Consulting services are sometimes described as being imported from abroad.

import credit: See letter of credit.

import duty: A tax levied by a country on products brought into it from abroad.

import license: A license issued by government, authorizing import of goods that are in some way regulated by government. That regulation may be pursuant to public policy favoring some home products by limiting imports of foreign products; may be limiting trade with unfriendly nations; or may be limiting trade in specific goods, such as some drugs.

import quota: A government-imposed limitation on imports of a product or products. That limitation may be on the quantity or the value of goods imported; may apply to some countries and not to others, or to countries unequally; and may impost different tax levels on different values and quantities imported.

impound: To physically take possession of and hold on behalf of the law and its agents, as in the taking and holding of actual or potential evidence by a court during legal proceedings.

imprest fund: A cash fund or bank account maintained for payments that are made in cash, most commonly used as a petty cash fund. A fixed maximum sum is kept in the fund, and, as the fund is depleted, that sum is periodically brought up to maximum.

impulse buying: Consumer goods buying that is done substantially at whim at the point of purchase, such as the purchase of a magazine at the checkout counter of a supermarket, or the purchase of a toy seen while walking by a store window. Such unplanned buying is often of nonessentials, but many consumers also buy essential goods on impulse, rather than by plan or budget.

impute: To attribute on the basis of an estimate or a construct based less on hard data than on informed guesses.

imputed costs: Costs that are estimated rather than specifically determinable through the generation of accounting information, such as cancelled checks and journal entries. Sometimes such costs are actually incurred, but are difficult to allocate and are therefore spread over several functions on an estimated allocation basis; sometimes such costs are not actual, but are figured as if they had been incurred, such as the foregone interest from other sources that might have been earned on the amount of an owner's investment in a business.

imputed income: Income that is not actual but equivalent to what might have been earned had something been paid for in cash rather than in non-cash equivalents, such as work performed in a family business by family members who are not paid in cash but in such non-cash equivalents as food, housing and clothing.

inactive account: A banking or brokerage account which has few or no transactions and modest balances over a substantial period of time, usually measured in years.

in-and-out trade: In the securities industry, a

quick sale following a securities purchase, usually in the hope of turning a quick profit on the transaction. Speculators often engage in in-and-out trading.

in-and-out trader: One whose pattern of securities trading is marked by a relatively large number of in-and-out trades; usually a speculator.

in bond: See bond.

inc.: Abbreviation for incorporated.

incentive: Anything moving people to the performance of desired actions, such as a rate of pay that increases as productivity increases or a prize for performance.

incentive contract: A contract that specifies extra rewards for better-than-contracted performance.

incentive pay: A compensation system based wholly or partially on performance rather than on time spent on the job, such as a piecework system in which workers are paid by the number of pieces produced rather than by the hour. Pay incentives can take many forms, and are often coupled with hourly and weekly pay systems to induce greater productivity.

income: 1. Total business or personal revenue received from all sources, usually within a defined period, such as a month, calendar year, or fiscal year. **2.** The total increase in net assets achieved by a business in any accounting period. **3.** In general, any item of determinable value received.

income averaging: As provided for in federal personal income tax law, the ability to lump current income and several previous years' income for figuring income tax rates; when current income is much higher than the average income, lower tax rates apply.

income bond: A bond bearing interest that is only payable out of the profits of its issuer, in contrast to bonds that carry interest as an unconditional debt obligation of the corporation.

income distribution: The spread of a nation's income among its population, indicated by the numbers of people earning or otherwise receiving income at a series of given income levels; used in analyzing changes in the apportionment of a nation's wealth over a period of time and also in comparing patterns of income distribution between countries.

income fund: A mutual fund oriented primarily toward the generation of current income for its holders, rather than toward growth securities.

income portfolio: A portfolio of securities carried by an investor or investing organization, oriented toward the production of current income, rather than toward rapid appreciation with little income.

income property: Real property used by its owner primarily as a source of income; for example, a farm leased to tenants or rental property.

income statement: An accounting statement, summarizing the income, expenses, and resultant profit or loss of a business organization for any accounting period; usually issued yearly, often quarterly and monthly as well; a profit and loss statement (P&L).

income tax: Any tax based on the income received, usually net, of any defined economic unit, including individuals and both business and non-business organizations. Income taxes are usually graduated with rates rising according to net income. Federal income taxes were levied during the Civil War, starting in 1861, and stopping after the War; modern federal income taxes date from 1913; state and local income taxes also developed after 1913.

incontestable: Firmly binding upon the insurer after a specified period following issuance of the policy; applied to certain policy protections, notably in life and health insurance. For example, a health insurance policy may waive the right to contest a heart condition as pre-existing, and therefore not covered, after one year from policy issuance; that policy protection then becomes incontestable.

inconvertible: Unable to be exchanged for precious metals, describing money which is backed only by the faith and credit of its issuer, as has been officially true of United States currency since 1971 and unofficially true for some decades earlier.

incorporated: See incorporation.

incorporation: 1. One of the three major forms of business organization, the others being sole proprietorship and partnership, and the form favored by most medium-sized and large businesses, as it provides for limited ownership liability, easy ownership transfer in the form of stock sale, multiple ownership by stockholders, maximum financing flexibility, and a wide variety of other advantages over the other two ownership forms. **2.** The process of becoming a legal corporation.

incorporation papers: See certificate of incorporation.

increment: Any increase of growth in steps, usually small, rather than continuous.

incremental: 1. In business, describing an increase, usually relatively small, tied to existing business operations, as in the addition of an element that costs little to an existing product line, with both the cost and the additional revenue being thought of as incremental. **2.** In accounting, marginal, describing a cost that results from the exercise of choices in production or marketing.

indemnity: 1. The amount of insurance coverage specified in an insurance policy. **2.** A governmental guarantee of immunity from prosecution in certain stated circumstances, normally by legislative action.

indemnity bond: A bond guaranteeing against losses caused by the employee or agent of the indemnifying party, who is the guarantor of that bond.

indent: A purchase order sent by a customer to an importer, authorizing purchase of specified goods either at specific prices or within a stated price range, from either a specific source or whatever source available.

indenture: 1. A deed owned by two or more parties which states their rights and obligations toward each other regarding the jointly owned property. **2.** An apprenticeship agreement, by which one party is legally bound to serve another for a specified period of time; common in colonial times, but now prohibited by law. **3.** An instrument naming a trustee to act for all holders of a bond issue and stating the amount, form, and conditions involved in the issue.

independent: An organization or individual operating alone, and not tied to a group, company, or association. Examples are an independent store operating outside of and competing with chain stores; an independent union or employer, operating outside the AFL-CIO or the trade associations; or a contractor who performs functions that are part of a job, but who is not an employee.

independent store: A store operating as a single entity, rather than as part of a group or chain of stores.

independent union: A union operating independently of the AFL-CIO.

independent variable: A known factor in an experimental situation; the value of an independent variable will be used to help predict the values of dependent, or unknown, variables.

index: 1. Any finding device functioning as a guide to the content of a body of information, such as a book or a computer data base. **2.** A measure of such factors as cost and performance, such as the Cost of Living Index and the Dow-Jones stock market indexes.

indexing: An investment technique, in a mutual fund or an individual portfolio, that attempts to organize and weigh its holdings so that it will perform much as a specific major stock index performs, such as Dow Jones or Standard and Poor's.

index number: A number designated as a marker within a body of developing statistical information, such as the Cost of Living

Index of the United States government, which gives data from the base year of 1967, an index of 100, and measures changes in the cost of living from that point, with the index having reached 200 during 1978.

indirect cost: A cost that cannot be directly attributed to a specific product made or service performed, but which is attributable to a related function. Indirect costs are usually allocated over several products or services in one or more overhead categories, such as maintenance or administration.

indirect labor cost: A labor cost, such as general maintenance staff, which cannot be directly attributed to a specific product made or service performed, but which is normally spread over several products or services in one or more overhead categories.

indirect liability: A potential liability, that may become a real liability in the future; for example, the co-signer of a note may become liable if the primary borrower defaults on the note.

indirect material cost: A material cost, such as the supplies used in general plant maintenance, which must be spread over several products and services as overhead because it cannot be directly attributed to a product made or service performed.

indirect taxes: Taxes on things, rights, and privileges, such as sales, franchise, and excise taxes, rather than taxes directly on people and organizations, such as income taxes.

individualized instruction: See programmed instruction.

individual proprietorship: See sole proprietorship.

Individual Retirement Account (IRA): A tax-advantaged pension plan arrangement available to individuals under Federal law. For many people this is the only kind of tax-advantaged pension plan available, although some are able to set up other kinds of pension plans, such as Keogh plans.

indivisibility: In accessing economy of scale, the inability of certain production factors to be subdivided, resulting in a necessary minimum scale of production. For example, steel of a given quality cannot be satisfactorily made in furnaces of less than a certain size, the size of the furnace setting the minimal scale of production.

industrial accident: An accident occurring on a job or connected with a job, and compensable through Workmen's Compensation insurance and court action.

industrial average: See average.

industrial bank: A commercial bank primarily oriented toward the extension of consumer credit, in contrast to commercial banks primarily oriented toward business banking. Sometimes called Morris Plan banks, after Arthur Morris, a pioneer in the development of consumer credit financing, they are called industrial banks because they were originally conceived of as appealing to workers in industry.

industrial democracy: A theory calling for the participation of workers in the management of their plants and industries, through participation at all levels of company and trade association management; it exists experimentally in Sweden and a few other countries.

industrial disease: An illness incurred due to the nature of work and the conditions under which that work is performed, such as the occurrence of "black lung" disease among miners.

industrial distributor: A wholesaler who sells primarily to industrial customers, rather than to retailers.

industrial engineering: The branch of engineering that specializes in the organization and development of the production process, attempting to organize all the factors of production most effectively and cost-efficiently.

industrial espionage: The covert and illegal seeking out of commercial secrets belonging to others; for example, the bribing of employees to reveal coveted secrets by a competitor or the wiretapping of a competitor's telephones or premises in pursuit of such secrets.

industrial hygiene: The branch of the health professions that focuses on the health and welfare of people at work.

industrialist: One who controls one or more industrial enterprises; usually implying the control of large enterprises and the management of large money and material resources.

industrialization: The development of widespread basic industry and mechanization within a country; a worldwide trend since the Industrial Revolution.

industrial migration: The movement of plants and whole industries to new geographical locations, spurred by such factors as the availability of less expensive labor, cheaper resources, and tax advantages.

industrial production index: A federally maintained index of the current level of national manufacturing, extractive, and utilities production, as measured against the currently used base period; a major indicator of the current state of the nation's economic health.

industrial psychology: The branch of psychology dealing with the behavior of those in the workplace, with major focus placed on the successful hiring, training, and management of workers.

industrial relations: The multiple relationships between all those in the workplace, with major focus on the relations between management and labor, both in collective bargaining and on the job day to day.

industrial revenue bond: A kind of municipal bond offered to investors, funding tax-advantaged arrangements as inducements for businesses to locate in municipalities. These arrangements are often very advantageous in terms of both taxes and plant construction costs. The bonds themselves are not federally tax-exempt to their purchasers.

Industrial Revolution: The beginning of the development of modern industry, in Western Europe as a whole and especially in England, during the 18th and early 19th centuries, and now often generally applied to any nation or group of nations in the process of industrialization.

industrial spy: One who is engaged in industrial espionage, full-time or part-time, amateur or professional.

industrial spying: See industrial espionage.

industrial stock: The common stock of an industrial company, as distinguished from the common stocks of railroads and utilities.

industrial store: See company store.

industrial union: A labor union organized by plant and industry, embracing all the kinds of workers in one union, rather than in several unions organized by craft. The United Auto Workers, for example, which attempts to organize and represent all the kinds of workers employed in an automobile plant, is an industrial union; the carpenters union, representing only a single trade, is a craft union.

industrial waste: The waste products associated with industrial production, such as the chemical byproducts of some industrial processes, which often pose hazards to the environment and must be disposed of at considerable cost.

industry: Firms involved in manufacturing, processing, and extraction; the term is used more loosely as a synonym for any kind of business.

industry-wide bargaining: Collective bargaining between unions and groups of employers representing all or most of the major employers within an industry, such as the steel industry.

inelastic demand: Demand for goods and services that does not fluctuate or that fluctuates relatively little in relation to price changes. For example, the demand for home heating oil is relatively inelastic in the short term; those who heat with oil can moderate their demand only slightly, even when faced with massive price increases.

in fee: See fee simple.

inflation: A rise in the general level of prices within an economy, accompanied by a decrease in the purchasing power of the unit of currency used in that economy. Inflation is often, but not always, accompanied by losses in real purchasing power, as when a cost of living index goes up by 10%, while average wages go up by only 5%, with a resultant 5% loss of purchasing power; in contrast, if average wages went up 15%, the net would be a 5% increase in purchasing power. But under conditions of rapid inflation, adulterations of quality and smaller quantities supplied at similar prices create hidden inflation as well, pulling the real purchasing power of the dollar down considerably more sharply than the standard figures indicate.

inflationary gap: The difference between available investment money from all private and public sources and the total amount of savings. In some economic theory, this difference is thought to be responsible for the pace of inflation.

inflationary spiral: A tendency within an economy experiencing inflation to accelerate the rate of inflation, as different interest groups struggle to raise their incomes to meet, and in some instances to exceed, the current rate of inflation. To increase their real incomes, businesses raise prices; workers demand higher wages; farmers demand higher prices; governments raise taxes; professionals raise fees, in a continuing spiral.

inflation hedge: An investment calculated to maintain the value of current holdings in spite of rapid inflation; examples are real estate when it is rising faster than the inflation rate, or government securities in a period when the interest paid on them is higher than the combined appreciation and dividends available in common stock investments.

informal organizational structure: The unofficial operating structure in an organization, in contrast to the formal structure set up in the organization chart. For example, the president or general manager of a subsidiary may be formally responsible for supervising production, while in practice an assistant, with neither title nor pay commensurate with the job, handles all production questions that arise.

information: See data.

information explosion: The worldwide expansion of data in all business, scientific, and technical areas in this century and especially in the period since the end of World War II.

information retrieval: The process of getting desired data out of any stored body of information, as in using a subject index to locate the page on which the answer to a specific question can be found. Much attention is currently being paid to the problems of retrieval of information stored in computerized data bases; while discrete bids of information and documents are being successfully stored and retrieved, success on "random access" questions—that is the direct answering of a wide range of specific questions by retrieval from a computer memory—is still "just around the corner."

information returns: Tax returns which must by law be filed with the taxing authorities, supplying information on payments made to others, for checking purposes, as when an employer files a form telling the federal government what wages have been paid and to whom.

information science: See information storage and retrieval.

information storage: The entry of information and holding of an accumulated body of information in any kind of data base; usually referring to the development of a body of information stored in computer-readable form and capable of being retrieved by computer.

infrastructure: The body of organizations,

people, and skills that binds together the economic operations of a nation and defines that nation's level of technology and socio-political sophistication. Infrastructure includes such factors as the level of technical skills available; the transportation industry; the telephone, telegraph, and broadcasting systems; the power systems; and the public health and education systems.

infringement: Violation by illegal use of the lawful rights of others who hold patents, copyrights, or trademarks.

inheritance: That which is received through a bequest from another; also that which is held and may be passed to another by bequest.

inheritance taxes: Taxes on the receipt of property by inheritance, and therefore paid by inheritors rather than the estate.

initial program loader (IPL): A program controlling transfer of the first portion of operating programs into the system, where they can proceed under their own direction.

injunction: A writ prohibiting a defendant from doing or continuing to do something which is, or can become, harmful to a plaintiff. An injunction is often issued by a court to restrain a defendant from pursuing a certain course of action while a legal proceeding is being adjudicated. For example, an injunction may be issued to restrain a defendant in a patent or trademark infringement case while the suit is pending, as continued infringement could cause irremediable harm to the plaintiff during the time it takes to complete the suit, even if the plaintiff ultimately wins. Injunctions have also been widely used by employers against unions in collective bargaining disputes.

inland bill: A bill of exchange drawn and payable entirely within one state, such as California, in contrast to a bill drawn or payable outside the state, known as a foreign bill of exchange.

inland marine insurance: See floater.

input: Originally, all data entered into a computer; now popularly used to describe any kind of information or opinion from any source.

input job stream: An ordered series of job control statements entering a computer system, sometimes including input data.

input/output control system (IOCS): A group of routines directing input and output operations within a computer system.

input/output equipment (I/O): Equipment used to access a computer, putting data in and taking data out.

insertion order: A formal order to place advertising in a publication.

insider: One who, because of his or her relationship to a firm, has access to private information that may affect the market performance of that firm's stock, such as an employee, member of the board of directors, attorney, or accountant.

insolvency: Inability to pay debts as they become due; usually a prelude to bankruptcy.

inspection: An examination aimed at determining whether defined standards have been met, as in inspection of a company's books by an independent auditor or the final inspection of an engine block on an automobile foundry assembly line to see whether or not it leaks or has cracks.

installment: A part payment on a financial obligation, often made periodically, as in part payment for a purchase or of a loan.

installment bond: A single bond that matures essentially piece by piece, the principal of which is paid in installments rather than all at once. It has the same net payment effect as a set of serial bonds, which mature one by one over a period of time, differing only in that it is a single bond.

installment buying: A widespread form used for the credit buying of consumer goods in which the buyer pays for goods purchased in a series of payments, usually equally spaced and of equal size; including interest to the seller. Once the main means of credit buying in the United States, installment buying has now been partly replaced by credit card buying, in which the consumer buys with credit extended by a commercial lender, usually a bank, and repays the bank, often on a revolving credit basis.

institutional advertising: Advertising that seeks to enhance the image of the organization advertising rather than to sell specific products directly, though it is often aimed at aiding the sale of the company's products in general, as when a company under attack for damaging the environment buys advertising stressing its social responsibility and public interest contributions.

institutional investor: An investing organization, such as a bank, mutual fund, pension fund, foundation, or other repository of substantial investment funds, that buys and sells large blocks of securities.

instruction: In computer systems, a direction to the computer to perform a specific act.

instrument: A document, embodying a formal and written legal entity, such as a contract, a will, or any of a whole range of financial obligations, such as checks, notes, and securities.

insurable interest: Any interest held by one in another's life or in property of any kind, to the extent of the loss that might be suffered if that life were lost or that property were damaged or destroyed. An insurable interest must be shown before insurance will be granted.

insurance: A legal agreement, by which one party, the insurer, agrees to compensate the other, the insured, for losses resulting from the occurrence of specified events and usually up to specified limits. Those insured must have insurable interests. Usually, the insurer is an insurance company, which covers the insured through an insurance policy, on which the insured pays premiums periodically.

insurance policy: A legally enforceable contract, in which an insurance company under-takes to cover the losses of an insured, in return for premium payments.

insured: One with an insurable interest whose potential losses are covered by a legally enforceable insurance policy.

insurer: One, usually an insurance company, undertaking to cover the losses of others by issuing insurance.

intangible assets: Assets that have no physical, determinable bodies, such as goodwill, patents, licenses, and trademarks, in contrast to such tangible assets as real estate, negotiable securities, and currency.

intangible value: The value of a business beyond its tangible assets, including such intangible assets as goodwill, patents, licenses, and trademarks.

integrated data processing (IDP): Data processing that is treated as a total system from the acquisition of data to its end uses.

integration: The extent to which related functions are joined in industrial enterprises, as in the instance of an aluminum company which is a producer, fabricator, and marketer of aluminum products, and therefore is responsible for every step of production and distribution.

intelligence: Developing information and insight into the plans and objectives of others, often of others who are thought to be in some sort of adversary position, such as competitors; often a combination of painstaking fact gathering and analysis and espionage, but quite often unaccompanied by espionage.

intelligence quotient (IQ): A score derived from a test purporting to measure individual intelligence; usually a ratio of mental age, as derived from the test score, divided by chronological age, then multiplied by 100.

intelligence test: Any standardized test attempting to measure intelligence by means of setting questions to answer or problems to solve.

INTELSAT: See International Telecommunications Satellite Consortium.

intensive cultivation: An attempt to maximize crop yields from land under cultivation, using the best available combinations of techniques, seeds, soil and plant nutrients, and irrigation; used where land is in short supply relative to the farm product needs of the population, in both technically advanced and developing nations.

Inter-American Development Bank (IDB): An international financing agency, formed under the auspices of the Organization of American States in 1959, in which most of the countries of North, South, and Central America participate. It raises money through bond issues and loans money for economic development purposes to both government and private organizations.

interchangeable parts: Those parts of a machine, production process, or product that are standard; for example, the carburetor of a particular make, model and year of a motor vehicle; the keys of a typewriter; or indeed most of the parts used in modern industrial society.

interest: 1. A legal right to all or part of something of value, as in an insurable interest, a beneficial interest under the terms of a will or trust, or an ownership interest, through ownership of all or part of a business. **2.** A sum of money paid for the use of money, usually expressed as a percentage of money borrowed, as in 10% over the principal of a loan charged for the loan.

interest inventory: An attempt to determine personal interests by means of interviewing technique or a standardized questionnaire.

interest rate: The interest percentage charged by a lender for a loan, which varies with the kind of loan, the money market, the general economic conditions, and the financial condition of the borrower, and therefore the amount of risk involved in making the loan. Stated and actual rates of interest being charged are often different, but true rates of interest charged retail borrowers must be clearly stated under the provisions of truth-in-lending laws.

interface: The facing and touching boundaries of two or more systems. Although originally used in business as a computer term, the term is now widely used to refer to the meeting place of any two or more contiguous systems, such as the government-business interface or the military-industrial interface.

interim: 1. Any period of time between fixed dates, such as the period between now and the first of next year. **2.** Describing a document, instrument, or function which by its nature is temporary, usually intended to be superseded by another, more permanent document, instrument, or function.

interim certificate: A temporary document, effective until a more permanent document is or is not issued, such as a temporary proof of insurance or automobile registration.

interim report: 1. A report covering less than a final report, issued as a temporary statement. **2.** In accounting, any report that covers less than a twelve-month period.

interindustry competition: Marketplace competition between industries producing different kinds of products aimed at meeting similar consumer needs, as between aluminum and steel or cotton and synthetic fibers, in contrast to competition between companies in the same industry.

interleaving: 1. The placement of updating pages into books of information. **2.** The placement of parts of one computer program in between parts of other computer programs, so that programs can be executed seemingly simultaneously, while actually executed during the pauses in other programs; also called multiprogramming.

interlocking directorates: Company boards of directors that are related to each other by the same individuals holding seats on those boards. Though holding of seats on the boards of competing companies is formally prohibited by law, in practice many American corporations are so related through major stockholders and directors in common, often through bankers, lawyers, accountants, and retired executives, who may hold a dozen directors' seats, some of them in competing corporations.

interlocutory decree: A temporary or partial judgment of a pending legal action, which will be replaced by a final decree on conclusion of the action.

internal auditor: An auditor who is an employee of the organization being audited, responsible to company management for the performance of audit functions.

internal code: A data representation system used in certain computers that is based on characters and computer words, rather than on bits and blocks.

internal organ: See house organ.

Internal Revenue Code: The body of statutes codifying the tax laws of the Federal Government.

Internal Revenue Service (IRS); That Federal agency responsible for the enforcement of the tax laws of the United States, except as to several excise taxes, and for promulgation of regulations interpreting those laws.

international balance of payments: See balance of payments.

International Bank For Reconstruction and Development: Also known as the World Bank, this is a major international financing agency, funded by a large number of participating nations, operating independently of, but affiliated with the United Nations. Formed at the Bretton Woods Conference of 1944, it has functioned since then to foster worldwide economic development, with special emphasis on the funding of economic take-off projects in the developing nations.

international commodity agreement: An agreement between nations producing basic commodities to set a common market stance vis-à-vis those who consume their commodities, to achieve the best possible economic results from sale of their commodities on the world markets, as when oil or coffee producers agree to limit production and set prices in common. Carried a step further, the nations participating in such an agreement sometimes develop more formal monopolistic combinations, as when oil-producing nations form themselves into a cartel.

International Confederation of Free Trade Unions (ICFTU): An international organization, composed of trade unions from many of the countries outside the Soviet and Chinese spheres of influence.

international corporation: A company that does business in several countries, usually having major offices, subsidiaries, and affiliated corporations abroad. The term has to some extent been superseded by the term multinational corporation.

international creditor: See balance of indebtedness.

international debtor: See balance of indebtedness.

International Development Association (IDA): An international agency affiliated with the International Bank For Reconstruction and Development, known as the World Bank; it functions as a conduit for funds from the major industrial nations to the developing nations, lending to those nations' governments money at little or no interest for a wide range of developmental projects.

International Finance Corporation (IFC): An international agency affiliated with the International Bank For Reconstruction and Development, known as the World Bank; it lends money to private investors in underdeveloped nations to further the development of the private economic sectors of those countries.

international investment: Investment abroad of capital from any private or public source, whether for anticipated economic or political profit.

International Labor Organization (ILO): An

international agency affiliated with the United Nations, taking up a large number of labor and social welfare questions throughout the world.

International Monetary Fund (IMF): An international financial agency, affiliated with the United Nations, which attempts to stabilize the world balance of trade and to smooth international money market fluctuations. Formed at the Bretton Woods Conference of 1944, the Fund has been especially active in attempts to aid the developing nations.

international payments agreements: An agreement between two or more nations specifying the terms by which payments due between them are to be settled, often resulting in conservation of available foreign exchange through use of goods and their own national currencies for such settlements.

international payments disequilibrium: A tendency on the part of a country to develop a continuously unfavorable international balance of payments, usually resulting from a medium or long-term tendency toward an unfavorable international balance of trade.

international representative: A full-time paid union employee, responsible for some area of union activity, such as the administation and representation of a group of local unions.

International Telecommunications Satellite Consortium (INTELSAT): The international organization governing the development of the world communications system, involving joint use of communications satellites.

international trade: The trading of goods and services between the nations of the world.

international union: A trade union that has affiliates in more than one country. Many unions functioning in the United States, for example, have Canadian affiliates.

interrupt: In computer operations, a signal causing a break in the flow of processing, whether from inside or outside the system.

interstate carrier: A carrier doing business in more than one state and therefore falling under Federal regulatory jurisdiction.

interstate commerce: Commerce involving two or more states, which therefore may be constitutionally regulated by the Federal government. Court interpretations of what constitutes interstate commerce have widened very considerably in the last several decades, with the effect of bringing more and more commercial and related matters within the Federal government's regulatory control.

Interstate Commerce Commission (ICC): An independent Federal regulatory agency, charged with interpreting and enforcing the Interstate Commerce Act of 1887, and with licensing, regulating the conduct of, and setting rates for all United States land and water carriers.

interview: A one-to-one discussion, whether face to face or over a communications channel, for any of a wide range of business purposes, including such matters as job seeking, market research, news media coverage, and data collection.

inter vivos: Between living people; usually in law applied to the voluntary transfer of property from one living person to another through the establishment of a trust or the presenting of a gift.

intestate: Having died without having made a valid will; also, the individual who has died without making such a will.

in the black: Describing a business that is operating at a profit, in contrast to "in the red," which describes a business operating at a loss. The term stems from the use of black ink by accountants when summarizing profitable operations, while red ink was used to summarize unprofitable operations.

in the red: In a loss position; operating a business at a loss; from the accounting practice of noting losses in red ink; contrasts with "in the black," or operating at a profit.

intrastate carrier: A carrier doing business

solely within one state, and therefore falling under state regulatory jurisdiction.

intrastate commerce: Commerce carried on exclusively within a state, and therefore not subject to Federal regulation. Court interpretations in recent decades have greatly narrowed the scope of intrastate and greatly widened the scope of interstate commerce.

intrinsic: That which is inherent in something by the very nature of the thing itself; usually applied to matters of value, as in assessing the underlying value of a silver plate in terms of what the silver in the plate would bring at current market prices if the plate were melted down.

inventory: To survey and record all things possessed; and the possessions so surveyed themselves. In this sense, a set of ideas, a body of trust property, a body of skills and people, or the material goods in the possession of a business may all be inventoried, and be inventory.

inventory change: The increase or decrease in the value of inventories carried from the beginning to the end of a given period. In economics, the quantity and kinds of inventory changes are thought to be important business cycle indicators.

inventory control: The process of accounting for and regulating materials moving into and passing out of inventory.

inventory management: The management of inventory for maximum profitability and efficiency of operation, as in carefully controlled buying to take advantage of seasonal price advantages, without risking shortage of necessary inventory items for use in production.

inventory turnover: The number of times inventory is used up and must be replaced in a given period, usually twelve months.

inventory valuation: The process of assessing the value of an inventory as of a certain time; the accounting method chosen, such as fifo and lifo, often greatly affects the value stated.

invested capital: The total value of the ownership shares held by the owners of a business.

investment: **1.** In the widest sense, any attempt to profit from the use of money or other valuables. Generally, investment is the attempt to use money to make money, but such things as time and love are in popular usage described as having been invested as well, often for anticipated non-monetary rewards. **2.** A store of value.

investment advisor: One who is in the business of offering investment advice, usually for a fee, and is registered to do so with the Federal government as well. Such advice may take the form of a published report, individual counselling, or both.

investment analysis: The evaluation of investment vehicles to determine key advantages and disadvantages in terms of profitability, risk, and investment goals, and the development of recommendations as to investment actions to be taken.

investment banking: The business of bringing securities to market, including both ownership equities and debt obligations, both private and public, either by issue to the public or by private placement to a few investors.

investment capital: See capital.

investment club: A group of investors who pool some resources and invest the resulting sum as a single fund, aiming to achieve better investment results than individual investing would bring.

investment company: A company formed solely for the purpose of selling shares in itself to investors, thereby creating an investment fund, either an open-end mutual fund selling as many shares as possible to the public or a closed-end fund which raises a fixed sum of money and uses only that fund for investment on the behalf of the fund's investors.

investment counsel: See investment advisor.

investment credit: In Federal taxation, tax credits allowed business for investment in machinery and equipment during a tax year.

investment property: See income property.

invisible export income: Income from both the sale of intangibles and investments abroad, in contrast to income from the sale of tangibles abroad, included in a nation's current account in computing the balance of payments. It includes such items as income from the sale of insurance, banking and other financial services; the proceeds of tourism; interest on deposits in foreign banks; and other investment income.

invisible import expenditures: Payments made by a country and its nationals for intangibles purchased from and investment return into other countries; included in a nation's current account in computing the balance of payments.

invoice: An itemized list of items purchased or sold; often attached to a bill for goods sold or services rendered.

involuntary bankruptcy: See bankruptcy.

IOCS: See input/output control system.

IOU: A written statement, signed by one, acknowledging a specific amount of debt to another, and constituting a legal, though informal and non-negotiable debt instrument.

IPL: See initial program loader.

IQ: See intelligence quotient.

IRA: See individual retirement account.

irregular: A piece of consumer goods, such as an item of clothing, which is in some way less than standard, though claimed by its maker to be entirely usable, and which is normally sold at a considerable discount and with less than normal quality guarantees.

irrevocable trust: A trust which is permanent, and may not be revoked by its maker; the main form taken by trusts, constituting passage of title to trust property and removal of that property from the estate of the trust's maker.

IRS: See Internal Revenue Service.

issue: In the securities industry, a new body of stock or debt instruments placed on the market for public or private sale.

issued capital stock: The amount of a company's authorized capital stock which has been issued to its shareholders; the balance of a company's authorized and unissued stock being held by a company as its treasury stock.

issue price: The price placed on a new stock or bond issue by those who bring it to market, usually its underwriters.

itemized deductions: A series of personal deductions taken on a Federal, state, or local income tax "long form" return, in contrast to the taking of a specified sum in lieu of that itemization, as on the popularly termed "short form."

iterate: In computer processing, to repeat the same processes over and over again until a specified point is reached; to loop.

itinerant worker: A mobile worker, who moves to follow a series of jobs, usually of a temporary or casual nature, such as unskilled jobs in agriculture.

COLLEGE OF THE SEQUOIAS
LIBRARY

J

jawboning: Discussion between a national administration trying to control the rate of inflation and those aiming to raise prices or wages more than that administration thinks healthy for the national economy, when such increases are legally uncontrolled; often accompanied by critical public statements from that administration.

JCL: See job control language.

JD: See juris doctor.

job: 1. A unit of work, consisting of a specific set of defined tasks, as in fulfillment of an order by a warehouse or by a computer system. **2.** A synonym for occupation. **3.** To sell to others in quantity lots, usually for resale by them to others in units; to function as a wholesaler.

job action: Concerted action by workers that is less than a strike, such as a mass sick call-in or a slowdown on the job, aimed at securing demands or protesting management action.

job analysis: The study of a unit of work or of many units of work comprising all or part of an occupation; usually conducted by management, aiming to get the job done most efficiently and profitably.

job analyst: One who is professionally engaged in the business of job analysis.

jobber: One who buys in large lots from a producer, wholesaler, or larger jobber and resells to either smaller jobbers or retailers.

job bias: See discrimination.

jobbing: See jobber

job classification: The categorizing of jobs within a company or industry by grades, usually with uniform pay scales corresponding to those grades, reflecting an attempt to group jobs by comparable skills and experience.

job control language (JCL): A computer language used to prepare programs that will run jobs in a computer system.

job description: A written description of all the main elements comprising a job, including responsibilities, authorizations, limits, and other job-defining elements.

job dilution: The separation of a job performed by a single skilled worker into its component parts, followed by reassignment of those parts among several workers, some of whom are substantially less skilled and lower paid than that skilled worker, resulting in less total payment to workers for the job performed.

job enlargement: The assignment of broader responsibilities to a worker on a job, aimed at making that job more interesting than before, encouraging fuller worker participation in the process of production, and thereby increasing productivity.

job enrichment: An attempt on the part of management to enhance worker productivity by supplying any of a number of new responsibilities, recognitions, and opportunities, all aimed at ameliorating job monotony and improving job attractiveness.

job evaluation: The process of placing a wage value on a job and the wage value itself; normally applies to a whole range of jobs within an enterprise, and is an attempt to develop a patterned structure of wages within the enterprise.

job hopper: A person who moves quickly from job to job, staying nowhere very long; generally regarded as a potentially unstable employee by those seeking to fill a job.

job lot: A body of merchandise sold as a single lot, usually at a discount, consisting of several kinds of goods grouped together in small quantities, which would normally be sold in larger lots by kind of goods.

job lot buying: The purchasing of only those materials needed for a particular job; often used by those fulfilling a specific contract, rather than manufacturing standard goods.

job order: An order or requisition, usually written, directing that something be done, such as the production of the number of units of a product needed to fulfill a customer order, or the accomplishment of a plant maintenance task.

job order costing: A cost accounting system that accumulates all costs associated with a single job as that job proceeds through the production process.

job posting: A procedure in which a firm advertises a job opening internally, by posting a notice of the job's availability for all employees to see, and by so doing solicits applications from current employees, usually in preference to outside applicants; sometimes a voluntary procedure on the part of the firm and sometimes mandated by union contract.

job rate: The rate of pay formally established for a specific task, functioning as the minimum which may by custom or contract be paid a worker performing that task.

job rotation: The planned moving of employees from job to job within a plant or company by management, usually to develop a pool of widely skilled employees, especially in middle management positions.

job satisfaction: Pleasure felt by an employee as a result of his or her job, such as the feeling of worth and fulfillment experienced by a doctor who has just saved a life, or an editor who has just salvaged a badly written manuscript.

job security: The kind and amount of security felt and actually experienced by an employee holding a job, in terms of the likelihood of being dismissed due to circumstances beyond the employee's control.

job shop: A firm that produces to fulfill specific orders, such as a custom builder of furniture.

joint account: A bank account held in common by two or more people or businesses.

joint agreement: A collective bargaining agreement between more than two parties; usually between a union and several employers who have bargained with the union as a group.

joint and survivors annuity: An annuity that pays two or more persons jointly during their lives and continues paying to the survivors after the death of any joint holder.

joint contract: A contractual obligation undertaken in common by two or more parties.

joint costs: Production costs that cannot be entirely split by product, but that can be attributed to two or more products rather than being necessarily spread out over all products made.

joint demand: Demand for two or more items arising from their joint use, such as shoes and shoelaces, typewriters and typewriter ribbons, nuts and bolts.

joint endorsement: Endorsement of an instrument by two or more parties, made necessary by that instrument being payable to those parties.

joint float: An agreement among several nations to attempt to stabilize their currencies in relation to each other, causing their several currencies to rise and fall roughly together in international money markets.

joint note: A note signed by two or more makers, for which they jointly assume responsibility, each for the full amount of the note should all other makers fail to pay any share of that joint obligation.

joint ownership: Ownership of property by two or more persons, each holding equally and each taking sole ownership if being the sole survivor.

joint products: Products resulting from a single industrial operation, such as the generation of several by-products from the production of coke from coal in a steel plant.

joint rate: The cost of shipping between two points via two or more carriers, quoted as a single price.

joint rate setting: In industrial relations, the setting of piece work rates jointly by agreement between labor and management, as provided for by contract.

joint return: A Federal, state or local income tax return that joins the income of wife and husband, who then file together as one; in most but not all tax situations thereby resulting in smaller total taxes than if they had filed separate tax returns.

joint-stock banks: British commercial banks, incorporated and privately owned, taking their name from the form of equity ownership.

joint stock company: A business organization that issues transferable stock, but carries unlimited liability for stockholders, thereby having some of the features of a corporation and some of a partnership; not a widely used form.

joint tenancy: See joint ownership.

joint venture: An undertaking for profit entered into by two or more people; usually but not always limited to the accomplishment of a single goal, such as the building of a factory abroad or the financing of a new mine; a general term, rather than a specific form of business organization, as such an undertaking may take any business form.

journal: In bookkeeping and accounting, any book originally recording transactions.

journal entry: In bookkeeping and accounting, any written entry recording a transaction in acceptable form and with enough information to be usable in constructing accounting data.

journeyman: A skilled craftsperson who does professionally competent work; in some trades, one who is so certified by a standard-setting group.

judgment: A court decision, complete and binding upon the parties to a matter before that court.

judgment sampling: See purposive sampling.

jumping: See branching.

junior bonds: Bonds which have less claim upon the issuer's assets than do other bonds, and which therefore in a default situation can make claims only after the claims of those other bonds have been satisfied.

junior mortgage: A mortgage, such as a second or third mortgage, which has less claim upon the property mortgaged than do other more senior mortgages, and which therefore in a default situation can make claims only after the claims of those other mortgages have been satisfied.

junk value: The value of goods as scrap, often the same as or little more than the underlying value of the materials in those goods minus the cost of preparing those materials for reuse.

jurisdictional dispute: A disagreement between two or more unions as to which union is legally entitled to represent a group of employees.

jurisdictional strike: A strike called by a union to enforce its claim of legal representation of a group of employees against the claim of one or more other unions.

juris doctor (JD): The bachelor of laws degree, and the basic degree granted after completion of law school; identical with the formerly granted LLB, or bachelor of laws, but presumably more status-generating.

jury of executive opinion forecast: A forecasting technique that compares the independent forecasts of several forecasters supplied with identical data, in an attempt to reach consensus; also called a Delphi forecast.

K

Keogh Plan: A kind of tax-advantaged retirement plan, named after Congressman Keogh, the chief sponsor of its enabling legislation, which allows the self-employed and those in unincorporated businesses to build tax-deferred retirement funds.

keyboarding: The process of printing or otherwise entering information through use of a set of keys, which when struck or pressed enter the information; used alike for all kinds of such devices, including typewriters, calculators, and computer systems.

keyed advertising: Advertising that carries a code identifying the media in which it is placed, and therefore identifies the source of returns from that placement, as when a coupon-carrying advertisement in the Chicago Tribune carries "CT" somewhere on the coupon, indicating on coupon return that this was from the advertisement carried in the Chicago Tribune.

key industry: Any industry that is centrally important to a national or international economy; usually either a basic industry, such as oil, coal, or steel; or an economically important industry, such as automobiles or food.

key man insurance: A kind of life insurance, bought by a firm on the life of a key employee and payable to the firm; aimed at compensating the firm for the loss of such a key employee.

Keynesian economics: A body of economic theory and proposed practice developed by John Maynard Keynes, aimed at control of unemployment and inflation and avoidance of depression by means of government taxing and spending policies; an important element of national economic practice in the United States and many other industrial nations.

keypunch: A machine that punches holes in cards as part of a data processing system, the punched cards then being used as information bits to be fed into the system.

kickback: An illegal payment made to someone in authority by someone who has benefited from use of that authority, as when a government contractor covertly pays a government officer for the illegal granting of a government contract or a supplier covertly pays a purchasing agent for received purchasing favors.

L

labor: 1. Those who, taken as a group, work for pay and are not primarily supervisors or owners, even though they may have minor supervisory tasks or ownership shares. **2.** Effort performed to produce and distribute goods and services; in this sense, a factor of production, like land and capital. **3.** Very widely, synonym for work.

labor agreement: A formal and written agreement between management and organized labor; a collective bargaining contract, covering such matters as wages, working conditions, fringe benefits, and grievance procedures.

labor attorney: See labor lawyer.

labor banks: Banks organized and owned by unions and their members. Such banks differ in no way from other banks in functioning or regulation.

labor contract: See labor agreement.

labor costs: The total gross wages paid to labor, which includes both direct and indirect costs, but does not include fringe benefits, clerical wages, or executive salaries.

labor dispute: Any dispute between labor and management relating to such matters as wages, hours, and working conditions, which are intrinsic to the work and to the relations between labor and management.

labor economics: The formal study of labor as an economic factor, including such matters as employment, work force composition, comparative productivity, wages, hours, and working conditions.

labor exchange: See employment agency.

labor force: All those over 16 years of age who are working or are looking for work, including both full- and part-time workers, while not including those who are employable but for any reason are not looking for work.

labor government: A government in which the dominant force is a party that identifies itself as a labor party, organized by and representing the interests of organized labor.

labor grade: See job classification.

labor intensive: Work that requires a great deal of labor relative to the amount of capital employed; applied to whole economies, industries, and sometimes even a single workplace. For example, excavating for the foundation of large building may be done largely by hand in a developing country and almost entirely by large earth-moving machines in an industrialized country. In the first country, that workplace, the building industry and probably the entire economy are labor intensive; in the second country, they are its opposite, capital intensive. Industries requiring personal service and hand production are labor intensive in all economies.

labor law: That body of statutes, regulations, and decisions applying to matters involving those who labor and those who employ labor, including collective bargaining, labor organizations, labor unions, worker protection, mediation and arbitration of disputes, and a wide range of similar matters.

labor lawyer: A lawyer who specializes in labor law matters, representing labor, management, or government. Like all legal specialties, no special licensing is involved, beyond clearance to appear before specialized agencies or courts; a lawyer may practice in several areas of the law at once.

labor market: The market in which those looking for work and those looking for workers meet; limited only by mobility factors. For example, the labor market may be a single city or metropolitan area for some kinds of factory jobs. But it may be worldwide for some kinds of engineers, with employers hiring and engineers seeking work wherever it is to be found. The labor market for even the lowest paid jobs may be international, as when agricultural producers in the United States recruit Mexican farm workers to harvest their crops.

labor mobility: The movement of those who work into other jobs, up or down in pay or status, between geographic areas, and between kinds of work; measured as the ratio between job changes of all kinds and total jobs filled in a given period.

labor movement: A very wide description of all organized actions by those who regard themselves as primarily workers, aimed at protecting and advancing their joint interests as workers, including all economic, political, and educational forms developed to further those interests. Unions, political action organizations, social welfare organizations, periodicals, and educational institutions are major features of the labor movement.

labor organizer: A person whose main job is to attempt to organize workers into the union represented by the organizer; usually but not always a paid union official.

labor relations: The ongoing set of relationships between those who labor and those who manage, including both a single relationship or transaction between supervisor and worker and a set of ongoing relationships between a major international company and a powerful international union.

labor theory of value: The theory that labor is the source of value, and that the real value of any goods or service stems solely from the amount of labor it has taken to produce it. Though widely attributed to Karl Marx, who used it as part of his body of economic theory, it was developed somewhat earlier and used in part by a number of other 19th-century economists, including Adam Smith.

labor turnover: The number of workers leaving a firm in a given period, measured as a percentage of those employed or a ratio of leavers to total jobs.

labor union: Any group of workers organized to pursue common goals as workers, whether as a craft or individual union, and whether the goals are primarily economic or political.

lag: In business, the time between two happenings; a shortening of the term "time lag," as when describing the interval between two assembly line or computer operations.

lagging indicator: An economic indicator that, by its nature, moves some time after other indicators of economic activity have moved, as in the instance of new plant and equipment spending plans, which must, given the nature of the planning process in companies, move behind consumer buying patterns.

laissez faire: The belief that government should interfere as little as possible in economic matters; once a belief that government should not involve itself in economic matters at all, beyond tax collections, but now an attempt to limit government involvement.

lame duck: One who holds office, but whose replacement has already been selected.

land: Earth, all but the great bodies of water that are seas; all that is below the surface of that earth and accessible, such as oil, coal, and other extractable substances; all that is permanently attached to that earth, by human or natural act, such as a building or a meteorite.

land banks: See Federal land banks.

land grant: A grant of land by government to private parties, for the accomplishment of purposes consonant with public policy; for example, the widespread granting of public land to private colleges in the last century, resulting in a number of colleges, such as Cornell University, popularly called land grant colleges.

landlord: One who has the right to lease property as proprietor of that property, and does so to a lessee.

land office business: A very active level of business, with a large number of transactions; usually, but not always, profitable business.

land poor: Describing those whose major assets are land, but who have insufficient cash to meet their cash flow needs, often because of cash demands caused by land ownership, such as taxes and maintenance.

land reform: Changes in traditional ownership arrangements as to land, usually by government decree, and usually resulting in the expropriation of large privately owned landholdings, either for redistribution among the formerly landless and small holding or for their retention by the state.

land tax: See property tax.

lapping: A technique used to hide thefts or other account shortages, in which an employee enters the amount to be hidden in a future accounting period, does the same in that period with another amount and covers the amount previously hidden with current receipts. The original theft or shortage is then repeated in each accounting period, or until the employee can make up the shortage—or until the procedure is discovered.

lapse: To be no longer in effect, applied to an insurance policy on which premiums are unpaid; under most circumstances the policy is cancelled after a specified time for failure to pay premiums.

last in, first out (lifo): A mode of inventory valuation that treats the cost of materials used in production as if those materials have just been purchased, no matter how long the materials have actually been in inventory. When prices are rising, the result is a considerable understatement of assets and profits, and a substantial reduction, therefore, in taxes paid.

last will and testament: The legal will of a decedent, superceding all previous testamentary dispositions.

latent defect: A defect in property sold, which cannot be perceived by the buyer even after reasonably careful scrutiny of the property purchased, as in the instance of a defective part deep in the engine of an automobile or a title to land which is fatally defective due to circumstances that could not be known by the buyer.

lateral transfer: A move to another job in the same organization that is roughly equivalent to the job left in pay and responsibilities.

laundered money: Money that has been illegally obtained and then passed through other economic entities to hide its true origin; for example, money obtained from narcotics sales which is fed as cash into such high cash turnover businesses as restaurants to reappear later as seemingly legitimate profits.

law: That body of rules governing the actions of people in a community, embodied in statutes, cases, rules, regulations, customs, and mores, and ultimately enforceable by the physical force of a nation or by nations acting in concert.

lawful money: See legal tender.

lawyer: One who is licensed in any state to practice law within that state. To practice law in any other state requires separate licensing, but legal specialties require no special licensing.

layaway plan: A mode of installment purchasing; the buyer pays the seller periodical installments, while the goods to be purchased stay in the seller's possession until the full purchase price has been paid, then passes by possession and ownership to the buyer.

layoff: A suspension of employment by management action, for either a specified or indefinite period, but short of outright discharge, as rehire is normally contemplated. However, many outright discharges are described as layoffs by management and workers, and the term is often therefore a synonym for discharge.

LCL: See less than carload.

lead: In selling, a prospective purchaser, to be followed up by direct selling efforts.

leader match: See contingency model.

leading indicator: An economic indicator that by its nature moves ahead of the business cycle, and can therefore to some extent be used as a predictive tool regarding business cycle swings; for example, new building permits and common stock price indexes.

lead-lag indicator relationships: The fairly predictable relationships between leading and lagging indicators, with changes in lagging indicators following changes in leading indicators within a predictable time range, often as a direct result of the leading indicator changes; an example is the change in the value of orders for new plant and equipment that follow a change in spending plans.

lead man: One who is primarily a worker rather than a supervisor, but whose job includes some independent planning for and supervision of other workers.

lead time: The time between formal initiation of an action or plan and its completion, as in the time between completion of research and development and the start of commercial production of an item or between the placing of an order and its delivery.

lean buying: See hand-to-mouth.

lease: A formal and written contract between one who has the power to rent property and one who wishes to rent that property, setting up the relationship between them of lessor and lessee, on terms explicitly stated in the contract. Realty and equipment are the main kinds of business leases.

leaseback: See sale and leaseback.

leased department: In a department store, a section that is leased to an independent proprietor, with the store supplying space, maintenance, and often financial and distribution services, and the proprietor running the department as a separate store. The relationship between store and proprietor is much like that between a market or bazaar and its lessees.

leasehold: That property interest possessed by a lessee, as defined by the terms of a lease, including such matters as rights, obligations, length of lease, renewal options, and termination conditions.

lease-purchase contract: A lease that carries with it an option to buy the property leased, often with some allowance for rental paid under the terms of the lease if the option to buy is exercised.

least-squares method: In statistics, a method of analyzing a linear relationship between a dependent and an independent variable that focuses on those points most closely related, minimizing the impact of values further from the line of regression, such as that shown in a scattergram.

leave of absence: A period of time spent away from a job, with the consent of the employer or by contractual right, in which the employee is not paid but retains any right to reinstatement and any seniority achieved as of the time of leaving.

ledger: A book of final entry used in accounting, into which is placed all information derived from original entry sources, such as journals and payment records; the size and complexity of a business' transactions will determine the number and kind of general and special ledgers needed.

legacy: In law, personal property that is passed by will; in general usage, anything, including both real and personal property, that is passed by will.

legal capital: The total value of the capital stock of a corporation, issued and unissued, stated as the total of that stock's par value; some part of the corporation's paid-in capital.

legal duty: A duty stemming from law or contract, and which undone may be found to breach a contract, violate law, or create liability for negligence.

legal entity: Any person or organization existing in law, and therefore capable of engaging in legal transactions, taking legal responsibility, acting, or being acted against in law.

legal interest: The highest rate of interest that may be charged by a lender; usually set by the usury statutes of the states, which have jurisdiction over interest rates.

legal investment list: An investment vehicle on a state-approved list of investments thought appropriate for fiduciaries and regulated companies, such as insurance companies and banks; usually composed of "safe" securities thought capable of withstanding almost all economic shocks.

legal liability: A liability enforceable at law, in contrast to a moral obligation, which although sometimes enforceable by mores and consequent social pressure, is not enforceable at law.

legal representative: One whom the law will recognize as representing another, as it does executors, administrators, and in some instances receivers in bankruptcy and some kinds of assignees.

legal reserve: The amount of cash or easily made liquid assets which must by applicable law be maintained by banks, life insurance companies and other firms as reserves against deposits and policies, and in compliance with other legal requirements.

legal residence: Any residence at which a person lives at least part of but not necessa-

rily most of the time and which is chosen by that person as a legal residence, synonymous with domicile.

legal tender: Money that is recognized by government as a lawful medium of exchange and usable for payment of sums owed, and which therefore must be accepted by creditors when offered in payment, unless the sums owed are defined in other than money terms or in terms of other currencies. For example, payment of a debt specifically stated in Japanese yen or German marks must be made in the specified currency if demanded by the creditor; payment in United States dollars at the current exchange rate may legally be refused.

legatee: One who is to receive a legacy by the terms of a will.

leisure class: Those who are in no way involved in the productive process, but only spend and consume; from Thorstein Veblen's economic theory.

lending institution: An organization wholly or largely in the business of lending money to others for profit, such as a bank or savings and loan association.

less-developed country: See underdeveloped country.

lessee: See lease.

lessor: See lease.

less than carload (LCL): A shipment that occupies less than a full railroad car; that may be moved from car to car as economy of shipment dictates, and on which higher rates than full carload lot rates apply.

less than truckload (LTT): A shipment that occupies less than a full motor truck, that may be moved from truck to truck as economy of shipment dictates, and on which higher rates than full truckload rates apply.

letter of credit: An instrument issued by banks and other financial institutions, guaranteeing payment of drafts up to a specified limit when made by the person or organization named in the instrument; commonly used in foreign trade transactions as a means of organizing payments between correspondent banks without large transfers of funds between them. In commercial transactions, letters of credit may be irrevocable or revocable at will by the issuing institution up to a stated date; may be guaranteed as to payment by the issuing bank and its correspondent bank or by the issuing bank alone; and may be for a fixed amount or constitute a line of credit. Individuals also widely use letters of credit when travelling; a traveller's check is such a letter of credit.

letters testamentary: A written instrument issued by a court of proper jurisdiction, authorizing an executor to proceed with execution of a will, and functioning as proof that the will has been through probate.

letter stock: Company stock that is unregistered with the Federal and state securities regulatory authorities and that is issued by letter between company and purchasers; may subsequently be transferred only by private sale and not by public sale.

let the buyer beware: See caveat emptor.

let the seller beware: See caveat venditor.

level of confidence: A statistical estimate of the likelihood that experimental results are correct, expressed as a percent; for example, a 95% level of confidence means that, statistically, there is a 5% chance that the results are incorrect. The range of values represented by the 95% is called the confidence interval.

level of significance: The statistical probability that experimental results occurred by chance alone, rather than for the reason being explored by the researcher, or for some other reason. For example, statistical evidence may indicate that a drug has the desired effect on a particular disease; Type I error might cause researchers to produce a drug that in fact does not work.

leverage: The impact on a common stock's market price of substantial corporate financial obligations which must be paid before common stock can be considered for dividends. A company carrying relatively heavy debt obligations, such as large direct debts and bonds outstanding, with consequent very heavy interest payments, is said to be heavily leveraged. In times of high earnings, the company is making money on the borrowed money, and earnings relative to capital invested are high, pushing the market price of the stock up; in times of low earnings, the company may make little money or actually lose money on the borrowed money, and earnings relative to capital invested may be extremely low, pushing the market price of the stock down.

levy: 1. Any claim by government upon the property of its citizens, including all taxes and seizures. **2.** An assessment by an organization on its members or stockholders to meet organizational obligations.

liabilities: 1. Amounts owed by debtors to creditors. **2.** All items appearing on the credit side of a double entry accounting system including all amounts owed.

liability: 1. In the law, one of the widest possible range of current, contingent, future, and possible responsibilities and hazards. **2.** In business, whatever is owed by debtor to creditor. **3.** In accounting, any item appearing on the credit side of a double entry accounting system, including both current owings and future owings incurred but not yet due, and including the net worth items carried.

liability insurance: Insurance covering risks associated with property and personal liability claims, including such risks as malpractice, product liability, libel and slander, and a wide range of casualty and surety lines.

liable: Legally responsible, or likely to be so, for satisfying the claim of another, and obliged to respond to that claim by either contesting or settling it.

libel: Defamation of character occurring in any published form, including writing, signs, pictures, or broadcasts, and in any form other than direct speech to others, which is slander.

license: 1. A permit by government to do something which by law requires such a permit; granted as a matter of governmental discretion, rather than as a matter of individual or organizational right, for a limited time and subject to conditions imposed by government. **2.** A permit granted by the owner of a patent or copyright to another to make use, usually commercial use, of patented or copyrighted materials or processes.

lien: A claim chargeable by one against the property of another, usually arising from a debt owed by the property holder to the lien holder. If that debt is unpaid, the claim may be pursued by legal action and the property sold to satisfy the debt, as when a mechanic holds an automobile for unpaid repair bills and is eventually satisfied out of the proceeds on sale of that automobile.

life annuity: A life insurance policy providing for premium payments by the insured for a stated number of years, and then payment of benefits to the insured for the rest of the insured's life.

life estate: An estate granted to one who is not an inheritor under the terms of a will, and which is limited to the life of its holder or some other person, the estate then reverting to its grantor or some other party designated by the grantor.

life insurance: Insurance providing for premium payments by the insured during life and payment of benefits to stated beneficiaries or to the insured's estate on death; it might far more accurately be called death insurance.

life tenant: See life estate.

lifo: See last in, first out.

lilliput: Very modest input into an analog computer; most commonly used in micro-economic and microcomputer applications.

limit: An instruction to a broker regarding

securities to be bought or sold, setting the top price that will be paid or the bottom price at which securities will be sold.

limited (Ltd.): A British term describing the limited liability to stockholders accompanying the corporate form of business organization; attached to corporate names in Great Britain and throughout much of the English-speaking world, and used synonymously with the United States "Incorporated" or "Inc."

limited liability: Any limitation on the liability of those jointly engaged in a business enterprise; the corporate form by its very nature offers limited liability to stockholders, whose liability as regards corporate obligations extends only to the value of their stockholdings.

limited line store: A retail store, such as a grocery or clothing store, that carries a single kind or a small number of kinds of goods, in contrast to a department store, which carries many kinds of goods.

limit order: See limit.

limited partnership: A partnership form in which one or more of the partners share liability only to the value of their holdings, take profits within stated limits, and participate only financially in the enterprise.

limited payment life insurance: A life insurance policy providing for a mode of premium payment in which all the premiums due on a life insurance policy are paid in less than the time between policy purchase and the insured's death, as when an insured takes a 10-payment policy on which premium payments may be completed when the insured is only 55.

limited price order: See limit.

limited price store: A retail store that wholly or mainly carries low-priced goods, usually promoting itself as a bargain or discount store.

line: 1. A kind of goods carried by a selling organization, such as a retail store, wholesaler, or manufacturer. **2.** That portion of a company's management group directly responsible for profitable operations, in contrast to staff, which carries mainly advisory functions. **3.** A shortening of the term assembly line.

linear programming: 1. The identification and mathematical examination of variables in a system, with the aim of securing the most effective and economic means of reaching desired goals; usually a computer-assisted activity, and widely used in operations research. **2.** In programmed instruction, the sequential presentation of material, in contrast to branching.

linear regression: See scattergram.

line function: A function for which line management, as opposed to staff, is responsible.

line management: That portion of a company's management directly responsible for profitable operations; controlling operating rather than advisory, administrative, and overhead-related functions.

line of credit: See credit line.

line officer: See line manager.

line of regression: See scattergram.

line organization: That portion of management's organization devoted to and responsible for profitable operations.

line production: See assembly line.

line supervisor: A manager who directly supervises workers engaged in any aspect of production, maintenance, or physical distribution.

liquid assets: Assets consisting of cash, notes minus an allowance for uncollectibles, and quickly marketable securities; for net liquid assets, current liabilities are also subtracted.

liquidate: 1. To terminate and dissolve an economic entity through sale of all assets, payment of all obligations, and distribution of the remaining liquid assets to those entitled by law to receive them. **2.** To pay and discharge a debt.

liquidated damages: An amount previously agreed upon by parties to a contract or court action, representing damages that will be paid on breach of contract or judicial decision.

liquidating dividend: The distribution of remaining assets to equity holders on corporate dissolution, on a pro rata basis after satisfaction of all prior claims, such as those of creditors and bondholders.

liquidation value: The estimated residual value of a business if it were to be terminated and dissolved, all assets turned into cash and all obligations paid.

liquidator: One appointed by law to liquidate a business; often used as a synonym for receiver.

liquidity: The ability to meet obligations out of liquid assets, rather than through debt creation or fixed asset sales.

liquidity preference: In Keynesian economic theory, the ongoing and ever changing relationship between the demand for cash for current needs and security desires on the one hand and the desire to invest in income-producing investment vehicles on the other.

list broker: A firm in the business of developing, managing, and renting mailing lists for use in direct marketing efforts.

listed security: A security traded on and listed by a recognized stock exchange, such as the New York or the American Stock Exchange.

listing: 1. In securities trading, full recognition of a security by an established stock exchange. **2.** In real estate, the placing of a property for sale with a broker or group of brokers.

list price: The standard price quoted on goods for sale, as listed in the manufacturers' or retailers' catalogues and other sales materials.

living cost: See cost of living.

living trust: See inter vivos.

load: 1. That portion of an insurance company premium or mutual fund investment which is attributable to selling and other business acquisition expenses. In some mutual funds, these expenses are taken from investors' funds very early in the life of an investment program, and investors attempting to sell out their holdings soon after starting such a program find that their recoverable funds have dramatically diminished in a very short time. **2.** To put a program into main computer storage, ready to run; also to move data into main storage from available auxiliary storage.

loading: See load.

loan: Property owned by one which, by mutual consent, is used temporarily by another; also the transaction resulting in that use. In business, that property is usually money, which is by formal agreement passed from owner-lender to temporary user-borrower, to be repaid at specified times and at specified rates of interest.

loan capital: The loaned capital of a corporation, as distinguished from its equity capital. Loan capital consists of debt instruments, such as bonds and bank loans; equity capital consists of ownership shares.

loan shark: A lender, operating illegally, charging usurious rates of interest, and normally indulging in unsavory collection practices.

lobby: A group organized to exert direct pressure on the legislative process, by influencing legislators and administrators to act as the group would like on specific issues.

local union: The union organization representing workers in a single location or relatively small area. A union organized along industrial lines, such as the United Steelworkers, will often have one or more locals at each plant; a union organized along craft lines, such as the bricklayers union, will often have locals organized by geographic area.

locked in: A condition in which someone cannot move because the move will cause more adverse results than preserving the status quo; in securities trading, usually referring to an investor who has capital gains on a stock and is unwilling to sell because of probable adverse tax consequences.

lockout: Stoppage of production by management initiative; a mangement strike, in which the workers are forced off their jobs by management's action, and usually part of a dispute between labor and management.

logical operations: Those operations within a computer, based on Boolean algebra, that allow the computer to make specified decisions on the basis of information generated during processing, without outside intervention at the decision point; for example, the computer might be asked to check if a variable X is equal to or greater than 10, or below 10, with the processing path specified in the program depending on the result of the computer's comparison.

logistics: The management of materials and people toward the achievement of stated goals, as in building a bridge or winning a war.

logo: An abbreviation for logotype, which is a symbol meant to identify and often to help create a public image for an organization; often protected as a trademark.

logotype: See logo.

logrolling: Within the legislative process, the practice of exchanging commitments among legislators and sometimes among other interested parties, in order to move favored legislation ahead toward passage; an often-criticized feature of that process when used to obtain passage of bills in favor of special interests.

long: Owning securities and commodities, usually purchased on margin and held in a margin account with a broker, which have been bought in expectation of a rise in their market prices.

longevity: See seniority.

long form: See itemized deductions.

long haul: The transport of goods over a relatively long distance, in contrast to a short haul, which is transport of goods over a relatively short distance; always a comparative matter, as the several hundred miles between two points in North America may seem a fairly short haul, while several hundred miles in western Europe may be a trip across several national borders.

long-range forecasting: Systematic attempts to predict future trends and events beyond four or five years into the future, often using mathematical models and computer technology.

long-term contract: Any contract which will take more than one year to complete, and must be accounted for in more than one accounting year. In collective bargaining, contracts longer than one year have been considered long-term, but the definition has been changing as more and more contracts are multi-year contracts, with long-term more often used to describe three- and five-year contracts.

long-term debt: Debts which must be paid one year or more after signing of the loan agreement, in contrast to short-term debts, which must be paid less than one year after the borrowing.

long-term lease: A lease that runs for several years, usually three or more; a relative term and not sharply defined as to length.

long-term liability: See long-term debt.

loop: In computer processing, a set of instructions that is to be repeated until a specified condition is reached; also to repeat such a set of instructions, or to iterate.

loss: 1. The difference between income and expenditure, when expenditure is larger; the net of the two is net loss, in contrast to net profit, which is the result when income is larger. **2.** The sudden, usually unexpected destruction of an asset without compensating payment, as in experiencing a fraud that is not adequately covered by insurance.

3. The substance of an insurance claim from the insurance company's point of view; the amount that must be paid to settle a successful claim.

loss leader: An item of merchandise sold at a loss, in the hope of bringing in customers who will buy other merchandise as well, resulting in net profitable sales.

lot: 1. A stated quantity of a specific kind of merchandise, as in a group of garments shipped from maker to retailer or a standard hundred-share block of traded stock. **2.** A defined piece of real estate of any size, but usually referring to a relatively small piece of land.

low bid: The lowest bid made among those competing for work on a bidding basis; often, but not always, resulting in securing the work.

low energy level: See energy level.

low-level language: In computer programming, a program that is relatively close to machine language, so it requires only a rather simple translation by an assembler into machine language before it can be used by the computer. Low-level languages are harder to program in than are high-level symbolic languages.

Ltd.: See limited.

LTT: See less than truckload.

lump sum appropriation: An appropriation stated as a total sum, specifying the purposes for which the sum is to be spent but not the specific expenditures that are to be made to accomplish that purpose.

lump sum payment: Repayment of a debt by single payment, rather than by any installment payment mode.

lump sum settlement: Settlement of an insurance claim by single payment, rather than by any installment payment settlement mode.

luxury goods: Expensive merchandise aimed

at satisfying desires rather than needs, as are most items of high-fashion merchandise.

luxury tax: A tax on relatively high-priced consumer goods, such as luggage and cosmetics; often a substantial tax, because of the nature of the goods and their satisfaction of desires, rather than needs.

M

M-1: The national money supply, defined in the most basic and narrow terms as the total of all currency plus all demand deposits.

M-2: The national money supply, using a somewhat broader definition than M-1, and including currency, demand deposits, and commercial bank time deposits.

M-3: The national money supply, using a somewhat broader definition than M-1 or M-2, and including currency, demand deposits, commercial bank time deposits, and savings held by savings institutions of all kinds.

machine hour: An hour of running time on a specific machine; used as an element of costing.

machine hour rate: The cost of running a specific machine or kind of machine for an hour during the production process; used as an element in determining the cost of goods in process.

machine language: A code that can be read directly by a computer, but is difficult for humans to read or write. Computer programs are usually written in a symbolic language such as FORTRAN or COBAL, which are easier for people to work with, and are then translated into machine language, also called the object language.

Machinery and Allied Products Institute formula: See MAPI capital returns formula.

machinery insurance: A kind of property insurance, covering losses caused by damage to or destruction of machines.

machine tools: Power-driven tools used for cutting, forming, smoothing, and otherwise working on metals and other hard substances, and capable of working to close tolerances.

macroeconomics: The study of economics in the large, using whole economies and large subsections of whole economies as objects of study, and focusing on how such large economic units behave; in contrast to microeconomics, or the study of small economic units.

macro instruction: A computer instruction that activates a sequence of other instructions.

Madison Avenue: A popular synonym for the advertising industry, after the New York street that was once, and to some extent still is, a center of that industry.

Mafia: An alleged criminal syndicate, operating in the United States and many other countries. In a wider sense, used to refer to any group operating covertly and using violent methods to exercise control over other people and organizations.

magnetic core: A tiny piece of metal, capable of existing in either of two states of magnetization; each core represents one bit (binary digit) of data in the main memory of the computer.

magnetic ink character recognition (MICR): In computer systems, a mode of storing computerized data, using ink that carries magnetized particles, which can then be read at high speed by automatic readers; in contrast to optical character recognition (OCR).

magnetic tape: In computer systems, a tape with a magnetized surface, used for the storage of computerized information, from which the computer can retrieve information at high speed.

mailing list: A list of mailing addresses, compiled by business activity, such as a customers' or subscribers' list. Most mailing lists are available for rental or purchase to selling organizations, then becoming prospective purchaser lists for those who attempt to sell their goods, services, or ideas by mail.

mail marketing: The process of marketing goods and services by mail directly to their prospective purchasers.

mail order: A purchase order that comes in by mail; usually solicited by mail as well.

mail-order house: A business organization that sells primarily, though not necessarily wholly, by mail.

mail selling: See direct marketing.

main core: See magnetic core.

main frame: See central processing unit.

main memory: The information storage capability of a computer system's central processing unit.

maintenance of membership: A collective bargaining contract provision requiring that those workers belonging to the union named in the contract must remain in that union as a condition of employment for the duration of the collective bargaining period; usually also providing a 15- to 30-day period after contract signing for any workers who wish to leave the union and still keep their jobs. Those hired during the contract period usually must join the union after a specified period, such as 30 days.

majority stockholder: One owning a controlling interest in a corporation; though earlier it referred to one owning more than 50% of a corporation's stock, it is now often used to describe those holding much smaller percentages, but in effective control.

major medical expense insurance: Insurance covering very large medical expense costs, usually taking over where such hospital surgical plans as Blue Shield, Blue Cross stop; for example, the costs of major heart surgery or the costs of a hospitalization lasting several months.

make a market: To act as primary trader for a specific stock, especially including moves aimed at regulating sharp fluctuations in the price of a stock, if possible. Dealers make markets in over-the-counter stocks; specialists make markets on the floor of stock exchanges.

maker: One who is the original signer of a promissory note, and therefore assumes prime responsibility for payment of that note.

make-ready time: The time needed to prepare machines and materials for production.

make work: Work that serves no productive purpose, but exists only to give idle people something to do, and often something to be paid for, such as performance of unneeded functions by too many workers to save jobs under the terms of some union contracts, or the assignment of endless reporting and task force development functions to redundant executives on overstaffed and badly managed management teams.

male chauvinist: A man who quite irrationally feels his sex naturally superior to women; often a man who displays those feelings overtly and covertly, in such areas as job discrimination, sexual harrassment on the job, and language.

male chauvinist pig: An especially pejorative term applied to alleged male chauvinists, but carrying no other meaning.

malfeasance: The commission of an illegal or otherwise wrongful act, the proving of which can lead to successful criminal or civil action against the malefactor.

malfunction: The failure or inability of machinery or processes to operate as intended and designed.

malpractice: Misconduct by a professional of such nature as to be actionable at law, including negligence, illegal actions, immoral intent and action, and breach of fiduciary duty; most often alleged against doctors and lawyers.

malpractice insurance: Insurance against successful malpractice claims arising from professional practice; most often successfully pursued against doctors, but sometimes also against lawyers and other professionals.

Malthusianism: A theory of population growth and its consequences put forward in the last century by Thomas Malthus, positing geometrical population growth, arithmetic resource growth, and consequent catastrophic overpopulation of Earth.

managed currency: Any currency which is manipulated by government or its agencies in pursuit of national goals, rather than being left free to respond solely to marketplace conditions. All modern currencies are so managed.

managed price: See administered price.

management: 1. In the widest sense, the operation and control of any function or organization, including the management of one's own time, a household, or the provisioning of an ocean liner. **2.** The operation and control of business organizations, aiming at attaining the overall goals of those organizations at minimum cost and maximum profit. Management may participate in overall goal setting and may in fact exercise many other ownership functions. **3.** Those who are responsible for the operation and control of business organizations.

management accounting: Accounting systems designed to help management perform effectively by reporting financial information quickly, simply, and in forms usable by nonfinancial management people; usually the function of an internal financial officer, such

as a controller, sometimes with the help of outside accountants.

management audit: A review of management's operations and control mechanisms conducted by independent outside reviewers, aimed at evaluating the quality of management's performance as compared with that of similar organizations, usually those headquartered in the same country.

management by crisis: A technique of management purporting to favor the development of operating crises as a means of most effectively clarifying issues, developing effective management, and moving organizations ahead; normally far more an excuse for poor planning and ineffective management than a coherent management style.

management by exception: A technique of managing that focuses major attention on variations from plans and previous business patterns, in the main assuming that if plans are working out as budgeted, little attention need be paid to them, leaving more time for attention to the unforeseen.

management by objectives (MBO): A technique of managing that focuses on formal goal setting and on reaching the goals set, featuring frequent planning, evaluation and reevaluation activities on the part of management people; usually accompanied by a good deal of organizational structuring and restructuring, as well as by the presence of a substantial number of internal and external consulting personnel.

management company: A company in the business of managing properties or investments.

management consultant: One who is professionally engaged in advising management as to the most effective ways of achieving management's goals. Most such consultants are independent contractors, whose value to management lies primarily in their independence and broad business experience.

management development: The process of attempting to train working managers to become better managers. Much of such development is self-development; much is relatively informal on-the-job skills training and self-training; some is formal in-company and outside professional training courses.

management game: Any problem-solving game using organizational models and case studies to develop alternative solutions to the kinds of problems managers face in real life; a widely used training and professional development technique.

management information system (MIS): A computer-based information system aimed at providing management with an ongoing flow of operating and financial data that will help provide the basis for consistently informed decision making.

management prerogatives: Those functions which management claims as solely its own, and not subject to the collective bargaining process, such as hiring, scheduling, and production control matters; all are very much matters of disagreement between labor and management in the United States and much of the rest of the world.

management rights: See management prerogatives.

management science: A body of formal techniques derived from the hard sciences and applied to the problems of management, most recently featuring mathematical models using computers as well as other complex mathematically based techniques; also called quantitative management or scientific management.

manager: One who manages; in small businesses one who manages at any level; in larger businesses, one who manages above the first-line supervisory or foremen's level.

managerial grid: A management self-assessment and development tool using a grid into which are positioned several variables, all within the constructs of "concern for people" and "concern for production" as major interacting factors in describing and evaluating management style and effectiveness.

mandamus: A court order commanding a court of lesser jurisdiction, governmental body, private corporation, other organization, or person to do or not do something, without delay; sometimes specifying the exact action to be taken and sometimes commanding that action in general terms, with the specifics left to the doer.

man hour: An hour of working time, usually referring to an average hour spent working on a specific job and used in costing that job. The term is also often used broadly, to describe the amount of time a specific piece of work has taken to perform, even though the work might have been performed at widely different speeds by different people working under various conditions.

manifest: A document listing and detailing the entire cargo of a ship, including all required information on origin, destination, and physical characteristics, as verified in writing by the ship's captain.

manipulation: In business the control or influence of market factors, such as the amount of a particular stock in public circulation or the price of a commodity or single product, for the economic benefit of those so operating. Some manipulations, such as the forcing up of a stock price, are illegal. Some, such as the control of world commodity prices by a group of commodity-producing nations, are merely factual, though deplored by those nations consuming the commodities in question. Some, such as control of money supplies by national governments, are widely regarded as beneficial instruments of national policy.

manning table: A table setting out organizational structure and the standard number and kinds of jobs needed to fill that structure; often a maximum rather than average or minimum projection.

manpower: The people available for work in a given geographical or functional area, including both employed and unemployed.

The area may be as large as a nation, industry, or profession, or as small as a lightly populated rural area.

Manpower Administration: A division of the United States Department of Labor, responsible for Federal activities in the areas of employment, apprenticeship, training, unemployment compensation, and a miscellany of development programs.

manual labor: Unskilled physical labor, as distinguished from skilled work of any kind, and from any kind of office work. As machines multiply, so do the skills necessary to run them, and less and less jobs consisting of manual labor exist.

manufacturer's agent: See manufacturer's representative.

manufacturers' new orders: The total of new orders for manufactured goods, collected by industry and nationally, and widely viewed as a leading indicator in the forecasting of future business conditions.

manufacturer's representative: One who functions as a sales representative for one or more manufacturers, and who is an independent businessperson, rather than an employee.

manufacturers' sales outlet: A sales outlet operated by the manufacturer and selling directly to those using the products sold, rather than selling to middlemen for resale to industrial and retail consumers.

manufacturing: The process of working materials to produce products for sale; also the total of the industries that do so. The New Mexico potter who produces and sells ceramic vases one by one, working alone, is a manufacturer; so is General Motors. Their joint output is part of the manufacturing output of the United States.

manufacturing costs: Those costs attributable to manufacturing, including materials, direct labor, and manufacturing overhead.

manufacturing inventory: See inventory.

manufacturing overhead: Those costs attribut-able to manufacturing, excluding direct labor and materials.

MAPI capital returns formula: A Machinery and Allied Products Institute (MAPI) formula that attempts to project investment returns resulting from investment in new machinery, stressing anticipated advantages and attempting to turn them into estimated cash savings and production increases, which can then be turned into a percentile return-on-investment figure.

margin: 1. The percentage of equity owned by an investor who has purchased stock on margin, that is by a combination of cash and brokers' loans; a 70% margin, for example means that the equity holder has paid 70¢ on each dollar of stock and the broker has loaned 30¢, with the broker holding a lien on the stock to the extent of the 30¢ per dollar loan. If the market price of the stock goes up, so does the owner's equity; if down, so does the owner's equity, with the 30¢ loan remaining stable in dollar amount but varying in percentage. **2.** A synonym for gross profit.

margin account: A brokerage account, in which credit is extended by broker to customer for the purchase of securities, within rules set out by Federal and stock exchange regulations, which the broker may sell out as made necessary due to market conditions. The securities in the account may be, and usually are, used by the broker as collateral for bank and other institutional loans to cover the loans made to customers.

marginal analysis: An attempt to analyze the impact of changes in economic variables, such as cost and productivity, by isolating changes in individual variables for study purposes, while assuming that all other factors remain constant; often rendered extremely difficult in practice due to the multiple impacts of any change upon many of the variables in any situation.

marginal business: A business that operates at or close to breakeven, generating very little profit or loss, carrying very little reserve for contingencies, and therefore always being close to failure.

marginal cost: The cost of adding a cost factor, assuming all other variables remain constant; often a theoretical rather than practical measure.

marginal costing: A costing technique that assigns only a marginal or incremental cost to a new cost factor, rather than assigning a full share of all costs being incurred; often used in evaluating new product results.

marginal productivity: The increase in amount produced caused by increase in a single factor of production; usually a theoretical rather than practical construct.

marginal revenue: The revenue resulting from a single additional sale. If revenue per sale remains constant, each additional unit sold yields as much as each previous unit, but if price decreases as units sold increase, revenue for each additional unit sold is less than a full unit price. For example, 5 units sold at $5 each yields $25. If 6 units are sold at $4.50 each, the yield is $27, which is only $2 more than $25. The marginal revenue is $2.

marginal utility: The theory that the usefulness and therefore demand for a product may lessen with its increased availability.

margin call: A formal request from lender to borrowing investor or broker, calling for additional payments into a margin account, usually because a stock has lost market value, making the proportion of loan to equity too large to conform with legal requirements or lender policy.

margin of safety: The extent to which loans secured by collateral, such as those in a margin account, are protected by the value of the collateral above the amount loaned. For example, stock used as collateral is always subject to loss in market value, and the amount accepted as collateral must therefore considerably exceed the amount of the loan. In a wider sense, any allowance for error and shortfall.

markdown: 1. A lowering of a retail price; literally the marking of a lower price on an item sold at retail. **2.** A lower evaluation of stores of value, such as factory inventories and securities held by institutions.

market: 1. Any place at which goods and services are publicly traded, such as an open air market in which dozens of fruit and vegetable vendors sell their goods, a retail store, or the New York Stock Exchange. **2.** To sell, as when a company markets its goods. **3.** The demand for an item, as when the market for microcomputers is booming. **4.** A total of all trading activity in a designated area or kind of product, such as the Australian wool market or the world market for manganese.

marketability: 1. The likelihood that a product will be sold; its salability. **2.** The speed at which an asset may be made liquid without the substantial loss of value that would be caused by a distress sale.

marketable securities: Securities easily converted into cash, and carried as a current asset on the balance sheet.

marketable title: A title to real estate good enough to be conveyed and without which a valid real estate transaction cannot be legally consummated.

market basket: The price of a group of consumer goods, which moves as the cost of living changes. For example, a typical group of consumer goods, costing $1,000 this year, might be used as a base for computing changes in the cost of those kinds of consumer goods. The same group of goods two years later may cost $1,200, an increase of $200 or 20%.

market concentration: The extent to which the demand for a kind of product is concentrated in a specific geographic or kind of business area.

market equilibrium: The theory that prices reflect a balance between supply and demand, and that as supply and demand change and react against each other, prices tend to move in response to those changes.

market index: Any of the several indexes of securities market prices, such as the Dow-Jones or Standard and Poor's stock price indexes.

marketing: In the widest sense, the distribution function, including buying, selling, transporting, financing, and collecting. In modern business organizations, however, the term describes a group of selling and sales-related functions, including advertising, promotion, and direct selling.

marketing concept: A business planning approach that stresses the primacy of customer needs and wants, and regards the main function of the business as satisfying those needs and wants.

marketing cooperative: A producer's cooperative, in which producers merge their marketing activities and selling efforts in an attempt to achieve marketing economies and greater selling strength.

marketing manager: One who is professionally engaged in developing marketing activities on behalf of a product or group of products.

marketing mix: The set of marketing activities chosen by those responsible for marketing that they believe will most successfully sell their product or products, including the kinds of activities to be pursued, the amounts to be spent on those activities, and the integration of those activities into a coherent marketing plan.

marketing plan: The total plan adopted by marketing management for moving company products to market, including budgets, personnel, advertising, promotion, and direct selling plans.

marketing power: The relative ability of a firm to successfully sell its products in its markets; usually describing firms with relatively strong marketing organizations.

marketing research: See market research.

market order: In securities trading, an order from customer to broker to buy or sell a security immediately upon receipt of the order at the best possible price then available in the market.

market penetration: The extent to which a firm has reached into a single market, and the share of that market to which it sells.

market position: The rank a firm occupies in its market relative to that occupied by other firms selling to the same market, assessed on the basis of such factors as sales volume, reputation and depth of penetration into specific areas. The term sometimes refers only to sales volume.

market potential: The sales possibilities for a product, in both present and future; a key assessment to be made by those developing new products.

market price: The price at which goods and services are currently selling in their marketplaces, such as the price of a security or commodity on an exchange.

market profile: A detailed description of the market or markets for a product, including such materials as demographic data and market survey results.

market rate of interest: The rates of interest currently being charged on loans by lending institutions.

market research: Information gathering and analysis bearing on any aspect of marketing, including such areas as consumer and industrial buying patterns and motivations, advertising, promotion, market definition, competition, and new product development.

market value: The price at which an asset or property will sell in its market now; often an estimate, as with real property, and sometimes a determinable amount, as with most securities.

Markov process: A type of statistical forecasting used in stochastic situations, that is situations in which a random variable is present; assumes that the probability of the random event can be calculated from present data, without need for any historical data.

mark sensing: The manual marking of a computer input card in a code capable of being punched by the computer and used as input.

markup: **1.** The amount added to the cost of a product to cover additional costs and profits; for example, the amount added to the wholesale cost of a product sold at retail by the retailer, to cover operating expenses, other selling costs, and profit. **2.** A raising of a retail price; literally the marking of a higher price on an item sold at retail, as when a publisher, jobber, or retailer places a $9.95 sticker over the $8.95 price shown on a book. **3.** A higher evaluation of stores of value, such as factory inventories, and securities held by institutions.

Massachusetts trust: A firm owned by investors who hold transferable shares representing the value of their investments in the business and who have only limited liability, just as do shareholders in a corporation, but who have no control over management or management policies. The firm is organized as a trust, with shareholders passing the assets of the firm to management, who are called trustees, and retaining only beneficial interest in profits commensurate with their investments.

mass communication: The process of disseminating information, ideas, and entertainment via such mass media as television and radio broadcasting, newspapers, and large-circulation magazines.

mass marketing: Marketing geared to the distribution of goods and services to very large numbers of consumers, through the employment of substantial marketing resources, including such vehicles as chain, department, and discount stores; catalogue selling; mass media advertising; and promotion.

mass media: The vehicles through which mass communications are disseminated, such as television and radio broadcasting, newspapers, and large-circulation magazines.

mass merchandising: See mass marketing.

mass production: The production of large quantities of standardized goods through use of standardized instruments, techniques, and specifications, as in the assembly line production of most motor cars in the United States.

master agreement: A multi-unit collective bargaining agreement covering more than a single union and a single company at one location; often a multi-company agreement with a single large union, covering most major contract matters, with local collective bargaining agreements covering a wide variety of local matters.

master policy: An insurance policy covering an insured operating in several locations at once, and supplemented in some locations by provisions meeting varying statutory requirements.

mat: See matrix.

matching grant: A grant of funds which will be activated only if a specified amount of funds are available to the grantee from other sources. For example, Federal or state funds for the arts may in some instances only be supplied if the intended recipients are able to raise some funds, usually stated as a percentage of the government funds, from private sources.

material control: See materials management.

material costs: The costs of all substances used in the course of doing business, including those materials directly used in production and those used in all other aspects of business.

materiality: Relevance to the matter at hand, as when evidence presented in a legal action relates directly to the matter being adjudicated rather than being irrelevant to the main issues to be decided, or when a matter taken up or omitted on an accounting statement is relevant to proper understanding of company affairs by those who must be informed, such as directors, stockholders, the general public, and regulatory authorities.

materials: Substances used in production, including raw materials and manufactured goods used as parts of other goods.

materials handling: The physical handling of materials used in a business, including all aspects of receipt, storage, internal moving, and shipping, as well as all the equipment needed to accomplish those functions, but not including movement of materials during the production process.

materials management: The management of the flow of materials into, through, and out of a business, including the equipment needed to accomplish that flow most effectively, and including such functions as purchasing, warehousing, inventory control, some aspects of production control, and shipping.

maternity benefits: Benefits accruing to an employee who is having a baby, including such provisions as maternity leave, hospital and surgical insurance, and pay for time lost; usually as specified by a collective bargaining contract, though sometimes a matter of law or employer policy.

maternity leave: A leave of absence granted by a company to an employee for the latter part of a pregnancy and for a period after the baby is born; usually covered by collective bargaining agreement provisions and sometimes by law as well, protecting the employee's seniority and sometimes providing specified maternity benefits.

mathematical economics: See econometrics.

mathematical model: A model set up on a mathematical, rather than a physical basis, which attempts to approach a problem by use of mathematical tools, often with the assistance of computer technology.

matrix: A form of holding, displaying, or developing any substance or body of thought, such as a body of mathematical symbols or a plate used in printing, often called a mat.

matrix management: The formal study and development of appropriate organizational forms to meet a wide variety of organizational and project development needs, using both existing departmental structures and developing temporary structures to achieve specific goals and accomplish specific projects in pursuit of those goals.

mature economy: An economy that has experienced very substantial industrial growth in the past and has to some extent shifted its current emphasis away from basic industrial growth to consumer goods and services.

maturity: The point at which a financial obligation becomes due and payable, such as the date at which a debt becomes payable, or an insurance policy becomes payable due to occurrence of stated conditions.

maturity date: See due date.

maximax: In quantitative decision making, the choice of a course of action that *maxi*mizes the *maxi*mum anticipated payoffs; an optimistic strategy. In contrast, maximin involves maximizing minimum payoffs and minimax involves minimizing maximum losses.

maximin: In quantitative decision making, the choice of a course of action that *maxi*mizes the *mini*mum anticipated payoffs; a pessimistic strategy. In contrast, maximax involves maximizing maximum payoffs and minimax involves minimizing maximum losses.

MBO: See management by objectives.

mean: A measure of the central tendency of a set of statistical observations, especially important in analyzing normal distributions. The mean is calculated by totalling the values and dividing the result by the number of observations, so the mean of 3, 7, 4 and 12 is 26 divided by 4, or 6.5 In popular usage, the mean is often called the average, though that term can also refer to the mode or the median average.

means test: A set of criteria applied to those applying for and receiving public assistance, to determine whether or not that assistance will be given or continued.

measures of central tendency: See normal distribution.

measures of dispersion: See normal distribution.

mechanic's lien: A legally enforceable claim for the value of work performed on property of any kind, and the right to hold or otherwise encumber that property until payment has been received, as when an automobile mechanic holds an automobile until payment for repairs has been received, with the ultimate right to receive payment out of the proceeds resulting from sale of the car after legal process.

mechanization: The development of machines, and production techniques and systems that depend on machines, to replace manual labor, techniques, and systems.

media: A group of forms through which things are done, as in communications media, artistic media, and media of exchange. In business, the term usually describes the means of mass communication, including television and radio broadcasting and newspaper and magazine publishing. It is increasingly used in referring to a single medium.

median: A measure of central tendency of a set of statistical observations; the median is the middle number of a series of numbers arranged in order, so in the series: 1, 2, 16, 44, 56, the number 16 is the median. In a normal distribution, the median is theoretically the same as the mean, but when the data is highly variable, references to the median as "the average" can be misleading, since that term popularly refers to the mean.

mediation: In labor-management disputes, and especially during the course of collective bargaining, attempts by outside agencies, such as government, to bring the parties closer together and to expedite the reaching of a settlement. Unlike arbitration, mediation is not binding upon the parties to a dispute.

medical insurance: See health insurance.

Medicare: A system of government-sponsored health insurance payments to those over 65, providing them with help in meeting the high cost of medical care but stopping considerably short of national health insurance.

medium of exchange: Anything that is accepted as money.

medium-range forecasting: Systematic attempts to predict the course of future trends and events, as far as two to three years into the future, often using mathematical models and computer technology.

melon: A relatively large sum of money to be divided among several people, whether proceeds or profits.

member bank: A bank that is a member of the Federal Reserve System.

member firm: A firm that is affiliated with the New York Stock Exchange.

memory: The capacity of a computer to store information; usually refers to the core storage capacity of the central processing unit, but sometimes includes some auxiliary storage capability, as in virtual memory.

mercantile agency: A company in the credit information business, such as Dun and Bradstreet and a substantial number of smaller firms.

mercantilism: A theory favoring extreme protectionism, in which trade barriers are encouraged, home industries are protected against competition from abroad and precious metal supplies are hoarded.

merchandise: Goods for sale or purchase at any level of distribution, but most often used in retail distribution.

merchandise broker: One who acts as a middleman, buying merchandise from a manufacturer or other broker and reselling it to a broker or retailer; part of the chain of distribution between manufacturer and consumer.

merchandising: Those marketing functions involved with presenting and selling goods, including advertising, displaying, promoting, and direct selling; most often encountered in retailing.

merchant bank: A bank engaged in a combination of investment banking, securities-related, and commercial banking functions, such as the international Rothschilds and Hambros banks; while active in Europe, they are not a United States banking form, for legal and historic reasons.

merchant marine: The total of all commercial vessels flying a single national flag. In the United States, and many other countries, shipping is a closely regulated industry, so many vessels that would otherwise be part of the United States merchant marine are registered in the less regulated merchant marines of other countries, such as Liberia.

merchant wholesaler: A merchandise broker who takes title to goods bought from manufacturers and other brokers and then resells those goods to other brokers and to retailers.

merger: The complete takeover of one business by another, whether accomplished by termination of the legal existence of the firm taken over or by its continued legal existence while under the complete control of the acquiring firm. A firm may maintain its name and be operated as a wholly owned subsidiary for public identification and marketing reasons, yet lose all legal existence in such a takeover.

merit increase: A pay increase based upon a person's general performance as evaluated by management, rather than an increase based upon promotion, seniority, or a change in job classification.

merit rating: The process of evaluating employee performance by management, often as part of a planned program of pay increase and promotion evaluation.

methods analysis: The examination of the flow of materials and sequencing of work within an enterprise, with the aim of increasing efficiency, thus reducing cost and improving profitability. As a practical matter, methods analysis covers much the same ground as time and motion study.

Methods-Time Measurement (MTM): As a practical matter, a synonym, or perhaps a euphemism, for time and motion study.

MICR: See magnetic ink character recognition.

microcomputer: Any small computer, made with miniaturized circuits, designed for use in small businesses, schools, or homes, and often costing as little as $1,000 or less; also called personal computers or home computers.

microdot: A very small printed area, literally a very small dot, on which is printed information invisible to the unaided eye; a kind of microform.

microeconomics: The study of small economic units, attempting to generalize about economic behavior from that study; in contrast to macroeconomics, which is the study of economics in the large, using economies and large subsections of economies as subject matter.

microfiche: A microform, in which many microfilms are reduced in size and placed on a single sheet. Such a sheet may contain as few as 30-40 images or as many as 4,000-5,000 images.

microfilm: A photographic image, greatly reduced in size, placed on a sheet, and capable of being shown on a viewer in readable size.

microfilm reader: A machine which displays microfilms in readable size.

microform: Any of several forms in which photographic images are reduced in size; placed on a sheet, roll, or other storage device; and made capable of being shown on a viewer in readable size.

micro instruction: A relatively simple and basic direction within a computer system; in contrast to macro instructions.

micromotion analysis: A time and motion study tool that involves examining motion pictures of work performed, especially by freezing or slowing down replay, to find more efficient, and therefore faster and more profitable, ways of working.

microsecond: One millionth of a second.

middleman: One who is part of the distribution chain between producer and retailer, buying from the producer or other middleman and reselling to a retailer or another middleman. Also one who acts as agent representing a producer or middleman.

middle management: Those managers holding jobs under those of top operating management and over those of first-line supervisors. The term is used rather indiscriminately, though; first-line supervisors are often described as part of middle management, as are some company officers who are part of top operating committees but are not part of a company's day-to-day top operating group.

migrant labor: Workers who follow a pattern of movement from job to job, usually unskilled, following agricultural work with the seasons, and including workers from other countries, such as Mexico, who are imported by American employers and their agents for such work.

milking: To systematically, intentionally and usually illegally strip a company of its assets; often prior to a change of ownership, bankruptcy, or dissolution; for example, by selling assets at bargain prices to a company owned by those in control of the company being looted.

milli: A prefix meaning one thousandth of, as in millimeter, or one thousandth of a meter.

millisecond: One thousandth of a second.

minicomputer: Any relatively small computer, aimed at meeting the needs of medium-sized and small businesses, and of individuals, in contrast to computers designed to handle the needs of large corporations and institutions.

minimax: In quantitative decision making, the choice of a course of action that *mini*mizes the *maxim*um anticipated losses; in contrast, maximax involves maximizing maximum payoffs and maximin involves maximizing minimum payoffs.

minimum markup: A price-fixing device mandated by law, in some jurisdictions, in which retailers are required to apply minimum markups to goods they have purchased for resale.

minimum price: A basic price, which will be charged by a seller for a product or service, even though the quantity or amount purchased is smaller than the basic price would pay for, as when a telephone company charges a minimum monthly rate even if no calls are made or a carrier charges a minimum single shipment price which is the same for a ten-pound as for a hundred-pound package.

minimum scale of production: See indivisibility.

minimum wage: The lowest hourly wage rate that may legally be paid to those doing a job, as defined by applicable federal and state laws.

minor: One who is not in law of legal age, and therefore is unable to exercise and undertake a substantial number of legal rights and responsibilities, such as contracts. The term is defined differently for different legal purposes, as when an 18-year-old may in one jurisdiction be able to drink alcoholic beverages, marry freely, vote, and die in battle, but in another, be able only to vote and die in battle.

minority interest: An ownership interest that is less than a controlling interest in a company. In some companies, a minority interest may be anything less than 50% of ownership; but in large companies, where a controlling interest may be as little as 10%, a minority interest may be anything under 10%. As a practical matter even substantial minority interests may be granted some share in policy making.

mint: A coinage-producing facility, as is the United States Bureau of the Mint.

MIP: See Monthly Investment Plan.

MIS: See management information system.

misdemeanor: A relatively minor crime, when compared to a felony, including all crimes not defined as felonies by statute or practice; but no longer definitively separated from the term felony.

misfeasance: The improper and sometimes civilly or criminally actionable doing of an act which if properly done would be lawful; in practice, the term is often used to describe the doing of an unlawful act, and in that context is synonymous with malfeasance.

misrepresentation: A false statement of fact that is material to a transaction of agreement; such a statement may be explicit or capable of being constructed from actions; and it may be intentional or unintentional.

missionary salespeople: Sales representatives who promote the purchase of their products by every means other than direct sale; usually due to the nature of the product or its distribution pattern. For example, a product sold by jobbers may be demonstrated to jobber sales representatives by a missionary seller employed by the manufacturer.

mixed economy: An economy including both public and private ownership of major industrial units, sometimes of units within the same industry, as when a government-owned postal industry and partially government-owned hospital system exist side by side with a telephone system and basic industries, such as steel and coal, that are privately owned.

mnemonic: A code, rhyme, or formula to aid memory, often used by students and computer programmers; for example, "Roy G. Biv" is a mnemonic for the colors of the rainbow; *r*ed, *o*range, *y*ellow, *g*reen, *b*lue, *i*ndigo, and *v*iolet.

mode: A measure of central tendency of the values in a set of statistical observations; in a data series, the number of value that appears most frequently; for example, in a series: 10, 11, 11, 11, 18, 19, 30, the mode is 11. A series of data in which two values appear with equal or near equal frequency is called bimodal.

model: A less-than-full-size representation, sometimes tangible, as in a ship's model; sometimes symbolic, as in a mathematical mode; and sometimes symbolic but cast in technological form, as in a computer model.

modem: A modulator-demodulator unit built into computerized data transmission systems, operating to translate transmitted signals into signals usable by computers, and vice versa.

modified union shop: A union shop agreement specifying that all employees must become union members after a certain period of employment, but exempting some employees, usually some of those employed before adoption of the union shop agreement, from union membership if requested by those employees.

modularity: Describing the quality of being interchangeable; for example, prefabricated housing units that feature interchangeable parts or computer hardware and software that may be used with many kinds of programs and equipment.

module: A self-contained, standard, and often interchangeable unit, such as a package of advertising services, a set of prefabricated offices, or a discrete part of a computer program handling a repeated, routine function.

mom and pop store: Any small family-run business.

monetary controls: Restrictions placed on the free exchange of currency between nations, by a single nation or a group of nations.

monetary policy: The set of policies by which a government attempts to manipulate the economy in pursuit of current national goals; in the United States, through the Federal Reserve System, and in many other countries, through their central banks.

monetary reserve: The stock of precious metal, usually gold, held by a government to secure its currency. The United States, in common with most other nations, secures its currency with only its full faith and credit, even though some gold stock is held.

monetary unit: A country's main unit of currency, such as the United States dollar, the British pound, or the Japanese yen.

money: A medium of exchange, generally accepted as having and holding a specified value against which the values of non-monetary items (stores of value) can be measured and expressed, as when a loaf of bread, which is non-monetary, can be bought for a dollar, which is a standard unit of money.

money market: A worldwide body of markets engaged in trading the short-term debt obligations of governments, financial institutions, and commercial firms, in such forms as commercial paper, bankers' acceptances, and treasury bills.

money market fund: A kind of mutual fund, trading mainly in the kinds of short-term debt obligations found in money markets, such as certificates of deposit, commercial paper, treasury bills, other United States Government securities, and bankers' acceptances.

money order: A money instrument purchased on a one-time basis and sent to its payee for conversion into cash; normally used as a means of sending money by mail by those without checking accounts or by those who want the payee to be able to use the proceeds of the order immediately,

rather than having to wait for checks to clear.

money supply: The total amount of a nation's currency and demand deposits denominated in that national currency available for use at any time. The size of a nation's money supply relative to its productive capacity is often viewed as an important factor influencing inflation and deflation, boom and recession, so governments often tend to use money supply manipulation as a key element of national economic strategy, as does the United States government through the Federal Reserve.

money wages: Cash wages received, without adjustment for such factors as real wage changes due to cost of living fluctuations or dollar value changes due to international currency value movements.

monitor: To watch; for example, to continuously survey the pace of inflation, Soviet or United States nuclear weapons tests, the performance of a production line, or the operation of a computer system. Also refers to a device used in such observations.

monopolistic competition: Competition between several sellers who among them dominate a market, and whose products and prices differ little in function and performance.

monopoly: Effective control over a market by a single seller or a group of sellers, with no substantial competition and therefore no major buying choices available to purchasers other than refusal to buy at all—and no choice possible in the instance of monopoly-controlled necessities. United States examples are telephone services, power utilities, and postal service.

monopsony: Effective control over a market by a single buyer or group of buyers.

Monthly Investment Plan (MIP): A New York Stock Exchange sponsored installment stock purchase plan, in which investors buy small amounts of listed stocks on a regular basis, usually monthly or quarterly, with title to the stocks purchased passing as purchased, even when only a fraction of a share is purchased.

moonlighting: The holding of another job by someone primarily employed elsewhere; often night work by those who work days. The practice is often frowned upon and sometimes even prohibited by public and private employers, so the term carries some implications of illegality or subterfuge.

moot: A legal question that has not yet been settled by judicial interpretation, is too abstract for such settlement, or is no longer relevant, having had its basis removed by operation of other factors.

moral debt: See debt.

moratorium: A government-sanctioned postponement of debt repayment for a kind of debtor or debt, issued pursuant to government policy, as in the instance of Presidential declaration of a bank holiday in 1933, to forestall imminent collapse of the banking system.

Morris Plan: See industrial bank.

mortality table: A chart listing life expectancy data, used to help set life insurance premium rates.

mortgage: A legally enforceable lien on property created by the pledge of that property as security for repayment of a debt or other obligation; also the legal document setting forth that lien, the terms of payment, and all other pertinent matters. In the common law, now largely superseded by state statutes, a mortgage was not a lien, but an actual transfer of property, voided by the mortgagee's performance of all obligations stated in the mortgage instrument.

mortgage bond: A kind of bond, secured by real or personal property, in contrast to unsecured bonds.

mortgage company: A company mainly engaged in the business of financing real estate and other property transactions through issuance of property-secured loans.

mortgagee: One who holds a mortgage on the property of another, being named as mortgage holder in the mortgage instrument.

mortgage insurance: A federally funded program which insures private lenders against losses stemming from some kinds of mortgage and housing loans. Administered by the Department of Housing and Urban Development, the program is intended to encourage lower down payments and interest rates and the availability of loan money to those of relatively modest means.

mortgage market: The aggregate of activity by those giving and getting mortgage loans in a given area; often referring to a state, as the states regulate mortgage loan rates and terms, but sometimes to the entire country. The term is sometimes used as synonymous with the rate of interest generally charged by lenders in a mortgage market.

mortgage premium: An extra charge, beyond the interest charges, attached to a mortgage transaction by the lender. It is often denominated in "points," that is, a specified percentage of the mortgage loan. For example, a bank or other lender might issue a mortgage loan of $20,000, at the going interest rate, plus 2 "points," or 2% of $20,000, for an extra charge of $400, payable on consumation of the mortgage loan.

mortgagor: One who mortgages a property, usually in return for a loan.

most favored nation clause: A kind of preferential tariff, in which two or more nations, when making a trade agreement, agree to apply any favorable tariff treatment given any other nation in future to each other as well.

motivation research: The study of consumer behavior; mainly used by companies to attempt to induce favorable reactions toward what they sell.

moving average: An average or mean that is calculated in timed sequence using the same number of time periods but, at each calculation, dropping the oldest and adding the latest data; for example, a securities price average computed from twelve monthly averages, which is recomputed each month with data added from the most current month and dropped from the oldest month.

moving sale: A sale of retail goods at discounted prices due to a planned change in place of business by the retailer, to avoid paying the cost of physically moving the goods to the new location.

MTM: See Methods-Time Measurement.

muckraking: The investigation and exposure of scandal and corruption involving special interests and public officials, sometimes separately and sometimes operating together.

multi-employer bargaining: Collective bargaining between one or more unions and more than one employer at the same time, but less inclusive than industry-wide bargaining, which includes all or almost all of the employers in a given industry.

multilateral trade: Trade between more than two countries.

multinational company: A major international company, with operations, often including subsidiaries and associated companies, throughout the world, and managed as a single massive entity for all major corporate policy purposes.

multiple-line insurance company: An insurance company that covers many kinds of property insurance risks, but not usually life, accident and health insurance; most major property insurers are multiple-line companies.

multiple listing: The listing of real estate for sale with a number of brokers, often an association of brokers covering a given geographical area, rather than with a single broker.

multiple regression analysis: See regression analysis.

multiplex transmission: The transmission of two or more bodies of information on the same communications channel.

multiplier principle: The theory that some kinds of expenditures impact on the economy far more strongly than the amounts expended, as when investment in new plant causes additional employment, retail purchasing, building, and other associated economic benefits.

multiprocessing: In computer processing, the joint operation of multiple processing units sharing a common memory, under the direction of one executive central processing unit; allows for time-sharing of computer equipment by many users at once.

multiprogramming: See interleaving.

municipal bond: A debt obligation of any unit of government in the United States, other than the Federal government, including state and all other lesser governmental units. Such debt obligations are, with a few exceptions, tax-exempt, and therefore are often attractive tax shelter devices for those of substantial income.

Murphy's Law: The colloquial expression that anything that can go wrong, will go wrong; it has become part of the everyday language of American management.

mutual benefit society: See benefit society.

mutual company: A company that distributes profits to its members in direct proportion to the dollar quantity of business they do with the company; there is no stock, but rather equitable holding that varies with that quantity of business, as when mutual savings banks distribute dividends to their depositors and mutual insurance companies distribute dividends to their policy holders.

mutual fund: An investment fund that pools the invested funds of others and invests those funds on their behalf, usually in a specific kind of investment, such as money market instruments, municipal bonds, or common stock.

mutual insurance company: An insurance company that issues no stock, but instead distributes its profits to its policy holders as premium rebates or dividends. Although

N

NAM: See National Association of Manufacturers.

nanosecond: One billionth of a second.

narrow market: A market, usually referring to a single security, that is characterized by a relatively small quantity of the security in circulation and relatively few trades and which is therefore vulnerable to wide fluctuations in price as trades are made.

NASA: See National Aeronautics and Space Administration.

NASD: See National Association of Securities Dealers.

national accounting: The development and issuance of summary national economic information, including data on gross national product, foreign trade, savings and investments, government finances, and personal income and expenditure.

national accounts: Large customers who buy products or services from a seller for use in many locations, often scattered nationwide, and who are handled as special accounts by the seller, often with separate sales representatives, pricing policies, and distribution handling.

national advertising: Advertising that reaches a national audience, usually through nationally circulated media.

National Aeronautics and Space Administration (NASA): A United States agency charged with responsibility for United States space exploration programs, and for aeronautics and space research.

National Association of Manufacturers (NAM): A major United States manufacturers trade association, engaged in a wide range of legislative and educational programs on behalf of its membership.

National Association of Securities Dealers (NASD): A securities dealers trade association, representing United States securities dealers, and holding some enforcement powers granted by the Securities and Exchange Commission, enabling it to regulate over-the-counter operations by dealers.

national bank: A bank chartered by the Federal government to conduct a commercial banking business, in contrast to a state chartered bank.

national brand: A consumer product brand name that is advertised and sold nationwide, which is widely recognized by consumers, and which is usually a household name, such as a well-known automobile, toothpaste, or deodorant.

National Bureau of Standards: See Bureau of Standards.

national debt: The total of a national government's outstanding debt obligations.

national income: See gross national product.

National Industrial Conference Board (NICB): A not-for-profit private business research organization, focusing on questions affecting American business, which conducts seminars and issues several research-oriented publications.

nationalization: The process of government

takeover of privately held property and organizations, with or without compensation, gradually or immediately. Examples are oil industry takeovers by nations in the Middle East and by Mexico, and industry takeovers following the Russian Revolution.

National Labor Relations Board (NLRB): A United States government agency charged with the responsibility of enforcing and interpreting Federal laws relating to collective bargaining, and functioning as a quasi-judicial industrial relations court for the accomplishment of these purposes.

National Mediation Board: A United States government agency charged with responsibility for mediating industrial disputes covered by the Railway Labor Act, and for appointing arbitrators when necessary.

national product: See gross national product.

National Railroad Adjustment Board: A Federal agency responsible for entering into and attempting to achieve settlement of disputes between railway labor and management.

national union: See labor union.

NC: See numerical control.

negative skewness: See skewness.

negligence: In law, failure to do what a reasonable person would do under the same circumstances, with consequent actionable damage to another.

negotiable: 1. Legally transferable to another merely by delivery or by endorsement and delivery, the new holder then becoming owner for all legal purposes. **2.** Open for bargaining, rather than being firm as stated; usually referring to prices and terms in a business situation.

negotiable instruments: Instruments, such as checks and promissory notes, which can be legally transferred merely by delivery or by endorsement and delivery, the new holder then becoming owner for all legal purposes.

negotiated price: A price fixed as a result of discussion and agreement between the parties to a purchase contract, rather than fixed by the seller.

negotiation: 1. The act of transferring a negotiable instrument. **2.** The process of collective bargaining. **3.** The process of bargaining in any business situation, as in the development of a trade agreement satisfactory to the contracting parties.

nepotism: The giving of unearned advantage to relatives; for example, giving jobs, salaries, and contracts to relatives even when others are far better qualified.

nesting: In computer programming, including a smaller program segment or block of data within a larger one, in a standard hierarchy.

net: The remainder, after all else has been added and subtracted; in business, always capable of being expressed discretely, almost always as a specific plus or minus number.

net assets: See net worth.

net asset value: In investment companies, the market value of all assets, minus all liabilities, divided by the number of shares, thus computing value per share.

net avails: The actual amount a borrower realizes from a discounted note, subtracting the amount of the discount from the amount borrowed.

net bonded debt: The net of bonds issued, minus bonds in any way paid, minus funds held in the issuing corporation or government as a reserve against repayment.

net business formation: The number of new businesses minus the number of firms going out of business for all reasons in any given period.

net change: The difference in the price of a security between the close of trading one day and the closing of trading the next day.

net earnings: See net profits before taxes.

net foreign investment: The net of all investments in other countries owned by a country and its citizens, minus all investments owned by foreigners in that country.

net income: The income remaining for the equity holders in a business after deduction of all expenses and other deductions from all revenues.

net lease: A lease which rents only land or land and structures, with the lessee paying for all other costs arising from that which is leased, including such costs as taxes and all maintenance; for example, a lease of an entire shopping center from its owner by an operating company.

net liquid assets: See liquid assets.

net loss: The net of expenditures and revenues during a given period, when expenditures exceed revenues.

net national debt: The net of all debts owed by the Federal Government; does not include debts owed by the country's citizens or by state and local governments.

net national product (NNP): The net of gross national product minus depreciation, or the wear upon and using up of capital goods used in the process of creating gross national product.

net-net: A final net figure; synonymous with bottom line.

net price: The actual price paid by buyer to seller for a purchased item, after all discounts, adjustments, and negotiations have been completed.

net proceeds: See net avails.

net profits: The net of revenues minus all appropriate costs. The term is often used as a synonym for net income, but in ordinary business usage may refer to either net profits before taxes or net profits after taxes.

net profits after taxes: The net of revenues minus operating expenses and taxes.

net profits before taxes: The net of revenues minus operating expenses but before deductions for taxes.

net sales: The net of gross sales minus all returns, allowances, and other appropriate deductions.

net weight: The net of the contents of a packaged item, minus the weight of all packaging materials, but including the weight of any substances in the contents even if not usable, such as water injected into packaged ham.

net working capital: See working capital.

net worth: The value of total ownership interest, the net of total assets minus total liabilities; expressed variously according to the form of business organization, as stockholders' equity, partner's equity or proprietor's equity. The net worth of an individual includes personal as well as business assets and liabilities, and is the net of all personal assets minus all personal liabilities.

New Deal: President Franklin D. Roosevelt's slogan, characterizing the very wide range of economic and social programs developed during his administration, in an attempt to help move the country out of the depths of the Great Depression of the 1930s; including such programs as social security, home relief, and a wide range of farm price supports.

New Frontier: President John F. Kennedy's slogan, characterizing the frame of mind he wanted the American people to adopt during his administration; characterized by such then new Federal programs as the Peace Corps and the Alliance for Progress.

new hire: Someone who has just been hired.

new issue: A securities issue that has just been put on the market, in contrast to a block sale of securities previously issued.

new plant and equipment spending: Total investment spending by the private sector on new plant and equipment; an important factor in smoothing out fluctuations in the business cycle, as actual spending in this area continues for some time after a period of high economic activity.

New York Curb Exchange: See American Stock Exchange.

New York Stock Exchange (NYSE): By far the largest stock exchange in the United States, and one of the world's largest stock exchanges. Often referred to as "the Exchange" or "the Big Board."

New York Stock Exchange Common Stock Index: A widely quoted common stock index maintained and reported by the New York Stock Exchange.

NICB: See National Industrial Conference Board.

Nielsen rating: The audience share achieved by television programs, as measured by surveys conducted by the Nielsen organization.

night depository: A device by which bank depositors may make deposits after a bank's regular business hours.

night differential: A premium paid for work performed on a night shift, as compared with substantially similar work done on a day shift, to compensate workers for a less attractive shift worked; usually included in collective bargaining agreements.

night shift: A work period that occurs mainly at night, usually as either a second or third shift; usually in the period 3 P.M.–7A.M.

nixie mail: Mail returned to the senders of mail order solicitations for any reason, such as improper address or insufficient postage.

NLRB: See National Labor Relations Board.

NNP: See net national product.

no contest: See nolo contendere.

no fault insurance: A kind of automobile insurance which eliminates or sharply reduces the potential liability of drivers involved in automobile accidents, assuming in most instances that neither driver is guilty of ordinary negligence, and so attempting to reduce insurance claims and amounts, thus reducing premium costs.

no load fund: A mutual fund that does not charge its investors heavy sales and management fees as soon as the investment is made, thus immediately sharply diminishing the value of the funds invested, in contrast to a frontloaded fund, which does make such charges.

nolo contendere: A plea of no contest made by the defendant in a criminal case, which operates for purposes of that specific case as a guilty plea, but which does not constitute an admission of guilt that can be used against the defendant in another case, criminal or civil.

nominal account: In an accounting system, any account containing balances transferrable to retained earnings at the end of a fiscal year, because of the completion of all transactions relating to that account, as contrasted to a real account, which carries forward from one fiscal year to the next.

nominal partner: Someone who gives every appearance of being a partner in a firm, such as being included on a firm's letterhead, but who in fact has no legal connection with that firm.

nominal price: 1. A price quoted on a lightly and infrequently traded security, reflecting a seller's estimate, rather than current market activity. **2.** A very low price.

nominal wages: See money wages.

nonassessable stock: Stock limiting the potential liability of its holders to the amount paid for that stock, and prohibiting the assessment of levies on that stock for additional monies by anyone.

noncallable bonds: Bonds that mature only at their stated maturity dates and that cannot for any reason be recalled or redeemed by their issuers before maturity.

noncontributory: Describing a fringe benefit, such as a savings plan, group life, or group health insurance plan, for which all expenses are paid by the employer, with no contribution made by employees.

noncumulative dividends: Dividends payable by a company to holders of its preferred stock which do not cumulate; if a specified date for dividend payment passes without dividend payment, the dividend is lost.

nondegradable: Substances that do not break down into harmless component parts when discarded after use, such as cans, some extremely harmful chemicals, and metals, but instead operate as continuing sources of pollution and in some instances direct causes of disease.

nonfeasance: Failure to perform a legal, usually contractual duty, but without intent to do so.

nonforfeiture feature: A feature of many life insurance contracts carrying the forced savings feature called cash surrender value, providing that the contract may not be cancelled for nonpayment of premiums as long as the cash surrender value in the contract can be borrowed against for premium payments, and further providing an automatic loan for premium payments from cash surrender value.

noninsurable risk: A risk that insurance companies are unwilling to insure, usually because of the nature of the risk involved. Risks considered noninsurable by some are viewed as insurable by other companies, which charge far higher premium rates. In some instances, companies legally required to insure risks they individually regard as noninsurable will pool such risks, as in the automobile insurance assigned risk pool.

nonmember bank: A commercial bank that is not a member of the Federal Reserve System.

nonnegotiable instrument: An instrument that lacks one or more of the requisites for being negotiable, and that therefore, while being an instrument of value, is not capable of being freely negotiated.

nonoperating company: A company that en-gages in no operations of its own, being dormant or having converted its assets into leases or investments.

nonoperating revenue: Revenue from all sources other than operations, such as dividends and land rental income for non-real estate companies.

nonparticipating policy: An insurance policy that does not carry with it any kind of ownership interest in the insurance company issuing it, and therefore does not share in dividends.

nonperformance: Actionable failure to perform obligations under the terms of a valid contract.

nonprice competition: The use of means other than price competition to compete in the marketplace, including such devices as prizes, premiums, exceptional guarantees, and credit extension.

nonprofit corporation: A corporation organized and chartered to be not-for-profit, from which no stockholder, manager, or trustee can legally take profit, and which often is wholly or partially exempt from federal and some state and local taxes due to the nature of their socially and legislatively approved activities, in such areas as education and charitable causes.

nonrecourse loan: A loan by the terms of which a borrower makes only a promise to pay, supported only by any collateral that may be stated in the loan agreement. Should default occur, the creditor has no other recourse or claim against the borrower, and that is so stated in the loan agreement.

nonrecurring charge: A one-time expense, so treated on accounting statements.

nonrenewable resource: See wasting asset.

nonstock corporation: A corporation which by its nature does not issue stock as evidence of equity ownership, as when a mutual insurance company, mutual savings bank, or fraternal organization confers equitable shares in direct proportion to and measured by premium payments, deposits, or membership.

nonunion labor: Workers who are not organized into or represented by unions.

no par value stock: Corporate stock which has no stated par value, but is carried on the books of the corporation at a value set by its board of directors.

no protest: An interbank practice, in which a bank stamps "no protest" on a check or other collectible so that another bank collecting the check will not protest in case of nonpayment, but will return the instrument unpaid; usually for instruments carrying small face amounts.

norm: A standard, such as a standard of performance or behavior. In statistics, the mean in a normal distribution.

normal distribution: In statistics, a frequency distribution, also called the Gaussian distribution, that has a characteristic bell shape—high in the middle, sloping sharply on either side, and then trailing off on both sides. According to the central limit theorem, for any kind of data, the larger the sample, the more likely the distribution will assume this normal—that is symmetrical—shape. In a normal distribution the main measures of central tendency—the mean, the mode and the median—all have the same value, and the measures of dispersion—the standard deviation and the variance—show the spread of data around that central value. Statisticians use tables based on the theoretical normal distribution to help them predict information about actual populations; applications range widely, from analysis of intelligence test scores to controlling quality of production processes.

normal probability distribution: See normal distribution.

no strike clause: A provision in a collective bargaining agreement prohibiting strikes for the term of the contract.

notary public: A state-licensed person, legally authorized to perform a variety of document-related functions, including the taking and certification of affidavits, depositions, and oaths; of payment demands and protests of several kinds of financial instruments; and certification of documents. The notary's seal is admissible legal evidence.

note: A negotiable instrument in which the note's maker promises to pay a specified sum, at a specified time or on demand, to the note's payee. The maker may defend against making the promised payment for lack of a valid agreement as between the original maker and payee, but not against other holders in due course.

notes payable: The sum of all notes promised and owed by a business to its creditors, such as banks and suppliers.

notes receivable: The sum of all notes promised and owed by others to a business, such as customers.

notice of dishonor: A document which is issued by a notary public at the request of a note holder who has been refused payment of a note by its maker, and which functions as legal evidence that the note has been dishonored, or unpaid.

novation: The replacement of an existing contract by a new contract, by agreement of the parties to both the existing and new contract. The new contract may alter the parties, the terms, or both.

no-win situation: A situation in which any course of action pursued, including inaction, will result in adverse consequences, and in which decision making is largely a matter of choosing between quite unpalatable alternatives.

NRC: See Nuclear Regulatory Commission.

Nuclear Regulatory Commission (NRC): A Federal agency responsible for the monitoring and regulation of all United States non-military activities involving nuclear energy.

nuisance tax: A very low-yielding tax, which is usually more trouble and sometimes expense to administer and pay than it is worth to the taxing authority; many taxes so considered by those taxed are considered well worth levying by taxing authorities.

null hypothesis: In research, the assumption that experimental results are due to chance variations alone; the researcher's aim is to get statistically significant results that cannot be explained by chance alone, the assumption being that the alternative hypothesis—the theory that the researcher sets out to prove—is then true, though subject to Type I and Type II error.

numbered account: A bank account designated by number, rather than by name, as a means of helping protect the anonymity of the account's owner, often as a means of soliciting bank business from those seeking to hide assets from their own government for tax avoidance and other purposes; available in several countries, notably Switzerland.

numerical control (NC): The control of production processes by machines programmed to work other machines, rather than being worked by humans; for example, the use of a magnetic tape to control the operation of a single milling machine or of a whole production line.

NYSE: See New York Stock Exchange.

O

OAS: See Organization of American States.

object language: Machine language that can be used by the computer, translated by an assembler or compiler from the source language, such as FORTRAN or COBOL, in which a program was originally written.

object program: A computer program, written in the machine language computers use, that has been translated by an assembler or compiler from the source program written by the programmer.

obligation: 1. Any kind of legally enforceable duty to another. **2.** Any kind of money debt to another, for a specific sum and legally enforceable.

obsolete: That which is no longer used, having been superseded by other devices or techniques. In business, the obsolescence of physical assets means a sharp reduction in their value, even though they may be entirely usable for many years.

occupation: The work one does, whether thought to be trade, profession, or job, and whether paid or unpaid.

occupational accident: An accident that occurs in the course of performing work or work-connected activities, and in any way attributable to those activities, whether or not on the premises of an employer or actually engaged in work at the time the accident occurred; for example, an accident occuring while directly at work and an accident occurring on a work-connected errand on company time off the premises have both been classified as compensable occupational accidents.

occupational hazard: A work-related human risk of any kind, including such health risks as black lung and cancer caused by industrial material and processes, as well as all kinds of industrial accidents.

occupational illness: An illness caused by the nature of one's job, such as tuberculosis caused by working in mines or lead poisoning caused by work in lead refining.

occupational mobility: The relative ability of workers to move from occupation to occupation, sometimes but not always carrying skills with them; most often found among unskilled workers.

Occupational Safety and Health Administration (OSHA): A Federal agency responsible for interpretation, regulation, enforcement, and education in the area of federally set industrial health and safety standards.

occupational structure: The total job situation in workplace, company, industry, region, or economy at any given time, focusing on the classification and quantity of jobs being done.

odd lot: Any quantity of securities other than 100 shares or a multiple thereof; trades of 10, 99, and 199 shares are all odd lot trades.

odd lot dealer: A stockbroker who buys securities in standard lots of 100 shares or some multiple of 100, and then sells odd lots, usually in amounts of less than 100 shares.

OECD: See Organization for Economic Co-operation and Development.

OEM: Original equipment manufacturer.

OFCC: See Office of Federal Contract Compliance.

offer: To make a proposal to another, involving but not limited to buying or selling. For example, in the securities industry, one may offer or bid to buy a security at a proposed price, or offer to sell at a proposed price; and contracting parties, both in commercial contracts and in collective bargaining, may make and counter with offers.

offering: A securities issue, offered by its sellers to the public.

Office of Federal Contract Compliance (OFCC): A Federal agency responsible for the execution of national policy forbidding employment discrimination by those doing business with the Federal government.

Office of Management and Budget (OMB): A Federal agency, charged with responsibility for helping Presidents develop Federal budgets and for exercising some control functions relating to administration of adopted budgets.

officer: One who is by charter and in law designated as a responsible official of an organization, capable of acting for that organization within specified legal limits; usual designations of officers in business include president, secretary, treasurer, controller, and vice president.

official exchange rates: A currency exchange rate set by a government, at which its currency is to be exchanged for other currencies.

off-line: In electronic data processing, machines that are not directly controlled by the central processing unit.

offset: 1. A sum balancing or reducing an opposite sum, as when damage claims and counterclaims by the parties to a lawsuit eventually, wholly, or partly negate each other, or when sums entered on both sides of a single account wholly or partly cancel each other. **2.** A widely used printing process.

off the board: A stock that is not listed on any stock exchange, but rather is traded directly in the over-the-counter market; an unlisted stock.

off the gold standard: See demonetization.

off the shelf: Goods purchased from stock, rather than those needing to be produced to order.

oligopoly: A group of producers effectively dominating a market, and engaged either in illegal collusive price fixing or wholly legal price fixing by unspoken but equally close consent.

oligopsony: A group of buyers effectively dominating a market, and using that domination to create favorable market conditions for themselves by driving down supplier prices and in some instances driving out small suppliers in favor of their own supply organizations.

OMB: See Office of Management and Budget.

omnibus clause: In liability insurance policies, a clause extending coverage to unnamed others beyond the insured, who may be, for all practical and policy purposes, standing in the shoes of the insured for coverage purposes, as when automobile coverage extends to the "guest" driver of an insured car.

on account: Characterizing the nature of a partial payment made on an account, usually one that is fully due and payable.

one-bank holding company: See bank holding company.

one-price policy: A pricing policy by which the seller sets a fixed price on a specified kind of merchandise and will not negotiate the price of that merchandise; often a stated intention and a tendency rather than a hard fact, as large customers tend to have considerable bargaining power.

one-stop banking: A slogan put forward by commercial banks offering a wide range of services to depositors, in an attempt to attract customers by distinguishing commercial banking from savings banking, which has historically offered a more limited range of services.

one-time rate: The charge for an advertisement placed only once, a higher rate than that charged per ad for multiple placements.

on-line: In electronic data processing, machines that are part of or directly in contact with a computer system, whether controlled by the central processing unit or in remote contact with that unit.

on the block: See auction.

on-the-job training: Training to do a job that occurs mainly while a worker is employed at that job, as when an assembly line worker learns how to handle the necessary tools, while employed to do that job; sometimes part of government-funded programs aimed at helping the unskilled and technologically unemployed gain marketable skills.

OPEC: See Organization of Petroleum Exporting Countries.

open account: A credit arrangement, in which a seller delivers goods sold to a buyer without demand for cash with order, and the buyer settles amounts due in cash later; while not intended as a credit vehicle, but rather as a convenience for both buyer and seller, it often serves as a means of credit extension from seller to buyer.

open credit: A line of credit, in which a lending institution or seller extends credit to a customer or buyer up to a set limit, so that the credit is available and ready to be used as desired, without specific approval by the creditor each time it is used.

open door policy: 1. In management, the maintenance of open access to superiors by subordinates; often symbolized by literally leaving an executive's office door open to all. **2.** In international trade, an attempt to maintain free access by all nations to a trad-ing area, rather than allowing some nations to obtain preferential treatment, such as tariff concessions; originating as American policy toward China in the late nineteenth century.

open-end contract: An agreement between buyer and seller, setting out most of the terms of their contract, but leaving some terms open, or indefinite. For example, all terms but maximum quantity may be agreed upon; then the buyer has the right to purchase the goods specified, at the terms and price set, in any desired quantity above a stated minimum.

open-end interview: An interview in which the interviewer has some fixed or "starter" questions, but in which those questions serve only to provide some basic data and pave the way for a wide-ranging discussion with the interviewee; usually an interview in considerable depth, rather than one reaching for large amounts of quantifiable material.

open-end mortgage: A mortgage that gives the mortgagee the right to borrow more from the mortgagor on the same mortgage, rather than being forced to undertake additional mortgages if a larger amount is desired.

open-end mutual fund: A mutual fund that sets no limit on the number of shares available for public sale, usually selling as many shares as possible continually; the most prevalent form of mutual fund.

opening: 1. A vacant job, which an employer is currently seeking to fill. **2.** The introduction of a new line of products, especially of seasonal lines, such as clothing.

opening price: The price of a security at the start of a trading day on a stock exchange, which may be and often is different from its price at the close of that exchange's previous trading day. Securities traded on several exchanges may open at different prices on different exchanges.

open listing: The listing of a property for sale with more than one broker simultaneously, without forfeiting the owner's ability to sell the property independently without any broker or brokerage commission.

open market: A market open to all potential buyers and sellers, rather than effectively controlled by statutes or business organizations; often describes a main tendency rather than a pure state, as most markets are in some ways restricted.

open market operations: Federal Reserve bank trading of United States government securities, usually short-term securities, in markets open to all traders; part of central bank manipulation of credit supply in pursuit of current national economic objectives.

open mortgage: See open-end mortgage.

open order: An order that has not yet been filled. In general business operations, that is often a back order, one placed previously but for supply reasons not yet sent to the customer. In the securities industry, it is a trading order that has not yet been executed by a broker, but that in most instances is executed within 24 hours of placement.

open shop: A workplace employing both union and nonunion members; in practice, either a nonunion shop or one in the process of being organized into one or more unions.

open stock: Goods stocked by a seller that are sold by the piece and have standard, substantially identical replacement pieces available, in contrast to goods that are unique or that are sold only in sets.

open union: A union that does not restrict its membership by placing obstacles to membership, such as unusually high membership fees, discriminatory practices, and current union member recommendation of prospective new members.

operating budget: A budget for current income and expenditures, rather than for capital items.

operating company: A company actively engaged in conducting one or more lines of business, in contrast to a nonoperating company, which is dormant or has converted its assets into investments or leases.

operating cost: A cost incurred while conducting business and attributable to the conduct of business.

operating expense: See operating cost.

operating profit: See operating income.

operating rate: The actual production of a company or industry compared to its potential to produce at full capacity, usually expressed as a percentage, as when a steel plant is described as operating at 75% of capacity. Capacity being hard to determine, the operating rate is almost always an estimate, rather than a hard and verifiable figure.

operating ratios: The relationships between items on an operating statement, usually expressing items related as pencentages and multiples of each other; for example, sales costs as a percentage of net revenue or divisional operating revenue as a percentage of company-wide operating revenue.

operating statement: A financial report on the operations of all or part of a business organization for a given period; for example, a rather detailed statement of income and expenditures or a cash flow statement.

operating system: In electronic data processing, a group of controlling programs which govern the functioning of a whole computer system, within which specific programs and groups of programs function to solve specific problems. Examples are the basic operating system (BOS) and the disk operating system (DOS).

operation: The carrying out of a single job, plan, or function, as in performance of a single kind of job on an assembly line; a computer response to a single programmed instruction; or the execution of a military or corporate takeover plan.

operations analysis: See operations research.

operations research: Research into the problems encountered by organizations and their systems, especially directed to the collection of information in quantity for use in analytical systems with a wide variety of models and mathematical approaches, as in a Presidential popularity poll run by an opinion sampling organization.

OPIC: See Overseas Private Investment Corporation.

opinion poll: A survey, usually using some kind of questionnaire, aimed at determining the views of some portion of a population on one or more questions.

opportunity cost: The best return that might be realized from an investment, taking investment goals into account, expressed as a cost and contrasted with the return that is currently being realized; for example, the ability to invest surplus company cash in relatively safe securities yielding 8-10%, as contrasted with current operating assets yielding 5%. The construct is often used in assessing major expenditures, such as new plants and acquisition possibilities.

optical character recognition (OCR): In computer systems the machine reading and input into the system of printed materials by scanning light patterns, bypassing punched cards and other intermediate steps; in contrast to magnetic ink character recognition (MICR).

optical reader: See optical scanner.

optical scanner: A machine capable of reading printed or written data directly into a computer system.

optimum lot size: See economic order quantity.

option: 1. The right to buy or sell something at a certain price within a specific time, usually as stated in a written agreement enforceable at law, in which that right has been conveyed in return for some kind of consideration; for example, a tradable option to buy a security or commodity; an option to buy company stock offered as part of an employee's pay package; or an option to buy land. **2.** A choice, such as alternative

contract terms during negotiations, or of modes of payment in settlement of a life insurance claim.

optional bond: A bond that may be called in and redeemed by its issuer at some time or times before its final maturity date; a callable bond.

optional dividend: A dividend that stockholders may take in more than one form, as they choose; usually a choice between stock and cash.

option period: The time during which an option may be exercised, according to the terms of the option.

options exchange: An exchange making markets in stock or commodities options, sometimes exclusively, sometimes as part of a regular stock exchange.

oral agreement: An agreement between contracting parties, that, in the absence of a written agreement, is legally binding upon the parties; sometimes but rarely, enforceable at law, though never against a legally valid written agreement.

order: A legally enforceable buy or sell instruction; for example, a written or oral purchase order, buying goods from a supplier, or a customer's instructions to a broker to buy or sell securities for the customer's account.

order bill of lading: See bill of lading.

order point system: A system of inventory control, in which additional stock is ordered when stock on hand reaches a previously determined level, taking the stock level up to what is thought to be maximum useful level, so that stock quantities move between minimum and maximum.

ordinal number: A number that holds a specific position in a series of numbers, as in first, second, or third position; in contrast to a cardinal number, which indicates amount or quantity, not rank.

ordinal utility: In some economic theory, the

extent to which consumers want products, ranked in order of preference.

ordinary depreciation: Losses in value occurring from normal aging and wear and tear, rather than from extraordinary factors, such as damage due to fire and natural causes.

ordinary life insurance: Life insurance that includes cash surrender value, and is therefore a combination of life insurance and savings.

ordinate: The vertical distance from 0 on the base line of a graph, or the number of units a point is from the origin on a y-axis; one of the two coordinates necessary to describe a point on a rectangular or Cartesian graph, the other being the abscissa.

organization chart: A chart showing the formal structure of an organization, sometimes also attempting to indicate overlapping relationships between structural components and informal structures of authority.

organization expenses: Expenses connected with the organization of a new business enterprise, such as legal fees, registrations, and deposits.

Organization for Economic Cooperation and Development (OECD): An international organization for economic studies, sponsored by its member governments, including the United States; disseminates information through meetings and publications, aiming at the development of international cooperation to meet common problems.

organization manual: A manual that attempts to describe every aspect of an organization's structure and parts, often also setting forth internal rules and procedures to be followed by the organization's employees.

Organization of American States (OAS): An international organization, formed by the governments of the countries of North, Central, and South America, which serves as both a forum and a vehicle for approaching such common problems as aid to the less developed nations of the hemisphere.

Organization of Petroleum Exporting Countries (OPEC): An international oil producers' cartel, formed by the governments of most major oil-exporting countries, which functions to set prices and fix other common policies in world oil markets.

organized labor: All labor unions and their associated and affiliated organizations, including political action, social, cultural, welfare, and educational groups; a general rather than specific description, as no single organization or group of organizations represents all such groups.

organizer: See union organizer.

original cost: The purchase price of an asset, as of its acquisition date, without any postacquisition costs.

original entry: An accounting entry, recording a transaction and entering it into an accounting system for the first time.

OSHA: See Occupational Safety and Health Administration.

other assets, deductions, income, or liabilities: Miscellaneous categories on accounting statements, summing up small amounts in all the major standard accounting categories.

outdoor advertising: Display advertising placed in outside locations, such as billboards and other kinds of signs.

Outer Seven: See European Free Trade Association.

outlay: An expenditure, in cash, cash equivalents, or property.

outlet: Any selling organization; usually describing a retail store.

out-of-pocket cost: 1. A cost, usually relatively minor, that is paid for in cash by an individual, as when an employee spends cash or uses a personal credit card on a business trip and is either advanced cash for the trip or is reimbursed afterward. **2.** A variable cost, as in costs incurred directly in the process of production.

output: 1. Any kind of production and any

materials produced. **2.** Data resulting from the operation of computer systems.

outside audit: See external audit.

outstanding: 1. A collectible or other current debt, due and collectible but as yet uncollected. **2.** Company ownership shares or debt obligations held by anyone other than the company's own treasury.

overage: Any amount more than is specified in a plan or on a document. The term may be used as either a plus or a minus; production may be over plan and budget, creating an overage; expenditures may be higher than plan or budget, creating an overage.

overbought: The condition of having bought more of something than was economically wise, and of now facing the necessity of selling at less than normal profit or at a loss, as when a retailer buys more merchandise than it can sell and is forced to hold a sale to move that merchandise; sometimes applied to a whole market, as when a company stock is bid up by speculators and has nowhere to go but down.

overcapitalization: The existence of capital stock in a company valued at more than the company's assets are really worth, creating a situation in which company assets cannot possibly yield even a minimally reasonable rate of return on capital, thus forcing a reassessment and reorganization of capital structure.

overdraft: The amount by which a call on established credit exceeds the credit available; usually the amount by which a check exceeds the balance in the bank account on which it is drawn.

overdue: Any obligation that has passed beyond the date it was due to be fulfilled; usually refers to a debt obligation that has become due and payable but has not yet been paid, but can also refer to some other kind of timed contractual obligation, such as completion of a construction contract.

overemployment: A condition said to exist when there are more jobs than people to fill

them, as when there is a shortage of skilled workers to do a specific kind of a job, or a boom caused by unusual peacetime economic expansion or a war.

overexpansion: The development of far more productive capacity than is justified by current and near-term business prospects; consequently a drain on cash, profits, and sometimes credit and stockholder relations.

overextended account: A borrowing account in which the borrower cannot pay obligations due and payable.

overextension: Spending or borrowing far beyond prudent limits, as when so much has been spent on plant expansion beyond sales prospects as to endanger company credit relationships; or an investor has bought far more stock on margin than that investor's net worth indicates prudent; or so much has been borrowed, reborrowed, and expended that current borrowings are far too great for prudent bankers to justify.

overflow: A quantity greater than a business or system can handle, usually met by an attempt to channel that quantity in other ways so that it can be specially handled; for example, too many diners for a restaurant to handle, or too much data for a computer.

overhead: All costs that cannot be directly attributed to the output of goods and services; therefore all costs other than direct labor and materials.

overhead rate: A preset rate at which overhead costs are charged against production and other operating units; can be charged as a percentage of overhead incurred within a unit or a percentage charged for company-wide overhead costs or both.

overheated: Describing the condition of an economy experiencing an unusually high rate and volume of economic activity, accompanied by inflation and credit expansion.

overinsurance: Property insurance of considerably greater value than the property insured, with resultant higher than necessary premium payments and sometimes unrealistic claims.

overlying mortgage: A mortgage that is subordinate to other mortgages, and therefore a junior mortgage.

overmanning: The assignment of more workers than are necessary to do a job; often the subject of considerable dispute in collective bargaining situations.

overnight loan: A short-term loan extended literally overnight by a bank to securities dealers, to finance securities transactions consummated by dealers on which payment has not yet been received.

overpopulation: The existence of more people than an economy or the world's entire economy can feed, clothe, house, and otherwise care for; a very real and growing concern throughout the twentieth century.

overproduction: More production than there is demand for goods and services; therefore always used as relative to consumption, dependent upon the level of consumption, and often called underconsumption.

override: A bonus paid to executives and managers, usually computed as some portion of revenue, profits, or compensation paid others, and most commonly as a percentage paid sales management for achieving specified sales goals or as a percentage of the commissions paid their selling staff.

Overseas Private Investment Corporation (OPIC): A Federal agency providing catastrophe insurance for American companies operating abroad, in such matters as nationalization, frozen bank accounts and damage resulting from terrorism.

oversold: Describing a stock or a market which is thought to have been sold more than is economically justified, and therefore to have declined in price to an unrealistic level.

oversubscription: Purchase by the public of more securities than the amount of a securities issue, resulting from simultaneous sale of the issue by a number of sellers; usually handled by pro rata cutting of buyers' purchases.

over-the-counter market: The market for securities not listed on any United States stock exchange, which are traded nationally and internationally directly between buyers and sellers, usually through dealers.

overtime: Working time beyond the regular work period or work week of hourly paid employees; in most unionized shops, overtime is paid for at higher than normal rates, such as time and a half beyond a scheduled 35-hour work week and double time on Sundays or time and a half beyond a scheduled seven-hour day.

overvaluation: 1. The placing of a higher than reasonable valuation figure upon property; often the subject of property tax disputes. **2.** Governmental support of a national currency at exchange rates higher than those which would occur if that currency were allowed to float freely, to reach its value against all other world currencies as economic and world currency market conditions would determine.

owner: One who has legal title to property.

owner-operator: One who owns and operates a vehicle, hiring out as transporter of people, goods, or both.

owner's equity: See net worth.

ownership: See owner.

P

package: A container, whether something physically holding goods or a document holding a group of ideas or agreements.

package goods: Goods that are sold at retail in prepackaged form.

package mortgage: A mortgage that includes some items of personal property, such as kitchen and laundry equipment in a house mortgage, that mortgage then becoming a loan on house, land, and personal property, all treated as realty.

package policy: An insurance policy that is actually a group of coverages that might be written in several different policies, but are written as one omnibus policy.

package store: Another name for liquor store, which sells all its goods in sealed packages.

packaging: 1. The material used to make a package. 2. That branch of marketing that concerns itself with the creation of packages that simultaneously help sell goods and physically hold products. 3. Image creation, applied very widely to anything from breakfast foods to movie stars.

padding: Adding nonexistent expenses, by falsely increasing real expenses or by stating wholly imaginary expenses; for example, adding imaginary cash out-of-pocket expenses to an expense account, or adding nonexistent workers to a construction contract and then billing for costs beyond original estimates. Padding is usually actionable fraud.

paid circulation: The number of copies of a publication actually sold, as of the date of a given issue, including both subscriptions and individual copies sold, as well as subscriptions purchased but not yet paid for; but not including unpaid circulation resulting from subscriptions and single copies given away.

paid holiday: A holiday from work in which the employer pays an employee as if the day were a work day.

paid-in capital: The total capital put into a corporation by its stockholders, including cash, property, services, and any other item of value that can be evaluated, and including both initial capital and any later contributions to capital.

paid-in surplus: The net of all capital put into a corporation by its stockholders minus the par value of the corporation's stock, including the difference between the par value of stock and the price at which it is sold to the public, plus all additional capital.

paid-up insurance: An insurance policy on which all premiums have been paid in advance of maturity date, and on which no other premiums will be due.

pallets: Storage platforms that can be stacked and are easily movable by such machines as the forklift truck; very widely used in materials handling and shipping.

P & L: See income statement.

panel: 1. A group of potential jurors from which a jury will be chosen. 2. A group of people gathered to discuss or decide any matter, as on a quiz show or county fair contest. **3.** A group of consumers participating in market research, queried by market researchers again and again on different matters over a period of time.

panic: A crisis in public confidence in the economy, triggering a depression, such as the Great Depression that started with the stock market panic of October, 1929. Often used as a synonym for depression.

paper: A general description of such short-term loans as those evidenced by commercial paper and treasury bills.

paper money: Money issued by a government on paper, rather than in coins, which may or may not be convertible to precious metals. United States paper money is not so convertible, and is backed only by the full faith and credit of the federal government.

paper profit: A so far unrealized gain; usually used to describe increases in the value of securities since bought by their current owner. In one sense, the profits are real—securities used as collateral are valued at current market prices rather than prior purchase prices.

paper tape reader: In computer systems, a machine that reads a roll of paper tape into the computer.

par: Full stated value, as indicated on the face of an instrument. Therefore, a stock's par value is its face value, and a check cleared at par is a check cleared at its full stated value, without discount or premium.

parameter: A value or characteristic that is constant in, and therefore limits or restricts, a particular system, mathematical expression, or body of statistics; in popular usage, often refers to a limit or boundary.

parent company: A company holding controlling interests in other companies, which are subsidiaries.

Pareto's law: The theory, developed by Vilfredo Pareto, that income distribution in a given economy tends to remain constant.

par exchange rate: See exchange rate.

parity: The principle, established as a matter of national policy, that prices for farm products shall be maintained by the Federal government through price support payments to farmers. Parity is aimed at providing farmers with prices which will give them purchasing power, as consumers, roughly equal to their purchasing power in the years 1910–1914, which are used as a base period in computing parity payment rates.

parity index: An index developed by the Department of Agriculture to help determine what parity prices should be paid to farmers.

parity prices: The farm product prices supported by the Federal government pursuant to the principle of parity.

Parkinson's Law: The rule that "Work expands so as to fill the time available for its completion," stated by C. Northcote Parkinson.

par list: A list of banks clearing checks at full stated value, without discount or premium, as published by the Federal Reserve, and consisting of most of the banks in the United States, including all Federal Reserve member banks.

parol contract: See oral agreement.

participating bonds: Bonds that combine debt and some measure of equity participation, by paying both a fixed rate of interest and, under some conditions, dividends out of company earnings.

participating policy: An insurance policy that carries with it a measure of ownership in the company issuing the policy, and thereby entitles its owner to participate in profits earned by the company, usually either in the form of cash dividends or policy premium credits.

participating preferred stock: Preferred stock carrying both a fixed rate of interest and the right to a share of profits, under some conditions.

participation: **1.** The share an investor or investing organization takes of a new securities issue. **2.** The share taken by a party to a joint venture, business organization, or any other pool of shared assets.

participation loan: A loan made by one bank in which another bank shares part of the risk and return, as when a large loan is made by several banks acting together, or when a large bank joins a smaller bank in taking a risk.

partition: The division of commonly owned or tenanted land, or of any commonly owned or held real or personal property, into separately owned units, as on dissolution of a partnership.

partner: One who has joined with others in some form of legal partnership.

partner's equity: See net worth.

partnership: The association of two or more people for the purpose of doing business together for profit. The main form is that of the general partnership, carrying with it unlimited liability, as well as the ability to bind and be bound by the commitments of individual partners, and needing no formal written agreements between the parties to be recognized in law as valid.

part-time employee: One who works less than full time, such as several hours a day or a few days a week, and is so classified on the employer's records.

party plan: A selling technique, in which sales demonstrations are given in sponsoring homes, with sponsors receiving some kind of compensation, usually merchandise, for their role in bringing their friends and acquaintances to the selling demonstration.

par value: The face value of a stock; usually quite different from market value, which normally is considerably higher.

passbook: A record-keeping book issued by a bank to its savings depositors, in which deposits, withdrawals, interest, and current balances are recorded and updated as transactions occur; also sometimes used in combined savings-checking accounts, but rarely in purely checking accounts.

passbook loan: A bank loan using as collateral the deposit balance in a savings account as shown in a passbook.

passed dividend: A regular dividend payment that, when due, is not voted by a corporation; usually due to business problems, and rarely otherwise done, as it is often seen as a clear indication that the corporation is in trouble.

password: In computer systems, the confidential code used to obtain access to the system.

past due: See overdue.

patent: A document issued and recorded by government, attesting that all rights to the invention patented belong to the specified patent holder, including manufacture, distribution, and licensing; patents are also protected by international agreements, signed by most nations.

patent medicine: Rigorously, a proprietary medicine that is a unique formulation, but in common usage a medicine of little or no value, sold by the use of fraudulent misrepresentation as to its curative powers.

patent pending: A statement by government that a patent has been applied for; usually printed or otherwise affixed to a product or process for which patent has been applied for and not yet granted to serve as a warning to others against patent infringement, because patent protection will be considered in effect retroactively since registration, when and if granted.

paternalism: A philosophy and practice in industrial relations, in which employers take on responsibility for the welfare of those working in their businesses, such as voluntary provision of health insurance plans; often criticized by employees, and employee organizations as a pattern of behavior aimed at discouraging union organization and maintaining employee dependence.

pattern bargaining: A collective bargaining approach, in which a union negotiates with a trend-setting company and uses the contract negotiated as a pattern for settlements throughout the industry, and even in other industries, often using the contract provisions themselves as models for similar provisions in other contracts.

patterned interview: See structured interview.

pawnbroker: One who lends money, holding personal property as collateral for the loan, and charging relatively high rates; used by those borrowers who are otherwise virtually unable to borrow from conventional lenders.

pay as you go: The payment of financial obligations on a current basis, rather than incurring debts; increasingly rare in modern business, personal and governmental financial practice.

payback period: The time it takes for a capital investment to return the amount invested, in terms of savings, increased productivity, or any other investment result that can be reduced to number quantities.

paycheck: The amount of pay actually taken home by someone working for wages.

payee: That person or organization to whom a debt instrument, such as a note, check, or money order, is made payable.

pay escalation: See escalation.

payload: That part of the maximum loaded weight of a vehicle that might be used for transporting goods and people.

payment: A sum paid another in settlement of an obligation, or pursuant to an agreement, whether complete or partial; also the action of paying.

payment terms: The way in which payment is to be accomplished, as specified in the agreement between payor and payee; for example, repaying of a loan in installments or cash on delivery in payment for a purchase.

payoff: Money paid for illegal purposes, such as bribes and kickbacks; also called payola.

payola: See payoff.

payor: One who is responsible for payment, and is so named on a debt instrument, such as a note, check, or money order.

payout period: See payback period.

pay package: The total compensation negotiated by the parties to a collective bargaining agreement, including wages and all associated features capable of being expressed in compensation terms.

payroll: The total wages paid to all employees during a given period.

payroll deductions: Those amounts withheld from employees' wages for tax and social security payments and for a variety of other possible reasons, such as group health insurance contributions, payroll savings plans, college loans and union dues.

payroll period: The length of time worked for which employees are customarily paid; for example, weekly, biweekly, or monthly.

payroll taxes: Taxes paid by employers to government, computed as a percentage of gross wages actually paid, used to finance the Social Security system.

PC: See professional corporation.

peak: The highest point, whether of a mountain, a business cycle, or work performance.

peak load: Maximum usage; usually referring to the ability of a machine or system to handle work volume, as when describing the maximum demand a power system can meet.

peak season: The period in which sales are normally best for a given business or kind of business; for example, summer is the peak season for amusement parks and December for toy stores.

peculation: See embezzlement.

pecuniary: That which relates to money, the word most often being used as a synonym for money, as in pecuniary benefit, meaning money benefit, or pecuniary exchange, meaning exchanging money or goods for money.

peddler: A traveling salesman; originally one who bought, sold, and traded goods from a horse and wagon, as in rural America; more recently, a somewhat derogatory epithet aimed at sellers in general.

pegging: Price fixing and price maintenance, using a variety of devices to hold prices at or very near a predetermined point; sometimes illegal, as in the instance of collusive price fixing by United States companies selling domestically; sometimes a matter of national policy, as in the fixing of currency exchange rates or farm prices; sometimes the result of international agreement, as in the fixing of oil export prices by an international cartel.

penny stocks: Very low priced, usually highly speculative common stocks, most often sold in over-the-counter markets, rather than on stock exchanges.

pension: A long series of payments made to a retired person or former employee, usually for the balance of a lifetime, by former private or public employers, or by government. Pensions may be payable only upon retirement from a job, upon a combination of retirement from a job and reaching a specified age, or only upon reaching a specified age, as in the instance of Social Security benefits.

peonage: A forced labor system, in which workers go into debt to their employers and are forced to continue to work for them to discharge their debts, which as a practical matter are never discharged. Widespread in agriculture, peonage originated in Latin America and was adopted in North America both in agriculture, as in sharecropping, and in other industries, such as mining and steel, using the device of the company town. Now illegal in the United States, but still surviving in many agricultural areas, using the device of the migrant labor camp.

per capita: Latin for "per head." An average, computed by dividing a total sum by the amount of people in a given group to find the amount per person; for example, per capita income is average income per person.

percentage depletion: A Federal income tax allowance for the depletion or using up of resources in the extractive industries, such as oil, gas, coal, metals, and minerals, allowing income tax deductions based on a specified percentage of gross income, with no direct relation to the cost of the property being so depleted. Percentages allowed vary with the kind of resource.

percentage lease: A business lease providing for computation of rentals to be paid wholly or partly as a percentage of gross business income; very often used in franchise agreements.

percentile: A 100-unit system of ranking items in a frequency distribution, often used in testing, with the percentile indicating the number of people at or below the point specified; for example, a score in the 91st percentile means that only 9 percent of those tested scored better. Related ranking systems are the decile, which uses a 10-unit ranking system, and the quartile, which uses 4 units.

per diem: On a daily basis; for example, payment of an expense allowance to a traveling sales representative on a fixed amount per day basis or rental of an automobile partly on a fixed daily fee basis.

perfect competition: See pure competition.

performance: The results shown by an investment vehicle or company, in terms of such indicators as market price, earnings, yield, and other key indicators of present health and future prospects.

performance appraisal: See job evaluation.

performance bond: A bond guaranteeing that work will be performed to specific quality and time specifications, and providing for forfeit if those specifications are not met.

performance fund: A mutual fund focusing on investments in speculative securities, taking high risks for anticipated high profits.

peril point: The maximum decrease in a particular tariff the United States Tariff Commission believes can be made without harming domestic producers; by law, the Commission is responsible for informing the President as to this view.

period cost: A cost that is attributable to a time period, rather than to a product; usually fixed costs, such as real estate costs and interest.

periodic inventory: A physical inventory, conducted regularly, as when a company closes its warehouse every year between Christmas and New Year's and physically counts its goods.

period income: Income attributable to a time period, and spread out for accounting purposes over the time properly attributable to it; for example, future interest on bonds already purchased.

perishable: Describing goods that are, by their nature, subject to quick spoilage, such as milk, meat, and fish.

perjury: The giving of false information knowingly, under a legally recognized oath in or out of court, before a judge, or any other official empowered to give an oath, or in legally sworn writing; a crime.

perk: See perquisite.

permanent disability: Inability to perform work previously performed, with no future ability to perform that work in view; but one may sometimes be so disabled and yet be able to perform other bodily functions, including strenuous exercise.

permanent injunction: See injunction.

perpetual bond: A bond that is an open-ended promise to pay interest indefinitely, and that has no maturity date; or a bond that has such a long life that it is effectively perpetual.

perpetual inventory: An inventory system that keeps detailed book records of all inventory on a current basis, aiming at having an accurate book count of all inventory items at all times.

perquisite: A fringe benefit. The term has fallen into disuse in the United States, but is current in Great Britain and elsewhere in the English-speaking world, where it is often "perks" in slang, and means both fringe benefits and such executive privileges as expense accounts and country club memberships.

personal check: A check drawn by an individual upon a checking account either in that individual's own name or one that is shared with one or more other individuals.

personal computer: See microcomputer.

personal consumption expenditures: Total national spending by the public for consumer goods and services.

personal finance company: See finance company.

personal holding company: A tax avoidance device, now little used because of tax law provisions attacking it, consisting of a corporation formed by a high-income individual to circumvent high individual tax rates by holding income in undistributed corporate earnings after paying the lower corporate taxes.

personal income: Gross individual income from all sources, including all income derived from work or property ownership, after expenses and before taxes.

personality tests: Tests designed to derive information as to the emotions and attitudes of those being tested, in contrast to intelligence tests, which are aimed at evaluation of basic learning levels.

personal loan: A loan made to an individual by a lending institution, such as a bank, credit union or finance company, carrying unlimited obligation to repay, with or without collateral; includes both specific sums loaned and lines of credit.

personal property: All property owned, other than ownership interests in realty and relatively immovable structures attached to realty; includes both tangibles, such as vehicles, books and toothbrushes, and intangibles, such as securities, copyrights, and insurance policies, as well as less-than-ownership interests in land, such as leaseholds.

personal property taxes: See property taxes.

personal selling: Direct selling by sellers to prospects, face to face or by other means of communication, but always on a one-to-one basis, in contrast to such broadcast selling efforts as mail sales and advertising.

personal service: Legally valid service of such legal process as a subpoena by personal delivery to the person for whom it is intended.

personalty: See personal property.

personnel: The people employed by an organization, including all employees.

personnel administration: See personnel management.

personnel management: Those functions associated with the management of personnel, including hiring, training, and evaluation; the development and administration of employee benefit programs; day-to-day handling of management-union questions and other industrial disputes; and compliance with appropriate laws and regulations.

PERT: See Program Evaluation and Review Technique.

Peter Principle: The rule that "In a heirarchy, every employee tends to rise to his level of incompetence," stated by Dr. Laurence J. Peter and Raymond Hull.

petition in bankruptcy: A document filed by a debtor or creditors in a court of bankruptcy, asking the court to place the creditor in a legal state of bankruptcy.

petrocurrency: Money paid to oil-producing countries by oil consumers, accumulated in very large quantities, and deposited in financial institutions throughout the world; used for a wide variety of purposes by the oil producers, including foreign investment and the purchase of goods and services.

petty cash: A small amount of cash kept on the premises of a business or a small bank account maintained as a matter of convenience in making minor expenditures for miscellaneous small items, such as the office coffee, messenger service, and minor stationery items.

phantom freight: Freight charges to a buyer that were never incurred or paid for by the seller, as when a buyer charges a seller for goods shipped to one destination that were actually shipped a shorter distance.

Phillips curve: A graph plotting the relationship between the level of unemployment and the rate of change in wage levels in Great Britain, and giving rise to the theory that the rate of wage level change increases as the level of unemployment decreases; that wages rise faster as workers are in shorter supply.

physical distribution: The physical movement of goods from producer to consumer, but not including advertising, selling, and associated techniques.

physical inventory: An actual count of all items held in inventory, and the resulting inventory listings.

physical life: The potential producing life of a machine or some other inanimate element of production, in contrast to its economic life, which may be cut short by such matters as technological developments causing obsolescence while it is still in good operating condition.

PI: See programmed instruction.

picketing: A public demonstration outside the premises of an employer, government, or other entity, aimed at gaining economic, political, or social ends. In industrial relations, it is usually in support of a strike over economic demands, over union recognition coupled with economic demands, or as a result of inter-union rivalry.

picosecond: One trillionth of a second.

piecework: A production and work payment mode in which production operations are evaluated for pay purposes by the operation performed, rather than on an hourly or any other time basis, though in practice piece rates are often combined with minimum hourly rates.

pie chart: A chart representing its object of study as a circle, and its components as wedge-shaped pieces of that circle in varying sizes to show their proportion to the whole.

piggyback shipment: The use of two kinds of vehicles at once in transporting goods, as when trailer trucks are driven to a railway line, and, instead of unloading their cargo for reloading into freight cars, are uncoupled and the trailers placed fully loaded in flat cars and then transported further. When the trailers are transferred to water transport, it is often called fishybacking.

pilot: Something produced for trial purposes; as when a single television program intended to be the first of a series is produced and shown to broadcasting company people so that a decision can be made as to series purchase, or when a new product or method is tested.

pink slip: A notice of dismissal from employer to employee.

pipeline: 1. A pipe, usually underground, through which are moved gases and liquids, such as natural gas and oil. Often refers more generally to long-term processes, as when a nuclear plant in its fifth year of a planned 10-year construction is said to be "in the pipeline." **2.** A channel, usually informal and sometimes covert, through which information and rumors are moved.

piracy: Once the illegal taking by force of vessels at sea by unaffiliated robbers, without the legitimization of war or national policy. In our time, the stealing of people, ideas, and processes, whether legally or illegally, as when a patent or copyright is illegally appropriated or an employee is quite legally stolen away by a competitor offering higher pay.

pit: The trading floor of a commodities exchange.

pitch: A slang term for a sales presentation.

pit trader: One who deals in commodities on behalf of his own account in the pit or on the floor of a commodities exchange.

placement: 1. A synonym for job **2.** The process of matching people and jobs, as when a school attempts to find appropriate jobs for its graduates.

plan: In business, the setting out of formal goals and a detailed statement of how those goals are to be met; often used synonymously with budget.

planned community: A large group of residences, built according to a master plan and often by the same builder, usually including the kinds of community spaces and maintenance services found in a small hamlet or village and sometimes including small independent businesses serving the community.

planned economy: An economy in which all major economic planning is done by the state, and in which supply and demand operate, if at all, only in some consumer products areas which do not significantly affect the main course of the state's economy; an example is the Soviet Union.

planned obsolescence: Any manufacturing policy and set of devices that are aimed at making products rapidly obsolescent that would otherwise be quite capable of further use, sometimes for years; examples are high-fashion clothing, designed and redesigned for quick replacement, and some United States automobiles.

planned presentation: An organized sales presentation, often assisted by prepared sales materials, and usually fully or partly memorized by the sales representative; often confused with a canned presentation which is a fully written and memorized presentation, with any sales materials used as part of the memorized presentation in place and without significant variation in timing or emphasis.

plant: In the widest sense, all fixed assets, including land, buildings, and equipment; but more often used to describe buildings or both land and buildings.

plant and equipment spending: See new plant and equipment spending.

plant capacity: The maximum productive capacity of a given plant, assuming that it is worked seven days a week, 24 hours a day, and 52 weeks a year, but including an estimate of down time for necessary repairs and maintenance.

pledge: The passing of collateral from borrower to lender as security for a loan, with the borrower keeping title but giving actual possession over to the lender, as when an object of value is pawned or securities are held by a bank as collateral on a loan.

PL/1 (Programming Language 1): A computer language, combining some features of FORTRAN and COBOL; widely used in business applications.

plow back: To use profits as money available for investment, rather than money to be distributed to owners; to put profits back into the business.

plunger: One who invests heavily in speculative securities, enterprises, or transactions.

point: 1. In United States securities trading, a dollar. When a stock starts a trading day at 100 and goes up to 102 by the end of that trading day, it is up 2 points for the day. In the stock markets of other countries, a point is the normal currency unit used for describing trades. **2.** A percentage point, as when a lending institution demands an extra "point," or 1%, of a mortgage, in a lump sum at the start of the payback period before granting that mortgage.

point method: In job evaluation studies, a scoring device that sets up a range of points that may be awarded for jobs, awards points for each function performed, and evaluates each job on the basis of the total number of points received, usually on a comparative basis as against all other jobs in the unit or company.

point of purchase advertising: Advertising placed where the advertised goods are bought by consumers; as when a book for sale is advertised with a banner on a display rack in a bookstore.

Poisson distribution: A frequency distribution used in calculating probabilities, especially in events randomly distributed in time and space; named after its originator, Simeon Poisson.

policy: 1. A general attitude toward a particular kind of matter, indicating what positions to take and actions to pursue when confronted with that sort of matter. In organizations, policies may be written or unwritten, and are normally generated by boards of directors and top management. **2.** A document evidencing an insurance contract, known as an insurance policy.

policy and procedure: The set of internal rules by which an organization operates, policies being set by the board of directors and top management, and procedures being developed by management to implement policies.

policy and procedure manual: Any formal, written body of policy and procedures meant to be an internal book of rules for employees, in their dealings with each other and with those outside the organization while representing the organization.

policy holder: The owner of an insurance contract; often but not always the insured, as when one spouse owns and pays premiums on an insurance policy on the life of the other.

political strike: A strike putting political demands to management and government, raising questions that can only be solved by government, such as tax rates and food price ceilings. In the United States, the overwhelming majority of strikes have been and continue to be economic, raising with management such questions as wages and working conditions.

pollution: The contamination of the environment by humans, often with poisonous or hazardous waste products, but also with normally harmless substances in excess of what the environment can break down and absorb by natural processes.

pool: 1. A group of companies formally working together to control any aspect of their business; for example a group of insurance companies may share risks and premiums on certain large and high-risk insurance cases, or a group of transportation companies may quite legally set prices together under the provisions of an applicable federal statute. All but a few such pools are outlawed as restraint of trade. **2.** A group working or moving together for common purposes; for example, a car pool or typing pool.

pool car: A freight car carrying several smaller-than-carload freight shipments, for which the railroad charges a rate lower than the normal rate for small shipments.

pooling of interests: A merger of interests, often for a limited time or specific purpose, in which those merging truly merge, rather than one party buying out another, with the resulting company reflecting the relative values of each party before merger.

population: The total number of people, people of a specific kind, or of other beings living in a place or area; for example, the number of people living in the United States, of trombone players living in New York City, or of deer in a national park. In statistics, a synonym for universe.

pork barrel: A derogatory description of the kinds of local projects funded by legislators aiming to satisfy their constituents by getting public money into their districts; often projects of little real worth.

portal-to-portal pay: Hourly wages payable for the period starting with the worker's entry into the plant and stopping when the worker leaves the plant, rather than only for the time spent actually on the job; of considerable significance in large, sprawling plants, such as coal mines and steel mills.

port authority: A governmental body having jurisdiction over all matters affecting port functions, often cutting across other local jurisdictions, such as cities, counties and states; may also have jurisdiction over other public works and functions, such as highways and bridges.

portfolio: 1. The total securities holdings of an individual or organization, including all stocks, bonds, options, limited partnership shares, and any other securities held; in a wider sense, all debts owed by others and all ownership equities. **2.** A group of art works, representing the output of a commercial artist.

port of entry: A port designated by a government to serve those people or goods entering and leaving the country, and in which government places regulatory people and organizations, such as the customs service, the immigration authorities, and the public health service.

positioning: Strategic placement to maximize opportunities and minimize risk; for example, a company considering introduction of a major new product or creating a market image for that product, must consider its positioning.

positive reinforcement: The encouragement of achievement by praise of work performed, aiming at the development of self-confidence and ever higher standards of performance.

positive skewness: See skewness.

postal money order: See money order.

postdate: To date a document later than the actual date it is executed; most often done on a check so that it cannot be cashed until the date specified, as banks cannot cash postdated checks until they become due.

postindustrial state: John Kenneth Galbraith's descriptive term for an economy thought to be past a major stress on industrialism and the development and maturation of basic industries, focusing more on the quality of life.

posting: The transfer of accounting information from a book of original entry into a ledger; also refers to an individual item so transferred.

poverty: The condition of being poor. In the United States, the government sets a minimum income as a poverty level, below which people are eligible for government aid programs. In world terms, much of the population of underdeveloped nations, as well as significant portions of the population of many developed nations, live in poverty.

power of attorney: Written authorization by one to another to act as an agent capable of making binding decisions regarding assets owned by the authorizer; may be limited to certain assets or for a limited time, or may be unlimited and revocable only by specific act of the authorizer.

power of sale: A mortgagor's or trustee's right, as specified in a mortgage or deed of trust, to sell mortgaged property at public auction to satisfy the debt when mortgage payments have not been kept up and the mortgage is thereby in default; the mortgagor or trustee satisfies as much as possible of the debt from the auction proceeds, with any remainder going to the mortgagee.

practice: The conduct of a profession by those trained to do so, usually involving guild or government certification, or both; examples include doctors, lawyers and accountants.

preapproach: Preparation to make a selling presentation, by learning as much as possible about a prospective purchaser before entering the face-to-face selling situation.

predate: To date a document earlier than the actual date it is executed; an act which may validate a contract, and which may in some instances lead to violation of law, as in the instance of checks predated to place deductions in a closed tax year for tax evasion purposes.

prediction: See forecast.

pre-emption: 1. The power of government to buy anything for sale ahead of its citizens, at a reasonable valuation. **2.** The power of a government at war to seize property belonging to neutrals and to conduct a forced sale of that property to its own citizens; just short of confiscation without compensation. **3.** The power of any individual or institution to buy ahead of others as a matter of right.

pre-emptive rights: The right of present stockholders to buy newly issued stock, as provided by corporate charter; usually granted in some fixed relationship to their current stockholdings.

prefabricate: To manufacture and assemble parts into a finished piece that otherwise is normally assembled on a building site, as when a building is put together out of factory-built, mass-produced rooms constructed whole and shipped to the site.

preference bonds: Bonds on which interest is payable only out of corporate earnings, after all other expenses, including more senior debt obligations, have been paid.

preferential hiring: The practice of giving preference to union members or others, such as veterans, in hiring, as against equally qualified job applicants, pursuant to collective bargaining agreement or statute.

preferential shop: A business that gives hiring and often rehiring preference to union members, as against equally qualified nonunion members.

preferential tariff: A tariff that provides preferential treatment for one or more nations as against all others, as when a country charges a former colony considerably lower import duties than it charges other countries.

preferred position: An advertising position,

such as inside front cover or center spread, which is preferred by advertisers, and for which publications usually charge more than for position in the body of the publication.

preferred stock: Stock conferring equity ownership senior to that conferred by common stock, in that it receives dividends in stated amounts before any dividends can be distributed to common stock; sometimes also in that it carries more control over corporate affairs than does common stock. It may be cumulative, receiving dividends owing from previous unmade distributions, or non-cumulative, losing past unmade distributions; it may be participating, sharing to some extent in profits beyond specified dividends, or non-participating, not so sharing; it may be convertible, or capable of being exchanged for common stock at the owner's option.

premium: 1. That which is paid for insurance coverage; usually used to describe a single payment made, but sometimes describing all payments due for the life of a policy. **2.** A gift or prize, distributed free as an incentive or merchandising device, as when a bank gives merchandise to those opening new savings accounts, or a company gives incentive awards in the form of merchandise to its top sales producers. **3.** The amount by which the price of a security or commodity is larger than its face value. **4.** The amount by which a new securities issue exceeds its selling price shortly after issue. **5.** The actual price of an option contract. **6.** Something of value, given by buyer or seller beyond the stated terms of a transaction, such as a toy enclosed in a box of cereal or an extra interest charge on a real estate transaction.

premium pay: Pay beyond the normal wage rate for the job being performed, as when an extra percentage of the wage rate is paid for hazardous or overtime work.

prepackaging: Packaging of goods before point of sale is reached, such as the packaging of some vegetables and most meats in supermarkets.

prepaid expense: An expense incurred currently, but properly attributable to future periods for profit and loss statement purposes, unless profit and loss are figured on a cash basis; for example, rent paid in advance for future occupancy; advance payment of insurance premiums or advance payments against anticipated royalties or commissions.

prepaid health care: Privately funded health coverage such as that provided by Blue Shield, Blue Cross and a substantial number of other nonprofit and profit-making firms, in which fixed fees are paid by those covered, buying individually or as groups, in return for specified health coverage.

prepaid legal fees: Legal fees paid by clients to lawyers on a periodic basis, for which clients receive certain legal services by prior agreement during the term covered by the prepaid fees; a standard lawyer-client arrangement known as a "retainer," now expanded to include individual clients and groups of clients purchasing legal services, much as health care is purchased.

prepayment: 1. Payment in advance for goods or services to be supplied in the future, such as rent, insurance premiums, and advances against royalties. **2.** Advance payment of obligations which will be due in the future, such as property taxes, mortgages, and debts. When such payment of future obligations operates to reduce future interest payments, there may be prepayment penalties; therefore prepayment is often a privilege specifically covered by contract.

prepayment penalty: A money penalty imposed by contract on a debtor prepaying an installment loan, to compensate for the lender's foregone interest.

prepayment privilege: The right of a debtor paying off an installment loan, such as a mortgage or personal loan, to pay all or part of the balance due earlier than the payment schedule specified in the loan, so effecting a total interest reduction, without a money penalty charged by the lender for prepayment, as partial compensation for that fore-gone interest.

presentation: 1. The physical presenting of an instrument due to be paid to the party responsible for paying it. **2.** A planned discussion, often accompanied by graphic representations; for example, a sales attempt.

presentment: A written communication from a grand jury to a judge, making an accusation of crime.

present value method: See discounted cash flow.

pressure group: See lobby.

pretax dollars: In popular usage, sums used to make payments that are tax deductible; for example, an automobile purchased for corporate rather than personal use is a tax deductible business expense, and may be described as having been purchased with pretax dollars.

pretax income: Net income before taxes for a business; personal income before deductions for an individual.

prevailing wage: The normal rate of pay for a kind of job in a geographical area; often includes compensation factors beyond hourly or weekly rates of pay, such as overtime rates, vacation pay, and holidays.

preventive maintenance: The continuing care of equipment, aimed at preventing and minimizing breakdowns, with their high repair costs and lost time.

prewrap: See prepackaging.

price: 1. The amount of money, goods or services offered or asked in return for goods, services or money that are for sale. Asking prices are prices quoted on that which is for sale; offering prices are bids by potential buyers. **2.** Also, the amount for which something is sold, which is often somewhere between what is asked and what is offered.

price control: The setting of maximum prices for goods and services by government, sometimes as a means of curbing wartime

excess profits, often as a means of fighting inflation.

price cutting: An attempt to establish prices lower than those of competitors, to gain competitive advantage; often used in sharply competitive marketplace situations and often by those who are economically strongest, as a technique for driving competitors out of business.

price discrimination: The practice of selling goods and services at varying prices to different kinds of buyers, even though these goods and services are of essentially the same quality and cost; for example, quantity pricing that favors larger buyers because of their greater bargaining power, whatever the rationale used by the seller. Some price discrimination practices are illegal, but enforcement is negligible.

price-earnings ratio: The relationship between the current market price of a stock and its most recent yearly earnings per share; for example, a stock selling for $20 per share, with previous year's earnings of $2 per share, has a ratio of 20:2, reduced and stated as 10:1.

price fixing: The setting of specific prices to be charged by groups of sellers for goods and services. It is legal when done by government during wartime, in peacetime to curb inflation, or in a regulated industry; if done by private industry, it is an illegal combination in restraint of trade.

price index: A measure of how prices for certain goods and services, or for all goods and services, have risen or fallen in a geographical area during a period of time, when measured against a previous period used as a base or comparison period. The consumer price and wholesale price indexes are major national and regional economic indicators.

price leadership: The pricing position held by one firm or relatively few firms in an industry, which act as trend setters for the rest of the industry when making price changes; for example, a few large banks will initiate prime interest rate changes, and most other banks will follow.

price level: The average price paid for any group of goods or services, or for all goods and services, in an area or throughout an economy, measured in money actually paid.

price quote: See quote.

price renegotiation: The reopening of a contract in being on the question of price, as provided by the terms of that contract, normally on occurrence of specified cost increases.

price rigidity: The tendency of some goods and services to hold prices within a relatively narrow range, without responding to supply and demand swings; a characteristic of markets dominated by a few large producers or suppliers.

price stabilization: The holding of prices within a narrow range; usually affected by government action, ranging from pressure on business to voluntarily hold current price levels to complete price controls.

price support: Government support of the price levels of specified goods or services, using any of a wide range of devices, including direct payments to producers and a variety of indirect means; used to support the prices of a substantial number of agricultural products.

price system: A pattern of collusive price fixing on the part of producers or suppliers.

price variance: A change in quoted price, usually caused by changes in cost factors, especially in periods of rapid inflation.

price war: A price-cutting contest between two or more sellers aiming to secure competitive advantage through lower prices; often results in little or no competitive advantage, but when sellers are of unequal economic strength the technique can drive some sellers out of the market.

pricing: The process of establishing prices which will be quoted for goods and services.

pricing policy: The price structure and selling arrangements quoted by a business for the goods and services it sells, usually including such matters as prices, terms, credit arrangements, and discounts.

prima facie: Something which will be presumed to be true unless there is evidence to contradict that presumption, as when evidence presented in a case at law builds a case that will stand, unless successfully rebutted.

primary boycott: An attempt by employees involved in a labor dispute to diminish the purchase and use of the goods and services sold by the employer or employers directly involved in that dispute, but with action limited to those employers, rather than extended to others buying those goods and services, even for resale.

primary data: Data resulting from original research rather than from other sources; for example, the tabulated results of a survey would be primary data, while the conclusions drawn from that data would not.

primary issue: A stock issue sold by a company directly or through its underwriters, in contrast to a body of previously issued stock being sold through any distribution channel, known as a secondary issue.

primary offering: See primary issue.

primary reserves: That portion of legally required bank reserves consisting of cash, money held in banks, and money held by the Federal Reserve.

prime: 1. Of very high quality; for example, beef, some bonds, and some commercial paper. **2.** Sometimes used as a contraction of the term prime rate.

prime contractor: See contractor.

prime cost: Direct cost, including materials and labor, but not including any items of direct cost, such as overhead.

prime mortgage rate: The lowest general interest rate charged on mortgage loans by lenders in a given period, extended to those thought to be excellent credit risks.

prime rate: The lowest interest rates charged by commercial banks to their most favored borrowers, usually extended only to large, well-established, and low-risk corporations. As the prime rate changes, all other interest rates in the private sector of the economy tend to follow suit.

prime time: In the broadcasting industry, those evening hours normally enjoying the largest listening and viewing audiences.

principal: 1. The amount of a loan or note, on which interest is charged. **2.** An amount invested, on which earnings, such as profits and interest, may accrue. **3.** One of the parties to a transaction. **4.** The holder of a substantial ownership share in an enterprise.

principle: A basic truth, moral belief, or general guide to action.

printer: A device that prints the output of a computer or calculator on paper.

priority: 1. A ranking in order of importance; for example, giving preference to a more urgent telephone message or computer program, or to a more important long-term task in a time management analysis. **2.** The order of preference enjoyed by creditors and other claimants against bankrupts and estates.

privacy acts: Federal and state statutes aiming to protect Americans from violation of their privacy by government and to some extent by business, providing for opening of Federal and state dossiers for inspection and correction, and prohibition of certain commercial uses of information in personal files.

private bank: A bank organized as a partnership or sole proprietorship, rather than as a corporation, and chartered under state banking laws; a very old and widely used form in European banking and in United States investment banking.

private brand: A brand originating with a single seller, usually a retailer, though some-times a wholesaler; for example, a radio sold under a Sears, Roebuck name or canned peaches under an A&P brand name, rather than as a nationally advertised brand sold by a manufacturer to many retailers.

private carrier: A carrier transporting goods or people for a single company, rather than making itself available for public hire as a common carrier.

private corporation: See closed corporation.

private enterprise: Businesses owned by individual owners, not by government, whether organized as sole proprietorships, partnerships, corporations, or in any other form; such enterprises may be highly regulated or even partly owned by government and still be in the main privately owned.

private enterprise system: See capitalism.

private placement: The selling of stock or debt obligations to a limited number of investors and investing organizations by an issuing company or by a securities firm, but not by public offering.

private practice: A law practice conducted as an independent business, in contrast to law practices conducted as employees of government or business organizations. Also applied to medical and some other professional practices.

private property: Property owned by individuals and private organizations, rather than by governments.

private sector: That portion of the national economy which is privately rather than publicly owned, including those portions of the economy that are substantially financed by government subsidy, but owned privately, such as portions of the health care industry.

probability theory: A large and complex body of theory that uses mathematical and statistical models to help estimate and predict future occurrences.

probability tree: See decision tree.

probate: The validation of a will by act of a

court of appropriate jurisdiction, and associated actions by a probate court.

probation: A trial period during which a person is tested for fitness to remain in a group, job, or organization.

probationary employee: An employee who is on probation for a limited period, and who will become a regular employee after passage of that period, either automatically or by employer action; usually a new employee during the first few weeks or months of employment, but sometimes a longer term employee whose employment is for some reason in question, and who is going through a new probationary period.

pro bono publico: Latin, meaning "for the public good"; often used to mean "in the public interest."

procedure: A planned mode of action, outlined in sequence and often in timing as well, and usually limited to the accomplishment of a single task.

procedures manual: See policy and procedure manual.

proceeds: The amount actually received by a party to a transaction, such as a borrower or a seller.

process: 1. A production system, in which a series of planned and codified steps results in an end product; usually so codified as to be patentable. **2.** To convert materials into other, usually more refined materials, as in the conversion of metal ores into metals, petroleum into oil products, or harvested agricultural products into fibers and food. **3.** A legal proceeding, including all the steps in that proceeding, from beginning to end. **4.** A legal document summoning a defendant to court.

process costing: In cost accounting, the averaging of cost per unit produced over many units, rather than specific attribution of costs to individual units; made necessary by the nature of the production process in some instances, as in chemical, steel rolling and oil refining operations.

procurement: See purchasing.

produce exchange: See commodity exchange.

producer cooperative: See cooperative.

producer goods: See capital goods.

product cost: See direct cost.

product development: The process of developing new products and processes, or changing the nature and sometimes the market images of old products, and of finding new uses for old products and processes.

product differentiation: The attempt by advertisers to distinguish their products from other similar products, by highlighting claimed unique or superior features and buyer benefits.

production: 1. The process of making goods, as in mining and otherwise extracting or growing raw materials, manufacturing, and otherwise creating finished goods. **2.** Any goods or services produced from work performed, as in the creation of a book or a play.

production bonus: A kind of incentive pay for production beyond standard or norm, paid to an individual or to a group of workers.

production capacity: See capacity.

production control: The process of planning the most effective possible production effort, aimed at rationalizing the flow of all the material and human factors affecting the production process.

production factors: See factors of production.

production flow: The movement of all material through the production process.

production line: In manufacturing, a sequence of production processes through which material moves, is worked on, and becomes a finished product, as when an assembly line performs a series of processes to turn materials into an automobile.

production management: That part of management directly involved in the production of goods and services.

production method of depreciation: Depreciation based on an estimate of the number of units that can be produced during the useful life of a machine, with each unit to be produced assigned a percentage of total depreciation and that depreciation taken as units are produced.

production planning: See production control.

production scheduling: The timing of production operations for maximum efficiency.

production worker: One who is directly engaged in production, as on assembly line or some other mode of manufacture.

productivity: The amount of output relative to input involved in producing that output; normally measured for land, labor, or capital, or any component thereof.

productivity clause: See productivity factor.

productivity factor: A collective bargaining contract provision calling for periodic wage increases during the life of the contract, as compensation for increased worker productivity; usually unaccompannied by any agreed-upon means of measuring productivity. So in practice functioning as a rationalization for placing a wage escalator in the contract.

productivity of capital: The yield produced by invested capital, as when money invested in securities nets 10% per year or money invested in capital goods yields 9%, but without adjustment for tax factors, which may very significantly alter the real money yield of an investment.

productivity of labor: The quantity and quality of goods produced by labor, usually measured as output per working hour, but varying with such factors as technical levels and techniques of production.

productivity of land: The crop yield of land, usually measured on a per acre basis; varies not only with the quality of the land but also with the quality of labor, machines, techniques and nutrients put into the land.

product liability: The liability of a product's maker or any others involved in the chain of distribution for damages directly or indirectly caused by that product; covers a wide range of possible causes of action, from food containing harmful foreign matter to construction materials containing cancer-causing substances.

product life cycle: The stages of a product's life in its markets, from introduction through maturity through eventual withdrawal by its maker.

product line: A group of related products. A single company may have several product lines; sometimes all of the products of a firm are described as its product line, even though not all products are related.

product manager: A marketing manager, responsible for marketing one or more products, usually through a variety of advertising, promotion, and direct selling personnel, inside and outside the manager's company.

product mix: The products sold by a company; sometimes the result of planning a series of complementary products, but equally often a group of loosely related products developed separately over the lifetime of the company.

professional corporation (PC): A corporation organized to conduct joint professional practice by several practitioners, such as doctors or lawyers; for many years barred by law, but now authorized in many states, and increasingly used by professionals in many fields.

profile: An outline, briefly describing main characteristics, such as a company profile, outlining the nature, personnel, products, financial structure, and prospects of a company.

profit: **1.** The net of revenues and costs, which may be expressed as a plus or minus figure. **2.** Any yield on capital or on entrepreneurial effort, such as the value of a small business built by a combination of a little capital and a great deal of time and effort.

profitability: 1. The net earnings of a business organization. **2.** The extent to which operations produce earnings, usually expressed as a percentage of sales.

profit and loss statement (P&L): See income statement.

profit center: Any portion of a business that is treated by that firm's management and accounting system as a source of costs and revenues, and therefore is capable of being evaluated in profit and loss terms; may apply to a very wide range of activities and unit sizes, and several profit centers may be included within a larger profit center.

profiteering: The taking of unconscionable profits through exploitation of a social or national emergency, such as war or epidemic; in normal times very much in the eye of the beholder.

profit margin: The net of revenues and costs, described in percentile terms.

profit sharing: A kind of additional compensation paid by a company to its employees, in the form of a distribution of some share of current profits to employees, usually as stock, stock options or cash, and often in deferred form, to be held until employee retirement or termination of employment.

profit squeeze: A situation in which profits are dropping, because costs are rising and, for whatever reasons, prices cannot be raised to offset those higher costs; often occurs while volume continues at previous or even higher levels.

profit taking: In securities trading, the selling of securities on which paper gains have been made, to turn those paper gains into real profits; often used to describe selling in a market that has been rising, helping to trigger a leveling off or downturn in prices.

pro forma: Latin for "as a matter of form."

In the law, a decision rendered to pave the way for appeal.

pro forma statement: 1. In accounting, a financial statement that, at least in part, makes assumptions as to future events, and that therefore serves only as a model, rather than as a financial statement reflecting reality. **2.** In general usage, a statement made for appearances' or forms' sake, such as a ritual denial of intent to run by one who is clearly a candidate for public office, but who has not yet publicly declared that candidacy.

program: See computer program.

Program Evaluation and Review Technique (PERT): A scheduling and production control technique that develops a graphically represented sequence of all the elements of a planned project, allowing those in control of a project to anticipate and plan for effective project execution in advance. Because the aim is to identify the critical path—the path that will take the longer time and that, if delayed, will hold up the entire project—it is often called the critical path method, or CPM.

programmed instruction (PI): A method of presenting instructional materials that involves the reader in applying skills and concepts as they are learned and provides immediate feedback on the reader's progress, either sequentially through the material, as with linear programming, or on a path dependent on the reader's responses, as with branching; a process that begins with analysis of what should be taught, setting of objectives, writing of materials, and testing and revising those materials until readers can reach the stated objectives. Also called self-paced instruction, individualized instruction, or, when the materials are presented on a computer, computer-assisted instruction (CAI).

programming: The preparation of computer programs, or of programmed instruction material, including design, writing, and testing functions.

Programming Language 1: See PL/1.

progression: The normal sequence of steps upward in pay and responsibility on a job or in a workplace; sometimes in timed sequence, and occurring automatically as various seniority levels are reached, but more often a general guide to advancement.

progressive tax: A tax that increases in percentage as taxables increase. For example, federal income taxes tax income at progressively higher rates as taxable income rises; in contrast, fixed rates of tax, such as many sales taxes, tax all purchases of the same kind at the same rate.

proletariat: In Marxian theory, those who do not own the means of production, but instead work as producers for wages, forming a working class; an expansion from Roman usage, which meant a poor subclass.

promissory note: A written promise to pay another or the bearer of the note a specific sum, at some time in the future or on demand.

promoter: One who takes an entrepreneurial role in the development of an enterprise, such as the development of a new company or of a single event, such as a boxing match; used most in describing those who organize sports events.

promotion: 1. A miscellany of marketing activities, including all but advertising and selling functions; for example, the development of point of sales materials and some public relations activities. **2.** A single marketing event, such as the introduction of a new product. **3.** A job advance in one's current employment.

promotional allowance: A payment or credit given to a wholesaler or retailer by a manufacturer, to help pay for promotional activities on behalf of the manufacturer's goods or services.

proof: A copy of material to be printed, supplied for inspection and correction before printing.

proof of loss: A written statement from an insured to an insurer, setting forth evidence of compensable losses and describing the extent of those losses.

propensity to consume: The proportion of income people tend to spend, at various income levels and as incomes rise.

propensity to hoard: See liquidity preference.

propensity to import: A country's tendency to import more as national income rises, but limited by government policy in planned economies.

propensity to save: The proportion of income people tend to save at various income levels.

property: That which can in any way be legally owned, by any individual, organization, or by the state, including real and personal property, tangible and intangible property.

property insurance: Insurance of any kind that covers property against loss from any of a large number of natural and man-made causes.

property tax: Any tax imposed by government on real or personal property; most often on real property.

proprietary: 1. Exclusively owned. **2.** Relating to a specific owner, or to owners and ownership generally.

proprietary accounts: In accounting, those accounts containing ownership amounts.

proprietary drugs: Drugs which by their very nature confer ownership interests in the companies developing and selling them, in contrast to generic drugs which are owned by no one, and may be sold and dispensed by all, though often subject to government regulation.

proprietary interest: An ownership interest, as in the interest held by an equity holder in a company or a patent holder who licenses use of the patent by others.

proprietary lease: A lease which grants certain proprietary rights to the lessee, but continues ownership in the lessor, as in the instance of a cooperative apartment lease.

proprietor: 1. An owner of a business or one who has legal title to something, such as a patented process or design. **2.** In general usage, any business owner.

proprietor's equity: See net worth.

proprietorship: See sole proprietorship.

pro rata: Proportional division of amounts, as in the division of overhead costs among several products or of utility charges among users sharing a single meter.

prospect: A possible purchaser of goods for sale, viewed by a seller as one who might reasonably be expected to consider purchasing on the basis of need or desire.

prospectus: 1. In the securities industry, a fully detailed description of every significant aspect of a business offering stock for public sale and of that stock, including financial matters, personnel, products if any, and all other pertinent business data. **2.** Generally, a written description of a proposed enterprise, such as a new book or new company.

prosperity: Good times, characterized by peace, growth in gross national product, growing real wages, increasing profits, a low inflation rate, and general optimism as to the economic future.

protective tariff: A tariff aimed at protecting domestic businesses from competition in domestic markets by products from abroad.

protest: A statement in writing and certified by a notary public, declaring that a negotiable instrument has been presented for payment or acceptance and has been rejected.

Protestant ethic: The somewhat ethnocentric theory that such qualities as work compulsion, saving and careful spending are characteristics formed in large part by the values of northern European Protestantism.

proximate cause: That which is the prime, immediate cause of the happening of an event, and without which the event would not have happened.

proxy: A written statement, legally authorizing another to vote stock capable of being voted by the authorizer; a normal arrangement in many publicly held corporations, with management routinely soliciting the proxies of shareholders, but also used by those trying to win control of a corporation away from its current management.

proxy statement: An explanatory written statement required by law to be attached to a proxy solicitation by whoever is soliciting the proxy.

prudent man rule: A general guide to legally acceptable investment action on the part of those investing funds in some sort of fiduciary capacity, indicating that those funds should be invested in such securities as a "prudent man" would invest in, rather than in speculative securities; in practice, the rule results in considerable conservatism on the part of those so investing.

pseudocode: A generalized computer code, used in planning program segments, that must be translated into a computer language before it can be operated on by the computer.

psychic income: Noneconomic benefits stemming from work performed or buying decisions made, as when an artist creates a work and is satisfied by the process of creation and the work itself far beyond any money that might be received from sale of the work, or when someone gets satisfaction from doing a job well.

psychometrics: Psychological testing, with emphasis on the accretion and evaluation of quantitative data.

public: 1. That which is in law or practice a matter of community interest, right, or ownership, or which involves those in a community and in those contexts is subject to government and court action. **2.** A people or portion of that people bound by common interests; for example, an audience for a kind of artistic work.

public accountant: An accountant in public practice who is not a Certified Public Accountant; in some states recognized for all practical purposes as equivalent to a certified public accountant.

public assistance: Most commonly used as a euphemism for welfare, but also embracing a wide variety of self-help programs for poor and disadvantaged people.

public corporation: 1. A corporation which has issued stock through general sale to the public, and which is therefore at least partially owned by those shareholders. **2.** A corporation set up by government and owned wholly or partially by government.

public debt: The total of all debts owed by every governmental body in a country; in the United States, the total of federal, state, and local debts.

public domain: 1. That which by its nature might have been or once was protected by copyright, patent, or trademark, or something never so protected, which is now unprotected and open to use by anyone; for example, a book written 100 years ago which once was copyrighted, but is now unprotected because its copyright period has run out. **2.** Land, such as national park lands, owned by government, rather than by private owners.

public finance: The formal study of the financial activities of government, in such areas as borrowing and spending policies and procedures, public debt management, and tax policy.

public grazing lands: Public lands that are used for cattle grazing by ranchers, subject to public regulation of grazing on those lands. In the United States, most western land was at one time public grazing land.

public housing: Housing that is financed, built under the direction of, and operated by government; usually but not always aimed

at meeting the housing needs of people of small to moderate income.

public interest: The idea that a community has an interest in those matters that affect all or some of its members, and that government has the right and obligation to intervene on behalf of community interests; for example, the obligation to intervene to prevent or remedy water pollution caused by industrial chemical dumping.

publicity: Whatever brings news of a person or product to the public, but is not directly paid for, in contrast to advertising, which is openly purchased. The term is often used even more widely to include advertising.

public lands: See public domain.

public offering: An offering of an original issue of stock through public sale.

public ownership: The ownership of any organization by government, as in a federally owned public utility, such as the Tennessee Valley Authority, or a city-owned transportation line.

public policy: The attitude of government on a specific matter or kind of matter, as expressed by statute and official statement.

public practice: An accounting practice conducted as an independent business, in contrast to accounting practices conducted as employees of government or business organizations.

public property: Anything owned by any government, including both real property and that which would otherwise be personal property.

public relations: The development of activities aimed at fostering a favorable public view of organizations and people, using all available means to do so, including publicity, advertising, and "good works."

public sale: The disposition of property at a sale open to the public, at auction or at fixed prices.

public sector: That portion of the national

economy which is occupied with the economic activities of government, including all ways in which a government spends or receives money and the entire public payroll.

public service advertising: Advertising which sells public goals and services, rather than products or company images, such as advertisements placed by nonprofit health organizations; but in some instances, such advertising is part of the public relations effort of a company and serves both public service and company image-building goals.

public service commission: The most common name for state agencies charged with the regulation of and rate setting for public utilities in the best interests of state citizens, while allowing the utilities reasonable profits.

public spending: The amounts spent by government for all or any purposes.

public television: Television broadcasters wholly or partially funded and to some extent supervised by the Federal government, and who operate on a nonprofit basis; they are organized into a fourth major television broadcasting system.

public utilities: Those basic functions so directly supplying public needs, and at the same time so prone to becoming monopolies, that government recognizes their essentially monopolistic nature and by law regulates their prices and other activities, such as telephone, power, water, and some transportation companies.

public utility bonds: The debt obligations of such public utilities as gas and electric companies; often secured by mortgages on company plant and equipment, and generally regarded as high-quality bonds.

public utility commission: See public service commission.

public utility stocks: Ownership equities in such public utilities as gas and electric companies; due to the protected and regulated position of these companies, usually regarded as high-quality, relatively stable stocks.

public warehouse: A warehouse renting storage space for public use.

public welfare: Those activities of government aimed primarily at helping the poor and otherwise disadvantaged to secure the basic necessities of life and at the same time to develop skills necessary for economic self-sufficiency.

public works: A wide range of projects funded by government to serve public interests, such as canals, bridges, dams, roads, and power projects.

publisher's representative: One who sells for a publisher, whether books to booksellers or advertising space to advertisers.

puffery: The making of false and misleading claims for a product or service by its seller, in both personal sales situations and advertising.

pump priming: An attempt by government to stimulate business activity and economic growth in times of recession or depression by direct spending, usually on the kinds of public works that create substantial numbers of immediate jobs for the unemployed.

punched card: See card.

puchase money mortgage: A mortgage accompanying a property sales transaction, given by buyer to seller as all or part of the purchase price.

purchase order: A document given by a buyer to a seller, specifying all the terms and conditions of a purchase, which, if accepted and verified as accepted by the seller, becomes a legally binding contract between buyer and seller.

purchase syndicate: See underwriting syndicate.

purchasing: The finding and buying of needed materials and equipment; a function performed in every organization, in larger organizations by a person or group whose sole job it is to buy what is needed most efficiently and economically.

purchasing agent: One who is authorized to buy needed materials and equipment for a company, and whose act of purchasing legally binds the company; usually a company employee.

purchasing power: How much a unit of currency, an individual, a group, or an entire economy can buy, relative to some previous period.

pure competition: A market in which all sellers compete equally, supply is high, and no one has any influence on supply, demand, or price; a largely theoretical construct.

purposive sampling: Sampling based on selecting a sample group judged by researchers to be representatives of the entire universe being examined; for example, the choice of the population of a single small town as representative of all Americans for purposes of market-testing a new product.

put: A stock option contract, enabling its holder to sell a stock at a specific price at any time during the contract period; often used as a hedge by bears, those who believe that the market or that particular stock will drop in value.

pyramiding: 1. The selling of dealerships, distributorships, or franchises essentially for resale, resulting in short-term high profits for promoters and early investors, and ultimately in the defrauding of later investors. **2.** The building of equity positions on paper profits, by using the profits in margined accounts to buy more stock. **3.** A corporate acquisition technique that builds a chain of controlled companies, by using the assets and borrowing power of some acquired companies to buy others.

Q

qualified endorsement: 1. An endorsement that in some way limits the free negotiability of the endorsed instrument, such as "for deposit only." **2.** An endorsement "without recourse," which attempts to remove or limit the liability of the current endorser if the instrument is ultimately unpaid or for some reason not accepted for payment.

qualified prospect: A prospective purchaser of goods or services for sale, who is known by the seller to be able to make or substantially influence a buying decision.

qualified stock option: An employee benefit, enabling employees to buy shares of their corporations at stated prices within a specified future period, making it possible for them to buy stocks at lower than market prices within the option period or to forego buying if market prices should drop below option prices; subject to legal restrictions imposed by laws and regulations, and qualifying for special tax treatment through compliance with those laws and regulations.

qualitative interview: See depth interview.

quality control: Those processes undertaken by a business to attempt to achieve and maintain high standards of quality for its products, including a series of inspections starting with the receipt of materials and ending with inspection of finished goods under conditions of use after sale.

quantitative interview: An interview in which all or almost all questions are set beforehand and are asked by the interviewer in a planned sequence.

quantitative management: See management science.

quantity discount: A discount offered by a business for purchase of multiple unit orders of its products; for example, a 10% discount on the entire purchase price on typewriter ribbons ordered in quantities of 100 or more.

quantity theory of money: The theory that the amount of money in circulation will directly affect prices and spending, less money in circulation causing higher prices and more money in circulation causing lower prices.

quartile: See percentile.

quasi-public corporation: A privately owned corporation recognized in law and practice as having public responsibilities, such as a public utility; therefore a corporation that is very highly regulated and expected to behave at least partly in the public interest.

questionnaire: A written group of questions, aimed at securing information on related matters; for example, a group of questions comprising a market research survey, or an employment application.

queued access method: In computer systems, an access method that consists of input/output statement and machine input/output statement in one step, in contrast to the basic access method, which requires two steps.

queuing theory: That body of mathematics concerned with the economical solution of fluctuating unit handling needs, such as the optimum number of bank tellers needed to serve a bank's fluctuating retail customer population or the optimum number of automobiles in a rental auto fleet.

quick assets: Assets that are quickly and easily convertible into cash, such as cash and readily marketable securities.

quick assets ratio: See acid test.

quickie strike: A strike called on very short notice or without any warning at all; usually a wildcat strike, that is in violation of existing union contracts, but sometimes a legal strike as part of a drive for union recognition.

quick ratio: See acid test.

quitclaim: 1. A release given by one to another, giving up any claim against the other as to a specific matter **2.** A release giving up claim to title; for example, title to land.

quitclaim deed: A deed given by one to another, passing claim, interest, or title to that other, but not claiming to have clear title to pass. If title is legally capable of being conveyed, the quitclaim deed serves to pass title.

quota: 1. A goal, such as the sales goals set for a sales representative by management. **2.** A limit, such as the maximum amount of a certain kind of import that may be brought into a country in a given period.

quota sampling: The selection of a sample population out of the total universe under examination by identifying and weighting subgroups within that universe, and then selecting proportional numbers of sample subjects out of each subgroup.

quotation: The current market price, both bid and asked, of securities and commodities.

quote: A price set by a seller; usually used in describing bids received on work to be performed under contract.

R

race discrimination: See discrimination.

racketeering: Any of a large number of illegal acts and practices in business or labor matters; for example, the taking over of legitimate businesses by organized crime, or the operation of union officials who take bribes from employers in return for favorable labor contracts or engage in theft from union pension funds.

rack jobber: A middleman who supplies retailers with goods and usually the racks and other display devices from which those goods are sold.

raid: 1. An attempt by one union to win members away from another union, and by so doing take over collective bargaining units from that other union. **2.** An attempt by securities speculators and traders to cause the price of one or more securities to drop; an illegal market manipulation.

Railroad Retirement Board: A Federal agency responsible for the administration of railroad retirement and unemployment insurance plans.

rail trailer shipment: A kind of piggyback shipment, in which fully loaded trailers are hauled by motor carriers to rail lines and then transferred to railroad cars to continue their journeys.

Railway Labor Act: A Federal law covering mediation of disputes between railway labor and management.

rally: A turnaround in stock market prices, in which previously dropping prices bound upward; applied rather indiscriminately by

traders to both large and small upward price movements.

R and D: See research and development.

random access: The ability to store and retrieve specific data in computer storage without reading through all stored data in sequence, as is necessary in sequential access.

random numbers: A group of numbers that have no statistical relation to each other; for example, the selection of numbers for a prize drawing by a blindfolded person. Tables of random numbers are often used to help researchers select subjects randomly.

random sampling: Sampling that uses subjects randomly selected out of a large enough sample population to be relatively sure that within a modest allowance for error, each has an equal chance of being selected.

random variable: A variable that may assume any of a range of values in a particular situation, independent of previous situations. Such a variable can be generally predicted by statistical analysis of historical data, but single occurrences cannot be predicted; for example, the number of times a pair of dice will come up "seven" in many thousands of throws is generally predictable, but how those dice will come up on any single throw is not.

range: 1. In general, the spectrum of possibilities in a given situation. **2.** In statistics, the breadth of a frequency distribution.

rank and file: The membership of a union, in

contrast to all elected or appointed union officials.

ranking: A job evaluation method that attempts to classify all jobs in a unit by their importance to the unit, from highest to lowest.

rapport: A relationship of mutual trust and respect; especially prized by sellers in a selling situation.

rate: 1. A seller's quoted price. **2.** To evaluate, most often in comparative fashion, as when a customer or evaluating organization judges one product as better constructed than another.

rate base: The amount thought to be invested in a public utility, which provides a base upon which a fair rate of return may be calculated, when determining a regulated public utility's proper rates.

rate bureau: A transportation industry organization that sets suggested rates for its industry or part of that industry.

rate cutting: The lowering of wage rates, usually incentive wage rates, by an employer acting alone, without agreement from workers or union; most often encountered in piecework situations.

rated capacity: See capacity.

rate of exchange: See exchange rate.

rate of interest: See interest rate.

rate of return: The amount of return on investment, calculated as a percentage of that investment.

rate regulation: The process of setting public utility rates engaged in by state and local public utility commissions.

rate setting: The process of developing incentive pay schedules through the placing of a price that will be paid by employer to worker for each job performed or piece produced; most often encountered in piecework pay schedules.

rating: 1. The process of evaluating insurance risks and setting prices that will be quoted by insurers on different kinds of risks and insurance policies. **2.** In broadcasting, the relative standings of different programs, as in television's Nielsen ratings. **3.** The evaluation of a security, such as a bond rating.

rating bureau: An insurance organization that sets proposed standard rates for some kinds of property insurance.

ratio chart: A type of statistical chart that presents relative, rather than absolute, changes, often using special types of graphing paper such as semi-logarithmic paper.

rationing: Government control of the distribution of goods in small supply, for such purposes as providing a fair share of goods to all users, balancing goods supply among users of unequal economic power, and providing relatively large supplies to some in preference to others for purposes of national policy; often used for the distribution of rare consumer goods, goods in wartime, and sometimes in peacetime.

ratio-to-moving-average technique: In statistics, a way of developing measures of seasonal and other fluctuations by comparing moving averages with historic trends.

raw materials: The materials from which other, more finished goods are made; goods may be made from raw materials only to become raw materials for other goods, as steel is produced from raw materials and becomes raw material for making automobiles.

reacquired stock: Stock that has been sold by the corporation to shareholders and then in some way acquired by the company to become treasury stock; usually because of a decision to buy back outstanding stock but sometimes due to gift or bequest.

readership: An estimate of all those who read a publication, usually referring to the readership of some sort of periodical, rather than that of a book; sometimes used more loosely as a synonym for audience.

readjustment: The restructuring of a corporation's debt and capital structure by voluntary act of the corporation; in contrast to reorganization, which is involuntary and results from legal process.

read-only access: Programmed access that allows data in a computer system to be read but not altered.

ready credit account: See charge account.

real account: In accounting, an account that is carried forward from one fiscal period to another, and is a balance sheet item, in contrast to a nominal account, in which transactions are completed within a single fiscal period.

real cost: 1. The cost of an item measured by its relationship to other items, as in a barter system; for example, one sack of grain is worth two bags of salt. **2.** The cost of an item measured in money terms, but adjusted to allow for that money's inflation or deflation; for example, one sack of grain worth $10 in 1967 may be worth $22 today, but its real cost may still be only $10 in terms of base year 1967 money. **3.** A synonym for opportunity cost.

real cost of borrowing: The net of true interest minus the rate of inflation, without allowing for hidden inflation, which does not show up in government figures indicating the current rate of inflation.

real estate: Land and anything held in law to be permanently attached to that land, including structures and some kinds of fixtures and equipment; real property, as distinguished from personal property.

real estate bond: A bond secured by a real estate mortgage; a debt obligation of its issuer backed by the issuer's promise to pay and further backed by the underlying value of the mortgaged property.

real estate broker: A state-licensed broker, who acts as agent, usually for the seller but sometimes for the buyer in real estate transactions.

real estate investment trust (REIT): A fund dedicated to real estate investments, and accorded special federal tax treatment; in practice operating much as does a mutual fund.

real estate tax: A kind of property tax, levied on real estate; part of a considerable body of state and local taxes.

real income: Income adjusted for the impact of inflation and deflation on purchasing power, usually calculated by comparing price changes with income changes, using a specified year as a base year for both; for example, apparent income may have doubled between 1970 and now, expressed in dollars, but prices as measured by the Consumer Price Index may have risen by 100% in the same period, yielding a net result of no change in real income—though such change may also be affected by changes in other factors, such as the proportion of income spent on tax payments.

realize: To convert something of possible or anticipated value into cash or near-cash equivalents; for example, to sell stock that has gone up in value since purchased, or to sell goods in stock to a consumer.

realized appreciation: The difference between the purchase price paid by the seller of something of value and a later higher selling price; for example, on stock or land sold.

realized depreciation: See recaptured depreciation.

real national income: See real income.

real property: An ownership or other legal interest in real estate, including land, structures and some kinds of fixtures and equipment.

real time: In computer processing, the operation of the system quickly enough to control ongoing processes, such as in controlling traffic or monitoring supply and distribution of commodities on a current basis.

realtor: See real estate broker.

real wages: See real income.

rebate: A repayment by a seller to a purchaser of part of an already paid purchase price, in contrast to a discount, which is a deduction from a purchase price before it is paid; for example, a promotional device may involve sending a check for $10 to a customer after receipt of the customer's payment of $200 for a camera—the net effect is precisely the same as a 5% discount in this instance, except that the customer pays a little more in sales taxes in the rebate situation.

rebating: 1. The promise of and return of part of a purchase price to a buyer as an inducement to buy; a widely used selling device. For example, a television set maker may return a $50 check to a consumer buying a $500 color television set, as a dramatic form of discounting. **2.** In insurance selling, the illegal practice of discounting insurance, in which the insurance seller returns to the insurance buyer, usually by direct payment, part of the premiums paid.

rebuilding: The process of taking a machine apart, such as an automobile motor, repairing it as necessary, replacing worn parts and reassembling it; sometimes resulting in a machine that has been substantially renewed throughout and sometimes merely a euphemism for relatively minor repair accompanied by rather substantial charges. Also applied to the process of developing a new staff or structure after a poor business period or loss of many employees.

recall: The calling back of products by their makers for repair or replacement, usually under pressure from Federal and state regulatory authorities; for example, the recall of hundreds of thousands of automobiles for the repair and replacement of unsafe parts.

recapitalization: A substantial change in the amount or nature of the securities issued by a corporation, especially as regards capital restructuring to cover debts or deficits with new capital.

recapture of depreciation: For Federal tax purposes, that part of the net selling price minus book value which is due to depreciation deductions taken by the seller while the asset was in its hands, and on sale is to be treated as ordinary income by the seller.

receipt: 1. A written acknowledgment that something has been received, capable of being used as legal evidence of such receipt; for example, a warehouse receipt for goods delivered to that warehouse, or a store receipt for goods purchased from that store. **2.** The act of receiving cash or any other assets, to be recorded on books of account.

receivables: 1. That which is now or will be collectible, in the forms of accounts and notes receivable. **2.** In accounting, a statement of the total of all accounts and notes receivable.

receiver: A court-appointed custodian of the assets of a debtor, charged with saving whatever of the debtor's assets can be used to satisfy creditors; limited to the custodial role, as the trustee in bankruptcy is appointed by the court to maintain and restore as much of a going business as is possible.

receivership: In law, the position of an insolvent business, one being managed by a court-appointed receiver, rather than by its previous management.

receiving: The receipt and acceptance of materials by a firm, and that portion of the firm's organization responsible for such receipt and acceptance, often a separate department in larger firms. Receiving and shipping functions are normally joined in actual operations.

recession: A strong and relatively long-term downturn in the national economy, characterized by increased unemployment and a lower level of business activity, but less deep and protracted than a depression, such as the Great Depression of the 1930's.

reciprocal buying: The policy of buying goods from customers, in preference to non-customers; for example, the purchase of raw materials from a customer that buys a firm's machine tools—a widespread, often rather unrewarding, sometimes denied practice.

reciprocity: A principle stated in some international trade arrangements, in which nations agree to supply each other with goods and services on mutually agreed-upon favorable terms.

reclamation: The process of attempting to make land, water and air that have been damaged by human and natural action, useful and healthful once again, through such activities as reforestation, water purification, irrigation, and flood control projects.

recognition: Formal acknowledgment by an employer that a union is accepted as bargaining agent for employees and that the employer will engage in collective bargaining with that union.

reconciliation: The process of balancing related accounts in a double entry bookkeeping system, and the documents evidencing that such balancing has been completed.

reconditioned: See rebuilt.

reconversion: After a war, conversion of a national economy from wartime production back to peacetime production.

record: 1. Any written or otherwise stored information, usually in sequential form for multiple items; examples include accounting information stored in books of record and legal proceedings, often referred to in the law as the record. **2.** To place information in storage, or in storable form. **3.** In computers, a single kind of information, one of many like it; for example, the record of a purchase in a store's computerized business handling system. **4.** The best, most, worst, or least, as in a record snowfall.

record date: The date officially set by a corporation for a dividends or rights distribution; stockholders must be recorded as such on the corporation's books on or before that date to participate in that distribution.

recorder of deeds: A government official responsible for the recording of documents re-

lating to real estate transactions in official books of record.

records retention policy: The policy of an organization as regards the length of time records will be kept for tax, business handling, and legal requirements purposes; usually varying with the documents and purposes concerned.

recourse: The extent to which one who has an obligation can be legally held to that obligation. For example, the maker of a personal note has unlimited liability to pay that note, but if the note is "non-recourse," the lender has agreed to accept only the borrower's promise to pay, backed by whatever collateral is specified, if any, and has no ability to compel payment from other borrower resources.

recovery: 1. Something, usually of value, awarded by a court to a plaintiff as a result of a successful action at law. **2.** The collection of all or part of a debt that had been treated as uncollectible. **3.** An upward move to a previous higher level, as when securities prices fluctuate. **4.** The move of a whole economy toward relative prosperity after a recession or depression.

recruitment: The process of finding wanted employees for an organization, pursued through such vehicles as employment agencies, newspaper and magazine advertisements, and college campus solicitations.

recycling: The use of scrap and used materials in the production of new materials; for example, the use of junked automobiles and other scrapped machines as sources of metals which can be refined and used again in new machines, an old established practice; also the newer practice of reusing paper, old cans and many other materials as sources of new materials, which has grown in recent years as part of the ecology and conservation movements.

redeemable bond: A bond that may be recovered by its issuer before its maturity date, on payment of its face value and usually an additional premium amount to its holders.

redemption: 1. The recovery of a debt instrument by its maker through repayment of the debt it evidences; for example, the recovery of a note after payment, or the retirement of a bond issue at maturity or at full payment before maturity. **2.** The right to buy back an obligation, by payment of money or performance of an obligation, as provided by law and the specific provisions of applicable contracts.

redemption fund: See sinking fund.

redemption price: The price at which something may be bought back; for example, the price at which a bond may be retired by its issuer before maturity.

red herring: A preliminary prospectus, offering a new issue of securities for public examination; but without some of the details offered in the final prospectus, which actually offers the securities for public sale.

red ink: Referring to a minus entry in accounting records, which was traditionally written in red ink; but in a wider sense indicating losses rather than desired profits.

rediscounting: The act of making second and subsequent discounts of commercial paper passing between banks or between banks and Federal Reserve banks; for example, the discounting of a note by a bank when paying it and passage of that note to a Federal Reserve bank to raise funds in a second or rediscounting transaction.

rediscount rate: The interest rate charged to member banks by the Federal Reserve on rediscounted paper only; synonymous with discount rate.

redlining: The refusal of banks, insurance companies, and other financial sources and insurers to make loans and insure property in some geographic areas and with some kinds of people and businesses, or willingness to do such business only at very high premium rates. For example, banks may refuse to make normal mortgage loans in some

poor, black, or Spanish-speaking inner city areas, citing very high default rates, but discriminating against a whole class of risks, rather than differentiating between individual risks; or an insurer may refuse to write fire insurance in the same kind of area.

red tape: Unnecessarily complex, difficult rules, regulations, and procedures; endemic to all large organizations and epidemic in governmental bureaucracies.

re-export: The export of goods that have been imported and held unaltered and usually unopened, sometimes without additional import duties being levied, as when held in a duty-free international area.

referee in bankruptcy: An officer appointed by a bankruptcy court, responsible for fact finding, hearing, and preliminary adjudication steps under the supervision of the court, and who, if bankruptcy is declared by the court, functions as temporary administrator of a bankrupt's assets.

reference: A recommendation, stating a person's character, qualifications, and reliability; often required of people seeking jobs, credit, and housing.

reference check: A verification of references supplied, aimed at affirming that the recommendations are legitimate; for example, a check of references supplied by a job seeker or of references supplied by a prospective borrower.

referendum: A vote by the members of a group on an issue, rather than leaving the resolution of that issue to those representing the group; for example, submission of a collective bargaining contract to the entire membership of the negotiating union, rather than letting union officials or representatives accept or reject the contract for the group.

referrals: Sales leads generated by the recommendations of customers or others, to be followed up by a seller, often but not always using the name of the recommending person as a means of introduction to the recommended prospect.

refinancing: The replacement of existing debts with new debts, usually extending the term of debt repayment, whether as a matter of convenience or economic necessity on the part of the borrower; for example, the replacement of an existing mortgage with a larger mortgage, supplying needed cash, more and smaller payments, or both; or the replacement of corporate or government bonds about to mature with new bonds carrying a maturity date years in the future.

reflation: A governmental policy aimed at moving economic activity, prices, and wages to higher than current levels, usually by means of inflationary money, tax, and credit policies and usually in the presence of recession or depression.

refund: A return of a payment, all or in part; for example, the return of money paid or the extension of credit for defective merchandise.

refunding: See refinancing.

regional differential: See geographical differential.

regional stock exchange: A stock exchange operating in a limited geographical area, listing the securities of companies headquartered in its region as well as those of companies listed on other, major exchanges.

register: A body of information about a specific kind of thing or transaction, maintained in writing in sequence or in a data base capable of being called forth in sequence. Examples are sequenced accounting entries, usually kept in book or journal form; a list of ships registered as vessels of a particular country; a list of lawyers, accountants, doctors, or dentists practicing in a geographical area; or a corporation's stockholders list.

registered bond: A bond carrying the name of its owner on its face, and so recorded on the books of its issuer. It may not be negotiated unless endorsed by its owner and transferred on the books of its issuer.

registered check: A check purchased from a bank rather than drawn on funds deposited with that bank, in practice functioning as a money order, though called a kind of check.

registered coupon bond: A type of registered bond that is registered only to its owner, but carries interest-paying coupons negotiable by delivery, as do non-registered bonds.

registered mail: Mail which is recorded, for a fee, at the post office where it is originally mailed and is checked at intermediate and delivering post offices as well, and for which a receipt is signed by its deliveree; such mail may also be insured against loss or damage.

registered representative: One who is licensed by the Securities and Exchange Commission to sell securities and is employed by a brokerage firm doing business on the floor of a stock exchange, through its own floor broker or by arrangement with another securities firm. Registered representatives buy and sell securities for customers through floor brokers.

registered stock: Stock that is recorded on the books of its issuer in the name of its owner, and which cannot be transferred without that owner's signature and transfer on those books.

register of deeds: See recorder of deeds.

registrar: An agent, employed by a corporation issuing securities, usually a banking organization, to perform all authentication and checking functions in relation to an issue, to prevent issuance of unauthorized, counterfeit, or otherwise illegal securities.

registration: **1.** The act of recording an official entry; for example, the entry of a newly constructed ship upon its national ship registry, the application for and granting of an automobile license, or official entry into a course of study. **2.** The process of officially registering securities with the appropriate Federal and state regulatory authorities, involving a series of documents and clearances, so that the securities may be offered for public sale.

registration statement: A document filed by

a prospective securities issuer with the appropriate regulatory authorities, which must grant official clearance before those securities are cleared for public sale; such a statement includes substantial financial, other business, and personal information relating to the securities issue, its issuer, and the leading people associated with the issue.

regression analysis: In statistics, a way of examining and predicting the behavior of unknown factors by casting them against the behavior of known factors, the unknown factor being called the dependent variable, and the known factor being called the independent variable. For example, assembly line error rate might be predictable if cast against the speed of the line, with the percentage of error increasing as the speed of the line increases. The casting of one known against one unknown is simple regression analysis; of one or more unknowns against one or more knowns is multiple regression analysis.

regression equation: In statistics, a mathematical expression of the relationship between variables, used in regression analysis.

regressive tax: A tax that is proportionately heavier on those of small income than on those of large income. For example, a sales tax, on which all pay equal amounts of tax per dollar spent, is regressive, contrasting with a progressive tax, in which tax rates rise with income.

regular dividend: A dividend that is customarily and regularly paid by a corporation, usually on annual, semiannual, or quarterly basis. It may be paid out of current profits or reserves; it may be unchanged in amount for many years, or raised or lowered at any time of payment by the corporation's Board of Directors. If not paid when scheduled, it is passed and lost.

Regulation Q: The Federal Reserve regulation specifying the top limit on interest payable by member banks on regular savings accounts.

Regulation T: The Federal Reserve regula-

tion specifying the top margin credit allowable by brokers and dealers to their customers.

Regulation U: The Federal Reserve regulation specifying the top amount of credit bankers may advance their customers for the purpose of buying listed securities; a companion to Regulation T, aimed at preventing the use of bank credit in circumvention of margin requirements.

reimbursement: To pay back money that has been spent by another; for example, to pay back money that has been spent by an employee on a business trip, on submission of an expense statement.

reinstatement: To restore something to its previous position; for example, to restore an insurance policy that has lapsed due to nonpayment of premiums to its previous position of coverage of the insured, when payment of the lapsed premiums is made within the period specified in the policy; to restore an employee who has been fired to employment on successful prosecution of a grievance against the company; or to restore a student who has been on probation to full status after the probationary period.

reinsurance: In the insurance industry, the transfer of all or part of a risk from the company originally insuring to another insurer, usually resulting in the sharing of a risk undertaken by one insurer with one or more insurers; a very common practice when underwriting major risks.

reinvestment: The investment of funds stemming from other investments rather than taking those funds out of investment; for example, the investment of funds resulting from maturing bonds or stock sales in other bonds or stocks; or the investment of funds resulting from dividends paid on stock and interest paid on bonds in more of the same stocks and bonds.

REIT: See Real Estate Investment Trust.

release: 1. To give up a legal claim or possible legal claim upon another; for example, the settlement of an insurance claim by agreement between claimant and insurer involves a renunciation of all current and possible future claims against the insurer by the claimant arising from the same set of circumstances. **2.** The document that is evidence of the giving up of an existing or potential legal claim.

reliability: The extent to which a person, machine or process can be relied upon to give consistently satisfactory performance.

relief: Government aid to those in need, especially to the unemployed during the Great Depression. The term has now largely been replaced by several other somewhat more specific terms, such as unemployment compensation and welfare.

remainder: 1. In publishing, to sell books still in the publisher's warehouse unsold, and likely to be unsold at normal prices, at large discounts to booksellers who will then resell them at retail at deeply discounted prices. **2.** A future interest in an estate after all prior interests have been satisfied. The person who holds such an interest under the terms of an estate, is called a remainderman.

remainderman: One who is to receive the remainder of an estate after all prior interests set up by the terms of the estate have been satisfied; for example, a child who takes the remainder of an estate that, on the death of one parent pays income to the other parents for life, with the entire estate and its income going to the child on the second parent's death.

remedy: The means by which a right is protected or a wrong righted; at law, the action taken by a court on conclusion of a case in favor of a plaintiff, as distinct from the case itself.

remittance: A payment, usually on a debt or other financial obligation; sometimes used more widely to describe any sum of money sent by one party to another.

remonetization: The restoring of a metal to the status of money, after having removed it from that status; for example, bringing back gold as money and issuing a currency fully recoverable in gold after having gone over to a paper money backed not by gold, as it once was, but rather solely by the full faith and credit of the government issuing that paper money.

remote: That which is located at some distance, often far away; in business, often used to describe that which is any distance from a machine which it controls or works with. For example, a television set may be controlled from a distance of a few feet and be described as being remotely controlled; a computer may be reached by telephone line from thousands of miles away and be described as being remotely accessed.

remote access: The ability to reach and work with a computer from some distance away; usually moving input and output through a terminal or some other computer.

remote batch processing: See batch processing.

remote control: The ability to direct the movements of a machine from some distance away.

removal bond: A security bond to cover import duties and other expenses, when imported goods are taken from a bonded warehouse for re-export.

remuneration: Pay, in whatever form; for tax purposes, including a wide range of noncash items, such as many, though not all, kinds of fringe benefits.

renewal: 1. The extension of a debt, by its replacement with another debt; for example, the replacement of a loan due to be paid to a bank with another loan to be paid later. A loan may be renewed again and again, in practice constituting a line of credit. **2.** The continuation of an insurance contract for an additional period. **3.** The replacement of an old machine, machine part, or any other tangible portion of plant and equipment, with new equipment, in contrast to repair of old equipment. **4.** The continuation of any contract, such as a subscription to a periodical.

rent: Payment for the right to use anything tangible, including land, buildings and equipment, usually for a specified period of time, but sometimes for the use itself, as when a machine is rented for a single use rather than for a period of time.

rent control: Governmental restriction on the amount of rent that can be charged, usually setting top rents or maximum increases that may be charged on residential rentals; under some circumstances, as in wartime, commercial rentals may be controlled as well.

rent escalation: See escalation.

rentier: From the French, someone whose income is largely dependent on the proceeds of investments yielding fixed dollar amounts, rather than varying with economic conditions; a highly vulnerable economic position in periods of inflation.

reopener: A contract provision setting terms and conditions under which a contract will be opened for renegotiation, and specifying which matters will then be eligible for renegotiation; for example, a collective bargaining contract providing for a wage reopening at the beginning of the second and third years of a three-year contract, or a government contract providing for a reopening on the question of costs under specified conditions.

reorder point: The point at which supplies must be reordered, as set by an internal inventory control system; for example, standing instructions in a company may indicate that 5,000 more units of a specific item are to be ordered when that stock reaches the 1,000-unit level.

reorganization: The involuntary restructuring of a corporation's debt and capital structure, as ordered by a court of law, under circumstances of insolvency and pursuant to the bankruptcy statutes; in contrast to readjustment, which is voluntary.

reorganization bonds: Bonds issued by a company as part of the process of reorganization, replacing previous debt obligations.

reparations: Damages paid by one side to another after conclusion of a war; usually, but not always, by the defeated to the victors.

repayment terms: See credit terms.

replacement contract: See novation.

replacement cost: What it would cost to replace an asset, usually part of plant and equipment, at current prices.

replacement insurance: An insurance contract providing for payment of the replacement cost of property destroyed, rather than its depreciated value.

replacement method of depreciation: The addition of straight-line depreciation and a factor for replacement cost, when replacement cost is estimated higher than original cost; for example, when replacement costs are estimated as $5,000 higher than the original cost, and the depreciable life of the item is 10 years, $500 per year for ten years would be added to the straight-line depreciation of the item. Generally not an acceptable mode of depreciation to accountants and taxing authorities.

repledge: To use a borrower's collateral as collateral for a loan to the original lender. For example, a bond that has been pledged as security for a loan may be used by the original lender as collateral for a different loan. Repledging requires some form of consent by the original borrower, who owns the collateral although it has been so pledged.

report: 1. To supply others with information and anlysis, orally or in writing. **2.** Information and analysis that is supplied to others, orally or in writing.

reporting chain: See chain of command.

reporting pay: See call-in pay.

reporting period: The period of time covered by a report; usually applied to a report issued regularly, such as a quarterly or annual report.

reporting relationships: See chain of command.

reporting structure: See chain of command.

report program generator (RPG): In computer processing, a method of programming that allows production of a wide variety of reports of tabulated data.

repossession: The act of reclaiming property that has been purchased on an installment basis, when the buyer fails to meet the payment terms of the loan.

representation: 1. A statement, expressed or implied, claiming something to be true which is material to a contract being made; for example, a claim about the worth or performance of a product that is material to the consummation of a sale, and which, if shown a' law to have been false and misleading, may cause a court to invalidate that sale. **2.** Any statement claiming to be fact.

representation election: An election held in a workplace or company to decide which union, or whether any union, will represent the workers as bargaining agent.

representative money: Paper money issued by a national government that is backed to its full value by stores of precious metal, in contrast to paper money that is backed wholly or partly only by the full faith and credit of the government.

reproduction cost: An estimate of the cost of reproducing a specific kind of fixed asset at current prices.

repudiation: The act of refusing to fulfill an obligation; usually a refusal to pay a debt. As a practical matter, legally enforceable debts cannot be repudiated, as legal process will result, but governments can and do repudiate debts.

repurchase agreement: A legally enforceable contract between buyer and seller that speci-

fies the seller's right to buy back what is being sold at specified prices and terms; a device often used in sale and leaseback agreements.

request for bid: A request from a buyer to seller for a bid on work to be performed, sometimes as sole bidder and sometimes in competition with other bidders.

request for proposal: See request for bid.

requisition: A written intra-organization request for goods or services; for example, for office supplies from a company warehouse.

resale: The second and subsequent selling of items purchased, with no significant change in their character.

resale price maintenance: The holding of the resale prices of goods to levels specified by their manufacturers; once supported by fair trade laws in many states, these attempts are now often unsuccessful.

rescission of contract: The cancellation of a contract, with all parties to the contract returning to their previous positions as to rights and duties, whether by agreement between the parties or by legally enforceable unilateral action for cause.

research and development (R and D): Investigation aimed at developing new products and processes, whether directly through applications research or indirectly through basic research.

reserve balances: Reserves held by member banks of the Federal Reserve system in the form of Federal Reserve Bank deposits.

reserve currency: A national currency recognized as so stable that many nations keep their foreign exchange reserves in that currency, as well as in gold or any other internationally recognized medium of exchange; for example, United States currency in the period following World War II.

reserve fund: A fund set aside for a specific purpose, consisting of cash or cash equivalents, and recognized as such for accounting purposes.

reserve price: See upset price.

reserve ratio: The relationship between the deposits of a commercial bank and its vault cash or deposits in a Federal Reserve bank; that ratio is set by each Federal Reserve bank.

reserve requirement: The amount of commercial bank deposits that each Federal Reserve bank requires be held by those banks in each Federal Reserve district; a primary means of federal money market manipulation.

reserves: 1. Actual funds held to meet obligations or potential obligations; for example, bank reserves, national gold reserves, company reserves held for special purposes, and legally required insurance company reserves held to meet potential claim obligations. **2.** In accounting, a series of accounts set aside for specific reasons, such as reserves against amortization, bad debts, contingencies, depletion, and repairs.

residence: A place where one lives or maintains some kind of abode. One may have many residences, in fact and for legal purposes, but only one domicile, which for legal purposes is recognized as the principal living place.

resident buyer: A buyer located in a main marketplace and serving one or more organizations located in places other than that main marketplace; for example, a clothing buyer in New York may serve several stores and groups of stores located in other parts of the country.

residuary estate: That portion of an estate that remains, if any, after disposition of all that has been specifically covered by the terms of a will and satisfaction of all debts and expenses in connection with the estate.

resistance level: Any securities or commodities price level, whether for a single security or a whole market, at which advances or declines have previously tended to stall.

resource allocation: Attempts by government to influence or direct the use of national re-sources in directions indicated by public policy, as in encouragement of research in alternate energy sources by the use of federal research grants.

restitution: The return of something to its rightful owner, or its replacement with something of approximately equal value; for example, the return of stolen property to its owner, the payment of money to a successful plaintiff in an action for fraud, or the return of a fine to a defendant after reversal of a lower court's decision by a higher court.

restraining order: See injunction.

restraint of trade: The concept that businesses may attempt to control competition, and by so doing limit freedom of competition; a basic concept in the development of the entire body of United States antitrust law, which attempts to make combinations and other actions in restraint of trade illegal.

restricted stock: Stock that by the terms of its issue cannot be freely traded; for example, stock offered under an employee compensation plan, which must be held conditionally for some time; or unregistered stock, which is restricted as long as it is held.

restrictive covenant: A contract provision limiting free use of property by its owner, usually encountered in real estate contracts; for example, requirements that new home styles in a housing development be approved by a homeowners' committee, or the now illegal restriction of the sale of homes to whites.

restrictive endorsement: An endorsement on a negotiable instrument that limits or destroys its further free negotiability; for example, "for deposit only to the account of . . . " is a common restrictive endorsement on the back of a check.

resume: A brief written business, and to some extent personal, biography, used to present a job-seeker's background to prospective employers.

retail business: A business principally engaged in selling goods to consumers; for example, a neighborhood clothing store, a mail-order business selling consumer products, or a door-to-door sales operation.

retailer: See retail business.

retail method of inventory: A mode of determining book inventory at the close of accounting periods and in between physical inventories, which involves holding inventories at listed selling prices, and adjusting inventory records periodically to reflect actual selling prices.

retained earnings: Company earnings after taxes that are held by the company rather than being distributed as dividends to shareholders; such earnings often fuel long-term capital needs.

retainer: A fee paid for professional services to be rendered over a period of time, rather than for specific services rendered; for example, a law firm may be paid by a client on a yearly fee basis, which will cover certain kinds of services rendered and will usually specify a maximum amount of time to be spent by the law firm on client affairs, beyond which additional fees will be charged.

retaliatory tariff: A tariff levied by one country on the products of another, or on products heavily exported by another, because of tariffs previously levied by that other; sometimes part of an escalating series of protective tariffs between several countries, sharply limiting trade for a period.

retire: 1. To remove from active use; for example, to retire obsolete machinery. **2.** To remove from circulation and end the life of financial instruments, such as bonds paid at maturity. **3.** To stop work at one's occupation and live without any major occupation. **4.** To stop work at an occupation, thus becoming eligible for any retirement benefits involved, though taking up other work; for example, a police officer who retires from police work at the age of fifty to become an English teacher.

retirement insurance: A major aim of the so-cial security system, which takes premium payments from those working during their working lives and pays them benefits after they reach specified retirement ages.

retrenchment: Cutting back on expenditures, usually in the face of adverse business experience or prospects.

retroactive pay: Pay due employees for work previously performed at a lower rate. Examples include pay won by women who have successfully prosecuted a claim for sex discrimination regarding rates of pay, in which the difference between what they received and what they should have received in the period covered by their complaint is awarded them in a lump sum; or pay following a wage settlement achieved some time after a contract expiration date, resulting in higher rates of pay retroactive to the date of expiration of the old contract.

return: 1. Merchandise sold and then returned to its seller by its buyer for credit or refund. **2.** A document supplying a taxing authority with information on matters relating to taxables and with tax computations; accompanied by tax payments as necessary. **3.** Earnings on investment, expressed as a percentage of investment; sometimes used imprecisely to describe also dividends paid relative to the current market value of a stock, even though the stock itself has fluctuated since its acquisition.

return on investment (ROI): Earnings on investments, expressed as a percentage of the amount of the investment; for example, an investment yielding a 4% yearly dividend and 2% in the form of increased market value in that year of the investment would have returned 6% if that investment had been turned back into cash at the end of a year.

revaluation: To change the stated value of a national currency in relation to the values of other national currencies by formal action of a national government.

revenue: The total income received from all sources, but the term is used variously in business and government; for example, in government it includes tax and miscellaneous income but not appropriations, while in public utilities it generally means only sales.

revenue bonds: State and local bonds backed by revenues to be received from state and local income-producing facilities, such as port authorities and power plants, rather than backed by the full faith and credit of the governments issuing them.

revenue stamp: A stamp placed by a taxing authority upon a taxed item, indicating that taxes have been paid.

revenue tariff: An import duty aimed mainly at raising money for government, rather than at protecting home products in domestic markets; in practice, many import duties perform both functions.

reverse discrimination: Alleged discrimination against majority group members, resulting from compliance with government and private policies that attempt to fight current discriminatory practices and make up for past practices by the use of affirmative action.

reverse split: The calling in of an existing stock issue by its issuer and its replacement by an issue containing less shares than the issue recalled, resulting in a smaller number of shares outstanding; in fact, a consolidation of shares rather than a split.

reversionary interest: An interest that reverts to an owner after an interest granted to another has ended, for whatever reason; for example, real property occupied by another under the terms of a lease.

revocable credit: A specific amount or line of credit extended by a lender, usually a bank, that may be revoked at any time and without notice.

revocable trust: A trust which may be revoked by its grantor; usually one that involves a trust fund paying trust income to its beneficiary while its grantor is alive and that is revocable either at will or under stated conditions.

revolving charge account: A charge account which is actually a line of credit, on which items may be purchased and charged up to a stated credit limit, and into which repayments go for crediting.

revolving credit: Any line of credit that may be borrowed against up to a stated credit limit, and into which repayments go for crediting.

revolving fund: A fund into which receipts go and from which disbursements are made, causing the size of the fund to continually change as funds flow in and out of it; for example, a government working fund, into which tax dollars flow and from which expenditures are made; in the widest sense, any current working fund.

rider: A provision added by the parties to a basic contract, such as an insurance policy, which takes up some special questions; such a provision may be signed at the time the contract is originally made or added later by the parties.

rigging: The manipulation of a price by collusion between two or more parties; for example, the manipulation of securities prices by stock speculators or the rigging of a bid by collusion between bidders.

right of privacy: The right of an individual or organization to withhold itself from public view and examination, and to avoid intrusion upon its life, to the extent that law and public policy permit.

right of rescission: The right of a consumer, under Federal law, to change his or her mind on a purchase within three business days, cancel the purchase contract, and receive money paid back from the seller; a limited right and dependent on certain conditions specified by law that have not yet been completely tested in the courts.

right of way: A legal right to move over land belonging to another; for example, the right to use a lane on another's land as access to otherwise inaccessible land, as provided by deed, or the right to build a road as purchased by government from private land-holders.

rights: 1. In general, justifiable claims, supported by law or tradition. **2.** The option, extended by a board of directors to current shareholders of a corporation, to buy a new issue of corporate stock at a discount; such an option is something of value, which can be bought and sold in the securities marketplace.

right-to-work law: A state labor law outlawing the union shop. Under a union shop employees must join a union by some designated time after employment; the right-to-work law eliminates this condition of continuing employment.

riparian rights: The rights of those owning land abutting waterways in regard to the use and enjoyment of those waterways and the land on which they flow.

risk: 1. The extent to which loss is possible. In a somewhat wider sense, the amount of danger of potential loss in a situation in personal and business terms. **2.** That which is covered by insurance, if it is insurable.

risk arbitrage: That branch of investment banking involved in taking risks associated with anticipated growths in securities values arising from corporate takeover situations; for example, when a corporation has just received a purchase bid from another company, the purchase of its common stock at a price considerably higher than the current market price of the stock, by arbitrageurs anticipating a substantial rise in that current market value.

risk capital: Capital invested in high or relatively high risk securities and enterprises, in expectation of commensurately high returns.

risk management: The management of insurable risks, including both insurance and the prevention of loss.

ROI: See return on investment.

role playing: The taking on of assumed roles during training and development, in order to explore actions and reactions in simulated business situations.

rollback: Return of any cost element in an economy to a previous and lower rate, as with a return to previous lower price levels, wage levels, or interest rates; usually but not always an act of government or forced by government.

rolling stock: Whatever is owned by a railroad that moves on wheels on rails; sometimes also used to describe whatever moves on wheels, such as a fleet of trucks or taxicabs.

rollover: A refunding of debt by the replacement of existing debt with new debt; used frequently by governments as a means of continuing debts, paying only interest on them, while at the same time normally incurring new debts as well.

rotating shifts: Work periods so organized as to have workers change the normal period worked on a scheduled basis; for example, to work a 7 A.M. to 3 P.M. shift for one week, a 3 P.M. to 11 P.M. shift the next week, an 11 P.M. to 7 A.M. shift the week after and then the whole sequence again.

roughneck: A relatively unskilled oil well employee.

round lot: A standard securities or commodities trading unit; for example, the standard New York Stock Exchange common stock trading unit is 100 shares, and most trades are conducted in multiples of 100 shares.

round off: To express a number approximately, by taking that number to the nearest number with less digits, as with changing figures using dollars and cents to the nearest dollars; with $10.12 becoming $10, and $10.51 becoming $11.

routine: A special-purpose computer program, or part of a program, designed to perform specific, limited functions; when kept in storage for use in solving standard problems, often called library routines or utility routines.

routing: The planned path to be followed; for example, the path a shipment of goods is scheduled to follow from London, England to Bombay, India or the movement of materials through a series of production processes.

row: A horizontally arranged body of figures or digits.

royalties: Amounts paid by one to another as compensation for the use of the other's property; for example, a percentage of net or gross receipts paid by a publisher to an author for use of the author's work, or a percentage of revenue paid to a landowner for the right to extract natural resources.

RPG: See report program generator.

rule of reason: See antitrust legislation.

runaway inflation: A very high rate of inflation that cannot be brought under control, even with use of whatever manipulative tools are available to government.

runaway shop: A plant or other business firm that leaves a unionized area to operate in a nonunion area, for the purpose of employing nonunion labor.

runoff election: An election between the highest plurality holders in a previous election, in an attempt to achieve clear plurality or majority; most often encountered in union representation elections involving several unions, when no single union has achieved a majority.

run on the bank: See bank run.

S

sabbatical: A long leave from work with full or part pay taken as a matter of custom or right; for example, the traditional college teachers' leave, normally at full or half pay, which may last up to two full semesters and be taken one year of each five to ten years, depending on the college involved. Some larger companies also provide sabbaticals for valued long-term management personnel.

sabotage: The damage of installations or disruption of procedures for political or economic reasons; sometimes charged by employers against workers in strikes.

safe deposit box: A vault in which valuables are kept, in some remote location, usually a bank.

safety stock: Inventory kept on hand to guarantee the unimpeded flow of production in the event of supply problems.

sag: A minor dip in securities prices.

salary review: A formal periodic evaluation of an employee's performance and comparative salary level, to help determine whether or not a salary increase is justified.

sale: 1. A contract passing title to goods or undertaking an obligation to supply goods or services in return for stated consideration, usually in the form of a price. **2.** A lower-than-normal price offer of goods or services by a seller to one or more buyers; for example, the offering of a body of goods at cut prices for a limited time by a retail store.

sale and leaseback: The sale of a property by its owner to a financing organization, accompanied by the leasing of that property on a long-term basis by its former owner; a financing technique used to remove both ownership and debt obligation from the books of the former owner, while allowing full use of the property for business purposes.

sale on approval: A trial sale under a revocable form of contract in which the seller supplies goods to a potential buyer, who can return the goods to the seller for full refund or credit as specified in the form of contract; not really a sale or a contract, as no legally binding contract is made by the parties involved.

sales: Income from goods and services sold, appearing as such on financial records and statements.

sales agent: An independent organization or proprietor that acts as agent for the goods or services of one or more firms.

sales book: A book kept by a seller recording sales made, before entry into books of account.

sales costs: See marketing costs.

sales forecast: An estimate of sales that will be made within a specified period; a guess that is a vital part of all budgeting and other planning.

sales management: That part of management responsible for meeting the sales objectives of an organization, by developing sales organizations and techniques that successfully sell company goods and services.

sales presentation: See presentation.

sales promotion: See promotion.

sales quota: See quota.

sales tax: A tax on goods and services sold, normally a percentage of the actual selling price. As the tax may be placed on sales occurring anywhere in the chain of distribution, including retail sales, the final price paid by a buyer at retail may reflect several accumulated sales taxes.

sales trainee: See trainee.

salvage: 1. The value of something tangible that is sold as scrap. **2.** To recover something of value, such as a wrecked ship. **3.** The value of recovered property when assessing the extent of compensable damage for insurance purposes. **4.** In accounting, the estimated value of property if it were to be resold, whether for use as originally designed or as scrap.

salvage value: See salvage.

sample: 1. A piece of goods or a service provided free as an incentive to purchase other goods and services. **2.** In statistics, a test group selected from a much larger group, in the hope that data derived from the smaller group will cast desired light upon the larger group.

sampling error: In statistics, error that develops because of the nature of the sample selected, because that sample somehow turned out not to be fully representative of the entire group or universe being studied. Such error, within defined bounds, is inevitable and usually acceptable; larger errors invalidate the studies containing them.

sanctions: Actions taken against other countries that stop short of violence, including such matters as refusal to trade, international boycotts, seizure of property, and abrogation of existing trade and treaty arrangements.

satellite banking: The development of a web of dependent relationships between relatively small banks outside a large metropolitan area and a larger, centrally located bank.

satisfaction: In law, the fulfillment of a contract or the execution of a judgment.

saturation: In marketing, the filling of a field. May describe an attempt to reach every possible buyer in a defined market, using every available advertising, promotion, and selling tool; or may refer to the condition of a market that has bought heavily in a product area, and will buy relatively little more, at least for a time.

saturation campaign: A massive promotional effort, aimed at using all available media to help sell a product in a specified market.

savings: Income held for future use, rather than being spent as received, forming a basis for accumulation and investment.

savings account: A bank account devoted to the accumulation of savings and paying interest on the money held in it, in contrast to a checking account, which is devoted to handling transactions and pays no interest; but the difference between the two is blurring, as more and more bank accounts combine both features.

savings and loan association: A savings banking institution specializing in home mortgage loans, and organized on a mutual basis, with account holders actually shareholders holding equity proportional to the size of their accounts.

savings bank: A bank that holds depositor's money in interest-paying savings accounts and uses that money in the main to make mortgage loans, as well as making relatively small investments in high grade securities; but the distinction between savings and commercial banks is blurring, as savings banks undertake more and more service functions, such as checking accounts and life insurance sales.

savings bond: A United States government bond paying a fixed rate of interest and holding a fixed value; it cannot be traded on bond markets, and can be redeemed only by the government.

SBA: See Small Business Administration.

SBIC: See Small Business Investment Company.

scab: One who works during a strike, taking the place of a striker; often applied to non-strikers and supervisory employees, but in the main aimed at workers recruited from outside during a strike for the express purpose of breaking that strike.

scaling: The placing of a series of orders to buy or sell securities at specific amounts and at specific price levels, in contrast to the placing of a single order to buy or sell at a specific price or at current market prices.

scalper: **1.** One who attempts to profit on small price changes in securities prices, buying and selling on a short-term, quick in-and-out basis. **2.** One who attempts to profit on the appreciation in the value of tickets to events between their time of issue and the occurrence of the event, by buying tickets at regular prices and selling them at whatever price they will command.

scarcity: The condition existing when the supply of specific goods or services is considerably short of current demand; for example an insufficient supply of oil, whether that short supply is a real condition or artificially created.

scatter chart: See scattergram.

scatter diagram: See scattergram.

scattergram: In statistics, a graph that shows the relationship between a known, or independent, variable and an unknown, or dependent, variable; the values of these two variables for each observation, such as the age and reaction time for each of a series of employees, are plotted as a set of points on a graph. The pattern of these points may indicate a linear, curvilinear, or no relationship; if the relationship is linear, called a linear regression, various methods of regression analysis are used, including the least-squares method, and the correlation coefficient.

schedule: **1.** In general a detailed list of any kind. **2.** A body of supporting data, especially as used by accountants in supporting financial statements. **3.** To plan the timing of a series of events, such as the steps in a conversion to a new computer system. **4.** In insurance, an enumeration of the specific risks to be covered in a policy, in contrast to general coverage of kinds of risks.

scheduling: The process of planning and timing a series of events.

scientific management: A body of theory aimed at applying empirical techniques to the practice of management, as popularized by the work of Frederick W. Taylor.

scintilla of evidence: A very slight amount of evidence, but just enough to raise a question that should be decided by a jury.

scrap: Manufactured goods, materials, and equipment that have no value beyond their salvage value; for example, junked cars. For accounting purposes, value is estimated at the net of value as scrap minus an estimate of the costs associated with converting these items into cash.

scrip: **1.** Substitute money issued by a government with promises to redeem it in real money at some future time; for example, the "occupation money" used by the victors in Europe after World War II. **2.** Substitute dividends issued by a corporation, constituting a promise to pay a specific amount per share at some future date.

SDRs: See Special Drawing Rights.

sealed bid: A competitive bid on work to be performed, offered to the buyer literally closed at some time before the date set for the close of bidding, to be opened by the buyer at the same time as all other bids.

seasonal discount: A discount offered due to the nature of the season; for example, a discount on ski equipment sold in late spring.

seasonal employee: An employee hired to meet the work needs caused by the season; for example, summer park department employees or autumn harvest hands.

seasonal unemployment: Unemployment due

to seasonal changes in the work available in an industry, region or country; for example, farm labor unemployment resulting from the need for harvesting labor only at certain times of year, or garment industry unemployment due to seasonal garment buying patterns.

seasonal variation: A change in economic activity that occurs regularly and relatively predictably in an industry, region, or country; for example, the surge in retail sales that occurs during the Christmas season, or the flow of business into ski resort areas during the ski season, and the employment swings that accompany and follow those surges.

seat: A membership on an organized stock exchange, such as the New York Stock Exchange.

SEC: See Securities and Exchange Commission.

secondary boycott: The attempted boycott of a company that does business with a company on strike, but has no current industrial dispute with the strikers; a practice outlawed by the Taft-Hartley Act.

secondary distribution: The offering for sale of a block of stock, one that is so large as to probably depress the market in that stock if offered on the open market, by means of a special sale to other brokers and dealers, after filing and receiving permission to do so from the Securities and Exchange Commission.

secondary market: See after market.

secondary offering: See secondary distribution.

secondary reserves: Bank reserves that can easily be turned into cash on very short notice; for example, short-term high-grade commercial paper and short-term government securities.

secondary storage: See auxiliary storage.

second generation computer: A computer using solid-state components, largely replacing the vacuum tube components of first generation computers.

secondhand: Describing goods that are sold for a second time; can apply to goods unused after original sale, but mainly refers to used goods for sale.

second mortgage: A mortgage on real property which already has a first mortgage. Such a mortgage is subordinate to the first mortgage, and in the event of foreclosure has no right to satisfaction until the first mortgage has been completely satisfied.

second mortgage bonds: Bonds secured by second mortgages and subordinate to bonds secured by first mortgages.

seconds: Goods of less than generally recognized quality standards, due to some irregularity in material or damage in manufacture, that are sold at substantial discounts; for example, drapery material that is slightly faded or machine-made carpeting of somewhat irregular weave.

second shift: The afternoon shift in a workplace, normally starting in midafternoon and ending at or before midnight.

secular trend: In statistics, a long-term trend in any time series, one measured in decades rather than in years, such as the basic and long-term trend toward inflation in all western European and North American economies.

secured bond: A bond that is secured by some kind of collateral, such as a mortgage, thereby becoming more than a mere promise to pay on the part of its issuer.

secured creditor: A creditor whose claim against the debtor is secured wholly or partially by some property of that debtor, or by a mortgage on some such property.

secured loan: A loan that is secured by collateral or mortgages capable of being liquidated in the event of default in order to satisfy the debt created by the loan.

securities: Documents of ownership or debt, such as common and preferred stocks, bonds, and notes, some of which are negotiable and tradable in securities markets.

Securities and Exchange Commission (SEC): A Federal agency responsible for registering and regulating securities traded interstate and people and firms engaged in trading or counselling others as to any aspect of those securities; the SEC carries wide investigative, regulatory, and quasi-judicial powers to help it carry out its statutory charge.

segmented program: A computer program written in sections, and put into a computer system section by section, rather than all at once, as is usually the case.

selective strike: A strike against only one or a few of a number of firms involved in industry-wide or area-wide bargaining with a union, aimed at breaking employer resistance by applying pressure to a limited number of firms and thereby dividing employer negotiating ranks, winning some strikes, and forcing the resisting employers to follow the lead of those who have already settled with the union.

self-employed: Those who are sole proprietors, deriving little or no earnings from salaries or wages paid by others; for example, many small-business owners and professionals.

self-employment income: Income that is defined for tax purposes as stemming from self-employment, and therefore subject to withholding and application of self-employment taxes.

self-insurance: Carrying no insurance with an insurer, but instead meeting insurance losses out of company assets, usually out of accounts and funds set aside for insurance claim purposes.

self-liquidating: Describing an investment or asset which is thought to be capable of repaying its purchase price in cash during some defined period; always an estimate, one that often fails to take properly into account the rate of inflation.

self-mailer: A mailing piece that can be addressed and sent without an envelope.

self-paced instruction: See programmed instruction.

self-service store: A retail store in which customers pick their own merchandise from open shelves, such as a supermarket or large discount store.

self-sufficiency: The ability to meet regional or national economic needs using only home resources; possible for a single kind of need, such as wheat in the United States, but not for all or even nearly all needs.

seller's market: A market in which sellers can command higher than normal prices and better than normal conditions because of relatively high demand or short supply.

selling against the box: A short sale against an equal amount of stock held, to guard or hedge against decline in the value of the stock held.

sell out: 1. To sell an existing stock of goods, without replacing the stock sold with identical or similar goods. **2.** The sale of holdings by an agent, such as a stock of goods held by a manufacturer's agent or of a customer's securities by a broker. **3.** To betray those who have trusted you, for personal gain.

semiskilled labor: People who do tasks that require some small degree of skill and are easily trainable; for example, some kinds of assembly line workers, who handle machines, but do the same job again and again; also can refer to the tasks such people perform.

senior bonds: Bonds carrying a primary claim upon a corporation, being secured by such assets as land and buildings, with no other bonds carrying prior claims; for example, first mortgage bonds, as contrasted with second mortgage bonds, which are junior obligations.

seniority: The length of time one is employed by a company, as recognized by union contract or company practice for such purposes as determining who will be continued in employment when layoffs occur, length of vacation, pay scale, shift preference, and promotion.

sensitivity training: A training and development method that uses small-group manipulative techniques to help participants understand and free their own emotions, while joining in the emotional liberation of the other participants; aims at better intra-group understanding in the hope that it will carry through to better human relations in the workplace.

separation: The termination of employment, whether by act of employer or employee.

separation pay: Any pay due an employee on termination of employment, often referring to a lump sum paid on layoff under the terms of a union contract or by company practice.

separation rate: The relationship, expressed as a percentage, between the number of workers leaving their jobs for all reasons during any given period and the total average employment during that period; usually quoted for whole industries, groups of industries, or an entire economy.

sequential access: Ability to locate data within a computer only by reading through the stored data in sequence, in contrast to random access.

sequester: To take possession of the property of another, by governmental process, holding that property for later return or disposition; for example, to hold a bank account by court order while litigation is in process, or to seize the property of enemy nationals during wartime.

serial bonds: Bonds that are issued at one time, but mature serially; for example, a $5,000,000 bond issue that matures in five equal $1,000,000 installments over a period of five years.

service charge: A special charge for services performed, beyond the price paid for goods or services; for example, an extra charge for sending a bill rather than being paid immediately, or a bank charge for handling a checking account that falls below a specified average minimum deposit.

service department: 1. A department that handles repairs and the servicing of items sold; for example, the repair and service functions of a new car dealership. **2.** An internal department that provides services such as repair and maintenance to other departments.

service industries: Those industries that produce services, such as the professions, and the finance, entertainment, and transportation industries, in contrast to those that produce goods, such as the steel, automobile, and mining industries.

service life: The anticipated useful life of an asset to its owner, forming a basis for computation of straight-line depreciation. Physical life does not always equal anticipated service life, because an asset may become fully depreciated and still be in use, or an asset may be not yet fully depreciated when it is scrapped due to obsolescence.

setback: 1. How far from a specified building line a structure is built; usually the minimum required by local law. **2.** Sometimes used synonymously with failure or loss.

settlement: An agreement between parties as to the terms and conditions of a matter that has been negotiated between them; for example, a labor agreement, a dowry, or a dispute over interpretation of an existing contract.

settlement options: Several alternative modes of paying a life insurance settlement, usually including a single payment and various installment payment plans, one of which is to be chosen by the beneficiary.

setup cost: The costs associated with starting a new machine or changing over to a different machine, operation, or process.

setup time: The time required to start a new machine, operation or process; or to change to a different one; used most often to describe changing machinery between jobs in a production process.

severance pay: See separation pay.

sex differential: Differences in pay for substantially similar work performed by men and women, with women receiving less pay than men because of sex discrimination; an illegal practice.

sex discrimination: Discrimination against those of one sex in favor of another, an illegal practice where provable; for example, failure to hire qualified women for sales jobs because they are women, even though some other reason is alleged by the employer.

shakeout: 1. A business or financial trend forcing some companies into troubled business positions, and others out of business. **2.** A securities or commodities market trend causing a downward price trend, characterized by substantial selling pressure.

shape-up: A hiring mode for casual and temporary workers, in which the workers come to a hiring place and the employer chooses those wanted on the spot; once used widely to hire dockworkers, but superseded by union contracts, and now used regularly only in some farm hiring situations.

share: An evidence of equity ownership in a corporation, that ownership being divided into equal parts.

sharecropping: A system in which a landowner rents land, equipment, and supplies to a tenant farmer, holds liens on future crops as security for those advances, and takes a large proportion of the tenant's crops as payment for advances; prices charged to tenants and paid for crops often bind those tenants to the landowner by a constantly growing burden of unpayable but legally enforceable debt. This was a popular system among landholders in the south for almost a century after the Civil War; though clearly not so popular among their former slaves and poor whites. It still exists to a limited degree in some parts of the United States.

shareholders' equity: See stockholders' equity.

shaving: 1. Discounting a note at a higher than normal rate, when that note is of relatively low quality or market conditons make such action possible for the lender. **2.** Making an extra charge for allowing late delivery of securities in securities transactions.

shift: A work period, usually but not always on a regular basis; for example, 7 A.M. to 3 P.M., 3 P.M. to 11 P.M., or 11 P.M. to 7 A.M.; also refers to a single work period.

shipping: 1. Waterborne transportation, and the ships that traverse the seas and inland waterways of the world. **2.** The act of transporting, on sea, land, or air, whatever the means of transportation used.

shipping department: That department responsible for the movement of goods from a company to others; usually also responsible for receiving goods as well.

shop: 1. A workplace of any kind, such as a machine or print shop. **2.** A retail outlet, selling goods or performing services for customers. **3.** To go to market, seeking or examining goods and services.

shopping center: A group of retail stores offering a variety of goods and services and usually including joint parking areas, public access, and shared facilities; often constructed as a complex and owned by a single owner, functioning much like a market that rents stalls to sellers.

shop steward: A union representative who handles day-to-day matters affecting workers in a unionized workplace; usually an elected representative, who also is an employee in the same bargaining unit.

shortage: 1. A lower than normal supply, usually of a specific kind of product, such as natural gas at a time of withholding of supply. **2.** A lower amount received than contracted for, as when a shipment of 100 cases actually contains only 98. **3.** A smaller amount of funds than should be in an account, necessitating refiguring.

short covering: The act of buying stock or commodities to cover the borrowings made by a short seller.

short form: See itemized deductions.

short haul: The carrying of freight over short rather than long distances; a quite relative matter. Freight carried 200 miles may be called a short haul in North America, but in Western Europe it may pass through four countries and be called a long haul.

short interest: The total of stock which has been sold short and is not yet covered on a particular exchange.

short interval scheduling (SIS): The planning and supervision of work in brief time units, resulting in assignment of specific jobs for completion within a relatively short period, normally measured in minutes rather than hours.

short squeeze: See short sale.

short-range forecasting: Systematic attempts to predict the course of future trends and events for only a year or less into the future, often using mathematical models and computer technology.

short sale: A securities or commodities sale in which the seller sells securities not yet owned, in expectation that the securities will go down in price between the time they are sold and the time the seller purchases equal amounts of the same securities for delivery to the buyer of the securities sold short. The seller will often, through a broker, borrow securities, on which interest must be paid, to deliver to the buyer if no purchase has been made to cover the securities sold short when they are due to be delivered; then delivery must eventually be made back to those from whom the securities were borrowed. Should the securities sold short go down before eventual delivery, as hoped by the short seller, the short seller profits; should they go up, the short seller must eventually cover at higher prices than the original sales price, and loses, sometimes then being in what has been called a "short squeeze."

short term: A relative description, depending upon the subject, but in all instances referring to a time period of less than one year.

short-term capital gain: For tax purposes, a capital gain that is treated as if it were ordinary income, because it has resulted from sale of an asset held too short a time to qualify for long-term, more favorable tax treatment.

short-term debt: 1. All debts and debt instruments maturing in less than one year. **2.** For accounting purposes, all debts maturing in less than one year, including long-term debts coming to maturity in that period.

shrinkage: Inventory losses caused by such factors as spoilage and petty theft, and by actual physical size or weight diminution, such as weight loss caused by the drying out of inventory items.

shyster: An unethical professional; a term usually but not exclusively applied to lawyers.

SIC: See Standard Industrial Classification Code.

sick leave: Time off for illness, paid or unpaid, pursuant to union contract or company practice.

sick pay: Pay received by a worker from an employer during a period of illness, in which that worker is unable to come to work; sometimes full pay for limited periods, and sometimes part pay for limited or more extended periods, depending on employer practice or collective bargaining agreement provisions.

sideways transfer:: See lateral transfer.

sight bills and drafts: Negotiable instruments payable on presentation.

significance level: See level of significance.

significant results: In statistics, results that

could not have occurred by chance alone, and which allow the researcher to reject the null hypothesis that variations are caused by random factors alone.

silent partner: A partner who is inactive in the conduct of a business and may be anonymous except to the other partners, but who is a general partner and therefore carries unlimited liability for the obligations of the business, as do all other general partners, whatever the extent of their activity.

silver certificate: A paper currency unit fully backed by national silver holdings; an important form of currency during the latter part of the nineteenth and early part of the twentieth centuries; now superseded by Federal Reserve notes, backed only by the full faith and credit of the United States, rather than by any precious metal.

silver standard: See silver certificate.

simple interest: An interest charge computed by multiplying the rate of interest by the principal, without any kind of compounding, or piling of interest upon interest.

simple regression analysis: See regression analysis.

simplex channel: A one-way communications channel, in contrast to multiplex.

simulation: The development of models and model processes in an attempt to duplicate as closely as possible real circumstances, test alternative hypotheses and multiple variables, and aid analysis and decision making.

sinecure: An easy, relatively well-paid job, with little power or responsibility, and correspondingly little ability to do much harm to the organization, beyond the waste involved in the existence of the job itself.

single entry bookkeeping: A bookkeeping system requiring only one entry for each transaction, rather than the standard double entry bookkeeping system; it is the most usual non-business system, while the double entry system is the only one generally recognized as acceptable for business purposes.

sinking fund: A fund created by an organization to pay long-term debts or retire preferred stock, consisting of earnings set aside in a separate fund and held in cash or quite conservative investments easily convertible into cash.

sinking fund bonds. Bonds that by their nature require that a sinking fund be set up to retire them, that fund to be deposited with an independent holder, such as a bank, and to be large enough, with anticipated interest, to pay principal in full at maturity.

SIS: See short interval scheduling.

sit-down strike: A strike in which those striking stay in the workplace and refuse to leave; a tactic developed and made popular in the 1930s, during the organization of the Congress of Industrial Organizations.

sit-in: A protest, in which those protesting stay at the seat of the protest and refuse to leave; a tactic made popular in the United States during the civil rights movements of the 1950s and 1960s.

skewness: Describing lack of symmetry in a frequency distribution, for whatever reason, with positive skewness indicating asymmetry on the high side of the graph and negative skewness indicating asymmetry on the low side of the graph.

skids: See pallets.

skilled labor: Tasks that require a considerable degree of skill and training; also the people who perform those tasks, such as tool and die makers, carpenters, and plumbers.

skip account: A customer who has moved, leaving no forwarding address, without paying bills due.

slander: Malicious spoken defamation of the character of another, actionable at law, which must be provable through evidence given by other than the one defamed; in contrast to libel, which must be published.

sleeper: Something unexpectedly popular, such as a product that suddenly catches buying attention or a moving picture that becomes an unexpected hit.

sleeping partner: See silent partner.

sliding scale: A ratio that changes as one of its two elements changes. Examples include a bonus based on profits that pays at an increasingly higher percentage of profits achieved as those profits go up; a progressive income tax in which rates increase as taxable income rises; and a quantity discount schedule that allows higher percentage discounts as increased quantities are ordered.

slowdown: 1. An industrial action, in which employees work at lower speeds as part of a campaign to achieve collective demands; for example, garbage collectors who work very slowly and let garbage pile up. **2.** A slowing in the pace of national economic activity.

slump: 1. When describing a whole economy, a synonym for recession or depression. **2.** When describing a unit smaller than an economy, such as an industry or regional economy, a slowdown in business activity, characterized by lower gross revenues and layoffs.

small business: Any very small to modestly sized business, such as a single pushcart or a family grocery store; but as defined by the Small Business Administration, may also refer to a manufacturing firm grossing some millions of dollars a year and employing scores of people.

Small Business Administration (SBA): A Federal agency responsible for administering a wide range of loan and information programs aimed at fostering the growth of small businesses, pursuant to statute and public policy.

Small Business Investment Company (SBIC): An investment company supplying capital, loans and management advice to small businesses; such companies are partially financed by Federal money, but privately owned.

smart money: Those presumed by others to possess expert knowledge and inside information on business and investment possibilities.

smuggling: The illegal importation of goods into a country, evading import duties and import restrictions; for example, the illegal importing of gems to avoid duties or of narcotics to avoid confiscation.

snake in the tunnel: A multinational agreement to float several currencies within an agreed-upon range, using one of those currencies as a center, around which the other currencies might fluctuate within that range.

SNOBOL: A computer language that is especially useful in dealing with symbolic equations, and especially strings, which are sets of symbols that are to remain exactly as they appear in a program and are usually enclosed in quotation marks for identification; an acronym for *string-oriented symbolic language*.

social insurance: Any insurance of citizens by a government; for example, social security, unemployment insurance, national health insurance, and workmen's compensation.

socialism: State ownership of major elements of the means of production and distribution, in such basic industries as mining, metalworking, and transportation, along with substantial central planning of economic activity. Some countries have mixed forms, including elements of both private and public ownership.

socialized medicine: A nationalized health care industry, in which most health care facilities are owned by the state and most people in the health care industries are employed by the state; to be distinguished from national health insurance, which pays federal insurance money to a privately held health care industry, as does Medicare.

social security: A massive national social insurance system in the area of retirement, disability, and medical assistance benefits, as well as a number of allied areas; funded mainly by contributions for employers and workers during their working lives.

socioeconomic: Describing matters in which social and economic factors are intertwined, as in the need to examine both social attitudes and economic impacts in analyzing white-collar crime.

soft currency: A national currency that is losing value relative to other, more stable currencies in a given period; for example, the American dollar in the late 1970s, which diminished in value very sharply relative to the values of the German and Japanese currencies.

soft goods: Consumer goods that are literally soft, such as clothing and bedding, in contrast to washing machines and refrigerators.

soft landing: A slowdown in national economic activity that does not turn into a recession; so far in the main only a theoretical construct.

soft loan: An international loan made on relatively easy interest and repayment terms, and often repayable in the currency of the borrowing nation; sometimes a lightly disguised grant rather than a real loan.

soft market: A market that is declining; often used to describe the short-term price tendencies of securities or commodities markets.

soft sell: An understated, empathetic selling style; usually contrasted with hard sell, which is thought to be an over-agressive selling style.

software: See computer software.

soil conservation: See conservation.

sole bargaining agent: A union recognized by an employer and at law as the only legal bargaining agent for a group of workers, even though individual workers may belong to another union or to no union at all.

sole proprietorship: A major form of ownership, in which a single person is the only owner of a business, and carries both unlim-ited rights and liabilities in regard to that business.

solid-state component: A portion of a machine, such as a transistor within a transistorized radio, which functions as a result of electrical processes occurring within solids, in contrast to processes occurring in other media, such as those within a vacuum tube.

solvency: The ability to pay debts, implying the ability to pay those debts when they are due out of relatively liquid assets without damaging the underlying structure of a business; for example, selling fixtures may enable a small store to pay current debts, but may make that store unable to continue in business, which in practical terms makes it insolvent.

SOP: See standard operating procedure.

source document: A document supplying primary information, rather than information secured from secondary sources. In electronic data processing, any document providing data used in a computer system.

source language: The language in which a computer program was first written, such as FORTRAN or COBOL, which must be translated by an assembler or compiler into the object language, or machine language, used by the computer.

source program: The program written by a computer programmer, usually in a symbolic language such as FORTRAN or COBOL; source programs are translated by an assembler or compiler into object programs, written in machine language that computers use.

sources and applications of funds statement: See flow of funds statement.

space seller: One who sells advertising space in printed media, such as newspapers and magazines; closely allied to but not identical with a time seller, who sells advertising time in broadcast media, such as television and radio.

span of control: The number of people directly reporting to someone; for example, an executive to whom six subordinates directly report has a span of control of six, even though those six may have a total of three hundred workers reporting directly to them.

special assessment: See assessment.

special assessment bonds: Special-purpose local and municipal bonds, issued to raise money for such projects as sewers, waterworks, and libraries, and backed by special taxes levied upon those within the area affected by those projects.

Special Drawing Rights (SDRs): An international reserve fund maintained by the International Monetary Fund for participating nations, serving as vehicle by which nations can pay their balance of payments deficits, with maximum loans set by the IMF; the values of the SDRs are determined by averaging current values of a group of the world's major country currencies.

specialist: A stock exchange member who works as a primary trader for very few stocks on the floor of that exchange, attempting to hold markets in those specialized stocks relatively stable, minimizing sharp price fluctuations.

specialization: The process of working in more sharply defined and narrow areas with increasing degrees of skill; for example, the movement of a general medical practitioner into a medical specialty such as cardiology or the movement of a metalworking shop making many items into production of a relatively few items.

special offering: See secondary distribution.

special situation: A security thought to possess unusual profit possibilities because of special circumstances accompanying it and the company issuing it; in many instances merely so described by eager brokers who want to sell these securities.

specialty store: A retailer carrying kinds of stock not normally found in most general merchandise stores; for example, cheese stores and pottery stores.

specie: Metal money, as distinguished from paper money; sometimes also used to describe any precious metals that may be used as money.

specifications: Detailed, written, and drawn descriptions of work to be done or products in being, used for several purposes, including job performance evaluation, repair information, and standard setting.

specific performance: The legally enforceable performance of contractual obligations precisely as agreed upon in that contract, with no material deviation.

specific tariff: An import duty stating a specific amount to be charged for each unit imported, as contrasted with a percentage of value; for example, a duty charging $2 for each bottle of perfume of a particular size imported, rather than a percentage of the value of the bottles of perfume, is a specific tariff.

speculation: High-risk purchases of any kind of property in hope of high profits at least commensurate with the risks; for example, purchase of volatile common stock in hope of quick, profitable sale or the purchase of land either for quick resale or coupled with willingness to hold it for a substantial length of time, but in either case risking large losses in hope of high profits.

speedup: An attempt by an employer to push workers to higher rates of production, with or without additional incentives for that production; the source of considerable industrial dispute. One example is the literal speeding up of a conveyer belt on an assembly line, forcing those working on that line to work faster to keep up with the speed of the belt.

spinoff: 1. The transfer of some portion of corporate stock and some corporate activities to a newly formed corporation, for such purposes as preparation for sale or liquidation of the operations involved, or for expansion of those operations. 2. The development of auxiliary products from a major product; for example, the sale of T-shirts bearing the name of a popular movie.

split: See stock split.

splitoff: See spinoff.

split shifts: A work period consisting of two or more shorter periods with unpaid time between those shorter periods; for example, a restaurant work period of 11 A.M.–3 P.M., followed by 5:30 P.M. to 9:30 P.M.

splitup: See split.

spoilage: Losses caused by the spoiling of goods due to such causes as the mildewing of paper in a warehouse, the rotting of food in transit, or errors during the production process.

sponsor: One who buys regular broadcast time in order to advertise goods or services.

spot: 1. Immediate, as in describing a spot market, which handles transactions involving immediate payments and deliveries, in contrast to future transactions. **2.** A single commercial broadcast time purchase, in contrast to commercial messages accompanying sponsored broadcasts.

spot market: A commodities market handling transactions involving immediate payments and deliveries of real goods.

spot prices: The prices of goods traded on spot markets; for example, the prices of quantities of crude oil bought and sold daily in those markets.

spread: The difference between two related prices; for example, between the bid and asked prices of stocks traded over the counter or between the price paid by a retailer and the price charged for the same goods.

squeeze: Describing a wide variety of situations in which some are caught by economic circumstances; for example, the kind of squeeze that occurs when profits are curtailed by rising inventories and faltering sales during a recession, the investment squeeze that occurs when short sellers who

have sold in expectation of declining securities or commodities futures prices are confronted instead with rising prices and have to buy to cover at ruinous prices, or the borrowing squeeze that occurs when lenders are less willing than before to lend at other than very high rates of interest.

stability: A condition in which economic fluctuations are rather narrow; production, real wages and employment rise relatively uninterruptedly; and neither inflation nor deflation characterize the period. Generally recognized as a goal rather than a set of actual conditions.

stabilize: The act of moving to moderate the pace of price changes, as when a government moves to ease the velocity of changes in the value of its currency in international markets or a stock exchange floor trader acting as a specialist buys or sells to smooth out fluctuations in the price of a single security.

staff: 1. Those employed by any organization, and the process of securing that body of employees. **2.** Those executives engaged in mainly service and advisory functions, such as legal, personnel, and internal consulting people, in contrast to those engaged in day-to-day management of organizations, such as factory managers and sales supervisory personnel.

stagflation: A combination of economic stagnation and inflation; coined by Gunnar Myrdal in an attempt to describe the condition of most Western economies in the last fifteen to twenty years.

stagnation: An economic condition in which annual growth rates are relatively small, capital formation and investment slacken, and real income diminishes.

stamp taxes: Taxes levied in the form of stamps that must be purchased and attached to items sold by sellers before legal transfer can be effected; examples include stamps on deeds, securities certificates, and cigarettes.

standard: 1. A comparative measure, used in

assessing quality or performance; for example, a government-set measure of acceptable auto emissions or of the quality of the peas in a can. **2.** A goal; for example, a degree of excellence as to such human qualities as bravery, humility, or morality.

Standard and Poor's Index: A composite index of the price movements of a group of 500 industrial, rail, and utility stocks maintained by the Standard and Poor's Corporation.

standard cost: The normal cost estimated for producing goods and services, serving as a comparative measure of efficiency and productivity.

standard deviation: In statistics, the square root of the variance; a basic measure of dispersion of values around the mean in a normal distribution, used in tests designed to determine if the difference between items or groups, whether test scores or the diameter of a bolt, is statistically significant at various levels of probability.

Standard Industrial Classification Code (SIC): A uniform classification scheme applied to all United States business organizations by the Federal government, providing part of the basis for government analyses of business conditions and development.

standardization: The development of uniform measurements and materials, so that products and processes can be compared with each other and against standards set for them, and so that industrial tools and materials can be used interchangeably, an indispensable step in the development of a modern economy.

standard of living: The level of material well-being of the people in an economy and of economic strata within that economy, as indicated by the goods and services consumed. An attempt to measure the quantity of life rather than its quality, it is by no means a precise or even a determinable measure, but varies both in level and goal structure between countries and regions.

standard operating procedure (SOP): The set of procedures used in an organization, developed by policy and custom to handle similar situations, such as hiring and termination procedures.

standby authority: The right to take specified actions, or actions within a specified range, conferred on officials by legislating bodies; for example, the right to impose certain kinds of tariffs, or to impose or lift some kinds of price controls, granted to an American President by act of Congress.

standing order: An order for repeated shipments of goods, to be sent without specific reorders, usually but not always up to a specified amount; for example, an order to send 1,200 units of an item a year indefinitely, at the rate of 100 per month, unless specifically instructed otherwise.

staple: A basic and necessary commodity, such as bread, salt, flour, or sugar.

state bank: A state-chartered commercial bank able to perform all commercial bank functions, in contrast to federally chartered commercial banks; sometimes state banks are members of the Federal Reserve System and usually they are members of the Federal Deposit Insurance Corporation.

stated value: See face value.

state holdings: Property and industries owned by a national government; in the main used to describe government holdings in wholly planned economies, but sometimes used to describe government-sector holdings in mixed economies as well.

statement: 1. In computer systems, a single instruction originating in a computer program. **2.** See financial statement.

statement of account: A listing and totalling of all transactions between a buyer and a seller during a given period; for example, a statement of charge account transactions between a department store and a customer for a month.

state planning: See centralized planning.

state trading: International trading conducted by a government organization rather than by a private trader, though it may be conducted with both other governments and private traders; for example, all the foreign trade conducted by the People's Republic of China is conducted through state agencies as are most major United States arms sales abroad.

statistical control: Monitoring and control of production processes by the use of statistical methods, comparing actual deviations from a normal distribution against standard deviations, within defined limits.

statistical model: See model.

statistical quality control: See statistical control.

statistics: That portion of applied mathematics concerned with the gathering, organization, analysis, and presentation of numbers; also refers to the data resulting from that process.

status buying: See conspicuous consumption.

status symbol: Something owned that is thought to bring enhanced status to its owner, such as a very expensive automobile, piece of jewelry, or home, and that has been acquired with status at least partly in mind.

statute of limitations: A law providing time limits within which certain classes of civil and criminal action may be legally pursued; such statutes cover a wide range of possible causes of action and time limits, but there is no statute of limitations on some kinds of criminal actions, such as murder and tax fraud.

statutory law: Law set by statute, within constitutional bounds, in contrast to the common law, which is developed by the accretion of case law; in many situations the practical distinctions between the two kinds of law blur.

steady: Describing a market or investment vehicle that is holding prices at roughly equal levels during a given period, with trading occurring within a relatively narrow price range.

sterling area: Those nations, located throughout the world, in which the British pound is used as the main reserve currency, many of them formerly members of the British Commonwealth.

steward: See shop steward.

stochastic: Describing a situation in which a random variable is present, the value of which will be determined by chance, in contrast to a deterministic situation, in which prior events determine present results; calls for special statistical analysis, such as the Markov process.

stock: 1. An ownership share in a corporation, whether that corporation is publicly held, privately held, or both. Ownership is divided into shares of equal value, and the quantity of shares held indicates the proportion of ownership held. 2. The inventory carried by a company, with particular reference to goods held by wholesalers and retailers for resale.

stockbroker: A dealer in securities, who buys and sells stocks for customers and sometimes for house accounts.

stock certificate: A negotiable instrument evidencing ownership of a specific quantity of stock.

Stock Clearing Corporation: A clearing house for securities transactions maintained by the New York Stock Exchange, organized as a subsidiary of the Exchange.

stock dilution: See dilution.

stock dividend: A corporate dividend paid to stockholders in the form of additional stock, rather than in cash.

stock exchange: An organized securities trading market, such as the New York Stock Exchange, in which members trade on behalf of their own and customer accounts.

stockholder: One who owns some share of a

corporation, through ownership of one or more shares of company stock.

stockholder list: A list of the current stockholders in a corporation, maintained by the corporation or its outside stock transfer agent, or both.

stockholder of record: A stockholder whose ownership interest is registered on the books of record of the corporation; significant in terms of dividend payments and other corporate actions which are often stated as applying to stockholders of record as of a specific date.

stockholders' equity: The value of total stockholder shares in a corporation, expressed as the net of assets minus liabilities.

stock insurance company: An insurance company organized as a stock corporation, in contrast to a mutual insurance company, in which those insured automatically become shareholders.

stock in trade: Goods normally and currently for sale in a business.

stock market: 1. Any stock exchange, which is an organized market for trade in securities. **2.** The New York Stock Exchange, widely described as "the market" for stocks and bonds.

stock option: A right granted by a corporation, usually to employees or underwriters, to purchase corporate stock, under specific price and timing conditions; for example, the right granted corporate officers to buy 1,000 shares of common stock at $10 a share, a right that must be exercised no later than 90 days from its date of issue. When the option is issued to an employee at a price below the current market price of the stock, it is compensation, and Federal tax law applies.

stockpile: A store of materials, usually of materials designated as necessary or strategic for national purposes; for example, a national emergency supply of oil, in contemplation of international oil supply problems.

stock purchase plan: A fringe benefit, in which a company encourages and sometimes contributes to the purchase of corporate stock by employees, usually on a regular payment basis, much like a savings program.

stock purchase right: See warrant.

stock split: A corporate action increasing the number of its own shares in being, by dividing the outstanding shares; for example, the split of 200,000 outstanding shares on a 2:1 basis, creating 400,000 shares out of the previous 200,000. A split does not directly affect the total market value of all outstanding shares, so that a share selling at $20 before a 2:1 split becomes 2 shares worth $10 each.

stonewalling: Adopting an attitude of complete innocence or incomprehension in the face of mounting pressure to acknowledge the existence of a problem, one notable instance being that of those in the Nixon administration who sought to ignore the fact of Watergate in the hope that the problem would somehow simply go away.

stoolpigeon: An informer, sometimes but not always a paid informer; often used in labor-management matters, and more recently in criminal matters involving corporate officers and public officials.

stoop labor: Work characterized by constant stooping over, most often referring to farm labor such as bean picking.

stop order: A customer instruction to a broker to buy or sell securities at a specified price, rather than at the market price at the time of the order; for example, to buy a stock at $10 if it goes down to $10 from its current $12 or to sell stock currently at $12 if it goes down to $10.

stop payment: An instruction to a bank from a depositor to withhold payment on a check drawing on that depositor's account, as when a check has been issued in error, or has been lost in the mail and must be replaced by a new check.

storage: 1. The holding of information or materials for future use; for example, the holding of bits of information in a computer memory or card file; the holding of raw materials in a warehouse for future shipment to manufacturers; and the holding of parts for future assembly or replacement of used parts. **2.** An area or device in which computerized data may be held, such as a specified area in the central processing unit, a disk, or a drum.

store: 1. A retail establishment, such as a grocery or department store. **2.** A stock of materials, such as goods stored in a warehouse. **3.** To put something, such as goods or information, away for future use.

stored program: A program that is stored in a computer's central processing unit and can be used as quickly as the data stored there.

stored program computer: A computer in which programmed instructions are stored in its own main core, rather than stored externally, as on cards or tape.

straddle: A simultaneously held put and call, specifying a price at which its owner will either buy or sell a security.

straight bill of lading: See bill of lading.

straight life insurance: Life insurance paid at the same level premium throughout the lifetime of the insured, and also carrying cash surrender value, thus combining both death insurance and savings features; in contrast to term insurance, which has no cash surrender value and carries rising premiums as the insured ages, but which has far lower premium payments for most of the time it is carried.

straight-line depreciation: A method of depreciating property that assigns equal proportions of value to each of the years it depreciates. For example, an asset worth $10,000 depreciating over a ten-year period will depreciate at the rate of $1,000 for each of the ten years.

straight loan: A loan granted on the basis of the anticipated ability of the borrower to repay, without any kind of collateral.

straight paper: Any note, acceptance, or bill of exchange, that is secured by nothing but its issuer's promise to pay.

straight salary: A salary that includes no incentive compensation.

straight time: Compensation purely on an hourly basis, with no bonus, incentive, or overtime components.

strategic materials: Materials designated by a government as essential for use in periods of national emergency, and often stockpiled for that potential use.

straw boss: Any first-line supervisor; usually applied to such supervisors as factory foremen and farm labor supervisors rather than to white-collar supervisors.

street name: The name of a broker, holding securities belonging to a customer at the customer's request, or as collateral for securities bought on margin. The securities are held and traded in the broker's name, rather than that of the customer.

stretchout: An employer attempt to speed up production without additional compensation; used synonymously with speedup.

strike: A work stoppage by employees in pursuit of collective goals, usually economic, sometimes political, and sometimes both. Such a stoppage may last as little as a few hours or as long as several years; may be legal and pursuant to contract, or illegal and spontaneous; may be in pursuit of a wide variety of ends, including union recognition, pay, working conditions, pensions, grievances, a political embargo, or a national political goal.

strike benefits: Payments made by a union to those on strike.

strikebreaker: One who works during a strike in the job of one on strike; applied by strikers to supervisors and nonunion workers, such as white-collar workers, who continue to work while a strike is on, but mainly used to describe outsiders hired by employers to take the places of those on strike while the strike is on, who are often also called "scabs."

strike fund: A fund set up by a union, usually out of some portion of dues collected from members, to make payments to union members on strike.

strike vote: A vote taken by the members of a union on whether or not to go on strike; sometimes by voice or hand vote during a union meeting, but often by secret ballot and supervised by an outside organization at the request of the union.

string: See SNOBOL.

struck goods: The products of an organization that is currently experiencing a strike.

struck shop: A company currently experiencing a strike.

structured interview: An interview, such as an employment interview, in which the interviewer follows a prepared pattern, often both as to the content of the questions and the sequence in which they are asked; such an interview may be rigidly structured, allowing the interviewer little or no deviation from a prepared path, or may be partially structured, giving the interviewer a series of key questions around which to develop the interview.

structured programming: Computer programming that emphasizes program segments placed in hierarchical order, as in the language Structured COBOL, rather than focusing on individual instructions in a fixed sequence.

subassembly: A part used in a finished product, which is in itself an assembled product, such as the door of an automobile.

subcontract: A contract to do work for one who has a larger contract to do a job; for example, the electrical work on a new house might be done on a subcontract with the contractor who has the contractual responsibility for the entire house.

subcontractor: See contractor.

sublease: A lease from a lessee, who in turn has leased from the owner, as when someone takes over the remaining portion of a lease; original leases normally specify that such a sublease requires the consent of the owner of the property.

subliminal advertising: An advertising technique that seeks to influence the actions of its audience by striking at the unconscious rather than the conscious, by such techniques as flashing an advertising message on a television screen so quickly that it can be registered by viewers without their becoming aware that it has been shown.

subordinated debenture: A debenture which by its terms of issue becomes junior to such other debts as bank loans in the event of bankruptcy, reorganization, or dissolution.

subordinate interest: An interest in property which, by its nature and from the start, is of lower rank than some other interest; for example, a second mortgage which may be satisfied by sale of the property securing it only after an existing first mortgage is fully satisfied.

subpeona: An order to appear before a court to testify in litigation before that court.

subpeona duces tecum: An order to produce a document in court relating to litigation before that court.

subprogram: A portion of a larger computer program, capable of being handled and translated into machine language independently.

subrogation: The substitution of one creditor or other claimant for another; for example, the substitution of one creditor for another when a note is made payable to another.

subroutine: A group of instructions within a computer system, operating to perform standard functions for many programs.

subscriber: **1.** One who agrees to buy a new securities issue. **2.** One who buys something to be supplied in series, such as a periodical publication, the right to access a body of information periodically, or tickets to a concert series.

subscription: 1. An agreement to buy a new securities issue. **2.** A contract to buy something which will be supplied in series.

subscription capital: Money received from subscriptions to capital stock.

subscription rights: The right to purchase capital stock; a form of stock rights.

subsidiary: A corporation that is wholly owned or directly controlled by another corporation.

subsidy: Direct or indirect financial support by government of business organizations or individuals, as directed by public policy and statutory authority, including a very wide variety of supports and insurances for farming and farm prices, domestic producers, transportation companies, and public utility companies.

subsistence: The least families and individuals need for economic survival in a particular economic system at a particular time, as defined by government; used in determining whether or not to grant any public assistance to those in need.

substitution: The replacement of difficult-to-secure or expensive ingredients with more readily available or less expensive ingredients; for example, the substitution of margarine for butter in restaurants or of composition board for wood in new construction.

substitution effect: The tendency of consumers to substitute other products to meet their needs when products they have been using increase in price, such as a move from steak to chicken to meet protein needs when the price of steak rises relative to the price of chicken.

suggestion system: A system in which employers encourage employee suggestions and criticisms aimed at improving any aspect of the employers' business, sometimes using an open system in which employees are compensated for suggestions adopted, and some-

times using a box into which suggestions and criticisms may be anonymously dropped.

summons: A notification that a court action has been started against a defendant, and that judgment against the defendant will be issued by the court if he or she fails to appear to defend the action.

sum of squares: In statistics, a method of weighting sample groups of unequal size when carrying out an analysis of variance.

sum of the years digits method: An accelerated depreciation method in which the estimated life of an asset is used to figure progressively smaller depreciation amounts; for example, an asset estimated to have a depreciable life of four years will have these digits—4, 3, 2, 1, totalling 10. First-year depreciation will be 4/10, or 40%, second year 30%, third year 20% and fourth year 10%.

sunk cost: A cost which for accounting purposes is recognized as arising from previous decisions, such as the decision to buy equipment which has now become obsolete.

sunshine laws: Federal and state laws requiring that meetings of elected officials be open to the public, in many cases also requiring that notice of those meetings be published long enough before meetings to make public attendance practical.

sunspot theory: 1. The theory that substantial sunspot activity adversely influences the weather and therefore the quantity and quality of crops, thus also adversely affecting economic activity. **2.** The theory that substantial sunspot activity adversely influences investing attitudes and causes stock values to decline.

supermarket: A large, mainly self-service food store, usually also selling a substantial number of non-food items; the main form of retail food distribution in the United States.

superseniority: A union contract provision giving a group of employees seniority status above that of other employees, even though they actually may have less time on the job;

for example, veterans after a war and the officials of some unions.

supervisor: One who directs the work of others, and has the authority to direct that work; usually used to describe first-line supervisors, those who have direct supervisory responsibilities for workers, rather than referring to those higher in the heirarchy of supervision, who are described as managers.

supervisory routine: See executive routine.

supplemental appropriation: A legislative branch appropriation adding additional funds to an appropriation previously made, in order to accomplish original purposes or for new purposes.

supplementary costs: For accounting purposes, all costs beyond direct labor and materials costs.

supplier: A firm or person selling goods to businesses, for use or resale; usually describing a firm that sells such goods to its customers on a long-term basis.

supply: The goods and services available for sale in any period in an area of economic activity, varying in the medium and long term with demand, resources, monopoly, and other economic factors.

supported price: A price that is in some way propped up by government, which will take action aimed at raising prices or compensating producers if the price-supported goods sell for less than a stated price.

suppressed inflation: Inflation that is held back for a period by governmental action, such as price and wage controls.

surety: One who agrees to guarantee the actions of another, usually the payment of a debt or the performance of a contractual obligation; such a guarantor may be an insurer acting for a fee or one acting without fee, such as the voluntary co-signer of a note.

surety bond: An instrument formally guaranteeing performance of an obligation, issued by an insurer to an insured for a fee.

surplus: 1. The net of assets over liabilities, constituting shareholders' equity in a corporation. **2.** Any net of pluses over minuses, such as a larger supply of wheat than there is demand for wheat.

surplus value: Created value that is unjustly taken by capitalists. According to Marxist theory, all value is created by labor, and all value created that is not paid to workers is value unjustly taken.

surtax: An extra tax, levied periodically on top of regular taxes; for example, excess profits taxes, which have been occasionally levied on top of regular corporate income taxes.

survey: A set of questions asked of the individuals in a group and aimed at deriving data from which group attitudes or behavior may be determined; for example, a set of questions aimed at determining such political preferences as current Presidential popularity or attitudes toward national health insurance; or a set of questions aimed at determining buying habits regarding soaps.

suspense account: For accounting purposes, an account that holds income and expenditures until they can be identified and properly entered on the books.

sustainable growth: An estimate of the rate of economic growth that can be maintained over a period of years by an economy, measured by increases in gross national product and real income.

swap agreement: When there are official exchange rates, an agreement between two countries to exchange their currencies at those official rates, in order to ensure supplies of each others' currency to meet currency outflow and valuation problems as they arise; normally these are agreements to swap as needed up to specified maximums, rather than actual exchanges.

swap fund: A mutual fund that under certain conditions may receive securities which have appreciated in value from their owners and issue fund shares in return, effecting a tax-advantaged sale of the appreciated securities.

sweatshop: A workplace, usually run by a nonunion employer, that has extremely low wages and poor working conditions, such as the garment factories in New York City at the beginning of the twentieth century.

sweetener: Additional consideration paid by borrower to lender to secure a loan; for example, an extra one percent of the entire amount of a mortgage loan, paid in a lump sum on granting of the loan, under conditions of tight mortgage money.

sweetheart contract: A collusive collective bargaining agreement, in which union and employer enter into an agreement that victimizes union members; usually accompanied by illegal bribes paid to union officials by employers.

swing: A financial or economic fluctuation, such as stock, commodity and currency price movements and economic activity movements.

swing shift: A working arrangement requiring shift rotation rather than the continuous working of a specified shift; for example, a worker may work the first shift one week, the second shift the next week and the third shift the week after, with days of the week altered as well; often used in continuous operations, such as steel mills and utilities.

switching: Moving to other securities and commodities, by selling holdings and buying new holdings with the money realized.

switching algebra: See Boolean algebra.

symbolic language: Language used in programming which is easily understood by humans, in contrast to machine languages which are far less easily understood by humans, but usable by computing machines.

sympathy strike: A strike by workers who are themselves not involved in a dispute, showing support for others engaged in a collective bargaining dispute.

syndicate: 1. In the securities industry, a group of investment bankers joined to handle the marketing or placement of a securities issue; a means of sharing risk and sharing marketing strength when bringing a large issue to market. **2.** A popular name for organized crime.

synergy: The achievement of far more through the combination of two or more factors than could have been accomplished by those factors alone; for example, the achievement of very substantial business successes resulting from the combination of two companies, successes that could not have been achieved by either company acting alone.

system: A body of related parts and processes, operating together as a whole different from the sum of its parts and processes, such as an economic, production, or computer system.

systematic advancement: In organizations, the planned advancement of personnel as they achieve preset levels of seniority and skill; usually a guide to management action rather than a rigid prescription.

systematic sampling: A sampling technique that draws samples from a universe in timed sequence, as in the testing of every twentieth garment as part of final inspection in a garment factory.

systems analysis: The examination of problems and organizations as total operating systems, such as computer, production, and national economic systems and the development of efficient problem-solving approaches on the basis of that analysis; often using statistical techniques, models, and simulations.

systems approach: The practice of looking at organizations as whole systems, rather than as collections of related and unrelated functions; widely used in organizational study and practical business, government, and other institutional operations throughout the world.

T

T account: A demonstration account physically set up in the form of a T, showing the accounting effect of a transaction, often for problem-solving purposes; the account name is placed above the T, with debits to the left and credits to the right below the T.

take a bath: To lose a good deal of money on an investment.

take-home pay: Employment earnings actually taken home in a paycheck or in cash, after all mandated deductions from gross pay, including social security, and income tax withholdings; such voluntary deductions as repayment of company education loans, payments for savings bonds, and Christmas club deposits are included when computing take-home pay.

takeoff period: The time in which an economy rapidly moves into industrialization, a period characterized by large investments in a rapidly developing manufacturing system and development of a large body of skilled people capable of handling the needs of a modern industrial state.

takeover: The acquisition of one business by another, whatever the form used in making the transaction, and whether or not the transaction was effected amicably.

takeover arbitrage: The purchase or sale of securities in hope of realizing gain from the stock fluctuations resulting from takeover attempts, having little to do with arbitrage and much more to do with speculation in takeover situations.

takeover candidate: A company that is being studied by one or more potential acquirers, in terms of the desirability and feasibility of a takeover attempt.

tangible assets: Those assets that have physical being, such as machinery, in contrast to assets that are not physical and therefore are intangible, such as goodwill.

tangible value: The value to a business of such tangible assets as plant and equipment, while that business is in operation, in contrast to their value once that business has ceased to be a going concern.

tare: The weight of anything used to ship material, including both packing material and vehicles; net weight is gross weight minus tare weight.

target company: A takeover candidate company that has been selected by a potential acquirer as a desirable and feasible takeover target, whether or not that company has evidenced any desire to be taken over.

target population: In research, the population that is being studied, or the population to which the results of an experiment will be applied.

tariff: 1. A tax by government on imports or exports, for revenue, purposes of national policy, or both. **2.** A list of transportation rates and regulations applying to that transportation.

task force: A group assembled to get a specific job done, in contrast to a continuously operating group performing ongoing functions.

tax: See taxes.

taxable estate: That portion of an estate remaining and subject to taxes after all deductions of any kind from the gross estate.

taxable income: That portion of income remaining and subject to taxes after all deductions of any kind from gross income.

tax accounting: That part of the field of accounting primarily concerned with the tax aspects of transactions, including both the levying and administration of taxes by government, tax planning aimed at legally minimizing taxes paid to government, and compliance with tax laws and regulations.

tax anticipation obligations: Any of several interest-bearing financial instruments sold by governments to raise money in advance and in expectation of tax revenues, and which aim to smooth out government income over the year, rather than having that income concentrated in periods of high tax receipts.

tax avoidance: The legal minimization of taxes due government by application of a large number of tax planning devices; in contrast to tax evasion, which is illegal.

tax base: For tax purposes, the value of all the property within a jurisdiction subject to taxes; for example, the value of all taxable real property in a township, which would not include such nontaxable property as church-owned land.

tax burden: The extent to which a kind of tax or group of taxes impact upon a group, usually stated relative to other groups; for example, one of the aims of the progressive income tax is to lessen the impact of the income tax on the poor and disadvantaged, compared to the impact on those thought better able to pay.

tax credit: A sum that may be directly deducted in full from taxes due, in contrast to a deduction, which is subtracted from taxables; for example, an investment tax credit allows businesses to deduct certain sums spent for capital investment directly from

corporate income taxes that would otherwise be due.

tax deduction: A sum that may be deducted from taxables, lowering those taxables; for example, certain sums spent for charitable purposes, taxes, and medical and dental payments are deductible from taxable income on Federal income tax returns.

tax equalization: The adjustment of property taxes payable among taxpayers in a taxing jurisdiction, in an attempt to fairly apportion taxes, usually by adjustments of valuations, rates, or both.

taxes: Charges imposed by government on those under its jurisdiction, including charges on income, imports, exports, sales, estate and trusts, gifts, licenses and fees, and property.

tax evasion: The illegal minimization of taxes due government; in contrast to tax avoidance, which is legal.

tax-exempt bonds: Bonds that pay income that is not taxable, including Federal, state, and local bonds that are not in any way taxable and Federal bonds not subject to state and local taxes.

tax exemptions: Sums deductible from Federal, state, and local taxable income for each taxpayer and each legal dependent of that taxpayer.

tax fraud: Failure to pay taxes legally due, with intent to defraud the taxing authority, through such actions as failure to report income and misstatement of deductions; no statute of limitations applies to tax fraud.

tax haven: A country that levies little or no income tax on foreign individuals and businesses and so, under some conditions, offers foreigners the possibility of legal tax avoidance in their own countries; but in many situations the line between tax avoidance and tax evasion is a fine one, and is subject to considerable litigation.

tax lien: A lien placed on a taxpayer's property by government for nonpayment of taxes due; the lien is satisfied by payment of taxes due or by forced sale of the property for back taxes.

tax loophole: A provision of a tax law that makes it possible to avoid taxes that might otherwise be due, sometimes due to government inadvertence, sometimes pursuant to legislative intent, and often as a result of special interest legislation with application far beyond the interests of the lobby that forced through the legislation.

taxpayer: 1. An individual or business liable for the payment of taxes, now or in the future. **2.** A property developed just enough to pay the taxes due on it, such as a single-story row of stores on a piece of prime commercial property that is awaiting development into an office building.

tax rebate: Government return of taxes already paid to a class of taxpayers, usually as part of an attempt to stimulate the economy.

tax refund: Government return of taxes already paid, due to overpayment or error.

tax roll: A record of all taxable property within a taxing jurisdiction, with ownership and tax information.

tax sale: A sale of private property by government to satisfy unpaid taxes.

tax selling: The selling of securities to achieve advantageous tax results, whether to take losses on which tax deductions may be gained or to take gains on which taxes will be paid; always a feature of the last quarter of the year, when tax planning is most often done, but a factor at other times of the year as well.

tax sharing: The sharing of Federal or state tax revenues with the governments of smaller jurisdictions; a means of moving some tax money back into localities, sometimes to provide a higher proportion of that money to the needier localities.

tax shelter: A form through which income can be developed tax-free or in a tax-ad-

vantaged way, such as a pension or profit-sharing plan, an investment in tax-advantaged oil drilling activities, or certain real estate investments.

teaching machine: A machine developed for individualized learning, using programmed instruction materials; in recent years largely replaced by computer-assisted instruction.

technical analysis: A school of stock market analysis stressing the primacy of such market data as price trends and trading volume in market trend analysis, and using a wide variety of charts and other graphic representations as tools of analysis.

technical assistance: Aid to other, usually underdeveloped, nations in using materials, techniques and processes and in developing those kinds of skilled people necessary to form the infrastructure of a developed nation.

technically strong market: A market featuring rising prices and relatively large volume when the general price level is rising.

technically weak market: A market featuring declining prices and relatively large volume when the general price level is declining.

technocracy: A technically trained aristocracy that is, in some theories, best equipped to run modern industrial society.

technological unemployment: Unemployment caused by the displacement of workers due to the development of new machines and processes which eliminate those workers' jobs; for example, the use of digging machines instead of pick and shovel workers in ditch digging and coal mining.

technololgy: The practical application of the scientific method to the solution of production and distribution questions, and to the development of all those machines and machine-oriented processes that characterize industrial society.

technostructure: The body of managers and technical personnel that collectively forms the infrastructure of large modern corporations, and provides their day-to-day management.

telecommunications: The transmission of messages or signals, including data in computer code, over considerable distances.

teller: One who is employed by a bank in the actual handling of currency for customers in a variety of transactions, including deposits and withdrawals.

temporary injunction: A preliminary injunction restraining a defendant from doing or continuing to do an act until such time as the injunction is dissolved by the court or replaced by a permanent injunction.

tenancy: A legal right or interest in the holding and occupancy of real estate, which may be with or without a written lease. Tenancy terms may vary widely, including a specified lease period, month-to-month and year-to-year terms; and tenancy may take many forms, including individual, joint and corporate tenancies.

tenant: One who has a legal right or interest in the holding and occupancy of real estate, with or without a written lease.

tenant farmer: One who rents land from its owner and works that land, paying rent in crops, currency, or both. Sharecropping is one form of tenant farming.

tender: 1. An offer to pay a debt or perform a contractual obligation. 2. An offer to purchase, often encountered in company takeover situations, in which one company makes an offer to buy the stock of another at a stated price.

tender price: The price at which an offer to buy is made; for example, the price at which a company offers to buy outstanding shares of a company it wishes to acquire.

Tennessee Valley Authority (TVA): A pioneer United States public power project, organized during the 1930s; the subject of considerable controversy between proponents and opponents of publicly funded and operated power projects, then and now.

tenor: The time period between the date a financial obligation, evidenced by a financial instrument, comes into being and the date it is due to be paid, at maturity.

tenure: 1. The length of time a job is held. 2. The right to hold a job permanently, as long as the job itself exists, barring serious actions, such as felony convictions, which create a presumption of unfitness; for example, the widespread practice in college teaching of granting this kind of job security after an extended probation period.

term: Any time period; in finance and investment, the length of time a debt or debt instrument, such as a bond, is in being.

terminal: A communications device which can be attached to a computer system from some distance away and used to access that computer, for both input and output.

termination: See separation.

termination pay: See separation pay.

term life insurance: Life insurance granted on a period-to-period basis, usually with guaranteed renewability, but with increasing premiums as the insured ages, and carrying no cash surrender value; in contrast to straight life insurance, which carries level premiums, cash surrender values, and much higher premium payments for most of the life of the insured.

terms of sale: The prices, arrangements for payment, and all conditions and guarantees attached to a sale, becoming part of the sales contract, including those implied by sales contracts that come under the jurisdiction of consumer protection laws.

testament: A synonym for "last will," meaning the legally valid last will of a deceased person; therefore "last will and testament" is redundant.

testamentary: Pertaining to a testament.

testamentary capacity: That soundness of mind and memory necessary for one to be able to make a legally valid will.

testamentary disposition: Property given by the terms of a will, and not passed until the testator dies.

testamentary trust: A trust created by the provisions of a legally valid will, becoming effective after the testator's death.

testator: The maker of a legally valid last will.

testimonial: An endorsement, such as a product user's recommendation that others use the product, or a politician's support of another politician running for office.

testing bureau: An organization in the business of testing products for adherence to accepted standards, compliance with regulations, and other factors relating to the quality, quantity, and reliability of products.

test market: A relatively small geographic area in which a new product is tested for consumer acceptance; for example, a new soap may be tested in four such markets—the Atlanta, Des Moines, Seattle, and Dallas metropolitan areas.

The Big Board: See New York Stock Exchange (NYSE).

The Exchange: See New York Stock Exchange (NYSE).

theft insurance: Property insurance against theft, whether included in general property insurances or as a separate schedule of specific items insured.

The Market: A general description of all securities markets; but when describing stock market fluctuation, usually used to describe price movements of securities listed on the New York Stock Exchange.

Theory X: Douglas McGregor's restatement of that theory of work behavior that supposes humans to be negatively motivated toward work, and in need of substantial coercion to accomplish work goals.

Theory Y: Douglas McGregor's restatement of that theory of work behavior that supposes humans to be positively motivated toward work, needing only a proper environment to liberate their creative energies, and somewhat frustrated and bound by the traditional conventions and organization of workplaces.

The Street: Wall Street, as a symbol for the entire New York City financial district, center of the American financial community.

think tank: A public or private organization primarily engaged in medium- and long-term analysis and recommendation in policy areas affecting government, business, and other major sectors of society.

thinly held: Describing a stock that is held by relatively few people and institutions, and which is therefore subject to considerable fluctuation on a modest transaction volume.

thin margin: Describing a security or commodity held with very little equity investment and very large borrowings.

thin market: A market for anything generally sold, such as securities and commodities, that is characterized by relatively few buy and sell orders, and for modest quantities, and is therefore subject to considerable fluctuation on a modest transaction volume.

third generation computer: A computer using miniaturization and microcircuits as major elements of construction, in place of the vacuum tubes of the first generation.

third market: A market in which large blocks of securities exchange hands, sold by dealer to dealer and customer at small negotiated commission rates.

third shift: The night shift, normally starting at 11 P.M. or midnight, and ending between 6 A.M. and 8 A.M.

Third World: Many of those nations of the world outside the main American and Western European, Soviet, and Chinese power blocs; most but not all of these nations are also underdeveloped nations.

through freight: Freight that moves mainly unopened and uninterrupted from origin to destination, and the rate that is charged for such freight.

ticker: A remote printer used to transmit messages simultaneously to many locations. Examples are a stock ticker, which transmits stock prices to brokerage offices, and news-wires, which transmit news stories to newspapers and broadcasters, often widely separated.

tickler file: A file of items kept in timed sequence, as a reminder of what must be done when; for example, an outside salesperson's monthly file, indicating which customers are to be called on and when in the coming month, which is added to and subtracted from as work proceeds.

tied loan: An international loan carrying the condition that the borrower must use all or a specified part of the loan proceeds to buy goods and services originating in the lending country.

tie-in sale: A sale requiring that the purchaser buy other goods and services from the seller; an illegal practice in the United States.

tie line: A communications channel directly linking two or more locations, rather than being part of a network.

tight money: A government policy that attempts to slow inflation by restricting the amount of money and credit in circulation through exercise of a number of money-manipulative devices, especially manipulation of the Federal Reserve rate, which directly affects the prime rate.

till money: See vault cash.

time and motion study: A careful and detailed study of a worker's performance of a job, aiming at finding optimum methods of performance and at wage and rate setting; often regarded by workers and unions as assaults upon wages and working conditions, and the source of considerable industrial dispute. More recently this technique has been called Methods-Time Measurement (MTM).

time bill of exchange: A bill of exchange payable at a specified future date.

time deposit: An interest-bearing bank deposit, which may be withdrawn only upon notice to the bank as specified by the terms of the deposit, and which pays a rate of interest dependent upon keeping the deposit in the bank for a minimum time; if the deposit is withdrawn early, there are substantial interest penalties.

time draft: A bank draft payable at a specified future date.

time loan: A loan repayable in full at a specified future date, in contrast to an installment loan, which is payable in a series of equal payments.

time log: A record of work performed, and of the time it took to do each definable job; used by lawyers, accountants, consultants, and others who bill their time to clients by the hour and sometimes by the minute, as well as by those attempting to do work measurement for industry.

time seller: One who sells advertising time in broadcast media, such as television and radio.

time series: In statistics, a body of data generated in timed sequence, over any period of time, such as daily sales for a year, or yearly production indexes over a period of decades.

time-sharing: In computer operations, the interleaving of programs so that many users may access the computer system simultaneously; made possible by the high-speed sequencing of users, and allocation of computer resources controlled by the central processing unit.

time study: See time and motion study.

tip: **1.** A gratuity, such as that paid to a waiter or hotel employee by a customer. **2.** An advice to take buying or betting action based on purported inside information as to the affairs of a company or the probable outcome of a horserace.

title: Legally valid ownership of real or personal property, and the documentary evidence of that ownership, such as a deed, certificate of title, or bill of sale.

title insurance: Insurance against passage of legally invalid title, issued by a title insurance company after a title search by that company has established that legally valid title exists in the seller, who then is able to pass that title to the insured.

tokenism: The practice of engaging a very small number of people from a group normally discriminated against, to create the appearance but not the substance of non-discriminatory practice in an activity or organization; for example, the hiring of a few blacks into a predominantly white business, or the placing of a single woman on a previously all-male board of directors.

token money: Metal money that is worth less than its face value, as is true of all United States coins currently issued; in contrast to some gold and silver coins currently being issued by other countries and to gold and silver United States coins formerly issued.

tolerance: The amount of variation from specification that will be accepted for industrial products, such as machine tools.

ton mile: A transportation measure, consisting of the movement of one ton of goods for one mile; for example, the transport of three tons of goods for 100 miles equals 300 ton miles.

tonnage: The number of tons of cargo a ship is able to handle under normal conditions and without overloading.

tontine: A kind of life insurance lottery arrangement, in which a group of participants each makes a contribution to a central fund and the last of the group to survive gets the entire remaining principal of the fund; a variation provides for payments to survivors after a certain period or the reaching of a stated age, with remainder to the survivor.

tort: A private or civil wrong to another, actionable at law for damages, such as unintentional harm to a person or property caused by negligence; such an action does not preclude a criminal action arising out of the same set of circumstances.

tortfeasor: One who is judged by a court to have committed a tort, that is an actionable private or civil wrong done to another.

total demand: See composite demand.

trace: In computer systems, a program or routine that records the actual operation of a system, providing historical information for diagnostic purposes.

tracer: A procedure aimed at tracking down a shipment or mailing that has not reached its intended destination within a normal length of time.

trade: The exchange of one item of value for another, including the exchange of goods and services for money; or money for money, as in a currency transaction; of goods and services for goods and services, as in barter; and of financial instruments for other financial instruments.

trade acceptance: A bill of exchange signed by the purchaser of goods in favor of the seller of those goods, usually functioning as a check drawn on the purchaser's bank; a negotiable instrument.

trade association: An association of companies in the same kinds of businesses, functioning to pursue common goals, including the dissemination of information; training, retraining and professional development; public relations; and legislative pressure for association goals, as by lobbying for specific legislation.

trade barrier: Any impediment to the full and free development of international trade among all nations equally, including protective tariffs, import quotas, currency restrictions, and political restrictions.

trade credit: Credit extended by business sellers to buyers on a regular basis, in anticipation of payment within a normal period, usually thirty days.

trade deficit: A larger volume of imports

than exports for a country in a given time period; one of the key elements in the balance of trade.

trade discount: A discount extended to those buying goods for resale; for example, the 40-50% discounts extended to retail booksellers by publishers of general fiction and nonfiction.

trade fair: An industrial exhibition, in which manufacturers, distributors, and sometimes nations exhibit their products and processes, sell their goods and services, and develop leads for future sales.

trade-in: The acceptance by a seller of used goods as part payment for new goods sold to the same buyer; for example, the widespread acceptance of used cars as part payment on new cars.

trademark: A mark, logo, or other design so distinctive as to be capable of being registered with the United States Patent Office and accepted as the mark associated with a company or product. Once it is so registered, others may not legally use that mark without the permission of its owners, and may be enjoined from use or be liable for damages resulting from illegal use.

trade name: The name under which a company markets a product or the name of the company itself; although not a trademark, such a name may be legally protected against misleading use of identical or substantially similar names by others to capitalize on the established business reputation of the company and its products.

trade-offs: The balancing of costs and benefits, when choices need be made between alternatives. Examples are a choice between quick delivery of a contracted job, which would involve high costs due to necessary overtime work, and somewhat slower delivery at lower costs; or a choice between the curative powers of a drug and its harmful side effects.

trade paper. See business paper.

trade publication: A printed publication focusing on matters concerning a particular industry or group of industries, such as *Women's Wear Daily.*

trade relations: The web of commercial and financial relationships between countries trading with each other, as expressed by treaties and other written agreements; by governmental presence in the form of embassies, consulates, and missions; and by a miscellany of public and private contacts and arrangements.

traders: Those who buy and sell goods, services, and instruments of value for themselves or on behalf of others; they often are also wholesalers and distributors, as in the securities and automobile industries.

trade school: See vocational school.

trade secret: A product, formula, recipe, or any other item which has been developed or legally acquired by business; which is held uniquely by that business; and which can be successfully asserted at law as unique and valuable, providing the basis for injunction or damage suit against any who might steal or otherwise illegally acquire it.

trade surplus: A favorable balance of trade.

trade union: Any organization of employees defining itself as a union; under some circumstances, an employee organization defining itself in some other way, such as an employees' association, may be considered a trade union, for legal purposes.

trade union movement: The long-term and historic movement of employees to organize unions; also the aggregate of all such organized workers.

trading area: The geographic area to which a business sells, such as the neighborhood served by a retail store or the communities served by a suburban mall.

trading down: Buying something less expensive and of presumably lower quality than what is currently owned; for example, the purchase of a small car after having owned a much larger car.

trading floor: That portion of a market on which trades are actually consummated, such as the floor of the new York Stock Exchange.

trading limit: The upper limit set by Federal regulatory authorities on the volume of futures that can be traded by one person in one trading day.

trading posts: A station on the floor of a stock exchange at which trades for designated securities are consummated.

trading stamps: Premium stamps bought from trading stamp companies and offered by retailers as bonuses with purchases, and redeemable for merchandise offered by the stamp companies; for example, a retailer may offer a stamp denominated as one unit for each dollar of customer purchases, which the customer may collect and later redeem for some desired item from the stamp company.

trading up: Buying something more expensive and of presumably higher quality than what is currently owned, the classic instance being the purchase of a more expensive model when trading in a used car for a new car.

trading volume: The total amount of stock or of a single stock traded on an exchange in a given time period; usually describing that volume in a single trading day.

traffic: 1. All goods and people transported; for example, air traffic, describing everything moved by air, including the vehicles themselves. **2.** Goods moving in commerce; sometimes describing the entire transportation of such goods, from origination to delivery.

traffic department: That department of a business responsible for moving goods produced to locations beyond the workplace; often called the shipping department, or shipping and receiving department.

traffic management: The preparation and shipment of goods to destinations outside the workplace, in the most cost-effective way possible, consistent with the firm's standards of quality.

trainee: One who is involved in a formal training process, and is so recognized by the organization in which he or she is working. Often a trainee works at a considerably lower rate of pay than those who do substantially the same work but who are fully skilled and experienced.

tramp steamer: A cargo-carrying ship that has no formal route or schedule, but instead moves cargo from place to place as that cargo is available; such a ship may also carry some passengers.

transfer: The legal conveyance of title to property from one party to another, whether by act of the parties or by operation of law.

transfer agent: An organization or individual engaged by a corporation to physically handle and record all transactions involving the stock of the corporation; such agents are often banks or other outside organizations, but sometimes are employees of the corporation.

transfer of control: See branching.

transfer payment: In national accounting, a payment that moves value from one holder to another, without relation to the production of goods and services, as in social security and welfare payments.

transfer tax: A Federal or state tax on the value of stocks transferred, payable each time the stocks are transferred.

transit number: The identifying number placed on checks by each bank as it moves checks into the clearing process; a uniform system throughout the United States, with each bank having its own number.

transloading: See transshipment.

transshipment: 1. The shipment of goods received by a wholesaler or distributor to some other wholesaler or distributor in a different selling area; for example, to meet sudden demand in the second dealer's area.

2. The transfer of goods in transit from one carrier to another.

travelers' check: A kind of money order purchased by travelers, to avoid the necessity of carrying large quantities of cash while traveling. Checks are issued for a fee by a selling organization, such as the American Express Company; are usable by travelers during a specified period; and are redeemable at face value at any time during that period.

traveler's letter of credit: A credit instrument issued by a bank on behalf of a depositor, guaranteeing the extension of credit up to specified limits; usually issued to named correspondent banks.

travel time: The time spent in work-connected traveling, as defined by practice and sometimes by collective bargaining contract; for example, time spent traveling from home to a workplace other than the employer's main place of business, or from a plant entrance to a workplace a mile inside the plant.

treasurer: The chief financial officer of an organization, responsible for the prudent handling of that organization's finances.

Treasury bills: Short-term United States government obligations issued by the Treasury Department, bearing no interest but sold at a discount, that discount therefore effecting a rate of return for investors; for example, a bill issued in denominations of $100, sold at a 10% discount, sells for $90. The rate of turn is 10/90, or 11.1%. Such bills are fully negotiable; Federal income taxes are payable on income derived, but that income is exempt from state and local taxes.

Treasury bonds: 1. Any bonds issued by the United States government through the Treasury Department. **2.** Bonds previously issued by a corporation, bought back before maturity, and held in the corporation's treasury.

Treasury certificates: Short-term United States government obligations issued by the Treasury Department, bearing interest and maturing in one year or less.

Treasury Department: That department of the United States government responsible for major policy formulation, administration, and regulation of a wide range of tax and financial policies and functions, including tax collection, administration, and enforcement; supervision and printing of the physical money supply; protection of the President and the President's family; participation in international financial organizations; and a wide range of other duties.

Treasury notes: Medium-term United States government obligations issued by the Treasury Department, bearing interest and maturing in one to five years.

treasury stock: Stock previously issued by a corporation, and then bought back; such stock may be held indefinitely, earning dividends, or may at any time be resold.

tree diagram: See decision tree.

trial balance: A listing and summary of all account totals in a double entry bookkeeping system, to determine whether total debits equal total credits, preliminary to balancing the books.

trial close: An attempt by a seller to determine how the prospective purchaser feels about purchasing the product or service; not necessarily a serious attempt to close the sale and often merely an attempt to produce reflexive agreement.

trial sale: A sale that is made subject to subsequent acceptance by a buyer, and that therefore is not really consummated until the buyer has either specifically approved the purchase or has by failure to disapprove the purchase after passage of a specified time, approved the sale.

trickle down theory: The idea that stimulants applied to a lagging economy by Federal, state, and local governments are best given to business to induce economic growth that will benefit citizens directly, rather than being given directly to consumers to spur purchasing power.

trough: A bottom reached in some area of economic activity; always an estimate and an approximation, even after the fact.

truckload: A measure used in setting highway cargo transportation rates, a full truckload costing considerably less to transport than a partial truckload.

truncation: The dropping of excess digits in a number, rather than rounding to the nearest number.

trust: 1. A right or interest in property held by one or more for one or more others; the holders, or trustees, have the right and responsibility to handle that property in the best interests of the others, or beneficiaries. Also refers to the instrument creating that right or interest. **2.** An illegal monopoly, the intended target of antitrust activities.

trustbusting: Federal antitrust activity of any kind, attacking trusts, combinations, and activities alleged to be unfairly competitive and in restraint of trade.

trust company: A financial institution, usually a bank as well as a trust company, which handles many kinds of trusts and trust investments; sometimes as trustee and sometimes as agent for trustees; commercial banks perform all major trust company functions, and the line between them and trust companies has now blurred so much as to practically disappear.

trustee: See trust.

trust fund: A fund set up under the terms of a trust, in which the trustee holds the principal and distributes some or all of the trust's income to the beneficiaries. Such a fund is often for the benefit of a surviving spouse for the remainder of a lifetime, with principal then to surviving children or others, and often to surviving children until they have reached specified ages, with principal then to them.

trust receipt: A financial instrument created for the purpose of financing purchase of goods by a bank's depositor for resale; a bank advances money to its depositor to buy goods, to which the bank takes title through the form of the trust receipt, with the bank then passing title back to the depositor or directly to the purchaser when the goods are sold.

Truth in Lending law: One of a series of modern consumer protection acts, requiring lenders to fully disclose the rates of interest, other charges, and all terms and conditions of each loan, in writing and clearly stated.

truth table: In logic, a table listing the resulting value—true or false—for all possible combinations of conditions for a logical proposition; through the use of Boolean algebra, such values are used by computers in making logical decisions.

turnaround situation: Describing a company thought to be capable of being moved from a losing or declining position to one of profits and growth; therefore a company very much worth investing in at its current low stock price levels; always a speculative move, as many such companies do not in fact turn around, but continue on their well established downward courses—as do the market prices of their securities.

turnaround time: The time it takes to do a job, from beginning to end.

turnover: 1. The number of times an asset or group of assets is replaced during a stated period, often a year; expressed, for example, as a ratio of sales to net worth, so that with sales of $1,000,000 and net worth of $200,000, the rate of net worth turnover is 5 to 1. **2.** The ratio of employees hired to replace those leaving a company for all reasons during a given period to the average number of employees working during that period. **3.** In Great Britain, a synonym for sales.

turnover tax: A tax on total sales made by the kind of business being taxed, usually as a percentage of those sales.

TVA: See Tennessee Valley Authority.

twisting: An unethical and illegal life insurance sales technique, which attempts to convince those insured to cancel existing policies and to take policies offered by the salesperson using the technique; used both to cancel existing policies initially sold by the same salesperson so that higher frontload commissions may be collected and to cancel policies sold by someone else. When straight life policies are so cancelled, the insured usually pays higher premiums than before, as insurance is being purchased at a greater attained age.

two bin system: An inventory control system in which two containers are kept for each item of supply, one for current use and one for reserve use. When the first bin is used up, an order is placed to fill it, and the second bin becomes the bin in current use.

two-dollar broker: A securities broker who handles orders for other brokers for a fee based on the value of the transaction.

tycoon: A powerful and wealthy financier or businessperson.

tying restrictions: See tie-in sale.

Type I error: In statistical analysis, the erroneous rejection of a null hypothesis that experimental results are due to chance; in Type I error, also called alpha (α) error, the researcher takes the results to support the alternative hypothesis, while in fact they are statistically significant by chance.

Type II error: In statistical analysis, the erroneous rejection of a researcher's alternative hypothesis in an experiment; in Type II error, also called beta (β) error, the results support the null hypothesis that variations are due to chance, while in fact the researcher's theory is true. For example, statistical evidence may indicate that a drug has no effect on a particular disease; Type II error might cause researchers to reject the drug, which in fact may work.

typing pool: See word processing.

U

ultimate consumer: The purchaser of goods and services for consumption.

ultra vires: Describing corporate actions that are beyond the legal power of the corporation to take, as they are beyond the corporate charter, which sets forth the purposes and therefore defines the legal limits of corporate action.

umbrella policy: A major liability insurance policy, picking up coverage where other liability coverages end, functioning much the same as a major medical insurance policy.

UN: United Nations. See individual departments and agencies.

unauthorized strike: See illegal strike.

uncertainty: The idea that individual events involve some element of unpredictability; a matter of considerable interest to those attempting to apply empirical methods to the study, prediction, and replication of events, including those events occurring in the business world.

uncollected funds: See float.

uncollectibles: Debts that cannot be collected due to the inability or unwillingness of the debtor to pay; reserve for such debts is normally carried by businesses selling products and services.

undercapitalized: Describing a business that has insufficient capital to properly meet its needs, and sometimes insufficient capital for survival. Often, the description is inapt, as what is really being described is a business that may have considerable capital and enough to meet its needs if that capital were easily made liquid, but has instead a cash crisis.

underconsumption: The idea that downswings in the business cycle are caused by economic inability to consume what has been produced, resulting in a downward production spiral, which is self-correcting only at the bottom of a business cycle. From the opposite vantage point, often called overproduction.

underdeveloped nation: A country that is economically less developed than the industrial countries of the world, as measured by industrial output, per capita income, infrastructure development, and capital available for investment; often characterized by an explosive increase in population and decreasing ability to feed that population.

underemployment: Employment at a lower level than that which one is qualified for, such as the employment of editors as editorial assistants.

underinsurance: 1. The carrying of too little insurance to cover potential losses, sometimes also resulting in failure to qualify for full insurance coverage under policy clauses requiring coinsurance. **2.** The carrying of insurance up to a specified percentage of real losses incurred.

underinvestment: A situation in which a smaller portion of available savings is used for investment than is healthy for an economy.

underselling: Selling at prices below those of

competitors for substantially similar goods and services, usually as part of an attempt to secure a market foothold, expand market position, or drive competitors out of business.

under the table: An illegal payment or bribe given to help consumate an agreement, such as a bribe given to a public official to influence a contract award.

undervaluation: 1. The placing of a lower than reasonable valuation on property; often the subject of insurance claim disputes. **2.** The lower than reasonable evaluation of securities being traded, or other property for sale, and consequent creation of investment opportunities.

underwriting: 1. The guaranteeing of the sale of a securities issue by a firm or group functioning as purchasers of the entire issue of that security. **2.** The taking on of insurance risks by an insurer; also the function of assessing and recommending a course of action as to the assumption of that risk.

underwriting syndicate: A group of investment banking firms joined together to purchase and resell a securities issue.

undistributed profits: Earnings that have been retained in the corporation rather than distributed to equity holders.

unearned income: 1. Revenue that has been physically received but is as yet unearned, such as payment for subscriptions not yet fulfilled, and therefore must be treated as deferred income for accounting purposes. **2.** For tax purposes, income that has not been earned for personal services rendered, such as rent.

unearned increment: An increase in the value of property that results from conditions out of the control of the owner of that property, rather than through additions to value brought about by action of the owner; but not including a general rise in property values due to the impact of inflation; for example, a rise in the value of real estate located near a superhighway entrance.

unearned revenue: See unearned income.

uneconomic: That which yields poor economic results, in terms of profits, growth, efficiency, and other economic factors.

unemployable: Describing those who could not hold a job if a job within their general skills area were offered to them, because of physical or emotional disability.

unemployment: 1. The condition of not having regular work, even though ready, willing, able and looking for employment. **2.** The extent to which workers seeking work are unable to find it in a country, industry or geographic area, stated as a percentage of those available for work.

unemployment compensation: A public insurance system, by which unemployed workers receive payments for periods of unemployment, up to specified time limits. Unemployment insurance is governed by state law, administered by the states, and funded by taxes on employers.

unencumbered: That which is entirely free of legal claims and obligations; for example, realty that is sold with clear title, and free of all debts and liens.

unenforceable contracts: Contracts which cannot be enforced by legal action, such as contracts creating obligations to do acts that are in themselves illegal, as well as contracts which are invalid for any of a wide range of reasons.

unfair competition: Competitive activities that create competitive advantages which are at law deemed unfair, and usually are illegal as well, such as deceptive competitive comparisons and the use of misleading trade names.

unfair labor practices: Actions which by law are declared unfair when practiced by employers against workers and unions, and other practices which by law are declared unfair when practiced by workers and unions against employers, including a considerable range of coercive activities on both sides.

unfavorable balance of trade: A balance of trade between nations in which a nation has more total imports than exports.

unfilled orders: Orders received but not yet fulfilled; a backlog of orders.

Uniform Commercial Code: A national codification of major laws concerning commerce and finance, which has been adopted by almost all states, covering a very wide range of matters, such as sales, contracts, commercial and bank paper, bank deposits, and receipts.

union: An organization of employees joined together to bargain collectively with their employers on a wide range of issues, including union recognition, wages, fringe benefits, job security, and working conditions, as well as to pursue a considerable range of other group goals, including political, social, and insurance activities.

union contract: A collective bargaining contract between a union and one or more employers, covering such matters as wages, hours, working conditions, fringe benefits, job security, and grievance machinery.

union dues: Dues regularly paid to a union as a condition of continuing membership, and therefore in many instances, such as in a union shop, as a condition of continuing employment.

union label: A label placed on goods made by unionized workers stating that fact with the consent of management; unions often attempt to encourage the public to buy union-made goods in preference to goods made by nonunion labor, and sometimes attempt to stimulate boycotts of nonunion-made goods, especially when supporting strikes for union recognition.

union labor: Unionized employees, in contrast to nonunionized employees; includes those in collective bargaining units who are not union members, for purposes of describing products as "union made."

union made: Goods made by employees in unionized collective bargaining units.

union organizer: One whose main activity consists of organizing workers into unions and representing those already organized into unions in industrial relations matters.

union security provisions: Clauses in collective bargaining agreements providing protection for the status of the union in the shop, such as the union shop and the hiring hall.

union shop: A shop in which a valid collective bargaining contract provides that all workers employed in collective bargaining units join the union relatively soon after employment, usually after 30, 60, or 90 days, and that dues must be paid to the union as a condition of continuing employment.

union steward: See shop steward.

unissued stock: Stock that has been authorized but not yet issued by a corporation; such stock is not treated as an asset, in contrast to treasury stock, which is also held by the corporation, but which has been issued and repurchased by the corporation.

unit cost: The cost to a producer, distributor, or retailer of a single designated unit in a group of substantially identical units; for example, the cost to the producer of automobile parts produced on an assembly line; or the per-ounce cost to the producer of instant coffee.

United Nations (UN): See individual departments and agencies.

United States depositaries: Those Federal Reserve and commercial banks used by United States government departments and agencies as sources of banking and financial services, and in which federal funds reside.

United States Employment Service (USES): Federal employment service administered by the states, which provides free employment counselling and attempts to bring together employers and those seeking employment.

United States Government (US): See individual departments and agencies.

United States Government bonds: All bonds

issued as debt obligations of the Federal Government.

United States Government securities: All securities issued by the Federal Government, including bonds, bills, certificates, and special debt issues.

unit record equipment: In computer systems, machines that transfer data on punched cards into and out of the system.

universe: In statistics, the whole body of units being examined, such as all Americans over 65 in a national study of over-65 retirement patterns; also called the population.

unlimited liability: Liability that extends to all of a debtor's business and personal assets; the corporate and limited partnership forms of doing business substantially limit liability, but the sole proprietorship and general partnership forms generally carry unlimited liability.

unlisted security: A security traded on the over-the-counter market, and not listed on any organized United States stock exchange; a corporation may be listed on an exchange functioning elsewhere in the world, but be an unlisted security in the United States.

unpaid dividend: A dividend which has been declared by a company and therefore is an obligation of that company, but which has not yet been paid to equity holders.

unsecured: Describing a debt instrument, such as a bond or note, that is not backed by any kind of collateral, but is backed only by the debtor's promise to repay.

unskilled labor: Work that requires little or no special skill or training to perform, such as dishwashing by hand and ditch digging with pick and shovel; also those workers who perform such work.

unsubscribed shares: That portion of a new securities issue which has not been sold by the underwriters; held by the underwriters for future sale, unless so much stock is unsold that a contractual provision cancelling the issue comes into play.

upset price: The minimum price at which a sale will be made, such as the starting price set at auction, to be met by bidders or the item will be withdrawn from that auction.

upswing: A turn upward in stock or commodity market prices, after a period of declining or relatively level prices.

urban renewal: Attempts to develop or redevelop sections of cities, often center city sections that have severely deteriorated; usually financed either directly by Federal, state and local governments or by private industry with substantial help from those governments in the forms of direct payments or tax concessions.

US: United States Government. See individual departments and agencies.

use factor: The rate of use of items in inventory, pointing the way to effective reorder timing; an essential element of inventory control and production planning.

useful life: See service life.

USES: See United States Employment Service.

use tax: A tax on the use of an item, rather than on its sale; for example, automobile registration fees in some states.

usury: The charging of illegally high rates of interest by a lender; such rates are governed by state laws, and allowable rates vary from state to state, creating some imbalances in periods of rapid inflation, when money may be available to borrowers in one state and very difficult to secure in another, because of higher allowable rates in one than another.

utility: 1. The usefulness of a good or service, as seen by its user. **2.** A company, such as an electric or telephone company, providing a public service and therefore highly regulated by government.

utility routine: In computer systems, a program used to help in the operation of the system, such as a sorting program.

V

VA: See Veterans Administration.

VAB: See voice answer back device.

vacancy factor: The percentage of rentable space in a structure or group of structures that is vacant in a given period, computed on either a space or rental percentage basis.

vacation pay: See holiday pay.

validation: Certification of the official or legal status of an instrument, such as the stamping on a newly issued passport.

valuation: 1. The process of establishing the value of an asset, usually for sales or tax purposes; for example, the highly formalized practices associated with setting real estate values for tax assessment purposes, or the process of evaluating items in an estate, including such items as antiques and collectibles. **2.** The value established for an asset, for sales or tax purposes.

value: 1. The worth of something, in terms of a reasonable assessment of what price it might bring if sold under current market conditions. **2.** The actual price paid for something just sold.

value added: The amount of value added to raw and semi-finished materials during the process of manufacture.

value added tax (VAT): A tax on the net of sales minus materials costs, levied successively at each stage of sale, from the first sale of processed raw materials to the final sale; for example, where value added taxes are in effect taxes are levied on the sale of paper to make a book, on the value added

by the publisher when that book is sold to a jobber, on the value added by the jobber when the book is sold to a retailer, and on the value added by the retailer when the book is sold to a consumer.

value analysis: A close examination of costs and functions, aiming at performing existing functions at acceptable quality standards and reduced costs; for example, the use of lighter, less expensive building materials that still meet industry and statutory standards, or the consumption of a less expensive aspirin identical with brand name aspirin.

variable annuity: An annuity on which premium payments are fixed, as on other annuities, but which pays varying amounts of benefits, depending on the fluctuation of the securities in which those premiums are invested.

variable costs: Operating costs that vary with changes in the levels of production and sales; for example, power, labor and materials, which depend significantly on the volume of business being done.

variable overhead: See overhead.

variable schedule: See flexible schedule.

variance: 1. The difference between estimates and actuality; for example, in accounting, the difference between sales forecasts and sales realities. **2.** In statistics, the square of the standard deviation; a basic measure of dispersion, of values around the mean in a normal distribution, used in tests designed to determine if the difference between items or groups, whether people or widgets, is statistically significant, at various levels of probability.

variety store: A retailer carrying a substantial number of low-cost and unrelated items and lines; this function in retailing is now mainly performed by the shopping mall or inner-city discount store, which often carries higher priced merchandise as well.

VAT: See value added tax.

vault: A security room, for keeping valuables; usually a literally armored room in a bank.

vault cash: Currency literally held by a bank in its vault and cash drawers to meet current operating needs, such as check cashing.

velocity of money: The rate at which money changes hands during a given period, usually a year; significant in terms of assessing the level of economic activity.

vending machines: Machines selling goods to consumers, such as cigarette, coffee, and candy machines.

vendor: In law, a seller of goods and services; in business usage, synonymous with supplier.

vendor's lien: See seller's lien.

Venn diagram: In probability and statistics, a method of illustrating the probability of various conditions within a certain area of interest, consisting of one or more circles, often intersecting, within a rectangle. For example, if the rectangle represents employees' ability to complete a project, each circle might represent various conditions under which the project would not be completed on time, such as a strike, lack of parts, or illness.

venture: A new business undertaking, whether a single move by an established business or a whole new business, and always implying some entrepreneurial risk.

venture capital: Capital employed in the establishment of a new business, always implying some entrepreneurial risk and hope of a relatively substantial rate of investment reward.

venue: The place in which an action is brought to trial, often the place in which the cause of action is alleged to have arisen.

verbal agreement: An alleged agreement between two or more parties, but not in writing, and therefore usually unenforceable as a contract; under some very limited circumstances capable of serving as evidence, which with proven actions might be used to successfully allege the presence of a constructive contract.

vertical integration: The process of acquiring or developing organizations handling more steps in the production process than the company has previously been able to handle; for example, the acquisition of ranching and cattle-feeding facilities by a company formerly solely in the business of wholesale meat marketing, or the development of retail outlets by the same firm.

vested interest: An interest arising from an existing right or set of rights; for example, the right to receive payments from a company pension on retirement after working for a company for a minimum number of years, even though leaving the employ of that company long before retirement and holding other jobs.

vestibule training: Employee training occurring after hire and before actual start of work; usually involving full payment for the training period, and often formal training in a central location.

vesting: The acquisition of a right to receive payments under the terms of a pension plan, usually achieved after employment for a minimum number of years.

Veterans Administration (VA): A Federal agency responsible for administering a considerable range of Federal benefit and rehabilitation programs designed to aid veterans of United States wars, and for administering a large number of hospitals and other physical facilities for veterans.

viable: 1. Feasible, workable, practical. **2.** Capable of survival, profitable.

virtual memory: The ability of the computer to access auxiliary storage directly, rather than through specific programmed instructions, to provide larger data storage capability than the main memory itself can provide.

visible item: Tangible goods traded internationally, and literally visible as exported and imported goods, in contrast to invisible items, which are intangibles, such as banking and financial services.

visual display: 1. Any display using mainly visual materials, such as an exhibit at an industrial fair. **2.** A display of computer output in the forms of charts, graphs, and other visual materials, whether on a viewing screen or on paper.

vocational training: Training and retraining for the performance of trades and jobs, such as machine repair and plumbing, in contrast to professional training, which is the designation for training and retraining in such professions as law, accounting, and medicine; distinctions between the two designations are historical and sociological, rather than functional.

voice answer back device (VAB): A machine connecting telephone and computer systems, and making it possible to query a computer by telephone and get back a computer-generated spoken answer.

void: Describing an agreement, document, or evidence of obligation which is not legally enforceable.

volume of money: See money supply.

volume of trade: See trading volume.

voluntary bankruptcy: A bankruptcy applied for by an insolvent debtor, in contrast to an involuntary bankruptcy, which is applied for by the creditors.

voluntary chain: A buying cooperative of retailers, working through an existing wholesaler or setting up their own wholesaler; the retailers all remain independently owned, in contrast to a chain, which is centrally owned.

voluntary compliance: Voluntary action by private parties to comply with government regulations, without threat of government sanctions for noncompliance.

voluntary export quota: A voluntary agreement by exporters of a country to limit exports of certain goods, usually arrived at through pressure and negotiation between themselves, their government, and foreign firms and governments.

voting right: The right of a stockholder to vote in corporate matters requiring a vote, usually on the basis of one vote for each share of stock owned.

voting stock: Stock which by its nature gives its owner the right to vote in corporate matters requiring a vote; common stock is voting stock, but preferred stock is not, except for exceptional circumstances specified in the corporate charter.

voting trust: A trust to exercise on a continual basis voting rights stemming from corporate stock ownership of stockholders who have passed those rights into the trust; in contrast to stockholders' passage of proxies, which enable proxyholders to vote stock owned by others only once.

voucher: A document evidencing receipt or payment of money, such as a petty cash receipt or a form evidencing cash disbursements while on company business.

voucher check: A check that details the particulars for which the payment is made, usually on a detachable portion of the check.

voucher system: An accounting system mandating the use of vouchers to cover all cash transactions, for accounting and financial control purposes.

W

wage controls: Controls imposed by government on wages, in an attempt to control the rate of inflation, on the theory that increases in wages are an important contributor to the rate of inflation; sometimes accompanied by controls on prices and profits.

wage differentials: The payment of different wages for work that is substantially identical, for such reasons as shift differences, in which the later shifts receive more pay to compensate for the less desirable hours worked; geographic differences, taking into account both varying costs of living and different degrees of unionization and union strength in different areas; and illegal discrimination against workers because of race, sex, age, or ethnic origin.

wage escalation: See escalation.

wage incentives: Compensation plans that are to some extent related to the production of individuals or groups of workers. Examples include piecework, which bases pay wholly or partially on the number of pieces worked or produced; and a variety of group bonus plans, based on group productivity, the value of that which is produced, or profit.

wage-price spiral: The idea that wages are the main cause of inflation, and that wage increases feed price increases, which in turn feed further wage increases, and so on; one of several theories as to the causes and cure of inflation.

wages: All compensation paid to employees, whether for regular work or a single piece of work, for an entire job performed or piece-work, and in whatever form that compensation is paid. Compensation can be on any periodic basis, from yearly to hourly or even a smaller measure.

wage scale: The rates of compensation prevailing within an enterprise; in larger companies often a carefully evaluated and negotiated set of comparable rates for the range of jobs performed within the enterprise.

wagon jobber: A wholesaler who sells goods to retailers from a truck.

waiting period: In a strike or potential strike situation, a period of time mandated by law or contract, during which the strike must be held in abeyance, while attempts to mediate and settle the dispute proceed.

waiver: The voluntary and unilateral abandonment of a right or claim which would have been legally enforceable.

waiver of premium: A life insurance policy clause providing for continuation in force of the policy by the insurer, without further premium payments, on the occurrence of specified events, such as the complete disability of the insured.

walking delegate: A union representative within a workplace; usually a shop steward, sometimes a union business agent.

walkout: Another term for strike, but implying a less premeditated action than a formal and legal strike that occurs after all attempts to settle a dispute, short of a strike, have been exhausted.

Wall Street: See The Street.

want: 1. Economic difficulty and personal privation, with inadequate supplies of basic necessities. **2.** Any desire for goods and services, whether or not to meet a basic need, and whether or not people are capable of buying or otherwise securing what they want.

want ads: Short-entry advertisements, sold on a small flat minimum basis, with additional charges line by line or word by word above the minimum, that describe job openings, merchandise, and other goods and services wanted or for sale.

war debts: Debts owed by some countries to others due to costs incurred while preparing for and making war, such as debts for the cost of munitions supplied to Israel by the United States while Israel was at war.

warehouse: A place used to store goods, whether those of others or those of the owner of the warehouse.

warehouse receipt: A receipt issued by a warehouse to an owner of goods stored there, stating that the goods are stored in the warehouse and are the property of the owner; if it further states that the goods will be duly returned to the owner or to anyone else indicated on the receipt, it is a negotiable instrument.

warehouse receipt loan: A loan accepting warehouse receipts as proof of collateral, in which the lender holds the receipts and the goods so used remain in the warehouse; a standard commercial loan form, but also the basis of several major financial frauds, when warehouse receipts so used have proven false.

warrant: 1. A process issued by legally constituted authority, such as a court or a grand jury, instructing or permitting an officer to arrest a named person. **2.** A stock purchase right, that gives its holder the right to purchase a specific amount of stock at a specific price within a specified period or in perpetuity. Such a right functions much as a stock right, but it is normally attached to debt obligations and preferred stock, and

can be exercised over longer terms. If attached by coupon to another instrument, it is non-negotiable; if issued alone, it is negotiable.

warranty: An assurance by a seller or other contracting party, whether express or implied, that property transferred is acceptable, using generally accepted standards of measurement; while not the central matter of the transaction, such an assurance is very often so material as to invalidate a transaction if a warranty is breached, or to give rise to successful damage actions.

warranty deed: A written statement accompanying a deed, stating that title to real property is clear, and that the property is unencumbered.

wash sale: A sale and purchase of stock at the same time and by the same party, creating a false impression of great activity in a stock, with the aim of manipulating the price of the stock upward; an illegal practice.

waste: Material fed into the production process, but not used in the finished product, because of such factors as spoilage, breakage, and trimming; for example, material trimmed from cloth used for a suit, which may later be sold as scrap material or thrown away. Material not used in the prime finished product, but used in subsidiary products, or byproducts, is not considered waste.

wasting asset: An asset that by its nature diminishes with use, such as oil or natural gas, and that is recognized as such by tax law, which makes allowances for the progressive depletion of such assets, thereby also creating tax shelter opportunities.

watered stock: Stock issued with aggregate par value very considerably higher than the total asset value of the issuer.

Watergate: The sequence of events starting with the break-in at Democratic Party headquarters, located in the Watergate building in Washington, D.C., during the 1972 Presidential campaign and climaxing with the resignation of Richard M. Nixon from the Presidency; now also used as a synonym for major political scandal, with variations such as Koreagate.

WATS: See Wide Area Telephone Service.

waybill: A written and detailed description of the contents of a shipment, issued by its carrier and accompanying the shipment.

weak market: A market experiencing a somewhat declining general price level, usually on a short-term basis.

wealth: The aggregate of personal, business, or national assets.

wealth tax: See ability to pay principle.

wear and tear: The loss of value caused by such normal factors as age and use.

weighted average: An average in which some of the items used to compute the average are figured in more heavily than some of the other items; for example, in a study of buying motives, comparative price might count twice as much as esthetic satisfaction.

welfare capitalism: The theory that, by seeking to enhance the lives and compensation of their employees, enlightened companies will minimize the impact of trade unionism; while popular as a general theory in the United States in the 1920s, it survives today mainly in the human relations approach to personnel management.

welfare economics: The application of economic theory and practice to an attempt to create the greatest good for the greatest number, in the main through state intervention in political, social, and economic affairs; for example, through the development of massive, federally funded social security and health insurance systems.

welfare state: An attempt to create a society and a state power that regards the economic and social welfare of its citizens as a prime national goal, and that creates very large and comprehensive social programs to accomplish that goal.

wellhead tax: A tax on the value of oil or gas, as it leaves its producing well.

wetback: A derogatory term applied to immigrants crossing the Rio Grande into the United States, whether legally or illegally, independently or with the illegal cooperation of those employers who exploit them.

when issued: The status of securities that have been announced to the public, not yet formally issued, and are being actively traded on a prospective basis.

white-collar crime: Those crimes committed by employees in administrative occupations, rather than those committed by outsiders or nonsupervisory plant employees; for example, embezzlement by a corporate officer, bank teller, or computer operator.

white-collar union: A union composed mainly of those who work in and from offices rather than in the production and distribution portions of industry.

white-collar worker: An office worker or office-related worker, in contrast to a factory or factory-related worker, known as a blue-collar worker; but as the trend toward skilled industrial work progresses, the distinctions between the two have blurred and begun to break down.

white knight: In corporate takeover situations, a company asked by the management of the takeover candidate to bid against an unwanted acquirer, in an effort to either frustrate the aims of that acquirer and keep control or to replace the unwanted acquirer with a presumably more friendly acquirer.

white noise: Noise that has equal intensity at all frequencies within a certain band; often generated deliberately to mask other noises, as in open modular office areas.

whole dollar accounting: The rounding off of all accounting figures to the nearest dollar; also known as cents-off accounting.

wholesale: The selling of goods to others for resale, sometimes to other wholesalers for further steps in the distribution process, and sometimes to retailers for sale to consumers.

wholesale banking: That aspect of commercial banking that handles accounts and transactions for large institutional and business customers and for wealthy individuals. Today most commercial banks handle both large and small customers, and the distinction between wholesale and retail banking has all but disappeared, except as a description of a commercial bank's thrust in building its business.

wholesale price index: A monthly national price index indicating wholesale price trends, using a weighted group of goods sold at wholesale; issued by the Bureau of Labor Statistics.

Wide Area Telephone Service (WATS): A service offered to substantial long distance telephone service users, in which a flat fee is charged for unlimited calls to designated areas.

wildcat strike: An unauthorized strike, in violation of a collective bargaining agreement; often illegal and actionable.

will: A legally valid document disposing of its maker's property after death; once accepted by a court of appropriate jurisdiction, the wishes of its maker are carried out as far as possible.

windfall: An unexpected gain, such as that resulting from a sudden price rise in a stock or commodity held.

wire house: A very large stockbroker, operating many offices throughout the United States and usually throughout the world, directly or indirectly through arrangements with other brokers; originally referred to a large securities house that maintained its own communications network.

wiretapping: The secret accessing of communications lines thought to be private by others; originally a term literally meaning cutting into a telephone or cable wire or line, it now describes any of the many means used by public and private parties to covertly listen to the communications of others, legally or illegally.

withdrawal: The reclaiming of funds held in a bank deposit.

withholding taxes: Tax payments withheld at the source of employment income by an employer, subtracted from gross paychecks, and remitted directly to the taxing authorities, including income and social security taxes.

word: In electronic data processing, a group of characters with one address and handled as a single unit for processing purposes.

word processing: The process of producing material in typed form within an organization, often including some editing of those words by the word processing staff; with the advent of new recording, storing, and retrieving technology, work formerly done by a typing pool has expanded to include enough new functions to justify a new name.

workaholic: A compulsive worker, to the virtual exclusion of all other substantial personal activities, and with little or no regard for health and social relationships.

worker's compensation: See workmen's compensation.

workfare: The policy of putting people on welfare to work on public projects as a precondition for receipt of welfare payments; usually put forward as intended only to apply to able-bodied welfare recipients.

work history: See employment history.

working capital: The net of current assets over current liabilities; a major factor in assessing a company's financial health.

working capital ratio: The relationship between current assets and current liabilities, expressed as a ratio; for example, a company with current assets of $1,000,000 and current liabilities of $500,000 has a working capital ratio of 2:1.

working class: As used by Marx, those who are engaged in physically operating the means of production; but the term is far more generally used to mean all those who work for wages except those in managerial and white-collar skilled positions.

working control: Ownership by an individual, group, or company of enough stock in a company to reach and maintain effective direction of the company's policies and activities; in many widely held companies, this is often far less than majority or near-majority stockholding, and can be as little as 10-20% of ownership.

working papers: 1. The research notes and other underlying data supporting a more formal and extended statement, such as those developed in connection with publication of a scholarly work or development of a substantial accounting statement. **2.** In some states, a set of formal statements and permissions required before a minor or alien may legally be employed in most occupations.

working poor: Those who are employed, but whose income from that employment is less than that required to sustain them and their families above the poverty level.

work in process: For accounting purposes, work that is currently being manufactured; generally, any work in the process of being produced.

work measurement: Another of the many names for time and motion study, and equally a source of considerable dispute between management and labor.

workmen's compensation: A body of state laws covering the compensation of workers by employers for work-related injuries or illnesses, in which employers purchase insurance to cover the cost of successful compensation claims and state compensation boards hear and adjudicate claims; now more correctly called worker's compensation.

Worker's compensation cases are not limited to such boards, and major cases have increasingly found their way into the courts.

work order: Within an organization, a written instruction or set of instructions ordering that a job be done.

work rules: A body of practices and procedures, covering acceptable work and work-related behavior while on company premises, established unilaterally by a company or negotiated with a union and included in a collective bargaining agreement.

work simplification: See methods analysis.

World Bank: See International Bank for Reconstruction and Development.

world trade: The trading of goods and services between the nations of the world, and the total of all such trade.

writ: A court-issued document directing or empowering a sheriff or other officer of the court, an official body, or any citizen, to act in some specified way or within specified bounds.

write down: To cut the value at which an asset is carried on the books of a business, to conform it with current estimated value, for such reasons as obsolescence, unusual depreciation, or price decreases.

write off: To cut the value at which an asset is carried on the books of a business to zero, reflecting that estimate of the current true worth of the asset; for example, an uncollectible debt.

write up: To raise the value at which an asset is carried on the books of a business, to conform it with current estimated value, for such reasons as unanticipated price increases on stock in inventory.

writ of certiorari: See certiorari.

Y

yardstick: A set of prices charged by one business that is used to set a standard for prices charged by other businesses in the same field; such use is generally informal, and in some instances would be quite illegal if formal, being considered price-fixing in restraint of trade.

y-axis: The vertical line through 0 on a rectangular or Cartesian graph.

year-end bonus: A formal or informal bonus arrangement existing in many businesses, by which employees are paid bonuses based on the company's fiscal or calendar year performance, often partly dependent on the employee's performance in that year.

year-end dividend: A dividend paid at year end to stockholders of record as of the end of the calendar or fiscal year, whichever is used. Usually it is a special dividend declared by the board of directors, regular yearly dividends normally being paid more frequently; for example, quarterly.

yellow dog contract: An agreement in writing not to join a union, signed by a new employee as a condition of employment; illegal since passage of the Norris-La Guardia Act of 1932.

yield: That which is actually returned by an investment, but not including the investment itself; examples are the rate of return on securities investments and the crops harvested from land under cultivation.

youth market: The portion of the population that customarily purchases goods and services especially favored by young people, such as certain kinds of records, clothes, and sports equipment; usually refers to people under 25 years of age, but often includes people in their late twenties and early thirties.

Z

ZBB: See zero based budgeting.

zero-based: The idea that in planning nothing should be taken as a given; that even seemingly mandated and unavoidable costs and other factors should be re-examined thoroughly in each planning period, considering each plan as a fresh start.

zero-based budgeting: The application of the zero-based concept to the budgeting process, with each cost treated as new, even though actually to a large extent historically determined; aims at taking a fresh look at each budget, creating the possibility of cutting seemingly fixed costs and finding new approaches to the solution of old problems.

zero defects concept: The application of the zero-based concept to the production process, by stating that no margin for defects is acceptable; normally used to attempt to stimulate higher product quality efforts in the workplace.

zero population growth: A goal of those who consider unrestrained population growth, with its attendant use of limited world resources, a major threat to humanity; the aim is to reduce population growth to zero, possibly even reversing the trend, to lower the human population of earth.

zoning: The fixing by government of geographic areas in which specified kinds of buildings and businesses may be developed; for example, many local districts, as authorized by state laws, prohibit commercial building in residential areas, specifying in which areas commercial building is permitted, and what kinds of commercial activities are permitted.

DISCARDED